Nuclear Politics

Nuclear Politics

THE BRITISH EXPERIENCE WITH

AN INDEPENDENT STRATEGIC FORCE

1939–1970

Andrew J. Pierre

London

OXFORD UNIVERSITY PRESS

New York · Toronto

1972

Oxford University Press, Ely House, London W.1

GLASGOW   NEW YORK   TORONTO   MELBOURNE   WELLINGTON
CAPE TOWN   SALISBURY   IBADAN   NAIROBI   DAR ES SALAAM   LUSAKA   ADDIS ABABA
BOMBAY   CALCUTTA   MADRAS   KARACHI   LAHORE   DACCA
KUALA LUMPUR   SINGAPORE   HONG KONG   TOKYO

ISBN 0 19 212955 4

Printed in Great Britain by
The Camelot Press Ltd., London and Southampton

The decisions which we make today
in the fields of science and technology
determine the tactics, then the strategy,
and finally the politics of tomorrow.

Sir Solly Zuckerman
Scientists and War

FOR CLARA

Preface

I first became especially interested in Britain's nuclear role in 1962 when I began two years on the staff of the American Embassy in London. The handling of the Skybolt missile cancellation and the subsequent Polaris agreement reached at the Nassau Conference in December of that year were disturbing. It seemed that Ministers and officials of Britain and the United States were acting out this 'high drama' without being fully aware of the past history and politics of nuclear weapons in Britain and the restraints which they imposed upon political action. A brief unofficial examination of British nuclear policy of the previous two decades confirmed this observation. So, also, did my subsequent years in London as I watched the national debate over Britain's possession of nuclear weapons and as I participated modestly in the Alliance debate over the multilateral nuclear force.

Intensive research began after I left the U.S. government. I am greatly indebted to Alastair Buchan for opening the doors to many interviews which would otherwise not have been possible, for making available to me the facilities of the Institute for Strategic Studies, and for his many spoken and written insights. Over the years others on the capable staff of the Institute have been most generous with their assistance and encouragement.

This study was considerably enriched and its judgements honed by a number of personal interviews. Among those I can publicly thank for responding to my questions are: The Right Hon. Julian Amery M.P., the Rt. Hon. Nigel Birch M.P., Ambassador David K. E. Bruce, Sir Frederick Brundrett, Hedley Bull, Lord Chalfont, Sir John Cockcroft, Julian Critchley M.P., Margaret Gowing, Vice-Admiral Sir Peter Gretton (Rtd.), Lord Harlech, The Right Hon. Denis Healey M.P., The Rt. Hon. Aubrey Jones, the Rt. Hon. Frederick Mulley M.P., The Rt. Hon. Duncan Sandys M.P., Lord Sherfield, Marshal of the Royal Air Force Sir John Slessor, Richard Taverne M.P., The Rt. Hon. Peter Thorneycroft M.P., Peter Wilkinson, John K. Wright, and Sir Solly Zuckerman.

In addition I learned a great deal from conversations of varying length with Leonard Beaton, Neville Brown, Joe Fromm, Michael Howard, Laurence Martin, Richard Neustadt, George Newman, Ian Smart, and Philip Windsor.

The manuscript has been read by Alastair Buchan, now Commandant of the Royal College of Defence Studies, Hedley Bull of the Australian National University and formerly director of Arms Control and Disarmament in the British Foreign Office, Wilfrid Kohl of the National Security

Council staff in Washington, and Leonard Beaton, journalist and student of British nuclear policy. I am deeply grateful for their comments. Professor William T. R. Fox, Director of the Institute of War and Peace Studies, Columbia University, and Professor Philip E. Mosely, Director of the European Institute, Columbia University, provided helpful comments on an earlier draft. Dr. Henry Durant, Director of the British Institute of Public Opinion, graciously allowed me to examine and use his files of public opinion polls. The newspaper clipping files of the Royal Institute of International Affairs were also most useful.

I am grateful to Hamilton Fish Armstrong for permission to draw upon my article 'Nuclear Diplomacy: Britain, France and America', which appeared in *Foreign Affairs*.

Although this book was written independently and before I joined the studies staff of the Council on Foreign Relations, my colleagues at the Council have offered advice and encouragement in its final stages. I am also most grateful to Herman Kahn for supporting the study while I was with the Hudson Institute. Paula Ohlsonn and Lucille Schwartz worked hard to move the manuscript through the typewriter and Andrea Kim helped greatly in many other ways.

All errors of fact or judgement are my own. Many corrections and insights are those of my wife, Clara, whom I met along the journey of this book and to whom it is lovingly dedicated.

Council on Foreign Relations   ANDREW J. PIERRE
New York
15 October 1970

Contents

PART THREE   *The Great Nuclear Debate, 1957– 1964*

PART FOUR *The Dénouement, 1964–1970*

PART FIVE *Conclusions*

Introduction

Nuclear proliferation is thought by many to be one of the gravest threats to the stability of the international system in the coming decades. Yet policy makers and political scientists have only an imperfect knowledge of what has or could lead nations to develop and continue an 'independent' nuclear weapons capability. This is an attempt to help fill that gap by examining in some detail the most complete experience existing to date of a middle level state as a nuclear power.

Britain has a special position in the nuclear age. The United Kingdom was the first nation other than the Superpowers to acquire nuclear weapons. In fact, the Churchill government of 1941 was the first to decide to take the necessary steps to manufacture an atomic bomb. The wartime decision was subsequently transformed into British participation in the Manhattan Project, but after the war the United Kingdom became the third nuclear power. In so doing Britain became the first junior member of an alliance to develop nuclear weapons independently of her senior partner. Britain was also the first nation to base her declaratory national security policy almost entirely on a strategy of nuclear deterrence.

The British experience is of interest for a number of additional reasons. The United Kingdom was the first country to be faced with the problems of a second-rank power in maintaining a credible 'independent nuclear deterrent' within a strategic and technological environment whose principal standards of deterrence are set by the two superpowers. In part because of the difficulties in maintaining a viable second-strike nuclear force as the complexity and cost of strategic delivery systems mounted, Britain was the first nation to have a serious and lengthy national debate about giving up its nuclear arms. The British were also the first to debate renouncing an already acquired nuclear capability in order to help avoid, through their own example, the spread of nuclear weapons. The dangers inherent in worldwide nuclear dispersion were recognized more widely and earlier in the United Kingdom than elsewhere, because Britain was the first atomic power to find herself relatively indefensible against a hostile, larger nuclear power. Moreover, Britain had considerable influence upon the evolution of the concept of nuclear deterrence and NATO's strategic doctrine, largely because she became a nuclear power in the early years of the nuclear age—before ballistic missiles and the thermonuclear bombs made the distinction between large and small nuclear powers more apparent. London's rhetoric and its actions also influenced the nuclear aspirations of other European countries, and helped determine the fate of various proposals for collective Atlantic nuclear arrangements. Finally, the Anglo-American special relationship in nuclear matters, as it was revived in the mid-1950s, constitutes the most important precedent to date of bilateral nuclear sharing within an alliance. It stands as an example of what may be the political impact of such a privileged arrangement upon third countries. It is also a case study of the possible consequence of one nuclear power becoming dependent upon the technology of another power for the continuation of its nuclear force.

The British experience therefore clearly constitutes a valuable body of material for the study of the actual experience of a middle level nation as a nuclear power. It is true that Britain's early start in the nuclear field makes its case unique. All particular cases have an element of uniqueness and this is more pronounced the fewer they are in number. But more significantly, the British experience is one of the only three middle level cases which a prospective nuclear power can examine. Among the three it is by far the most complete in length, depth, and richness of nuclear experience.

The principal aim of the study is to describe and analyse the British experience in the creation and maintenance of an 'independent' nuclear force. An examination is made of the political, economic, military, scientific, and bureaucratic incentives for pursuing the atom; the strategic assumptions upon which decisions were made; and the continuing goals and interests which guided policy makers after a rapidly changing technology drastically altered some of the original assumptions and incentives.

Questions are raised concerning the relationship between the nuclear force and Britain's conception of its role in the world. We look at motivating forces in terms of the role of national pride and the desire to retain Great Power status, the perception of the nuclear force as an instrument to enhance leverage and bargaining power in international affairs, including the desire to gain influence over American policy. We also examine the incentives relevant to military security, and discuss the strategic doctrine of the nuclear force and its credibility. Conclusions are drawn concerning the effect of the nuclear force upon Britain's alliance relationships; the inherent conflict between the stated aims of *independence* and *interdependence*; Britain's impact upon nuclear proliferation and the curious manner by which the British and French nuclear programmes fed upon each other by providing additional incentives one for the other—Britain at first stimulating France to seek equity with her in the Anglo-American nuclear relationship, only later to find herself unable to concede the sole nuclear role in Europe to France; and the interaction of technological innovation with nuclear strategy as demonstrated through Britain's trying experience with nuclear delivery systems.

There are two pitfalls common to many writers on strategic problems. One is to ignore political factors by constructing tightly knit theoretical models which have discipline and logic but fail to relate to the realities of domestic or international politics. The other is to look at all strategic nuclear issues as based solely upon a confrontation, usually that of the superpowers. The perspective of this analysis is the identification and evaluation of the individual and group interests, motivations, and values which shaped the evolution of the British nuclear force. It is suggested that there is no clear dividing line between the 'rational' requirements of national security policy and the political, economic, scientific, and bureaucratic interests and pressures which help shape defence policy. This is particularly true in a country such as Britain: a Great Power in decline, with sharply limited economic resources, attempting to adjust its commitments to its capabilities. Here, from the viewpoint of those who must make choices, the practical issues of defence policy—such as individual weapons decisions—become intertwined with other aspects of public policy and at times become the subject of national debate. This may appear obvious; but to the Europeans it has often seemed that the policy prescriptions of American strategists and policy-makers as to what should be, according to 'strategic logic,' the 'rational' nuclear weapons policy for the allies have not always given sufficient attention to this assumption.

Most studies of nuclear proliferation are in agreement that the critical element in the future decisions of potential nuclear powers will be one of political choice rather than technical capacity, national will more than resource availability. Particular attention is therefore devoted to the nuclear force as a political issue within the domestic national debate. Although the decision to acquire a nuclear capability was taken in secret, and when it was revealed five years later received surprisingly little public attention, the continuation of the 'independent deterrent' later became a principal issue of inter-party and intra-party dispute. It was the major foreign policy issue in the General Election of 1964, which brought the Labour party into power after thirteen years of Conservative rule. An effort is made to determine the 'feedback' effect upon the nuclear force of its having become the subject of domestic political debate. Moreover, in the late 1950s and early 1960s, the British nuclear force also became the subject of contention in the broader arena of international politics. This was especially the case after the United States adopted the twin doctrines of controlled response and limiting independent nuclear forces, and promoted the multilateral nuclear force (MLF). An effort is made to gauge the relationship between official British attitudes on defence policy and nuclear strategy, and the internal political pressures and economic restraints which influenced them.

It should be noted that there are limits to the ability to draw generalizations from the British experience which might be applicable to the likely experience of existing or potential nuclear powers. Other states may find it instructive to look at Britain's nuclear history. But their decisions will be guided primarily by their own perceptions of their international role, their own appraisal of their security requirements, and their own judgement of the military and political value of nuclear weapons. The particular problems of India, Israel, and Japan, for example, have only limited elements in common with Britain or with each other. Each country has its own special collection of fears and inherited political perspectives. Although one should refrain from reading the British experience too directly into the likely experience of other nations, this is not to say that the reader acquainted with another national setting may not find here concepts and examples which will lend themselves to interesting comparisons. France is an obvious example and some comparisons have been cited where relevant. It is likely that in the future, even with the Non-Proliferation Treaty, there will be an increasing number of distinctive national debates on nuclear arms. If more studies of this genre are undertaken, it should then be possible to make some valuable comparative generalizations.

The sources of evidence used in the study are varied: parliamentary debates; Defence White Papers and other official documents; memoirs; the writings of scholars, strategists, and polemicists; the daily and weekly press and other topical commentaries. In addition, interviews were conducted in London over a number of years with a cross section of the principal Ministers, senior civil servants, scientists, and commentators concerned with defence policy since World War II. In a number of important cases the interviews provided fresh materials, but their greatest over-all value was in providing the author with insight with which to make judgements on how to interpret or weigh the significance of portions of the already available evidence.

The study is organized into five parts. It contains both chronological and subject analysis although its basic structure is chronological, following the dictum of Descartes that 'it is easier to understand something when one watches it grow than when one looks at it fully formed.' The British nuclear force is an evolutionary entity, and as such it has seemed important to record how problems have arisen and been resolved. In order to provide the needed background to understand the reasons for the decisions taken, it has been necessary to reconstruct the political and strategic environment of the time. There has been an attempt to relate technological and strategic innovations to their national and international political environment. The circumstances in the years when consequential choices were made, in for example 1941, 1947, 1957, and 1964, have been too disparate to be lumped together. Within the main parts and within the chapters may be found analysis by topics, especially in Chapter 8 which analyses the range of issues at the height of the great debate.

Part One deals with the wartime genesis of the atom bomb from the viewpoint of British participation and motivating interests. Many of the assumptions and attitudes which influenced the British after the Second World War in developing a nuclear weapon capability had their origin in British thinking about the atomic bomb during the war. Conversely, considerations regarding the post-war world were an important element in the British interest in nuclear collaboration during the war. These are the primary reasons for examining the period prior to Hiroshima. A secondary reason arises out of the controversy which grew after the war concerning nuclear collaboration between Britain and the United States. According to widespread thought, the intimate collaboration during the war was suddenly and unfairly brought to a halt by the passage of the McMahon Act in 1946. Closer examination, however, suggests that there was as much conflict as co-operation during the wartime years, and that much of the discord was the result of the distrust by each nation of its partner's post-war intentions.

Part Two is concerned with the dozen years during which the United Kingdom came to base its national security policy upon nuclear deterrence, without much questioning and without foreseeing the difficulties ahead. The post-war decisions to manufacture independently the atomic and the hydrogen bombs are discussed and placed in the broader context of defence policy. The concept of the British 'independent deterrent' is examined as it evolved from a particular set of economic, political, and strategic conditions in the mid-1950s. Separate chapters are devoted to more extensive analysis of the development of the nuclear and delivery systems capabilities, respectively. The breakdown in Anglo-American atomic collaboration is described and appraised, as are the negotiations which eventually led to the revival of nuclear co-operation between the two countries. The creation of the V-bomber force is discussed and put into the context of the R.A.F.'s doctrinal heritage of strategic bombardment and its self-image in the nuclear era.

Part Three investigates the 'great nuclear debate' of 1957 to 1964. A systematic discussion of the principal issues is undertaken. For analytic purposes there is a separation of the questions of: (a) nuclear strategy, i.e., in what circumstances should nuclear weapons be used?; and (b) nuclear possession, i.e., should Britain retain her nuclear weaponry? The strategic and political justifications given for retaining nuclear arms are discussed, as are the multifarious arguments for renouncing them. The interests and groups debating the issues and responding to the arguments are identified. Subsequently, there is a description and analysis of the events within the continuing debate: the Skybolt crisis, the confrontation at Nassau and the resulting Polaris arrangement, Whitehall's reaction to the MLF proposal, and the debate between the Conservative and Labour parties before the General Election of 1964 on 're-negotiating Nassau'.

Part Four deals with the dénouement of the debate following Labour's accession to office. The decision to continue the nuclear force by not cancelling the Polaris missile arrangement is explained in terms of its explicit and probable implicit reasons. The political tactics involved in the apparent reversal of Labour policy are analysed and the decision is placed in the context of the Wilson proposal for an Atlantic Nuclear Force. The Polaris submarine programme is discussed, as is the Labour government's handling of the dilemmas which were raised concerning the Poseidon missile and Anglo-French nuclear collaboration.

Part Five begins with a summary of the conclusions of the study and closes with a discussion of the prospects for the future of the British nuclear force. Britain in the early 1970s possesses a new strategic nuclear force of four Polaris submarines. This flotilla was completed, however, just as the superpower arms race was moving on to a higher technological plateau. The advent of anti-ballistic missiles (ABM) and multiple independently targeted re-entry vehicles (MIRVs) is viewed by some analysts as making small, independent nuclear forces obsolete. This assumption is disputed in the study. But the coming strategic environment will undoubtedly create additional difficulties for the maintenance of credibility, and present political opportunities for new nuclear arrangements. By 1974, or thereabouts, the British government will have to begin making some important decisions concerning the long-term future, if it is to be assured of possessing a viable nuclear force in the following decade. In reaching these decisions Whitehall planners and Westminster politicians will want to weigh such broad and complex issues as the steadfastness of the American commitment to the security of Europe, the impact of any agreement on strategic arms limitations (SALT) between the United States and the Soviet Union, the future of the Anglo-American 'special nuclear relationship', Britain's place in Europe and the future role of 'Europe', and the prospective nature of East–West relations. These parameters of policy will provide the basis for the choices which will have to be made. Britain's selection of strategic weapons systems after Polaris will involve the choice of future nuclear partners or a policy of deliberate self-sufficiency. The study ends with an analysis of six alternative political and technological options open to Britain in deciding on the future of the nuclear force.

PART ONE
The Wartime Genesis
1939–1945

1 | The Decision to Begin the British Atom Bomb Project

Britain was the first country to decide to build an atomic bomb. The original British decision was overtaken by a subsequent decision to merge the effort into a joint Anglo-American project. Nevertheless, history will probably record that the government of Britain was the first to recognize and act decisively upon the military and political implications of atomic energy.

1. Can the Possible be Left Untried?

The decision of September 1941 to proceed on what appeared certain to be a risky and expensive programme of research on the development of a 'uranium bomb' was made after seventeen months of research and deliberation by a relatively small group of scientists and public officials. It was made at a sombre time in the history of Britain when the nation stood alone in the West and its very survival was subject to serious doubt. This was eminently a wartime decision made in the midst of a situation of scarce resources and competing demands. Its basis was scientific, involving as it did questions of feasibility. But above all this was a political decision reflecting to a surprising extent estimates of the post-war environment as well as considerations concerning the immediate wartime situation.

Without the threat of Germany to Britain's national survival research on uranium might well have led eventually to the making of an atomic bomb, but certainly Germany served to compress the scientific timetable. Once it became clear that a 'decisive weapon' was a realistic possibility and that there would be no guarantee that the enemy was not working on it, there was no real alternative but to proceed on a British project. Furthermore, the implications of atomic energy, if it could be developed, were so great that subsidiary considerations could not be overlooked. Thus it was that at the highest levels of the British government in the summer of 1941 some thought was also given to the uranium project as both the progenitor of a post-war 'international police force' and as an important source of energy for industrial purposes.

Prime Minister Churchill sent to the Chiefs of Staff on 30 August 1941 his famous minute in which he wrote: 'Although personally I am quite content with the existing explosives, I feel we must not stand in the path of improvement, and I therefore think that action should be taken in the sense proposed by Lord Cherwell. . . . I shall be glad to know what the

Chiefs of Staff think.'[1] Four days later, when Churchill met with his military advisers, they recommended immediate action with the maximum priority on the development of an atomic bomb. It was determined that the project was to receive complete support with necessary manpower, materials, and money. Thus Britain, several months before the equivalent American decision, set about to develop as rapidly as possible the weapon it could not afford not to develop.

In order to identify the considerations which led to the decision to begin work on an official British nuclear research programme one must look at the incentives and disincentives as they presented themselves to the scientists and public officials. Decision-making cannot be adequately understood save in the context and environment in which the decisions are reached. 1939 was a landmark year in uranium research. Although important discoveries in nuclear physics had been made throughout the 1930s in laboratories in Germany, France, Britain, and the United States, the world's leading science journals in 1939 were replete with notes and articles which illustrated the flurry of experiment and excitement at the time in nuclear research. The authoritative British scientific journal, *Nature,* carried no less than twenty contributions on the subject of uranium in the first six months of the year.

C. P. Snow, then editor of another British scientific journal, *Discovery,* discussed the possibility of a nuclear weapon in the editorial of the September 1939 issue. He wrote:

Some physicists think that within a few months, science will have produced for military use an explosive a million times more violent than dynamite. It is no secret. . . . It may not come off. The most competent opinion is divided upon whether the idea is practicable. If it is, science for the first time will at one bound have altered the scope of warfare. The power of most scientific weapons has been considerably exaggerated; but it would be difficult to exaggerate this.

Snow then asked what could be expected if a new means of destruction, far more effective than any then existing, came into being. He suggested that most scientists who had thought about this were pessimistic about the result. 'We have seen too much of human selfishness and frailty to pretend that men can be trusted with a new weapon of gigantic power.' Could

---

[1] Margaret Gowing, *Britain and Atomic Energy, 1939–1945* (London, Macmillan, 1964), p. 106. This is the first volume of the official history of the United Kingdom atomic energy project. The author, who is Historian and Archivist of the United Kingdom Atomic Energy Authority, had full access to classified government documents relating to Britain's atomic energy activities during the Second World War and in quoting liberally from them declassified a large amount of material hitherto not made public. Part One draws heavily upon the excellent official British history. See also Winston Churchill, *The Second World War*, Vol. III, *The Grand Alliance* (London, Cassell, 1950), Appendix G, p. 730.

then the making of the weapon be prevented? Looking at the state of the world, Snow did not think so:

It must be made, if it is really a physical possibility. If it is not made in America this year, it may be next year in Germany. There is no ethical problem; if the invention is not prevented by physical laws, it will certainly be carried out somewhere in the world . . . such an invention will never be kept secret.[1]

Science, it is often said, is international. The original stimulus to British governmental action came from France. When a letter from three French scientists at the Laboratoire de Chimie Nucléaire describing an experiment which indicated an emission of three neutrons from the splitting of each uranium nucleus was published in the 22 April 1939 issue of *Nature*, Professor George Thomson, then professor of physics at Imperial College, London, was immediately struck by the importance of the discovery. After consultation with a colleague he concluded that if a sufficiently large mass of uranium were put together it would be a source of heat and power greater by many times than anything yet known and there was also the possibility that it might become an explosive of extraordinary strength. Britain was not yet at war, but Thomson quickly thought of the availability of uranium supplies. It was known that uranium ores from the Belgian Congo had been sent to Belgium where the radium had been extracted. The completed process left fairly pure uranium compounds which had up to then seemed useless. Thomson considered it a matter of the greatest urgency that any large amounts of uranium in Belgium be denied to Germany and if feasible brought under British control. So urgent did this matter seem to him that the 'normal channels' of Whitehall would not do. Accordingly, Thomson made contact with General Ismay, then Secretary of the Committee of Imperial Defence, who in turn, brought in Sir Henry Tizard, then Chairman of the Committee on the Scientific Survey of Air Defence.

Tizard, one of the first great 'scientific administrators,' agreed with the scientific hypothesis but was so doubtful that it could have a successful

[1] *Discovery*, New Series, Vol. II, No. 18, September 1939, pp. 443–4. The antecedents to C. P. Snow's prognosis are of interest. In 1925, Winston Churchill painted in Orwellian colours a world with warheads of great destruction carried by guided missiles: 'Might not a bomb no bigger than an orange be found to possess a secret power to destroy a whole block of buildings —nay to concentrate the force of a thousand tons of cordite and blast a township at a stroke? Could not explosives even of the existing type be guided automatically in flying machines by wireless or other rays, without a human pilot, in ceaseless procession upon a hostile city, arsenal, camp, or dockyard?' From *Thoughts and Adventures*, quoted in Colin Coote and Denzil Batchelor (eds.), *Churchill's Maxims and Reflections* (London, Eyre & Spottiswoode, 1947), p. 91. In 1932, Harold Nicolson published *Public Faces* (London, Constable), a novel in which the cabinet is faced with a grave crisis provoked when a British 'Rocket Aeroplane' carrying an 'atomic bomb' accidentally sinks a United States Navy cruiser and creates a tidal wave on the coast of South Carolina in 1949.

military application that he personally put the odds at 100,000 to 1. Nevertheless he recommended to Ismay that the Government should quickly buy the uranium in Belgium or acquire an option upon it, because the single chance which he believed the odds were so heavily against could not be ignored. Tizard reasoned that Britain could not risk not acting on a possibility that could have such important consequences. Lord Chatfield, Minister for the Co-ordination of Defence, to whom Ismay was responsible, was impressed by the argument that the new discoveries raised possibilities that could not be ignored and on 26 April, only four days after the publication of the letter from the French scientists in *Nature*, the Foreign Office and Treasury were approached. As it happened, little came from this early concern. Investigations revealed that existing stocks of uranium in Belgium were not of a large quantity and that there had been no unusual demand for them. A report from the Admiralty commented that 'the fact that other people have apparently not already started buying up stocks of uranium must not be ascribed to ignorance but either to the fact that foreign nations have limited funds to gamble with or that they have decided that the possibility of developing an explosive of unprecedented power from uranium is so remote as to be negligible.' In an apparent change of mind, Tizard decided against recommending that the government take on the considerable expense of buying all available stocks. It was agreed, however, that existing research should be encouraged to go forward under Professor Thomson and should be monitored by the Committee on the Scientific Survey of Air Defence.[1]

Britain's entry into the war did not serve to accelerate uranium research. As physicists were recruited from the universities to deal with urgent problems of what is now termed conventional warfare, there was even some thought of discontinuing uranium experiments altogether. Tizard reiterated his conviction that a usable bomb made from uranium was highly improbable. A similar belief emerged from quite another quarter.

Winston Churchill in August 1939 feared that the Chamberlain government would recoil from entering into a war with Germany if Poland was attacked. He was especially concerned that Hitler might try a bluff with some 'novel agency or secret weapon' which would befuddle the weak British cabinet. From time to time Churchill's close friend and scientific adviser Lord Cherwell (then Professor Lindemann) had spoken to him about uranium research. Now, after asking Lord Cherwell where things stood, he wrote to the Secretary of State for Air, Kingsley Wood. Churchill noted the recent speculation in one of the Sunday papers regarding the immense amount of energy which might be released from uranium by the

---

[1] Gowing, op. cit., pp. 34–6. For a critical study of Tizard's career see Ronald W. Clark, *Tizard* (Cambridge, M.I.T. Press, 1965).

recently discovered chain of processes which take place when the uranium atom is split by neutrons. He wrote that there were indications that 'tales would be deliberately circulated when international tension becomes acute about the adoption of this process to produce some terrible new secret explosive capable of wiping out London. Attempts will no doubt be made by the fifth column to induce us by means of this threat to accept another surrender.' Churchill, without any layman's modesty, then set out the 'true position': According to the 'best authorities' only a minor constituent of uranium was effective in these processes and it would take many years to extract this before sufficient amounts were available for large-scale results. Such an endeavour could not be kept secret, especially since only a comparatively small amount of uranium located in Czechoslovakia was under German control. The chain process could take place only if uranium was concentrated in a large mass. Before the large mass could be fully activated it would explode so that it was unlikely to produce anything much more dangerous than existing explosives. Churchill concluded, 'It is essential to realize that there is no danger that this discovery, however great its scientific interest, and perhaps ultimately its practical importance, will lead to results capable of being put into operation on a large scale for several years.'[1]

There is no evidence that Churchill's letter had any effect on the cabinet. Neither, in the early weeks of the war, does there seem to have been much concern in Whitehall about a uranium bomb. In press speculation about Hitler's 'secret weapon', the uranium bomb was sometimes mentioned. It was also discussed in British scientific circles but the general view seems to have been that it should not be taken seriously. Nevertheless, at a meeting of the War Cabinet Lord Hankey, Minister without Portfolio, asked Dr. Edward Appleton, the head of the Department of Scientific and Industrial Research, what information he had. Appleton, forgetting that Professor Thomson was continuing his research for the Tizard Committee, wrote to Professor James Chadwick of Liverpool University. Chadwick, who had discovered the neutron in 1932, was considered Britain's greatest nuclear physicist. Four years later Chadwick, as head of the British scientific mission in the United States, was to be one of the strongest supporters of a post-war British nuclear programme. In the autumn of 1939, however, it seemed to him that although an explosion might result from the uranium fission process, questions of feasibility and lack of data left serious doubts about the possibility of a controlled chain reaction. Consequently when Appleton sent Chadwick's observations to Lord Hankey, the latter felt able to inform the Minister for the

[1] Winston Churchill, *The Second World War*, Vol. I, *The Gathering Storm* (London, Cassell, 1948), p. 301.

Coordination of Defence that he gathered 'we may sleep fairly comfortably in our beds.'[1]

Similar scientific advice came from another source. Thomson in his experiments at the Imperial College was coming to the conclusion that a wartime uranium project was not worth pursuing.[2] A report along these lines was in fact submitted to the Director of Scientific Research at the Air Ministry. As Gowing observes, by the spring of 1940 'practically everyone had more or less ruled out a uranium bomb as a serious proposition for the Second World War.'[3]

Then, unexpectedly, a report arrived from the University of Birmingham which was to change the whole pace and direction of work on a uranium bomb. Two refugee scientists, Otto Frisch and Rudolf Peierls, by asking the right questions had theoretically explained how a bomb could be practically constructed. In three pages they suggested how U-235 could be separated, analysed the criticial size of a bomb, discussed how it could be detonated, and predicted the enormous radiation effects.[4] The interest of Thomson and Tizard was quickly aroused by the report, and it was further increased by a visit to London of Lieutenant Alliers, a French intelligence officer from the Ministry of Armaments. He told British scientists of experiments in Paris using 'heavy water' which had implications for an atomic bomb. Alliers further reported that Germany was making great efforts to learn about uranium research in France and had been seeking to acquire heavy water stocks in Norway.

In combination the Frisch-Peierls Memorandum and the Alliers visit served to initiate action in several directions. The Ministry of Economic Warfare was asked to try to remove from the Continent stocks of uranium oxide which could be captured by the Germans. The Intelligence Bureau was asked to learn about the present activities of nuclear scientists still in Germany.[5] New experiments were started and the British Scientific Attaché in Washington was queried on the current state of uranium

---

[1] Gowing, op. cit., p. 39.

[2] The history of early atomic energy research in Britain is given in the White Paper released shortly after Hiroshima, Great Britain, Treasury, *Statements Relating to the Atomic Bomb* (London, H.M.S.O., 1945). A more descriptive and complete account may be found in Ronald W. Clark, *The Birth of the Bomb* (New York, Horizon Press, 1961).

[3] Gowing, op. cit., p. 42.

[4] For the text of the Frisch-Peierls Memorandum see ibid., Appendix I. According to Gowing (p. 42) it stands as the 'first memorandum in any country which foretold with scientific conviction the practical possibility of making a bomb and the horrors it would bring'.

[5] British intelligence had good reason to believe that Germany was working on a bomb. The fission process was discovered in Germany by Otto Hahn in December 1938, and another German published the first paper on the theory of the chain reacting pile. The Alsos mission which advanced with the United States Army into Germany in 1944–5 found, however, that the 'race' was a rather one-sided affair. The Germans were nowhere near producing an atomic bomb and did not believe anyone else could. See Samuel A. Goudsmit, *Alsos* (New York, Henry Schuman, 1947).

research in the United States. Most important, as it turned out, a uranium sub-committee of the Committee for the Scientific Survey of Air Warfare was officially organized. Thus in the early months of the war the threat that an atomic bomb might be possible and therefore could be made by the enemy forced the British, somewhat reluctantly, to take another look at the entire matter.[1]

2. The Maud Report

The Maud Committee, as it came to be known,[2] must certainly rank as one of the most important scientific groupings of modern times if it is to be judged by its long-term effect. By providing the impetus for setting Britain on the road toward the development of an atomic bomb, it strongly influenced the later American decision to do likewise. Although it can probably be said that the long thread of uranium research in the 1930s made the development of the bomb 'inevitable' in the wartime 1940s, there is considerable evidence to suggest that without the sense of urgency and efficiency which the Committee imparted to uranium research in Britain in 1940–1, the atomic bomb would not have been ready for use until well after the planned invasion of Japan in the fall of 1945.

It is all the more noteworthy, therefore, that the Maud Committee as it was organized in April 1940 was essentially an informal, academic group made up entirely of scientists and only loosely connected to the Whitehall apparatus. The Committee addressed itself to two critical questions: Can scientists produce a uranium bomb? If so, could Britain and her allies make one before Germany? The Frisch-Peierls Memorandum had been a wholly theoretical prediction, an 'inspired hunch'. The task now was to decide if an atomic bomb was a practical possibility.[3]

In order to answer these questions much brilliant and original scientific

[1] Clark, who interviewed many of the principals involved, notes 'the harrying spur of fear—fear that somehow, someone within the frontiers of the Reich, might after all discover the trick of the thing.' *The Birth of the Bomb*, p. 41.

[2] As German troops were invading Denmark Niels Bohr, who had done important research with uranium, sent Frisch a personal telegram which ended with 'Tell Cockcroft and Maud Ray Kent'. The final three words were interpreted by the scientific and military authorities to be an anagram for 'radium taken' and were seen as strong evidence that Germany was active in this field. Only years later did it become known that the message was intended for his children's former governess, Maud Ray, living in Kent. These were the circumstances which suggested a name for the Committee. Ibid., pp. 76–7.

[3] The original members, most of whom were to have important parts in subsequent atomic energy developments both during and after the war, were Professors George Thomson (Chairman), James Chadwick, John Cockcroft, Mark Oliphant, and Dr. P. B. Moon; Professors Patrick Blackett, Charles Ellis, and William Haworth were added soon after it first met. Subsequently other scientists were to become involved in its work. Gowing, op. cit., pp. 45–8, 67.

research was undertaken in the leading British university laboratories
during the next fifteen months. The research was co-ordinated during the
meetings of the Maud Committee at the Royal Society in London.[1] At
the same time the Committee looked over its shoulders on uranium
research in Germany. Information about German scientific institutes,
German periodicals, and lecture programmes was examined by members
of the Committee for any clues of the whereabouts and research interests
of certain scientists. German interest in Norwegian heavy water, in
Portuguese uranium, and the placing of orders for a large number of fans
suitable for a gaseous diffusion plant was observed. The Committee even
discussed developing devices for the detection of the explosion of radioactive bombs. The evidence gathered did not give any signs that the
Germans were working on an atomic bomb. Nevertheless, the British
scientists 'felt the breath of their German competitors hot on their necks'.[2]

The report of the Maud Committee said specifically that it believed it
was possible to make an 'effective uranium bomb' which would be a
'very powerful weapon of war'. It noted that the Committee had begun
its work with 'more scepticism than belief' but felt that it was a matter
that 'had' to be investigated. Such a bomb, the report said, was 'practicable' and could be ready by the end of 1943 at an estimated cost of
£5,000,000. In retrospect, the estimates of cost and time were optimistic.
More accurate was the estimate that a uranium bomb would have a
destructive effect equivalent to 1,800 tons of T.N.T. and that it would
release large amounts of radioactive substance which would make the
area where the bomb exploded dangerous for some time.

The Committee did not feel constrained from making specific recommendations on the broader political considerations at the beginning of its
report, although the bulk of the report dealt with scientific and technological matters. Having said that a bomb was feasible, it also strongly
urged that it be constructed. The destructive effect—moral and material
—was so great that 'every effort should be made to produce bombs of
this kind.' It mentioned evidence of German interest in securing supplies
of heavy water and noted that 'the lines on which we are now working

[1] One of the first problems to arise regarded security. British regulations did not permit the
inclusion of aliens in secret wartime scientific work. Thus at first even Peierls and Frisch were
excluded from knowing about the deliberations of the Maud Committee. Many of Europe's
leading nuclear physicists, including Dr. H. von Halban and Dr. L. Kowarski, former colleagues
of Dr. F. Joliot-Curie, and Dr. Klaus Fuchs, were then refugees in Britain. Loopholes to this
bureaucratic problem were found by creating a Technical Sub-Committee of the Maud Committee and by placing the scientists under contract to the Universities rather than a Ministry.
Since most of the wartime scientific research was undertaken by scientists directly on the government payroll, there is some irony in a situation whereby the greatest of all wartime secrets
was entrusted to scientists who were excluded for security reasons from other war work. Gowing, op. cit., pp. 46–8, 53–4.
[2] Ibid., p. 87.

are such as would be likely to suggest themselves to any capable physicist.' Then the Committee looked at the post-war world and made what at the time must have appeared as an eerie statement, the full significance of which would not become apparent for some years: 'Even if the war should end before the bombs are ready the effort would not be wasted, except in the unlikely event of complete disarmament, since no nation would care to risk being caught without a weapon of such decisive possibilities.'

The time had now been reached, the report said, when it was important that a decision be made as to whether work was to be continued on the increasing scale which would be necessary if Britain could hope to have an effective weapon for 'this war'. Work on uranium was being undertaken in the United States but the bulk of that effort was directed towards the production of atomic energy as a source of power rather than towards the production of a bomb. It was important and desirable that development should proceed on both sides of the Atlantic irrespective of where it may be finally decided to locate a plant for separating uranium. The conclusions and recommendations of the Maud Report said:

1. The committee considers that the scheme for a uranium bomb is practicable and likely to lead to decisive results in the war.
2. It recommends that this work be continued on the highest priority and on the increasing scale necessary to obtain the weapon in the shortest possible time.
3. That the present collaboration with America should be continued and extended especially in the region of experimental work.[1]

The Maud Committee was basically a committee of scientists asked to answer scientific questions, although as we have seen it did address itself to some of the broader political questions. In the weeks following its submission the Report was discussed at several levels of government. Within the Ministry of Aircraft Production it was considered by Sir Henry Tizard, by Dr. David Pye the Director of Scientific Research, and by Colonel Moore-Brabazon the Minister of Aircraft Production. Next it was sent to the Defence Services Panel of the Scientific Advisory Committee of the War Cabinet which had been set up in October 1940 under Lord Hankey and which included some of the most eminent scientists in Britain, including three Nobel prize winners. This committee submitted its report to Sir John Anderson, the Lord President. By that time, however, the Prime Minister, acting under the advice of Lord Cherwell, had already sent the minute cited above to the Chiefs of Staff and the basic decision

---

[1] The Maud Report was published for the first time in ibid., Appendix II. There were actually two reports made at the same time, one on the 'Use of Uranium for a Bomb' and the other on the 'Use of Uranium as a Source of Power'.

to proceed on a British nuclear programme had been taken. It is not our purpose to give a step-by-step discussion of the questions taken up as they arose. Rather, we shall identify the major considerations which weighed upon the individuals as they deliberated the future of a British nuclear effort.

One of the fundamental considerations was the question of feasibility. An unusually high degree of risk was entailed since, unlike most major scientific endeavours, it was not possible to run the project through a test case on a small scale. It would therefore be necessary to spend large sums of money long before any practical results could be achieved. The list of scientific uncertainties was long; for example, no weighable quantity of U-235 had yet been isolated, nor as yet had there been an attempt to separate it from the uranium ore by the proposed method. Tizard remained sceptical, believing that it was highly improbable that anything of military importance could be developed during the war although he conceded that no one could exclude the possibility.

Closely related was the question of the amount of time necessary to develop a usable bomb. The Maud Committee had estimated two and a half years, but P. M. S. Blackett in a minority statement had said that the magnitude of the technical problems had been underestimated and insufficient allowance had been made for the inevitable delays which would arise. He doubted that an atomic bomb could be developed in time for 'this' war. Tizard supported Blackett on this point saying that he was in disagreement with the 1943 date suggested in the Maud Report. Dr. Pye commented that a fully developed bomb with all the unforeseeable problems of its handling and control might well be the work of a decade, even if the estimates of the physicists did not need serious revision. Consequently, the recommendations that went from the Ministry of Aircraft Production to the Science Advisory Committee were largely based on Blackett's view that an atomic bomb would not be ready for use in World War II. The available record does not indicate how long the war was expected to last. The Science Advisory Committee's report simply said that 'The estimates before us of the time required to bring it to fruition varied from two to five years. We expect that the lower estimate will be found to be too short.'[1]

If the successful development of an atomic bomb was considered uncertain in terms of feasibility and unlikely, if achieved, to be ready for use in the war the outcome of which remained so unpredictable, what, one must ask, were the considerations which ultimately led to the British government to decide to embark on this costly endeavour?

Certainly one, though not necessarily the most important, was the

[1] Gowing, op. cit., p. 105.

possibility that the bomb *might* still be ready for use in the war against Germany. As Lord Cherwell[1] wrote to Churchill:

People who are working on these problems consider the odds are 10 to 1 on success within two years. I would not bet more than 2 to 1 against or even money. But I am quite clear that we must go forward. It would be unforgivable if we let the Germans develop a process ahead of us by means of which they could defeat us in war, or reverse the verdict after they have been defeated.[2]

The Scientific Advisory Committee was also strongly influenced by this argument: 'We have to reckon,' it said, 'with the possibility that the Germans are at work in this field and may at any time achieve important results.' The Committee further said that the destructive power of the weapon which would be created and the ultimate importance of the issues at stake needed no emphasis. It was 'strongly of the opinion that the development of the uranium bomb should be regarded as a project of first class importance and all possible steps should be taken to push on with the work'.[3]

Clearly another consideration was the post-war implications of atomic energy. When Moore-Brabazon sent the Maud Report to Lord Hankey he had attached to it a personal letter. In the letter he suggested that a long-term, as well as a short-term, look be taken in deciding on the project. An atomic bomb would present at last the real possibility of an

[1] Lord Cherwell was the sort of controversial, mysterious, and influential personal adviser to the Prime Minister who makes the study of politics fascinating and frustrating. An Oxford physicist of Swiss extraction, an aesthete, vegetarian, and bachelor, he had formed an intimate, absolutely loyal relationship with Churchill at the time of the latter's wilderness years. During the war Lord Cherwell was asked by Churchill to form a 'statistical branch' which, with a small group of brilliant scientists and economists, dealt with subjects on which a quantitative approach would make a new contribution. This Lord Cherwell developed into a mandate covering the entire war programme, excluding only military operations and personnel appointments and promotions. He sent over two thousand private minutes to Churchill during the war years and was in closer and more continuous daily contact with the Prime Minister than any other individual—yet he was not a minister, and did not sit with the War Cabinet. Inevitably he was accused of substituting personal bias for scientific reasoning, of blocking alternative ideas, of 'court politics'. A considerable proportion of the British scientific elite opposed this man who, according to C. P. Snow, had more direct power than any scientist in history.

Lord Cherwell had watched the Maud Committee's deliberation from the sidelines, occasionally attending a meeting, at other times sending a representative. The Committee, in turn, had taken care to 'carry him along'. Until very late a sceptic as to the possibility of developing an atomic bomb, his recommendation to press ahead may well have been the decisive factor in Churchill's decision. For, as scientists have since testified of Lord Cherwell, he was 'the one man who could have stopped the whole project'. Gowing, op. cit., pp. 47, 82, 96. Clark, *The Birth of the Bomb*, pp. 104–7, 135. For a severe criticism of Lord Cherwell's role, which in turn led to some controversy, see Charles P. Snow, *Science and Government* (London, Oxford University Press, 1960). Two favourable biographies are: Earl of Birkenhead, *The Prof in Two Worlds* (London, Collins, 1961), see especially pp. 211–61, 295–7, and Roy F. Harrod, *The Prof: A Personal Memoir of Lord Cherwell* (London, Macmillan, 1959).

[2] Gowing, op. cit., p. 96.

[3] Ibid., p. 101.

CNP

'international police force'. America and Britain with their overwhelming superiority of power would have the ability to police and control the world. They would be able to stop any other country from developing a similar weapon, thereby presumably being able to check the proliferation which the Maud Report foresaw. Atomic energy could bring important future benefits to civilization. Hankey had been having somewhat similar thoughts although he appears to have been less sanguine regarding the expectation of the United States joining Britain in policing the world, remembering America's retreat into isolation following the First World War. The long-term implications had also struck Sir John Anderson, to whom it appeared essential that the project go on so that Britain and her 'associates' keep control over the enormous potentialities which atomic energy offered.[1]

Thus in 1941, eleven years before the first British atomic test, many of Britain's important scientists (Maud Committee, Scientific Advisory Committee) and her most important scientific administrators (Cherwell, Anderson, Tizard) favoured for a number of reasons, not all related to the current war, that the nation begin a serious atomic bomb project. Although it would be an uncertain and costly effort, they felt that Britain simply could not do otherwise. Perhaps subconsciously they agreed with the Maud Report's reasoning that, to repeat, 'even if the war should end before the bombs are ready the effort would not be wasted, except in the unlikely event of complete disarmament, *since no nation would care to risk being caught without a weapon of such decisive possibilities.*' (Italics mine.) A generation later, the military historian Michael Howard referred to this as 'the basic principle of British policy ever since'.[2]

3. Britain and America Compared

When one compares American research on uranium with British research in 1940–1, one is impressed by the striking contrast between the relatively relaxed and diffused nature of research in the United States as compared to the intensity and cohesiveness of research in Britain. The results of the basic research in nuclear physics of the 1930s were equally available on both sides of the Atlantic. Yet two groups of scientists and public officials —sharing the same information, facing basically identical technical problems, and holding essentially similar common values and ideals—differed in their reactions and conclusions because of the differing political environments within which they were working.

[1] Gowing, op. cit., pp. 94–7.
[2] In his review of Gowing in the *Sunday Times*, 27 September 1964.

The difference, of course, was largely due to the fact that Britain was at war and America was not. The effect of this could clearly be observed by contrasting the focus of research in the two countries. Uranium research in Britain since early 1939 had been geared to examining the feasibility of manufacturing a nuclear weapon. This is not to say that the potentialities of atomic energy as a source of power had been overlooked. On the contrary, in two appendices to the Maud Report, Imperial Chemical Industries, Ltd., had dealt at length with the great importance of nuclear energy as a potential source of power for the United Kingdom and the British Empire. The Maud Committee and the Scientific Advisory Committee in their reports both agreed on this, but they had also indicated that this was a matter of long-term development which was of substantially lower priority than an atomic bomb. Uranium research for the purpose of opening up a new source of energy was thus relegated to the somewhat vague category of post-war industrial considerations.

By contrast, much of the research in the United States until the fall of 1941 appears to have been concerned chiefly with atomic fission as a source of energy. In April 1941, Vannevar Bush, Chairman of the National Defense Research Council, asked a committee of the National Academy of Sciences to review the state of uranium research in the country. Although the committee discussed the possibility of the military application of atomic explosives, its reports of May and July 1941 disappointed Bush in their emphasis on atomic fission as a source of power and their relative lack of attention to its military significance. As late as September 1941 some members of the National Defense Research Council, not believing that there were any significant military applications in sight which could be of use in the war, argued for putting the entire uranium project 'in wraps' for the duration.[1]

Furthermore, research in the United States was clearly behind research in Britain although there were a substantial number of scientists scattered around the country working on uranium. Professor John Cockcroft of the Maud Committee had found on a visit to the United States that uranium research was several months behind that being carried out in Britain and was not proceeding as fast as the British work. He thought that American research should be carried out at a more vigorous pace.[2] Fundamentally, the authors of the official American history observe, the difficulty was that because the United States was not yet at war there was a lack of interest

---

[1] Richard G. Hewlett and Oscar E. Anderson, Jr., *A History of the United States Atomic Energy Commission*, Vol. I, *The New World, 1939–1946* (University Park, Pennsylvania State University Press, 1962), pp. 36–9. See also James Phinney Baxter, *Scientists Against Time* (Boston, Little, Brown, 1946), pp. 423, 426; Arthur H. Compton, *Atomic Quest* (New York, Oxford University Press, 1956), pp. 8, 45–9.

[2] Gowing, op. cit., p. 65.

in producing a military weapon. American scientists found it unpleasant to turn their thoughts to weapons of mass destruction. They were aware of the possibilities involved, but they had not placed them in sharp focus. 'The American programme came to grief on two reefs—a failure of the physicists interested in uranium to point their research toward war and a failure of communication.'[1]

In Britain the Maud Committee had provided an appropriate vehicle for organization and action. The stimulus, as we have seen, had come from across the Channel. As James Phinney Baxter wrote: 'Scientists who had survived the blitz were acutely conscious of what it would mean if Germany had atomic bombs at her disposal.'[2] Yet it was the highly effective work of the Maud Committee which placed the drive behind the British effort.[3] For fifteen months a small group of eminent scientists had smoothly co-ordinated and directed a programme of research in the nation's leading laboratories. Then in a masterly synthesis of scientific observation and theoretical reasoning they had written a report that was readable to the layman. This report was expeditiously brought to the policy-making level of government where its implications were carefully weighed and decisions were taken by a group of men peculiarly well suited for policy decisions of great scientific-political significance. The Maud Committee had brought to uranium research in Britain a sense of urgency and unity of purpose which was lacking in the United States.

It is not surprising then that the report of the Maud Committee had a significant impact in the United States. Some liaison had been established between the Maud technical subcommittee and the National Defense Research Council. Papers had been exchanged and a member of the Council had attended a meeting in London. Receipt of the Maud Report —which was freely transmitted by the British—marked, however, an important turning point in the American atomic energy effort. Bush and his deputy, Dr. James Conant, now had for the first time 'what they had been looking for':[4] a scientific estimate that there was a reasonable chance for something militarily useful to come from uranium research during the war then in progress in Europe. In addition, the British report made specific proposals and outlined a concrete programme—something which had hitherto not been done in the United States.

The Maud Report, together with information on British research obtained during the visit to the United States of Professor Mark Oliphant,

[1] Hewlett and Anderson, Jr., op. cit., p. 43.

[2] Baxter, op. cit., p. 426.

[3] Gowing, whose official history is notable for its balanced judgements, believes that the Maud Committee was 'one of the most effective scientific committees that had ever existed'. Op. cit., p. 80.

[4] Hewlett and Anderson, Jr., op. cit., p. 43.

a Birmingham University physicist, quickly led to a re-examination of the entire uranium question. Two distinguished American physicists, Professors G. B. Pegram and H. E. Urey, members of the uranium committee of the National Academy of Sciences, were sent to England to investigate at first hand. They visited the appropriate university laboratories where they were given full access to information. Bush, in order to obtain an independent check on the British work, enlarged the committee of the National Academy by adding more uranium experts and asked it to review the situation once more. He asked Arthur Compton, its chairman, to concentrate on the critical mass and destructive effect of a U-235 bomb and to provide full documentation on the necessary scope and direction for an intensified American effort. This time the committee reported that a fission bomb of 'superlative destructive power' was possible, thus confirming the conclusions of scientists in Britain that U-235 could be separated and made into an effective bomb. The American report was more conservative than its British counterpart. It estimated a lower destructive power, a longer time interval before production could be started, and expected that total costs would be much higher than in the British figures.[1]

There is little doubt that the Maud Report significantly influenced the American decision to pursue its atomic quest. When Bush saw President Roosevelt in October 1941, he used the British report to win presidential support. Roosevelt asked Bush to prepare a letter which would open the way to discussion with the British 'at the top'. There should be complete interchange of information with the British and when the time came to engage in large construction projects, this might be jointly done in Canada. No decision actually to produce an atomic bomb was made before Pearl Harbor; after that day, none seemed to be needed.

Looking back, one must admire the ability of the British to ask the right questions and draw the appropriate conclusions. The contrast to Germany and the Soviet Union is even more striking than with the United States. In both countries atomic research had undergone roughly parallel development to that of Britain and the United States. But because the organizational ingenuity and political will were lacking, the decisions to enter into a major bomb project were not taken. German scientists made the mistake of concentrating on heavy water rather than graphite to produce a chain reaction based on uranium, but more important still than this miscalculation was the lack of commitment and organization.[2]

[1] Henry DeWolf Smyth, *Atomic Energy for Military Purposes: The Official Report on the Development of the Atomic Bomb Under the Auspices of the United States Government, 1940–1945* (Princeton, Princeton University Press, 1948), pp. 53–4; Compton, op. cit., pp. 56–64; Hewlett and Anderson, Jr., op. cit., pp. 40–9, 259; Baxter, op. cit., pp. 427–8.

[2] David Irving, *The German Atomic Bomb: The History of Nuclear Research in Nazi Germany* (New York, Simon Schuster, 1967).

Similarly in the Soviet Union, where there appears to have been no equivalent of the Maud Committee, the political leadership does not seem to have been aware of the military aspects of atomic energy until much later, too late for the Second World War. Because of competing wartime programmes, the Soviets dropped their nuclear project in the summer of 1941 and did not recommence it, with its new aim of producing weapons, until the autumn of 1943.[1] As a result of the British research and the early Maud Report, the United States made decisions which if taken later could have delayed the availability of the first atomic bomb, thereby probably making necessary the invasion of Japan and the prolongation of the costly war.

[1] Arnold Kramish, *Atomic Energy in the Soviet Union* (Stanford, Stanford University Press, 1959), pp. 34–6, 63, 106.

2 | Setting the Terms of Anglo-American Nuclear Collaboration

Problems in collaboration on atomic energy between Britain and the United States—persistent problems which in one form or another have consistently had a configurative influence on the creation and maintenance of a British nuclear capability—began at the earliest stages of nuclear development in the two countries. There is a popular but mistaken belief that close and full collaboration during the war was abruptly and crudely terminated with the passage of the McMahon Act in August 1946. This myth has been slow to fade. At the time that the world learned of the atomic bomb, it also became known that it was the result of a collaborative effort. Later, with the passage of the McMahon Act and the subsequent break in co-operation, and with the publication of certain memoirs, it emerged that collaboration during the war was not without its difficulties. Not until the recent availability of the official histories of the respective atomic energy projects have the materials become available with which it is possible to study the true course of Anglo-American collaboration during World War II.

These histories reveal that from the issue of the Maud Report in the summer of 1941 to the signing of the Quebec Agreement on 'Tube Alloys' in August 1943, officials of the two countries strove towards setting some terms of collaboration on atomic energy. There were no formal negotiations; rather, as the difficulties in the development of nuclear energy unfolded themselves in each country, the policy makers attempted to work out guidelines for the type of collaboration which would be of the most benefit to their respective national programmes. The deliberations within each country, therefore, often led to discussion of the national purpose and objectives to be sought through nuclear research. They also led to misunderstandings and friction between the allied countries.

The statesmen and scientists involved were not unaware of the immense transformations in military and industrial technology which were likely to result from the successful exploitation of nuclear energy. Clearly, these transformations were certain to have an important effect on world politics and the standing of nations in the post-war international system. The discussions between the British and Americans reflected to a considerable extent expectations as to the role of atomic energy in their post-war national security. Indeed, many of the arguments in Britain in subsequent years supporting or opposing an 'independent' nuclear role are traceable to considerations first brought out in the policy debate in the years before Hiroshima. With the stakes so high, it should not be surprising that collaboration was not easily achieved.

1. Britain Rejects United States Proposal for a Joint Project

It was the United States which first took the initiative in proposing that the two countries produce the atomic bomb together and it was Britain which first shied away from such a joint venture.[1] After the Maud Report was read in Washington in August 1941, Vannevar Bush and James Conant called in Dr. Charles Darwin, director of the newly created British Central Scientific Office in Washington. They suggested that the possible development of an atomic bomb be regarded as more than merely a subject of information exchange and co-ordinated research, but be undertaken as a joint project by the two Governments. Bush and Conant proposed a bi-national committee to decide on the prospects of building a bomb together within two years. When he transmitted the proposal to Lord Hankey, Darwin recommended that a mission be sent over from England immediately to make this joint inquiry and that if the results were affirmative the atomic bomb be considered a joint project.

Hankey's reaction could not have been very favourable for the letter was not answered until seven months later, after Darwin returned to London. Then it was answered by Sir John Anderson, who in a letter to Bush and Conant allowed the opportunity for a joint project to slip by. Existing co-operation between scientific groups in the two countries, he wrote, was 'very good indeed'. With the technical situation fluid as it was now, it seemed inadvisable as yet to decide on any detailed plans for full-scale development. He assured Bush and Conant 'we would like our collaboration with you in the later stages of this project to be as complete as it now is.'[2]

A second American initiative towards establishing close collaboration, this time at the heads of state level, also failed to kindle British interest. President Roosevelt on 11 October 1941 wrote to Churchill that 'it

---

[1] The wartime exchange of general scientific information between the two countries began in the fall of 1940 when Tizard led a scientific mission to Washington which brought with it a 'black box' containing drawings and details of important weapons and inventions. At the time the British were primarily interested in exchanging information on radar, which had immediate wartime importance, but the Tizard mission also broke the ice on the exchange of reports on uranium research. Vannevar Bush, *Modern Arms and Free Men* (New York, Simon & Schuster, 1949), p. 39; Baxter, op. cit., pp. 119–20.

[2] Gowing, op. cit., pp. 94, 132.

appears desirable that we should soon correspond or converse concerning the subject which is under study by your Maud Committee and by Dr. Bush's organization in this country in order that any extended efforts may be co-ordinated or even jointly conducted.'[1] A reply was not received until December, at which time Churchill simply gave a general assurance of 'readiness' to collaborate and said that he had arranged for the scientific liaison officer of the American Embassy in London, Mr. Hovde, to discuss the matter with Lord Cherwell and Sir John Anderson.

What then followed, given the subsequent post-war American mistrust of British security procedures, was not without irony. Anderson told Hovde that the British government was anxious to collaborate with the United States as fully as possible but was 'disturbed about the possibility of leakage of information to the enemy'. The United States, he said, did not have the same means of preserving secrecy as Britain which was organized for war. It was therefore important to consider how the American project could be best organized in order to ensure the maximum secrecy. Thus, instead of making progress towards some sort of a joint project, the Anderson-Hovde meeting simply produced an agreement to exchange information on organizational structures in the two countries. Subsequently the British made some detailed suggestions as to how the American organization might be improved by adopting some features of their own organization.[2]

The reluctance of the British to merge their atomic energy project with the United States had been foreshadowed in the internal Whitehall debate concerning the most suitable location for the large-scale plants when it came to the time for their construction. The Maud Committee had felt that a 'boiler' project of Dr. Hans von Halban, which it thought would have civil power but not military application, might be transferred to America. As to the location of a large plant for separating U-235 for the bomb its recommendations had begged the question by simply saying that development work should proceed on both sides of the Atlantic. In his dissent from the Maud Committee's optimistic estimate of the time necessary for building a bomb, Professor Blackett had suggested that the project was so novel and large that a separation plant would have to be constructed in the United States. The Ministry of Aircraft Production's recommendations to the Scientific Advisory Committee espoused Blackett's view and proposed that a small delegation should go to America to discuss erecting a full-scale plant there. Tizard and Anderson, concerned with the allocation of scarce resources, also felt that it would be necessary for the British project to move to the United States. Tizard was worried about the drain which construction in Britain would impose upon highly skilled

[1] Ibid., p. 123.   [2] Ibid., pp. 123-5.

workers who would otherwise be used on aircraft, while Anderson had given thought to the risk of damage through bombardment.

Lord Cherwell, however, raised important political considerations regarding the location of the plant in the minute he sent Churchill recommending a British project. Even though large-scale manufacture would absorb skilled engineering labour, he strongly believed that if it was decided to go ahead on the project the plant should be erected in Britain, or as a last resort in Canada. Lord Cherwell wrote that:

However much I may trust my neighbour, and depend upon him, I am very much averse to putting myself completely at his mercy and would therefore not press the Americans to undertake this work: I would just continue exchanging information and get into production over here without raising the question of whether they should do it or not.[1]

Later before the Scientific Advisory Committee Cherwell again discussed the undesirability of being dependent on another country, noting that while scientists and engineers in the United States were perfectly competent they tended to be 'slow starters'.

Lord Cherwell's views were shared by Hankey. The Scientific Advisory Committee had concluded that Halban's long-term power project might be sent to America. If and when it was decided to erect a large separation plant it also must be built in North America although on political grounds 'it might be thought best' that the plant should be in Canada rather than the United States. Meanwhile a pilot plant should be built in England as well as one in Canada. The decisive argument against building a large-scale plant in England had been the danger of air attack as production of U-235 would necessitate a large sprawling plant above ground. Thus it would seem that it was not the technical-scientific factors which weighed against closer collaboration with the United States, but the political motivations. Gowing tells us that among those who believed the plant should be built in England, or if necessary Canada, were some who were 'fearful of the consequences of making America the one nuclear power'.[2]

In retrospect, the occasion for a fusion of the British and American atomic energy efforts appears to have arisen in 1941 and not been seized. At a time when Britain was ahead of the United States in both the substance of uranium research and the amount of policy-oriented thinking about its long-term implications, no need was felt to react enthusiastically to American proposals for a joint project. If the opportunities offered by the Conant-Bush initiative and the Roosevelt letter had been quickly accepted, the United States might well have later found herself willy-nilly locked into close and continuous collaboration.

[1] Gowing, p. 97.   [2] Ibid., p. 125; see also pp. 78, 92–7, 102–3, 125.

Instead, the British allowed the American overtures to pass by. When they did decide to opt for a joint project in mid-1942, the United States had progressed so far on its own that the inducements for close collaboration were relatively few. Gowing suggests that the failure to anticipate the fast growth of the American project was to affect profoundly Britain's own atomic energy project for at least a decade. This may be true, but to this must be added the postscript that it is doubtful whether any American seer could have foretold the fantastic progress of the Manhattan Project.

In identifying the reasons for the British reluctance to bring together the two projects despite the obvious economic benefits of a merger, the stated concern for secrecy seems plausible when looked at from the viewpoint of a nation desperately fighting for its survival while dealing with the America of 1941. Another reason may have been confidence in British science and the justifiable assumption that later would not be too late to take up the option for a joint project with the United States. The primary motivation, however, was probably the desire to remain independent by retaining complete control over their own project.

2. Britain Reluctantly Changes her Mind

By the summer of 1942 British policy on nuclear collaboration had undergone a substantial transformation. The British had come to the conclusion that the fusion of their atomic energy project with America's was necessary and desirable. They had been led to this conclusion by the rapid technological progress made in the American programme and the scarcity of resources available for such a large-scale endeavour at home. Moreover, the British were not unmindful of the long-term benefits to be dervied from joining forces with the Americans now.

Nuclear research in Britain following the Maud Committee's report was placed under a new organization, the Tube Alloys Consultative Council, which was to direct the British nuclear programme until after the war. 'Tube Alloys', as it came to be known,[1] was lodged in the Department of Scientific and Industrial Research.[2] Churchill named as its chairman Sir John Anderson, then Lord President and as such the official

[1] The cover name of 'Tank Alloys' had originally been suggested as a meaningless name which would include a top priority word, for tanks were then of utmost importance. Sir John Anderson pointed out that tanks would not retain indefinitely their high priority and suggested instead an important piece of equipment to be found in almost every weapon connected with the war—the tube. See Gerald Pawle, *The War and Colonel Warden* (London, Harrap, 1963), p. 128.

[2] For its history, work, and organization, see Henry Melville, *The Department of Scientific and Industrial Research* (London, Allen and Unwin, 1962).

holding ministerial responsibility for a number of governmental scientific bodies. This was a fortunate choice and Anderson was to have an important role in the development of Britain's nuclear programme for more than a decade. By an extraordinary coincidence Anderson, who was not a scientist by profession, had gone after graduating from Edinburgh University in 1903 to Leipzig for postgraduate work in chemistry where he had decided to do research on uranium, the radioactivity of which had been discovered by the French scientist Henri Becquerel a few years earlier. Although his later career was essentially as an administrator he had thus acquired a special interest and understanding for science, and particularly uranium research, which was to serve him well.[1] The person selected to have full-time executive responsibility for Tube Alloys was Wallace Akers, director of research at Imperial Chemical Industries. The appointment of Akers was to have an adverse bearing on future Anglo-American negotiations. Although chosen for his personality, drive, and knowledge, his former employment in an industry which could substantially benefit from the commercial uses of atomic energy became a source of suspicion to a number of important Americans.

In early 1942 Akers went to the United States accompanied by Professors Halban, Peierls and Simon from the Tube Alloys Technical Committee for an extended visit to the leading uranium research laboratories throughout the country. The British scientists were greatly impressed by what they found and were especially struck by the sheer size and rapidity with which the American effort was progressing. In England, work was being undertaken on one possible method of producing fissile materials, by gaseous diffusion. In the United States, research was under way on this and three additional methods: electromagnetic separation, centrifugal separation, and the production of plutonium. The British scientists found what they considered an impressively large number of able physicists and chemists

[1] Anderson (later Viscount Waverley) was an eminent example of that extraordinary type of professional administrator for which the British civil service is well known. He had joined the Colonial Office in 1905 and had peripatetically progressed through Whitehall in a variety of positions including the Irish Office, Treasury, and Home Office, where he became Permanent Under-Secretary. Having reached the top of that tree, he then spent five years as Governor of Bengal. Returning home, he was elected to Parliament to represent the Scottish Universities and in 1938 became the cabinet minister responsible for civil defence. In the War Cabinet as Lord President of the Council he took charge of sundry economic as well as scientific matters and in 1943 became Churchill's Chancellor of the Exchequer. Although he was an important member of the opposition to the Labour government after the 1945 election, he was nevertheless selected by Attlee as chairman of the United Kingdom Advisory Committee on Atomic Energy, a post he held until 1948. Churchill in 1953 asked Anderson to chair the committee which drew up the plans for the new United Kingdom Atomic Energy Authority. Not surprisingly he finished his career in the House of Lords. The success of Britain in atomic energy is due in part to the continuous able guidance, leadership, and foresight of Anderson. For his biography see John W. Wheeler-Bennett, *John Anderson: Viscount Waverley* (London, Macmillan, 1962).

working on atomic energy and supplied with ample funds. America's scientific resources, including the trained scientists and technicians in university and industrial laboratories, were much larger than in Britain. Furthermore, nuclear research did not suffer competition from other pressing wartime research requirements in the same manner, for example, as research on radar drained scientific resources in Britain. From America, Akers wrote to London: 'One thing is clear and that is that an enormous number of people are now on this work so that their resources for working out schemes quickly are vastly greater than ours.'[1]

By late spring the conclusion was being drawn in London that the United States was no longer behind Britain in the quest for the bomb and indeed was forging ahead. The British scientists who had been to America returned home with a proposal similar to the Bush-Conant proposal of the previous year. They suggested a combined Anglo-American effort directed by a joint technical committee with a council to advise on policy. The scientists were not unmindful of the need for merging the two programmes quickly. At present Britain could still make a substantial contribution to a joint project but with every passing month the relative importance of the British contribution would diminish. Akers, becoming convinced of the necessity of starting a joint endeavour while the British were still in a strong bargaining position, brought before the Tube Alloys Consultative Council in June 1942 precise proposals for a joint Anglo-American nuclear project. They called for a single organization to direct the project; the merging of Halban's 'boiler' team with the equivalent American team, or failing that, its transfer to Canada; joint experimental work on U-235; and a definite decision not to build a uranium separation plant in the United Kingdom but to consult with the United States about a possible location there.

The Council's reaction was one of hesitation. The proposals, it felt, were momentous, for they would in effect make the British programme dependent upon the Americans. Lord Cherwell remained unconvinced that it would not be possible to build a full-scale U-235 plant in the United Kingdom within a reasonable time. Further cost studies were called for as well as new estimates of the scale of work on atomic energy in Germany. Anxiety was expressed about fusing the research activities before an Anglo-American patent agreement was concluded. It was therefore decided to defer any decisions on a joint programme.

Soon thereafter Michael Perrin, Akers' deputy, made a trip to the United States. Four days after his arrival he wrote Akers an alarmed letter: the Americans were making 'enormous' progress and would very soon 'completely outstrip us in ideas, research and application of nuclear energy,

[1] Gowing, op. cit., p. 131.

and that then, quite rightly, they will see no reason for our butting in.' He had the strong impression that 'the time available for making any plans for co-ordinated work between the Americans and ourselves is extremely short and probably less than a month from now.'[1] An additional source of alarm resulted from President Roosevelt's decision, while Perrin was in the United States, to expand the American programme by building pilot plants on all four methods of producing fissile materials and to place the entire development programme in the hands of the United States Army. Perrin rightly recognized that this would make the merger of the two projects much more difficult. The Americans were rapidly overtaking the British in almost all aspects of the race for an atomic bomb and their project was soon to be reorganized in such a manner that it might prove difficult to fit the British in. Perrin urged quick action on the part of the British. The only hope which he saw for closer collaboration was an immediate and unhesitating offer.

When Akers proposed to the Tube Alloys Consultative Council for a second time a 'fusion' of the two projects, the reception was more favourable. Detailed suggestions to be made to the Americans were drawn up which included the appointment of British representatives to the policy-making and scientific levels of the American programme. The United States would be asked to construct a pilot plant for the British method of gaseous diffusion in America. A substantial portion of the British nuclear scientists and technicians would be transferred to the United States but some, particularly those working on more long-term research, would remain in Britain. Lord Cherwell was unhappy that such a large portion of the British programme should leave the country. He hoped, 'principally for sentimental reasons', that it would not be necessary to send Halban's 'boiler' team, which was not thought to have a wartime potential, to Canada, but Anderson prevailed upon him to withdraw his opposition. 'At last,' Gowing observes, 'the Council had decided that the British must throw in their lot with the Americans.'[2]

Reluctantly, Anderson asked Churchill to approve the Council's decision that the atomic programme be pursued as a combined Anglo-American effort and that most of the work be carried forward outside Britain. There was no real choice, for the construction and operation of even a pilot plant was beyond the nation's wartime capacity. Furthermore, Britain had to 'face the fact' that her pioneering work was now a 'dwindling asset', which if not quickly capitalized upon would soon leave her without any significant contribution to make to a merger. Anderson's realistic but melancholic minute to Churchill tells much of the financial and technological squeeze in which the British project had been caught:

[1] Gowing, op. cit., p. 139.   [2] Ibid., p. 144.

2. It has now become clear that the production plant will have to be on such a huge scale that its erection in this country will be out of the question during the war. Even the erection and operation of a pilot plant would cause a major dislocation in war production.

3. Meanwhile, the Americans have been applying themselves with enthusiasm and a lavish expenditure, which we cannot rival, to experimental work over the whole field of Tube Alloys. They are working on four alternative methods, and are making increasingly rapid progress. It is still considered probable that our method is the best; but it has little chance so long as work on it is handicapped by the limited resources available in this country.

4. In these circumstances, I have come to the conclusion, after discussion with my Consultative Council, that we must now make up our minds that the full-scale plant for production according to the British method can only be erected in the United States and that, consequently, the pilot plant also will have to be designed and erected there. . . . Henceforth, work on the bomb project would be pursued as a combined Anglo-American effort.

5. I make this recommendation with some reluctance, as I should like to have seen the work carried forward in this country. We must, however, face the fact that the pioneer work done in this country is a dwindling asset and that, unless we capitalise it quickly, we shall be rapidly outstripped. We now have a real contribution to make to a 'merger'. Soon we shall have little or none.[1]

In conclusion, Anderson noted that British scientists sent to the United States would be able to keep abreast of developments in the entire field of atomic energy. After the war they would be in a position to resume the British project, not where it was left off, but at the point where the combined Anglo-American effort had brought atomic research.

Churchill approved the minute and on 5 August 1942 Anderson wrote to Bush proposing the virtual merger of the two projects. Apparently unknown to Anderson, Churchill had briefly discussed Tube Alloys with Roosevelt on his visit to Hyde Park six weeks earlier. In what in retrospect appears as a significant tactical step, he had raised the subject on his own initiative with the somewhat unprepared President and had committed him to close collaboration on a 'research plant'. Churchill later wrote that he had 'strongly urged that we should at once pool all our information, work together on equal terms, and share the results, if any, between us.' In discussing the location of a plant, Churchill noted the disadvantages of construction in Britain. In addition to the diversion of precious financial and manpower resources from competing parts of the war effort, the factories would be subject to German air reconnaissance and bombardment. He was pleased when Roosevelt said the United States would build the plant, presumably as a common project. 'We therefore took this decision jointly and settled a basis for agreement.' Churchill further wrote that he had 'no doubt that it was the progress that we had made in Britain

[1] Ibid., Appendix III, p. 437.

and the confidence of our scientists in ultimate success, imparted to the President, that led to his grave and fateful decision.'[1]

In little over half a year's time there had been a complete reversal in the British attitude towards collaboration. America had entered the war and her nuclear programme had undergone rapid transition. In size, diversity, and rate of progress it had already surpassed the British. Thus the relative bargaining strength of the two nations had drastically changed. Only later, and somewhat bitterly, were the British to come to understand the real extent to which their influence in atomic matters had diminished.

3. United States Rejects British Proposal for a Joint Project

The need to react to the British proposals and subsequent representations led to a re-examination in the United States of the intended purpose and methods of collaboration. From this emerged a markedly reduced desire for collaboration and a new American policy of restricting the exchange of information. In part, this was a result of the changed balance of the United States vis-à-vis Britain in terms of accomplished nuclear research to date and the nature and extent of the commitment of scientific resources to future development. In part, also, this was due to American suspicions of the motives for collaboration of the British, especially with regard to their post-war intentions. At this time Anglo-American relations on atomic matters became embroiled in a sea of mutual suspicions and misunderstandings from which they were not fully to emerge for more than two decades.

In the view of the Americans, collaboration on a joint project as proposed by the British had become appreciably less attractive. By October 1942 it was felt that Americans were already doing ninety per cent of the work. The entire American effort was guided by a single consideration—

---

[1] Churchill, *The Hinge of Fate*, pp. 341–3. Like other examples of personal diplomacy, this discussion was a source of later misunderstanding at the 'working level'. According to Gowing, there is no record in the British files of any discussion of Tube Alloys on this trip. British officials first heard of the Hyde Park talk when collaboration broke down. See Gowing, op. cit., p. 145, fn. 1. An exception, apparently, was General Ismay who was told by the Prime Minister after his return to Washington from the Roosevelt home of the 'very satisfactory' agreement reached on Tube Alloys. See Lord Ismay, *The Memoirs of General Lord Ismay* (London, Heinemann, 1960), p. 254. Bush, a month later, received a memo from the President saying that he and the Prime Minister were 'in complete accord'. There was no written agreement and evidently no effort had been made to spell out the details; the only other participant in the discussion had been Harry Hopkins. (See Hewlett and Anderson, Jr., op. cit., p. 261.) Possibly both national leaders had forged ahead of their advisers and did not wish to commit themselves on matters on which they were not fully briefed. Possibly, also, Churchill was aware that trying to get a written agreement would push the matter to the Bush-Conant level from which objections might well emanate.

to have the atomic bomb as quickly as possible. 'Every other consideration,' according to General Leslie Groves, the top military officer of the Manhattan Project, 'whether the advancement of knowledge for the sake of knowledge or the maintenance of friendly diplomatic relations with other powers . . . [was] subordinated to achieving the project's single overriding aim.'[1] This criterion of speed encouraged American scientists to decide to construct large-scale plants on minimum data. Accordingly, plans were made to construct a gaseous diffusion plant on the basis of available information without awaiting the results of a pilot plant using the British method of gaseous diffusion. The question of locating a British pilot plant in the United States would therefore not come under consideration. Neither would the British scientific contribution be essential.

Bush and Conant came to believe that the exchange of information with the British could only be justified when it would contribute directly to the war effort. A joint project, as suggested by the British, could bring little but trouble and was not likely to save time. In addition, the British were only working on one of the four possible 'routes' to the bomb. Bush and Conant were reluctant to give the British information on the other three methods, all completely American in origin and development.[2]

Another factor which helped move American policy away from desiring closer collaboration was the increasing emphasis on security which came with the reorganization of the American programme and its partial placement under military authority. General Groves, in an effort to limit the amount of information on the Manhattan Project known to any individual or group of scientists, instituted a policy of 'compartmentalization'. Under this concept, individuals should only have what information they needed for their jobs, and none for the purpose of 'satisfying their curiosity' or increasing their scientific knowledge. Groves also believed it would improve efficiency by making the scientists, in his words, 'stick to their knitting'.[3] After the Quebec Agreement, the British who were working in the United States were reluctantly 'compartmentalized'. Before then, they had argued that it could not be applied to the British team because their numbers were too small and their talents too varied. But to the Americans it seemed unfair to 'compartmentalize' their own compatriots while allowing the group of British scientists to receive more information on the Manhattan Project through reports or travel around the several locations where American scientists were at work.[4]

---

[1] Leslie R. Groves, *Now It Can Be Told: The Story of the Manhattan Project* (New York, Harper, 1962), p. 11.

[2] Hewlett and Anderson, Jr., op. cit., pp. 263–5.

[3] Groves, op. cit., p. 140.

[4] The security precautions of the Manhattan Project were especially invidious to the British temperament. After the war Professor Oliphant, the eminent Australian scientist who worked

The most important obstacle to closer collaboration, however, was the developing suspicion of the British motive for wanting it. Conant and Bush were becoming convinced that the British were primarily interested in collaboration in order to ensure that they would have all the knowledge on nuclear energy in the post-war era. Ironically, they felt the British were deeply concerned with the *commercial* benefits of nuclear energy. Their objection to this was that full collaboration would divert the attention of the British away from the immediate and pressing goal of developing an atomic bomb. When in order to counter this suspicion Lord Cherwell told Hopkins and Bush at the White House that the British were really interested in having all the information not for its commercial aspects but so that they could manufacture a *British* atomic bomb promptly *after the war*, this seemed to him to be an argument which would sway the Americans towards closer collaboration.

The appointment of Akers as the executive director of the Tube Alloys project, thereby making him chief negotiator with the Americans, generated a substantial amount of suspicion. Bush, Conant, and Groves all judged Akers to be an Imperial Chemical Industries man at heart, really more interested in power plants than in bombs. Akers was a subtle and persistent negotiator and the more forceful his arguments in favour of greater exchange of information became, the more the Americans were convinced that the British were primarily moved by commercial interests. According to Groves:

if the British, particularly Akers, had not displayed such an interest in, and had not insisted on obtaining material of value solely for postwar industrial possibilities, the existing interchange of information might not have been affected. Negotiations broke down not because of American policy but because the British refused to accept our view that collaboration should be for the purpose of winning the war—not for postwar purposes.[1]

With American thinking developing in this direction, it is not surprising that the letter which Bush wrote Anderson two months after the British proposals for a joint project were made was termed by Conant a 'masterly evasive reply'.[2] When Akers subsequently came to Washington in November 1942, the interchange of information which had existed between the two countries since the days of the Maud Committee had been reduced

on electro-magnetic separation at Berkeley, characterized 'compartmentalization' on a BBC broadcast as 'a rigid system of secrecy . . . creating the atmosphere of a secret service thriller . . . barbed wire and guards appeared overnight'. M. L. Oliphant, 'The American Story', in *Atomic Challenge* (London, Winchester Publications, n.d.), pp. 22–3. Gowing acknowledges that General Groves became the 'Aunt Sally' of the scientists against whom they pinned their resentments and frustrations. But Groves is also seen as having been competent and fair, even though single-minded and tough. Gowing, op. cit., pp. 236–7.

[1] Groves, op. cit., p. 130. See also Hewlett and Anderson, Jr., op. cit., pp. 265–71.
[2] Hewlett and Anderson, Jr., op. cit., p. 264.

to a trickle. In their discussions, Akers and Conant were unable to agree upon terms for collaboration. Conant said information given by the United States was to be restricted to information which could be useful to Britain in the current war. Under this 'need to know' basis, the British were not to receive information on processes on which they were not actually working. This also meant that British scientists and engineers would receive some theoretical information, but would not have access to the bomb design laboratory and some of the production plants.

Akers' protests against these restrictions were of several sorts. First, British scientists should have complete access to all American plants, because information on one method would have direct bearing on programmes under consideration for other methods. Second, the President and the Prime Minister had always intended a co-operative effort, regardless of the country of origin of the ideas and methods chosen or of the location of the plants to be erected. Third, Akers suggested that, as after the First World War, America might become isolationist. Britain would then have the responsibility for keeping the peace in Europe and thus must have full knowledge of the processes of manufacturing the ultimate 'police weapon'.[1]

It became clear to Conant, Bush, and Groves that they would have to ask President Roosevelt for a directive on future relations with Britain on atomic matters. In their view, the only criteria which justified interchange of secret information was furthering the military effort. It appeared to them that Britian would not be in a position to embark on the development of a large-scale atomic programme during the war. Since it was therefore unlikely that they would produce any fissionable materials, passing information to the British on plants and production would be of no direct assistance in prosecuting the war.

The Military Policy Committee of the Manhattan Project sent a report in late December 1942 to President Roosevelt, along with a letter from Akers which set forth the British case in great detail. The report reviewed the background to the exchange of information and included a summary of the two positions. Three possibilities were suggested for future collaboration: (1) cessation of all interchange; (2) complete interchange not only in research but also in development and production, including the exchange of personnel; (3) restricted interchange to the extent that information could be used by the recipient for immediate wartime purposes. The third possibility was strongly recommended although if it came to a choice between the two extremes, cessation was thought to be preferable to complete interchange.[2]

[1] Ibid., pp. 265–6; Gowing, op. cit., pp. 152–4.
[2] Groves, op. cit., pp. 129–30; Hewlett and Anderson, Jr., op. cit., p. 267.

President Roosevelt approved on 28 December 1942 the third recommendation for a policy of restricted exchange of information. To what extent he recalled the general understanding with Churchill of the previous June is not known. What is known is that by a curious turn of fate there arrived on his desk two days earlier an Anglo-Russian agreement for the exchange of new weapons, both those currently in use and those which might be discovered in the future. This was the first time Roosevelt or Stimson had heard of this agreement and it seems to have added to the distrust of the British.[1]

The new policy of restricted information transfer was set forth in a memorandum written by Conant. It set the 'basic principle' that interchange was to be carried out 'only to the extent that the recipient of the information is in a position to take advantage of this information in this war'.[2] Under its detailed provisions, information would be withheld from the British over the greater part of the American atomic energy programme. Thus not only was the joint project to which the British had aspired completely out of the question, but existing collaboration was to be severely restricted.

4. Britain Reconsiders an Independent Project

Britain's reaction to America's refusal to enter into effective collaboration was one of shock, dismay, and determination not to allow itself to be edged out of the drive for an atomic bomb. As soon as Anderson learned of the new American policy he wrote to the Prime Minister: 'This development has come as a bombshell and is quite intolerable. I think you may wish to ask President Roosevelt to go into the matter without delay.'[3] The British, who were by now deeply involved in co-operative wartime planning with the United States on many matters of strategy and logistics, were hopeful that a more reasonable policy on nuclear matters could be achieved at the heads-of-state level. Failing this, they could either accept the American terms for collaboration or make an attempt to 'go it alone'.

There appears to have been a difference in the British and American assessments of the reasons for the new American policy of restricted exchange of information. In Washington Akers was told by Conant, Bush, and Groves that the reason for the use-in-current-war limitation

---

[1] Hewlett and Anderson, Jr., op. cit., pp. 267–8. According to Gowing, the agreement had been made with the knowledge and approval of the United States and it was intended that the forthcoming Anglo-Russian discussions would include only items approved by the United States, op. cit., p. 155.

[2] For the text of the Conant Memorandum see Gowing, op. cit., p. 156.

[3] Ibid., p. 157.

to interchange was the speedy prosecution of the war. In London, on the other hand, the Tube Alloys Technical Committee, after examining the American policy, felt certain that it was designed to give the United States sole control of atomic energy both as a military weapon and for industrial purposes. Moreover, there was suspicion of the American military services. 'The pretext for this policy,' Anderson wrote to Churchill, 'is the need for secrecy, but one cannot help suspecting that the United States military authorities who are now in complete control wish to gain an advance upon us and feel that having benefited from the fruits of our early endeavours they will not suffer unduly by casting us aside.'[1] Thus there was a reciprocal character in the suspicion of each other's motives: the Americans were convinced that the British were primarily interested in post-war commercial advantages, while the British suspected the Americans of wanting to establish a post-war nuclear monopoly.

In the spring of 1943 the British re-examined the estimated costs in money and resources of an independent project to build a British bomb. Lord Cherwell proposed an intensified study of the possibility of erecting a diffusion plant and a heavy water plant and pile in Britain. Churchill in turn asked Anderson for a report on the implications of pressing forward on such a project, including estimates of time, money, manpower requirements, and the disruption that would be caused to other items of war production. To the authorities in London, the military and industrial potentialities of nuclear energy seemed so important that, if necessary, Britain would probably go ahead on its own.

The results of the studies of the estimated costs, however, were discouraging. The nation did have the scientific base necessary for an independent atomic project. But to take off from this base into full technological development would consume large amounts of manpower and material resources that were badly needed elsewhere. The extent of various types of costs would be so formidable that they led everyone concerned to the conclusion that it was essential to make another attempt towards achieving full Anglo-American collaboration. Another consideration also existed: Akers and Perrin were convinced that competitive British and American projects would make the problem of post-war atomic control far more difficult. Anderson, who was mindful that the Russians might also be working on Tube Alloys, joined Lord Cherwell in asking the Prime Minister to make a direct appeal to President Roosevelt.[2]

[1] Ibid., p. 159.   [2] Ibid., pp. 161–3, 229–30.

5. The Quebec Agreement of 1943

So it was that the British launched a veritable diplomatic offensive which culminated in the Quebec Agreement. In the process some of the mutual suspicions and misunderstandings were set straight, at least temporarily. As in most processes of negotiation when important issues are at stake, agreement was achieved through compromise. The road to that agreement is worth examining, for it reveals much about the motives and interests of the two nations, especially their early expectations regarding the post-war world. It is also important to examine it because the terms of collaboration set forth in the Quebec Agreement were to contribute to the post-war Anglo-American controversy on nuclear matters.

Churchill raised the issue of atomic energy at the Casablanca conference of January 1943, expressing considerable concern that the previous Anglo-American co-operation and exchange of information seemed to be drying up. Hopkins promised to look into the matter on his return to Washington, but when a month later Churchill had not heard from him he sent a telegram asking for news. Hopkins in his reply of 24 February said that his inquiries revealed that the Americans directing nuclear affairs believed that there was no continuing agreement which had been reached with the British. In response to Hopkins' request for a British statement concerning the present misunderstanding Churchill sent within seventy-two hours two long cables. In the first he reviewed the complete history of Anglo-American interchange and the assumption held in London of collaboration at all stages. In the second he agreed that there was no question of a formal breach of agreement. Interchange of information had hitherto taken place on the basis of complete mutual confidence and with the conviction that the most rapid conclusion of the project could be attained only through complete co-operation. Churchill recalled his conversation with President Roosevelt at Hyde Park in June 1942 and said that his whole understanding was that everything was on the basis of fully sharing the results as equal partners. He had no record, but he would be surprised if the President's recollection did not square with this. He merely wanted Hopkins to review the American position and restore the original policy of joint work. Churchill said that 'urgent decisions' about British programmes at home and in Canada 'depend on the extent to which full collaboration between us is restored, and I must ask you to let me have a firm decision on United States policy in this matter very soon.'[1]

Churchill received no answer. Several weeks later he sent another tele-

[1] Robert E. Sherwood, *Roosevelt and Hopkins* (New York, Harper, 1948), p. 704. See also pp. 593, 703; Hewlett and Anderson, Jr., op. cit., pp. 270–1; Gowing, op. cit., p. 159.

gram: 'Time is passing,' he observed, 'and collaboration appears to be at a standstill.' Not one to lose track of his objective, Churchill kept pressing. On 1 April, he cabled Hopkins again saying that he was much concerned about not hearing from him about Tube Alloys. 'That we should each work separately,' he observed, 'would be a sombre decision'.[1] Foreign Secretary Eden added his support, reminding Hopkins on 13 April that the British have 'various decisions to take if there has to be a separate development'. Hopkins wired that he had found that the subject had many ramifications and that he would send a lengthy telegram giving his view fully. The telegram never arrived, and was overtaken by Churchill's visit to Washington in May.[2]

Although Hopkins did not answer Churchill, he was very concerned about the state of affairs. Bush was shown the Churchill correspondence and asked to suggest a reply. After canvassing the situation with Secretary of War Stimson, Conant, and the Military Policy Committee, Bush found a consensus that the American position should remain unchanged. The 'need-to-know' formula which restricted information to those able to use it in furthering the war effort was neither new or unusual. It was standard procedure in American and British wartime projects. Bush suggested that the real reason the British objected was that the United States was withholding information which they could use after the war. He was thinking primarily of the commercial uses of atomic energy, especially as a replacement for the dwindling coal supply of the United Kingdom.[3] Hopkins, in a private conversation with the British Ambassador, Lord Halifax, which he asked not be reported to London (it promptly was), confided that he had very little doubt that on both the American and British sides there was a tendency to hold back information from one another. This he attributed to the fact that much of the scientific research was in the hands of persons who had been and would again be in the employ of big business and who therefore had their eye on the post-war interests. Hopkins was inclined to think that the only way of handling the situation was for the President and the Prime Minister to agree on the broadest lines that the pooling of information should not be confined to the war but carry over into the post-war times. The issues involved were too big to be handled by lower officials.[4]

Summit diplomacy, however, runs its risks. When the 'chiefs' and the

---

[1] Gowing, op. cit., pp. 159–60; Sherwood, op. cit., p. 704; Hewlett and Anderson, Jr., op. cit., pp. 271–2.

[2] Anthony Eden, *The Reckoning*, (London, Cassell, 1965), Appendix E, p. 569.

[3] Hewlett and Anderson, Jr., op. cit., p. 271. See also Vannevar Bush, 'Churchill and the Scientists', *Atlantic Monthly*, Vol. CCXV, No. 3 (March 1965), p. 96, and *Pieces of the Action* (New York, William Morrow, 1970), pp. 281–5.

[4] Eden, *The Reckoning*, Appendix E, p. 569.

'indians' are acting independently of each other, the results can be unfortunate as was illustrated by events at the White House on 25 May 1943.
This was the last day of Churchill's third wartime visit to Washington,
during which many arduous days had been spent hammering out an
over-all strategic concept for the prosecution of the war. An agreement
satisfactory to Churchill had been reached on this in spite of serious differences of view at the staff level and this he attributed to his close personal
contact with the President. Now he raised the question of atomic energy.
Churchill discussed the matter privately with Roosevelt, while Lord
Cherwell met in conference with Bush and Hopkins.

Churchill evidently elicited from Roosevelt a sweeping promise on
interchange. The next morning as he left for Gibraltar, he sent a message
to Anderson saying that Roosevelt 'agreed that the exchange of information on Tube Alloys should be resumed and that the enterprise should
be considered a joint one'. He understood that the President's ruling
would be based 'upon the fact that this weapon may well be developed
in time for the present war and that it thus falls within the general agreement covering the interchange of research and invention secrets.'[1]

Lord Cherwell, Bush, and Hopkins did not hear about this promise
until after Churchill left Washington; the meeting of the advisers produced
startlingly different results. Lord Cherwell, upon being closely questioned
by Bush concerning the reason for Britain's objections to the use-
in-current-war principle, fully admitted that his Government wanted complete interchange now so that Britain could manufacture an atomic bomb
of its own promptly after the war. The commercial benefits of nuclear
energy were of no immediate importance to Britain as it would take five
or ten years before their practical applications could be developed. An
amazed Hopkins and Bush maintained that the exchange of information
for post-war *military* purposes was a subject that needed to be approached
on its own merits because of its broad implications for future international
relations. Lord Cherwell countered by noting its direct connection to the
current war: in order to insure Britain's national security in the post-war
years, it might be necessary to divert some of the country's present efforts
to building production facilities for nuclear weapons.

When Roosevelt later heard from Bush about the meeting with Lord
Cherwell he was astounded to learn that Churchill's adviser had placed
the matter on an after-the-war military basis. Several times the conversation returned to the British position and each time Roosevelt seemed
amazed, remarking once on the extraordinary nature of their stand. But
a month had passed since the two meetings of 25 May during which time
Hopkins had not told Roosevelt of the discussion with Lord Cherwell

[1] Churchill, *The Hinge of Fate*, p. 723.

and the President had not told Bush of his pledge to Churchill. Thus there quite probably was discomfort on all sides. When the President discovered that he had acted on the basis of an incomplete understanding of the situation, he drew back from giving instructions for complete interchange. Bush willingly interpreted this to mean that there was to be no change in the policy of limited collaboration.[1]

Viewed from London, Anglo-American relations on Tube Alloys were once again in a quagmire. The relief felt when Churchill returned from Washington with Roosevelt's promise on collaboration turned to disillusionment and scepticism as the Americans failed to suggest ways of implementing it. Akers, who had been quickly dispatched to Washington to settle on the arrangements, was not called in for consultation. When Churchill returned to London he had written to Hopkins to confirm his discussion with the President and to express the hope that the decision could be implemented as soon as possible. Hopkins had replied that he expected the Tube Alloys matter to be completely settled within a week, but nothing further was heard from him. Anderson urged Churchill to send another message to the President. 'It is becoming most urgent', he wrote the Prime Minister, 'that we should either resume effective collaboration or part company on friendly terms which will ensure for us an adequate share of vital materials on which the Americans have secured a stranglehold.'[2] Churchill, prodding Roosevelt, asked him to let him know of any difficulties that might have arisen in case the British could help in solving them.

Roosevelt was on the spot. For several weeks he procrastinated, hoping to find some way out of the dilemma that would satisfy both Churchill and Bush. He turned to Hopkins who felt obliged to advise that having made a firm commitment to Churchill there was nothing to do but go through with it. Finally, on 20 July, eight weeks after his promise to Churchill, he sent instructions for Bush to 'renew' in an inclusive manner the complete exchange of information with the British.[3] As the British had long wanted, the use-in-this-war principle was to be cast aside.

But now an accident of history occurred. Five days earlier Bush had arrived in London with Secretary of War Stimson for a discussion on anti-submarine warfare. When Roosevelt's instructions to Bush were forwarded from his Washington office to London by coded telegraph the word 'renew' was garbled into 'review'. As it turned out, it was during this visit to London that the ground was laid for the Quebec Agreement. If the message had arrived as sent, and if Bush had acted in accordance with

[1] Hewlett and Anderson, Jr., op. cit., pp. 272–4; Groves, op. cit., p. 130.
[2] Gowing, op. cit., p. 165.
[3] Hewlett and Anderson, Jr., op. cit., pp. 274, 277.

the terms and intent of the President's instructions, the entire course of post-war Anglo-American nuclear relations might have been different.[1]

Some of the British had long suspected that the Churchillian method of dealing directly with the President stiffened the resistance of the American scientific administrators and the United States Army. As Churchill himself was to tell Bush, the President had given him his word of honour on sharing equally in the effort, but every time he got an agreement to alter the present arrangements, somebody in the American organization knocked it out. He had been at this for months, he complained. Bush, in turn, made it clear to the British that they had caused offence to some Americans by their direct appeal to the President. Now in London the Prime Minister had the opportunity to use his considerable powers of persuasion directly on America's chief scientific administrator and the Secretary of War. At an initial meeting between Churchill and Bush, and at a subsequent conference which also brought together Anderson, Lord Cherwell, and Stimson, some of the issues were finally discussed between the right people.

The Americans explained that their rationale for interchange remained set on the supposition that its sole purpose should be hastening the end of the war. What the British were asking for was information which they could only use in the post-war commercial development of atomic energy. For the first time the British now came to understand the full reason and depth of the American suspicion of their motives. They were completely bewildered, they said, by the American charge that they seemed primarily interested in commercial uses after the war. True, they had been talking about the question of patents, but they had seen patents only as a means for achieving a system of international control of atomic energy. Anderson suggested that the American concern stemmed from the fact that some of the British scientists had been encouraged to indicate interest in commercial possibilities of nuclear research as a cover for the real war-time objective. Churchill gladly asserted that Britain was interested in winning the war, not in commercial 'advantage'.[2]

In a masterful tactical stroke Churchill cleared up the misunderstanding and stressed his commercial disinterest by offering to enter into any arrangement which Roosevelt considered equitable. Churchill proposed that he and the President sign an agreement on the terms of collaboration which would include the following set of propositions:

[1] Bush and Roosevelt were probably both embarrassed by the turn of events, FDR for having had his hand forced by Churchill, Bush for seeming not to have followed instructions. Although they were on cordial terms, the episode was never mentioned between them. 'I have long wondered', Bush wrote, 'just what he thought having told me to do one thing and being presented by something quite different. I suspect he did not fully realize the dynamite in his letter, or possibly he did and wished he had not written it.' Bush, 'Churchill and the Scientists', p. 95.

[2] Hewlett and Anderson, Jr., op. cit., pp. 275–7; Gowing, op. cit., pp. 166–9.

1) A free interchange would be established to the end that the matter would be completely a joint enterprise.

2) Each government would agree not to use this invention against the other.

3) Each government would agree not to give information to any other parties without the consent of both.

4) Each government would agree not to use atomic energy against other parties without the consent of both.

5) Information passing to Great Britain concerning commercial or industrial uses would be limited in such manner as the President might consider fair and equitable in view of the large share of the expenses born by the United States.[1]

The unilateral British concession on post-war commercial applications paved the road to agreement. The 'Articles of Agreement Governing Collaboration between the Authorities of the U.S.A. and the U.K. in the matter of Tube Alloys' signed in Quebec on 19 August 1943 are essentially similar, though set in more elegant prose, to the proposals made by Churchill in London.[2] When Anderson arrived in Washington soon after the London meeting to settle on the provisions of the draft agreement he suggested adding a clause providing for a Combined Policy Committee to meet in Washington to work out the programme of collaboration, including the allocation of materials, apparatus, and plant, and the interpretation of the Agreement itself. There would be full interchange of information between members of the Policy Committee, but at the working level of scientific research and development there would be full interchange of information only between those scientists of the two countries engaged in the same activities. In the design, construction, and operation of large-scale plants, interchange of information and ideas would be regulated by such *ad hoc* arrangements as might be necessary for the speedy fruition of the project. This was agreed to by the Americans although Anderson was not successful in persuading them to accept an additional document setting out in greater precision and detail the arrangements to cover interchange.

The Quebec Agreement was an effort to resolve 'a conflict as intricate and divisive as any in the long annals of Anglo-American discord'.[3] The result of two years of informal bargaining, it was a loosely worded agreement. In subsequent years it was to become the subject of much criticism and difficulty chiefly because of a lack of specificity which permitted divergent interpretation. 'In the cold light of history it [the Quebec Agreement] may seem a little naive', it was later written.[4] At the time,

---

[1] Groves, op. cit., pp. 132–3.

[2] Text in Appendix A.

[3] Hewlett and Anderson, Jr., op. cit., p. 279.

[4] Leonard Bertin, *Atom Harvest: A British View of Atomic Energy* (London, Secker & Warburg, 1955), p. 74.

however, its generality was probably a prerequisite for agreement. The imponderables in the field of atomic energy were such that a 'tight' agreement would have been unwise, even if feasible.

To the Americans, the Quebec Agreement offered a number of benefits. Roosevelt and Stimson were anxious to remove this irritant in Anglo-American relations which threatened to poison the atmosphere of wartime co-operation. There were a number of seemingly more urgent disagreements to be resolved at the Quebec conference which competed with atomic energy for the issues on which the President should make his stand: Far Eastern strategy and Britain's part in the war against Japan; the invasion of France; Britain's claim to the command of Overlord, etc. . . . Indeed, Bush and Conant could be pleased that the President did not give the British all they wanted on Tube Alloys, as in fact he seemed inclined to do, and they feared he might. Roosevelt's instruction of the previous month to 'renew' complete interchange had been quietly 'forgotten' by Bush and there was uneasiness in Washington when the President left for Quebec without taking along anyone familiar with atomic energy problems. According to Groves, the Military Policy Committee was 'extremely concerned' lest the President enter into an undesirable agreement.[1]

Bush and Conant approved the draft agreement for mixed motives. The American project could well use British assistance, especially with their experience in the gaseous diffusion method. The British seemed strongly determined to succeed in acquiring a share in the American project, and given this attitude, their concession on commercial application was of importance. The President's advisers seem to have been concerned that without this commercial concession the President would be opening himself up to charges of having abused his wartime power by allowing the American taxpayers' money to assist in the creation of a great new British industry. Conant explained to Anderson that because of the vast sums of money spent on the Manhattan Project there would surely be a searching congressional investigation after the war, and that he was anxious there be a 'clean slate'. There was a prevalent idea in the United States, said Conant, that when the American and the British get together on a deal, the 'British always come out on top'.[2]

For the British, the Quebec Agreement enabled their scientists to continue nuclear research at a time when the continuation of the Tube Alloys project in the United Kingdom was threatened. By the summer of 1943 it had become clear that the war in Europe was certain to finish

---

[1] Groves, op. cit., p. 135.
[2] Gowing, op. cit., p. 175. See also Groves, op. cit., p. 135; Hewlett and Anderson, Jr., op. cit., p. 275.

before a British atomic production plant could be built. Thus questions were being raised as to the wisdom of allocating large sums of money for Tube Alloys while other wartime projects, the results of which could be expected to contribute directly to the war's end, were short of funds.

Churchill's concession on commercial uses, therefore, seemed a reasonable price to pay. He had no reason to believe that Roosevelt would not treat the British fairly after the war, when the two nations would be allied in planning for the control of atomic energy. As Attlee later explained, it did not seem wise to press too hard in 1943 for a firm agreement on Tube Alloys. 'We were allies and friends. It didn't seem necessary to tie everything up.'[1] In the two years between the Quebec Agreement and the end of the war British scientists and engineers in the United States were to gain far more knowledge than they would ever have been able to acquire through an independent British project.

6. In Retrospect

Central to our inquiry is the question: What considerations were given to the development of nuclear weapons in Britain in the post-war era prior to Britain's entry into full collaboration with the United States through the Quebec Agreement?

In retrospect, the determined, sometimes desperate, British effort to continue to have a significant role in the creation of the first atomic bomb stemmed from an awareness of the effect that nuclear weapons would have upon world politics. That nuclear weapons would be an important index of strength for a Great Power in the post-war pecking order was seen, if perhaps only hazily, by the leaders of a nation that had long been accustomed to being on top.

The original stimulus to pursuing nuclear research under wartime conditions had come from the threat presented to Britain's national security by Nazi Germany. By the summer of 1941, by which time some serious doubts had been cast upon the feasibility of producing an atomic bomb before the end of the war, the idea had already become prevalent among the policy makers that atomic energy would be so important after the war that Britain could not afford not to pursue a nuclear programme. The scientists, it should be noted, while conscious of what splitting the atom might lead to, were not adverse to continuing down the path of uranium research. When the United States entered the war and suggested collaboration on the atomic project the British recoiled from entering into any joint venture which might affect the autonomy of their project

[1] Francis Williams, *A Prime Minister Remembers* (London, Heinemann, 1961), p. 108.

or limit their freedom of action. Against all the economic and technological reasons for merging the two projects, the British set their reluctance to become dependent on their ally in this matter.

After a time, however, the rapid progress of the American programme and the competitive demands of wartime resource allocation at home, in effect, turned the tables. The British came to realize that they had much more to lose than to gain by not joining forces with the Americans. They were thinking primarily of where they would stand at the war's end. Conversely, in the United States, when the benefits to be gained by collaboration were no longer so great, there was reluctance to enter into it. Faced with American recalcitrance, the British were determined not to be edged out of the nuclear business. After re-evaluating the possibility of going ahead alone and finding they could not afford this during the war, they waged a desperate, and ultimately successful, struggle to push the Americans into collaboration.

By mid-1942 it was quite certain that the United States would devote enormous resources to the Manhattan Project and would spare no effort in its drive for the bomb. Since there was no likely requirement in the existing war for an independent British nuclear capability, one must conclude that the British were thinking primarily of the post-war era. From the start, the British never wavered in their intent to develop nuclear energy; never did they seriously consider leaving it completely to the Americans. Yet the American dominance in nuclear matters, which loomed so large after the war, had already come into being. In Tube Alloys, as in so many other areas, the years 1942–3 marked a shift in the balance of power between Britain and the United States.[1] The political, economic, scientific, and technological constraints under which the British nuclear programme found itself during the war form a microcosm of the problems which beset the British in the development of nuclear weapons after the war.

While the British may have fallen behind the Americans in the development of nuclear technology, they were considerably advanced in thinking about its implications for international politics. If in the United States there was an uneasy general awareness among a few people that there would be a post-war problem in the control of atomic energy, little concrete thought was given to planning for it. Among the reasons discussed in Washington for restricting collaboration with the British none appears related to avoiding a second national nuclear weapons capability. While this may be understandable, it should none the less be noted that in

---

[1] For an extensive analysis of the wartime power relationship see William H. McNeill, *America, Britain, and Russia: Their Co-operation and Conflict, 1941–1946* (London, Oxford University Press, 1953), especially pp. 754–7.

negotiating the terms of the Quebec Agreement no effort was made to limit Britain's *military* nuclear capacity after the war. American concerns were focused on developing the bomb quickly, on military security, on accountability to Congress, and on the commercial aspects of atomic energy. Indeed, the Americans, in suspecting the British of harbouring grandiose schemes for the commercial exploitation of nuclear energy, failed completely to identify the true British motivation.

'It was not the carrot of post-war commercial possibilities that drove Churchill, Anderson, and Cherwell on,' writes the official British historian, 'but the stick of the post-war military possibilities.'[1] If this were not so, would the British so readily have conceded to the American President in the Quebec Agreement the arbitrary authority to decide what share of the commercial benefits would be theirs? The Maud Report, as far back as the summer of 1941, had said that even if the war should end before an atomic bomb was ready, no nation would subsequently care to risk being caught without such a decisive weapon. Anderson, with great foresight, later pinpointed this argument more concretely when he wrote: 'We cannot afford after the war to face the future without this weapon and rely entirely on America should Russia or some other power develop it.'[2] Lord Cherwell, in rebutting Bush's suggestion of commercial motivation, had frankly avowed that Britain wished after the war to be in a position to manufacture nuclear weapons. Churchill, in disclaiming commercial interest at the London meeting prior to the Quebec Conference, said that something much more important was at stake—Britain's independence in the future. To British statesmen, Great Power status in the post-war environment would require nuclear weapons. Gowing comments: 'The idea of the independent deterrent was already well entrenched.'[3]

[1] Gowing, op. cit., p. 168.   [2] Ibid.   [3] Ibid.

3 | Wartime Planning for a Post-War Nuclear Programme

In the two-year period between the signing of the Quebec Agreement and the end of the war, the British gave much thought and attention to what might be the organization and direction of their post-war nuclear programme. This came as a natural consequence of their collaboration with the Americans. The ostensible purpose of collaboration was to help produce an atomic bomb as early as possible. But it was widely recognized in Britain that collaboration had the additional advantage of enabling its scientists to acquire far more knowledge and experience than they could ever have hoped to acquire in the same amount of time from an independent British project. Thus wartime planning for a post-war nuclear programme proceeded side by side with collaboration. Indeed, the very frame of mind with which the British approached substantive aspects of collaboration was often conditioned by post-war considerations. In this chapter we look at the plans laid *during* the war for Britain's own project *after* the war, and the political and diplomatic steps taken to assure its achievement. It is necessary to begin by discussing and evaluating Britain's contribution to the American programme and to the Anglo-Canadian programme set up in Montreal and Chalk River from the viewpoint of the effect it had upon British planning for their own post-war nuclear programme.

1. Collaboration in America—the Balance Sheet

The British may have had a premonition that the harvest of collaboration would be bountiful. When it seemed certain that an agreement would be signed at Quebec, a cable was sent by Anderson to London asking Professors Chadwick, Simon, Oliphant, and Peierls to leave for the United States at once. They arrived in Washington the day the Quebec Agreement was signed—with indecent haste, it appeared to the Americans. The Combined Policy Committee which had been created to co-ordinate the collaboration did not have its first meeting until several weeks later. By that time Bush and Conant had let it be known that Akers, who was expected to be the Technical Adviser to the British members of the Combined Policy Committee, was considered *persona non grata* because of his former affiliation with Imperial Chemical Industries. Anderson was deeply distressed by what appeared to him as an unfair attitude towards a person of high integrity and ability, but for the sake of Anglo-American co-operation he replaced Akers with Professor Chadwick and also made the latter director of Tube Alloys Mission in Washington.[1]

This step typified the British attitude towards the Americans: smooth collaboration was to be maintained even if at a sacrifice. The British were aware, as their Embassy in Washington reported, that on nuclear matters 'the salad is heaped in a bowl permanently smeared with the garlic of suspicion.'[2] Because of their constant attention to American sensitivities, the British succeeded in achieving generally friendly and harmonious relations. The Combined Policy Committee, which made arrangements for British scientists to work in American projects, promoted a Combined Development Trust to organize jointly the acquisition and allocation of raw materials, sponsored an agreement concerning patents, and arranged for American assistance to the Canadian project, conducted its business without any serious differences of opinion. This Groves attributed in large measure to the 'awareness' on the part of its British members of the measure of their contribution in contrast to the 'magnitude' of the American programme.[3] An additional factor was the excellent personal relationship established between the mild-mannered Chadwick and the tough Groves, based upon a mutual respect for each other's task and the discretion exercised by the scientist in dealing with the general.[4]

Chadwick believed that without doubt the British must undertake a major atomic energy project after the war. When, after Quebec, the British learned the full extent of American progress, they were amazed. Chadwick was quick to realize that the British contribution was not necessary for the rapid completion of the American project. The British scientists, relatively small in number compared to the Americans, could expedite progress, improve design and operating methods, and contribute new ideas; but their participation was far from crucial to the goal of the Manhattan Project. Chadwick therefore reasoned that the British were fortunate to be allowed to join the enterprise and that it was to their advantage to send the greatest possible number of scientists to the United States, so that they could acquire knowledge and experience in as many aspects of the project as possible.

Chadwick successfully urged Anderson, who obtained Churchill's assent, to send to the United States the best men obtainable, whether or not they had worked on Tube Alloys. The remaining Tube Alloys project in Britain was sharply reduced for the duration of the war. High priority was given to releasing qualified experts from other war work. After collaboration had been resumed, Chadwick realized that the help the

---

[1] Gowing, op. cit., pp. 171–3.   [2] Ibid., p. 235.
[3] Groves, op. cit., p. 136.   [4] Gowing, op. cit., pp. 236–7.

British were giving, however substantial, was relatively unimportant compared to the knowledge they were gaining through their participation. Indeed, the British were acquiring information which it would have taken them years of effort to get on their own.[1]

Teams of British scientists worked in various parts of the Manhattan Project. An important British contribution might have been expected in the gaseous diffusion process, on which the British had done the initial theoretical and laboratory work, but the Americans had already fully committed themselves to their own method. Groves asked the British to discuss their experience in gaseous diffusion and to give an independent assessment of various unresolved questions. Although the British assisted in solving some technical problems the basic method was, to the chagrin of the British, not the one they had developed. At Berkeley, Oliphant headed a small British group which assisted Lawrence on the electromagnetic separation process. Although this was the large-scale American project for producing fissile material to which the British had the fullest access, enabling them to acquire knowledge of its entire technology, it was not the one which they developed after the war. At Los Alamos, the most secret of the American projects, where the physics and design of an atomic bomb were under study (and, as it turned out, the hydrogen bomb was first conceived), the British had more than twenty scientists, with at least one in most of the divisions of the large laboratory. Chadwick wrote to Anderson that he could not stress too strongly the importance to Britain of participation in the ordinance work at Los Alamos. Consequently, William Penney, who was to devote his career to weapon research and development after the war and ultimately became chairman of the United Kingdom Atomic Energy Authority, was with great difficulty prised from his war research and sent to the New Mexico desert. From Los Alamos the British took with them knowledge of the techniques of the construction of an atomic bomb and the fundamental theory of the hydrogen bomb.[2]

To assess the British contribution is a difficult task. In part this is because the American programme in sheer size so dwarfed the British effort. Even at Los Alamos, to which they sent some of their best scientists, the British, according to Groves, did not play a major role because their numbers were relatively too small, although their work was of high quality. Initially, as we have seen in the first chapter, the British optimism based on theoretical data and laboratory work influenced significantly the American decision to expand its nuclear programme. The British contri-

---

[1] Gowing, op. cit., pp. 238-42.

[2] Ibid., pp. 250-67; Hewlett and Anderson, Jr., op. cit., pp. 134-5, 281-2; Groves, op. cit., pp. 117-19.

bution to the Manhattan Project often consisted of incommensurables: providing secondary opinions, critical or reassuring; increasing the 'reservoir' of scientific talent and skills; use of special machinery at a plant in Wales for producing gaseous diffusion equipment; shepherding Niels Bohr, considered by some to be the greatest living physicist, from occupied Denmark to the United States.

Groves declared that the British were 'helpful but not vital'. Nevertheless he writes that he 'cannot escape the feeling that without active and continuing British interest there would probably have been no atomic bomb to drop on Hiroshima'. Churchill emerges as the 'best friend the Manhattan Project ever had'. He was 'our project's most effective and enthusiastic supporter; for that we shall always be in his debt'. Groves also points out that the British realized from the start what the long-term implication of the project would be. They were aware of the relevance of atomic energy to their continuation as a Great Power, but they also realized that they were unable to do the job themselves. The British saw in collaboration with the United States, Groves suggests, a means of accomplishing their purpose.[1]

For the British, the rewards of collaboration turned out to be substantial. Considering the condition of the British nation—high war mobilization, scarce scientific and industrial resources—their contribution was impressive. But the inherent imbalance in the resources which the two nations could marshal meant that in a joint project the British were to receive far more than they could give. The expectation of this was implicit in the British desire for collaboration and it proved to be correct. The first director of the post-war United Kingdom atomic energy project believed that, judged by the results, the Quebec Agreement was well justified. In addition to making an effective contribution to the American atomic bomb project, the British acquired an 'almost complete knowledge of its technology'.[2]

[1] Groves, op. cit., pp. 456–8. The British-Groves relationship remains somewhat unclear. Chadwick reported that he found Groves' door always open, with the General willing to listen to any suggestions which would lead to quicker production of the bomb and always appreciative of British participation. The British considered Groves tough but fair. Gowing, op. cit., pp. 236–7. After the war, however, Groves said that he 'did everything to hold back' on collaboration, strongly disclaiming any responsibility for the policy. But he was a realist: 'There was not any use in trying to keep them out, as I saw the picture. . . . I didn't try to oppose the administration when I knew I was going to get licked. After all, I had been in Washington for many, many years.' See U.S. Atomic Energy Commission, In the Matter of J. Robert Oppenheimer (Washington, GPO, 1954), pp. 175, 177. According to the official American historians, the collaboration arrangements went a good deal further than Groves would have liked. Although he was eager for British help when it might advance the project, he 'detested' the joint enterprise. He did not go out of his way to expedite interchange, remaining carefully but unenthusiastically correct. See Hewlett and Anderson, Jr., op. cit., p. 282.

[2] Sir John Cockcroft in his book review of Gowing, op. cit., in Disarmament and Arms Control, Vol. III, No. 1 (Spring 1965), p. 89.

2. The Anglo-Canadian Project—Prototype for the Future

In one sense, the cornerstone of the post-war British nuclear programme was set not in the United States but in Canada. British scientists in the United States gained knowledge of the theory and the technology. In Canada they acquired experience in running an atomic energy establishment. There they worked on the problems of constructing a pile and controlling radioactive effluents. The Anglo-Canadian project became in fact a prototype for Britain's future atomic energy establishment.

This also was in a large measure the result of Anglo-American collaboration. In 1942 a British slow neutron team under two Frenchmen, Hans von Halban (born in Austria) and Lew Kowarski, was moved to a Montreal laboratory where it was merged with a group of Canadian scientists. It had been hoped that the Montreal group would be integrated with an American slow neutron team then under Arthur Compton and Enrico Fermi at Chicago. But because the British were using heavy water as a slowing down agent whereas the Americans were using graphite, and because of the almost total breakdown in collaboration in the winter of 1942–3, the Anglo-Canadian project, unable to receive American assistance, practically ground to a halt.

After the Quebec Agreement, the British proposed in the Combined Policy Committee that an atomic reactor using heavy water be built in Canada to produce plutonium. The Americans had good reason to oppose it as they had already begun to build an experimental heavy water pile at Argonne. The suspicions which Groves had of the British on security matters were doubled when it came to the French scientists who had earlier worked with the Communist Joliot-Curie, and all of Washington was unhappy with de Gaulle and the Free French with whom the French scientists had some ties. Most important, the proposed reactor could hardly be justified on the basis of assisting the war effort. The Americans realized that it was not likely to be operational before the end of the war and therefore went beyond the terms of the Quebec Agreement.

Nevertheless, after long delay and some paring down of the British proposal, the Americans agreed. Chadwick, who recognized that this was essentially a post-war project, believed that the proposal would not have been accepted had it not been for the willingness of Groves to co-operate. In London the new Anglo-Canadian enterprise received top priority. John Cockcroft was selected to be its director and with an eye to the future he added to the Montreal team a number of British and Canadian physicists and engineers. The United States supplied uranium ore and heavy water

and established a liaison office in Montreal although the terms of interchange still created problems. Conant and Groves made every effort to
restrict the flow of information to an agreed set of subjects (the British
attributed this attitude to the familiar bogy of fear of a post-war congressional inquiry), but to the Americans it seemed a losing battle.[1] A month
after Hiroshima, 'ZEEP', the first atomic reactor outside the United
States, became active at its Chalk River location in Ontario.[2]

The Anglo-Canadian project laid the groundwork for the post-war
British nuclear capability in many ways. A Future Systems Group was
formed to consider possible atomic piles without specific reference to
where or when they were to be built. In the course of its work it discussed
every type of reactor system to be considered in England in the next
fifteen years. When it became necessary to identify the purpose of the
piles, Chadwick gave it as his opinion that the primary requirement
would not be nuclear energy as a source of power. It would be to accumu-
late an adequate stock of pure fissile material for military purposes.

The United Kingdom Atomic Energy Research Establishment set up
in Harwell, Berkshire, in 1946 owed much to its Canadian forebear.[3]
Knowledge of nuclear reactor technology acquired at Chalk River was of
great importance in the founding of Harwell.[4] 'GLEEP', the first nuclear
reactor in the United Kingdom, was similar to 'ZEEP'. The post-war
plutonium separation plant at Windscale had its origins in the Montreal
chemical laboratories.[5] The director of the Anglo-Canadian project
became the director of the British project and many of his former colleagues joined him in England.[6]

One result of Anglo-American nuclear collaboration in North America
during the war was that afterwards the British did not start their nuclear
programme anywhere near from scratch. Neither did the Canadians. Nor,
because of the participation of French scientists in Canada, did the French.

The important contribution of the French created problems for the
British, especially in their relations with the Americans. These difficulties
got French-American and French-British nuclear relations off to a bad start,
the effect of which is felt to this day. The British had made a number of
agreements concerning future atomic energy patents with the French
scientists and had expressed their willingness to continue collaboration
after the war. Unfortunately, they neglected to inform the Americans of

[1] Gowing, op. cit., pp. 269–89; Hewlett and Anderson, Jr., op. cit., pp. 282–4.
[2] Compton, op. cit., pp. 194–5.
[3] See United Kingdom, British Information Services, *Nuclear Energy in Great Britain* (London,
Cox and Sharland, 1962), p. 7.
[4] Cockcroft, op. cit., p. 89.
[5] See Christopher Hinton, 'British Developments in Atomic Energy', *Nucleonics*, Vol. XII
(January 1954), pp. 6–8.
[6] Clark, *The Birth of the Bomb*, pp. 201–2; Bertin, op. cit., pp. 88–91.

their obligations to the French at the time the Quebec Agreement was signed. Subsequently, when American officials learned of some of these ties they were quite upset, citing the obligation under the Quebec Agreement not to communicate information to third parties except by mutual consent. Attempts were made to block some of the Montreal French scientists from visiting France in 1944–5 and the French were quickly cut off from British and American nuclear developments after the war. This left the French understandably embittered, for in their eyes the British at Quebec broke an earlier British-French understanding on post-war nuclear co-operation.[1]

3. Planning for Britain's Own Project

Throughout the period during which their atomic activities were merged with the nuclear programmes of the United States and Canada, the British were giving thought as to what should be the size, shape, and purpose of their own post-war project. Because the British scientists were widely dispersed in three countries, the process of discussion and decision making was more difficult than usual. Nevertheless, the Technical Committee of the Tube Alloys Consultative Council managed to assemble three times before the war's end, twice in Washington and once in London. Its deliberations inevitably turned to the relationship with the Americans. Indeed, no realistic discussions could take place without taking into consideration the nature of post-war Anglo-American nuclear relations.

The London-based officials had come to believe that the Americans were opposed to the development of nuclear energy in Britain after the war, suspecting that the Americans wished to establish an atomic monopoly. They therefore felt that once the British scientists in the United States had assisted as much as they could to produce an atomic bomb usable during the existing war, they would have done their duty under the Quebec Agreement and should thereupon quickly return to England—to develop large-scale British atomic plants. This view was shared by Oliphant in Berkeley. Starting in early 1945, he believed that his electromagnetic separation team was doing work which could no longer be used during the war and that his scientists should therefore return to England to continue their work. 'What we are doing now', Oliphant wrote to London, 'gives only the impression that we are trying to muscle in on a racket we have been too dumb to develop ourselves.'[2]

[1] Bertrand Goldschmidt, *Les Rivalités atomiques 1939–1966* (Paris, Fayard, 1967), pp. 85–93; Gowing, op. cit., pp. 209–15, 289–96, 342–6; Robert Gilpin, *France in the Age of the Scientific State* (Princeton, Princeton University Press, 1968), pp. 170–1.
[2] Gowing, op. cit., p. 323.

The Washington-based British officials saw the situation in a different light. In the American support for the Anglo-Canadian project they saw evidence that the Americans were not opposed to the development of atomic energy in Britain after the war. Chadwick had never attempted to hide the fact that Britain intended to develop atomic energy vigorously and Groves had never objected to this. Chadwick believed strongly in the necessity for the fullest collaboration between the two countries in atomic matters after the war. In order to avoid any misunderstandings which might affect later collaboration he thought it essential for British scientists to remain associated with the Manhattan Project until its culmination. Chadwick told Whitehall that British support must be wholehearted and remain visible. He had been warned by Groves that any indication of half-heartedness in the war against Japan after the end of the war in Europe would only serve to feed the suspicions which some Americans had of the British.

The British, then, were conscious of the psychological danger of returning to their own programme too quickly. Their representatives in Washington stressed the importance of candour in dealing with the Americans by informing them of any plans for development in the United Kingdom. Consequently, Churchill told Roosevelt at Yalta in February 1945 that Britain would pursue an atomic energy project after the war on a scale commensurate with her resources, and that discussions would take place within the British government on what might be done during the war without impairing their contribution to the Manhattan Project. Roosevelt made no objection.[1]

The fear of creating an adverse climate of opinion in American officialdom was one reason why the Tube Alloys Consultative Council adopted a cautious policy towards the post-war project. Another reason was that questions now arose as to the purpose of such a project and the scientific methods to be used.

It had always been implicitly assumed that Britain needed her own atomic bomb as soon as possible. This assumption was given explicit form when the Tube Alloys Technical Committee meeting in Washington in May 1944 recommended a programme 'which would shorten as much as possible the time required to produce in the United Kingdom after the war a militarily significant number of bombs, say ten.'[2] Once stated on paper, however, the assumption came to be questioned. Sir Henry Dale,

---

[1] Ibid., p. 324. There is no record in the published United States diplomatic papers that the British discussed atomic energy matters with the Americans at Yalta, or at the preceding Anglo-American conference at Malta. No written records, however, were kept of the private Roosevelt-Churchill meetings. See Foreign Relations of the United States, *The Conferences at Malta and Yalta, 1945* (Washington, GPO, 1955), p. 383.

[2] Gowing, op. cit., p. 325. The magnitude of such a goal becomes clearer when one notes that in 1945 the United States had only managed to make two atomic bombs.

who as President of the Royal Society represented the general interests of science on the Consultative Council, noted that an assessment determining the value of atomic bombs to Britain had not been made. For what purpose was the bomb to be used? Dale suggested that British scientists after the war would be free agents and that they would ask such questions. He was also alarmed about the drain of an atomic bomb project on scientific resources and noted the need for the university physics departments to regain and consolidate their position of leadership in fundamental physics. Tizard was similarly worried about the potential appetite of atomic energy and its probable effect on British scientific life.

The Tube Alloys Consultative Council was not the place and this was not the time for deciding on questions of such weighty implications. Their very asking, however, altered the atmosphere of the discussions and re-oriented the thinking about a post-war project. The quick production of a military weapon was no longer assumed to be the overriding objective. As to nuclear power, everyone agreed that it might become important and that Britain must try to develop it but there was also recognition of the long road ahead. For the moment, planning for Britain's post-war programme was to be geared directly neither to bombs nor to bulbs but to the development of atomic energy along the broadest lines.

Scientific considerations reinforced this cautious approach. At the Technical Committee meeting in Washington in May 1944 all the possible methods of producing a bomb were studied and debated in the light of the then existing knowledge. Of the four possible methods of separating uranium, the British scientists believed they could develop three. But unlike their American counterparts, they were in general agreement that not all the various methods could be developed simultaneously. The costs were prohibitive and the pressing wartime need which spurred the Americans to work on all the methods at the same time did not apply. As the British scientists sought to choose the separation method best suited to their pocket and needs, their calculations were constantly upset by new and unexpected pieces of information on the still-developing American plants which often contradicted earlier estimates. In the end it proved impossible to make a rational choice with any degree of assurance. The wisest course seemed to be to postpone the choice and in fact no decision was made until after the war.

It was decided, however, to set up an 'Experimental Establishment'. Anderson told the Council that in his view Tube Alloys 'was so pregnant with possibilities for the future, both military and industrial', that it was necessary to embark soon on a broad programme of research and development.[1] A wide-ranging programme which did not include the construction

[1] Gowing, op. cit., p. 331.

of large plants for producing fissile material was considered to be acceptable to the Americans and when they were informed at a meeting of the Combined Policy Committee no objection was raised. Beginning in the fall of 1944 the British on both sides of the Atlantic made plans for the Experimental Establishment. Care was taken to assure that it would remain complementary to the Anglo-Canadian project and it was agreed that there should be the closest co-operation and interchange between the two projects. Possible locations for the Establishment were visited and Sir John Cockcroft was asked to be its Director.

In a sense British planning for their post-war project was cautious. With their eye on the reaction of the Americans and remembering only too well past difficulties, they did not wish to appear too eager or hasty in their preparations. Furthermore, as they progressed in their thinking they increasingly uncovered technical and political uncertainties. Since it was expected that in the aura of goodwill following the war questions of political goals and technical methods would be more readily resolved, there was a normal tendency to avoid or postpone decisions. But underlying their cautious and pragmatic approach, there existed the firm conviction that nuclear energy would be too important, militarily and industrially, for Britain not to develop it. This was reinforced by the reassuring knowledge that through their own research and through their collaboration in America and Canada, the British by the end of the war were close to the 'take off' stage on the full-scale development of atomic energy.

4. Preparing for Continued Anglo-American Collaboration

Just as it was assumed by the British that they must have an atomic project of their own after the war, it was similarly assumed that Anglo-American collaboration must continue. There was some anxiety about the future, for the British knew well that under the terms of the Quebec Agreement they were dependent upon the sense of fair play and generosity of the President of the United States, whoever he might be. Although thought was given to discussing with the atomic energy people in Washington the question of future collaboration, there seemed to be good reason for not raising the issue. The British felt that the Americans were 'positively suspicious' about any undue interest shown in post-war arrangements. Furthermore, their Washington Embassy reported that the Americans did not wish to take the future into account in present action and 'hardly in present thought'.[1]

[1] Ibid., p. 340.

Nevertheless, before Churchill left England for the second Quebec Conference in September 1944, Anderson and Lord Cherwell asked him to sound out the Americans on their intentions. The advantages of continued collaboration were clear, especially to Churchill. In addition to its substantive benefits, collaboration would help cement post-war Anglo-American political relations. Churchill discussed atomic energy with Roosevelt at Hyde Park on 18 September 1944. In the preceding days at Quebec Roosevelt had developed an understanding for the economic troubles that would face Britain with the end of the war. The United States could not allow the economy of its ally to collapse in the hour of victory. Economic aid and continued lend-lease would be one way to buttress the British economy, and atomic energy could be another. With such thoughts in mind, Roosevelt apparently readily agreed to full collaboration after the war in the military and industrial applications of atomic energy.[1] The following day the two leaders initialled an aide-mémoire which was to bedevil Anglo-American relations for the next decade. Paragraph two stated that:

Full collaboration between the United States and the British Government in developing tube alloys for military and commercial purposes should continue after the defeat of Japan unless and until terminated by joint agreement.[2]

The Hyde Park Aide-Mémoire was, in the words of a former Commissioner of the A.E.C., 'clouded in its own private mystery'.[3] When two months after Roosevelt's death, the British representative on the Combined Policy Committee, in urging that preparation for post-war collaboration be started, referred to it for the first time the Americans were mystified. Not a single person in Washington knew of it and numerous file searches failed to uncover a copy. Many years later when the Roosevelt papers at Hyde Park were being catalogued the single American copy of the Aide-Mémoire was discovered in a folder on naval matters, 'tube alloys' apparently having been mistaken for a type of naval equipment. Meanwhile the embarrassed Americans asked the British for a photostatic copy.[4]

Roosevelt, for reasons upon which one can only conjecture, had not told Stimson, Bush, Conant, Groves, or apparently anyone else of his agreement with Churchill.[5] A few days after returning from Hyde Park

[1] Gowing, op. cit., p. 341; Hewlett and Anderson, Jr., op. cit., p. 327.
[2] For the full text see Gowing, op. cit., Appendix VIII.
[3] Lewis Strauss, *Men and Decisions* (Garden City, N.Y., Doubleday, 1962), p. 369.
[4] Groves, op. cit., pp. 401–2; Hewlett and Anderson, Jr., op. cit., p. 458.
[5] Admiral Leahy was the only other person present at Hyde Park when atomic energy was discussed. In his book he recalls that the President offered to share atomic energy for industrial purposes but notes that no similar understanding was reached on military uses. William D. Leahy, *I Was There* (New York, Whittlesey House, 1950), pp. 265–6.

the President called Bush, with whom he had not conferred about atomic matters for some months, to his office, where he also had Lord Cherwell. Without mentioning the Aide-Mémoire the President spoke of his belief in the necessity of keeping the British Empire strong and of continuing the partnership in atomic energy development. It would be up to the governments of the day at some time in the future to dissolve the partnership if they so wished. The only thing which now would interrupt it, said Roosevelt colourfully, would be if he and the Prime Minister, Bush, and Lord Cherwell were all killed in one railroad accident. Cherwell in his later account noted that Bush had kept quiet. Indeed Bush had been most uncomfortable while the President was discussing in front of Lord Cherwell matters that he had not previously considered with his own advisers.[1]

What neither the President nor the British knew was that Bush and Conant had just begun the American government's policy planning for a system of domestic and international control of atomic energy. In a letter to Stimson, written the day Churchill and Roosevelt were discussing Tube Alloys at Hyde Park, they had outlined some of their early thoughts on the subject: a treaty might be signed with the United Kingdom and Canada which would put the interchange of information on a permanent basis, determine the future commercial benefits which under the Quebec Agreement the President would authorize for Britain, and insure for the establishment of civilian control of atomic energy in all three countries. Bush and Conant did not wish the United States to commit itself so completely to Britain as to prejudice its relations with Russia. They felt that without an international system of control the semblance of an Anglo-American monopoly might only be an incentive for the Russians to develop the bomb secretly and to precipitate a nuclear arms race.[2]

In Britain, also, thought had been given to a post-war system of international control. It had run foul, however, of Churchill's cardinal precept in the last year of the war on all matters concerning atomic energy: nothing should be done which might upset future Anglo-American collaboration. Whenever a proposal was put to him his first question was always: 'Does this conflict with my Agreement with the President at Quebec?' This to Churchill was the 'bedrock of policy'.[3]

Thus when Anderson proposed to Churchill that the Foreign Office undertake a study of the practical and political problems of international control of atomic energy after the war, and suggested that the Prime Minister break the ice on the subject in a message to the President, he

[1] Hewlett and Anderson, Jr., op. cit., pp. 328, 346; Gowing, op. cit., p. 341.
[2] Hewlett and Anderson, Jr., op. cit., pp. 326, 328, 346.
[3] Gowing, op. cit., p. 341.

received a sharp rebuff. Further urging from Anderson and a pointed minute from Lord Cherwell suggesting that any preparations for the post-war world or for the peace conference were utterly illusory unless this crucial factor was taken into account fared little better. Churchill was concerned most of all with—one might almost say blinded by—Anglo-American relations, and he was loath to do anything which might disturb the Quebec Agreement.[1]

The British were cautious in their dealing with the Americans so as to to do nothing which might upset the Quebec and Hyde Park Agreements. This was well illustrated by their reluctant acquiescence in a disagreement which arose over the publication of the Smyth Report. When the Americans, for reasons of their own primarily relating to the desire to justify to the Congress and the American people the great expenditures of the Manhattan Project, decided to publish an open report, there was alarm in London. The British saw no need for releasing such a full, coherent report which could be used as an effective guide through the labyrinth of wartime nuclear developments, and they considered using Britain's rights under the Quebec Agreement to prevent its release. Unknown to them Stimson shared some of their misgivings but under considerable pressure from Washington the British decided not to force the issue. When shortly after the war's end the Smyth Report was released, the British thought it so neglected their own contribution that they were led to publish a supplementary report outlining in greater detail the work of British scientists.[2]

Similarly, caution was demonstrated in the decision not to insist upon any significant consultation in the decision to use the atom bomb on Japan. Under the terms of the Quebec Agreement the two nations had agreed not to use a nuclear weapon 'against third parties without each other's consent'. But because the American share in both the development of the bomb and the Pacific War was so overwhelming, the British left this decision wholly to the Americans. They had no role in the deliberations of Stimson's Interim Committee and there was no equivalent discussion in Whitehall. To the British this was essentially a military, not a moral, decision, and as Churchill later recorded 'there was never a moment's discussion as to whether the atomic bomb should be used or not.'[3]

[1] Professor Niels Bohr was the innovator of much of the early attention given to this problem in Britain. When he made a direct personal plea to the Prime Minister, Churchill viewed this intervention as a criticism of the Quebec Agreement and an attack on the Americans. When, upon leaving, Bohr asked if he might send a memorandum on the subject, Churchill said that he would be honoured to hear from a learned professor but hoped that it would not be about politics. See Wheeler-Bennett, op. cit., p. 297; Gowing, op. cit., pp. 351–5.

[2] Gowing, op. cit., pp. 364–5; Clark, *The Birth of the Bomb*, pp. 196–7; Strauss, op. cit., pp. 250–1. For the British report see Great Britain, Treasury, *Statements Relating to the Atomic Bomb* (London, H.M.S.O., 1945).

[3] Winston Churchill, *The Second World War*, Vol. VI (London, Cassell, 1954), p. 553.

Nevertheless, the modalities of diplomacy necessitated that the British approval be formally recorded. Churchill was anxious that the British should not appear to be insisting on a legalistic interpretation of the appropriate clause of the Quebec Agreement. The British were conscious that some Americans had grave doubts about the wisdom of that clause both on constitutional grounds and for political reasons, Roosevelt's administration being open to the criticism that the Government had spent two billion dollars on a weapon which it could not use without the consent of another nation. British consent to the use of the bomb was therefore quickly and quietly given at a meeting of the Combined Policy Committee.[1]

The end of the Second World War came with an atomic bomb first conceived by the British out of fear of a German bomb and in the context of the war in Europe, but built by the United States and used in the Pacific against Japan. The wartime years of Anglo-American collaboration were marked by as much conflict as co-operation. There can be little doubt, however, that perceived British interests were well served. The United Kingdom emerged from the war possessing the theory and the technological knowledge of the atom bomb, as well as the fundamental concepts of the hydrogen bomb. Many of its scientists had acquired invaluable experience in the United States which was to be used at home immediately after the war, and the project in Canada was used as a model for the post-war British nuclear establishment. All of this could not have been achieved in the British Isles under wartime conditions. More important still, considerable thought had been given to the political role of atomic armaments in the post-war world. Those who were close to the wartime project assumed that if Britain was to retain the status of an independent and Great Power, she must possess her own nuclear weapons.

[1] John Ehrman, *Grand Strategy*, Vol. VI of the *United Kingdom History of the Second World War* (London, H.M.S.O., 1956), pp. 295–9. See also Gowing, op. cit., pp. 371–2; Michael Amrine, *The Great Decision: The Secret History of the Atomic Bomb* (New York, Putnam, 1959), p. 124; Herbert Feis, *Japan Subdued: The Atom Bomb and the End of the War in the Pacific* (Princeton, Princeton University Press, 1961), p. 46.

PART TWO

Towards the 'Independent Nuclear Deterrent' 1945–1957

4 | Defence Policy: The Pre-Detonation Period

Part Two deals with the period, from 1945 to 1957, during which Britain came to base much of its national security policy upon nuclear deterrence, and developed the first generation of its strategic nuclear force. The evolution of defence policy and strategy before and after the first British atomic detonation is discussed in Chapters 4 and 5. We then deal more extensively with the development of the nuclear capability in Chapter 6 and examine the creation of the delivery capability in Chapter 7.

1. The Post-War Setting

The primary factor shaping Britain's role in world affairs in the twentieth century has been her decline in power. This has been so obvious that it has often been overlooked. For a nation in the 'habit of power' it does not come naturally to recognize diminished status. 'Nations which have known empire', wrote John Strachey, 'may simply break their hearts' if they do not find another ideal.[1] In the historical consciousness of most living Englishmen, British statecraft and military strength weigh heavily in the world balance of power. Britain's self-image has only gradually adjusted to the nation's new circumstances. For most of the time since the Second World War, Britain's psychological involvement in international relations has remained quite high; and her defence commitments have outrun her existing military capabilities. The creation and maintenance of the British nuclear force has been closely intertwined with the nation's self-image and the reduction in her power and influence.

It was probably during the Second World War that Britain and the United States 'switched roles'. Before the six-year conflict the two nations were powers of roughly equal political strength and prestige; afterwards they were not. The United States emerged from the war with its economic power greatly enhanced; Britain with its political power, though not its prestige, considerably reduced. 'The United States became heir to Britain's world position, a change that brought considerable embarrassment to most Americans and regret to most Englishmen,' observed William H. McNeill.[2]

The shift in the balance of power and responsibilities between the two

[1] John Strachey, *The End of Empire* (London, Gollancz, 1959), p. 229.
[2] *America, Britain, and Russia: Their Co-operation and Conflict*, pp. 754–5.

nations was not immediately recognized on either side of the Atlantic at the war's end. The initial American attitude was one of disengagement from her wartime alliances. Britain, in addition to her worldwide imperial commitments, had troops engaged in restoring order in such diverse locations as Greece, Indonesia, Syria, and Lebanon. The Mediterranean was virtually under British control. Greece was dependent upon Britain economically as well as militarily, and the Anglo-Turkish Alliance was the cornerstone of Turkey's national security. In 1946 the burden of the developing tensions between the Western nations and the Soviet government was borne by the British.[1] At the United Nations it was Britain that most often clashed with Russia. Attlee was the first to criticize publicly the Soviet use of the veto in the Security Council in October 1946. As Foreign Secretary, Ernest Bevin told the House of Commons:

His Majesty's Government do not accept the view . . . that we have ceased to be a Great Power, or the contention that we have ceased to play that role. We regard ourselves as one of the Powers most vital to the peace of the world and we still have our historic part to play. The very fact that we have fought so hard for liberty, and paid such a price, warrants our retaining this position; and indeed it places a duty upon us to continue to retain it. I am not aware of any suggestion, seriously advanced, that by a sudden stroke of fate, as it were, we have overnight ceased to be a Great Power.[2]

A number of circumstances in the early post-war years served to conceal the real extent of Britain's decline. The prestige attached to membership in the victorious 'Big Three' was skilfully used by Bevin, who thereby projected an image of national strength greater than Britain's resources. The massive power of the Soviet Union had not yet become apparent. The destruction of the war on the continent left Britain by far the strongest of the nations of Western Europe. In 1946 the competitive advantage of British industry over its rivals on the continent was absolute. The devolution of Empire which began with the grant of independence to India and Pakistan in 1947 appeared to ensure for Britain through the Commonwealth link a continuing voice in the affairs of nations in the Middle East, Africa, and Asia. Not until the shock of Suez in 1956 did many Englishmen place their nation in the rank of a second-level power.

Britain's decline from her nineteenth-century eminence had begun half a century earlier. Notable landmarks in the process included: the accommodation with the United States in the Venezuelan crisis of 1902, and the

---

[1] See C. M. Woodhouse, *British Foreign Policy Since the Second World War* (London, Hutchinson, 1961), pp. 13–21; Matthew A. Fitzsimmons, *The Foreign Policy of the British Labour Government 1945–1951* (Notre Dame, Notre Dame University Press, 1953).

[2] Hansard's Parliamentary Debates, fifth series, House of Commons, Vol. 437, col. 1965 (16 May 1947). Cited hereafter as H.C. Deb.

reduction of naval forces in the Far East and Caribbean on the basis of agreements with Japan and the United States; the end during the First World War of the myth of maritime supremacy which for the hundred years following the Napoleonic Wars had appeared to many as the major source of Britain's influence and dominant position; the reduction of the economic base of British influence abroad in the interwar period with the rise of several rivals in the manufacturing industries, and the lessening of confidence in the City following the sterling crisis of 1931; and, most important, the loss of insularity which had in the past permitted Britain to be the uncommitted balancer and mediator between the European powers.[1]

The structural weakness of the economy after the Second World War was the most significant indicator of Britain's new situation. Britain in 1945 was in many respects far poorer than in 1938. The heavy damage to her productive plants from bombardment and to the merchant fleet from torpedoes was considerable. More importantly, wealth which had been accumulated over decades had been rapidly consumed. Gold and dollar reserves had dropped from £864 million to £453 million; over a quarter of the overseas investments which had long played a role in balancing Britain's international account had been sold to pay for war supplies; external liabilities in the form of debts had risen from £760 million to £3,353 million; exports had gone down thirty per cent. At home the war had delayed the replacement of obsolescent equipment in many sectors of industry.[2] Abroad the traditional foreign markets and trade patterns upon which Britain had formerly depended to sell manufactured goods had been disrupted. Nor did the economic situation improve immediately after the war. After 1945 the unfavourable balance of payments worsened, the wartime rationing of food and clothing continued, and bread and potatoes were added to the list of rationed items for the first time.

The abrupt termination of lend-lease as unilaterally announced a week after the Japanese surrender by the new American President 'gravely embarrassed' the Labour cabinet[3] and was seen by Lord Keynes to be 'without exaggeration a financial Dunkirk'.[4] The urgent effort to alleviate

[1] See Harold and Margaret Sprout, 'Retreat from World Power: Processes and Consequences of Readjustment', *World Politics*, Vol. XV, No. 4 (July 1963), pp. 655–88; Lionel M. Gelber, *The Rise of Anglo-American Friendship* (London, Oxford University Press, 1938).

[2] The war also brought some beneficial results: new industrial machinery was produced, factories were constructed, the labour force was expanded, and managerial attitudes and methods were improved. See M. M. Postan, *British War Production, History of the Second World War* (London, H.M.S.O., 1952), pp. 385–6.

[3] Emanuel Shinwell, *The Labour Story* (London, MacDonald, 1963), pp. 177–8.

[4] Quoted in Woodhouse, op. cit., p. 122. The British public suffered a 'nearly traumatic experience' with the halt in the shipment of lend-lease supplies and the new Labour government went through one of its most discouraged times. See Leon Epstein, *Britain—Uneasy Ally* (Chicago, University of Chicago Press, 1954), pp. 36–7.

the economic situation which resulted in the Anglo-American Financial Agreement of December 1945 was disappointing to the British government because of the hard terms upon which the United States insisted. Lord Keynes had argued that the United States was under a special obligation to deal generously with Britain because she had voluntarily agreed, according to allied wartime production plans, to forgo the manufacture of the export goods which were so important to her economy in order to concentrate on munitions for the allies. Moreover, Britain had borne the major economic brunt of the war prior to America's entry. But although it was conceded that Britain's financial difficulties were largely due to her war effort, the United States did not appear to consider her economic welfare as a matter of continuing responsibility.[1]

Indeed, the 'special relationship' which Churchill and Roosevelt had so carefully cultivated was substantially reduced in the year following the war's end. The mood of America was one of disengagement from alliances and all the abnormalities of war. In some quarters there was suspicion of the new 'socialist' government in Britain; to many Americans the electoral defeat of Churchill had come as a surprise. In September 1945 President Truman approved a policy statement calling for the early abolition of the several Anglo-American Combined Boards which had implemented the wartime partnership by pooling resources, combining staffs, and co-ordinating operations for the two countries.[2] With the signing of the McMahon Act in August 1946 the 'special relationship' had suffered a major curtailment.

2. Defence Strategy and the Decision to Build the Bomb

In the first two years after the war British defence policy was clearly in a period of transition. The new structure of world politics was not yet discernible; the imperative need of Britain was economic rehabilitation at home. The 1946 White Paper on Defence, the first after an interruption of several years, was described by Anthony Eden as 'not a statement relating to defence but a progress report on demobilization'.[3] Attlee

---

[1] See 138 H.L. Deb. col. 779–80 (18 December 1945); Herbert G. Nicholas, *Britain and the United States* (Baltimore, The Johns Hopkins University Press, 1963), p. 37; Richard N. Gardner, *Sterling-Dollar Diplomacy* (Oxford, Clarendon Press, 1956), pp. 184–254.

[2] Included among the boards dissolved in 1946 were the Combined Munitions Assignment Boards, Combined Raw Materials Board, Combined Shipping Adjustment Board, Combined Food Board, and the Combined Production and Resources Board. The Combined Chiefs of Staff were formally kept in existence, awaiting the signing of the peace treaties, but there was a marked reduction in the flow of information and a new restraint on the part of American officers in discussing questions of military policy. McNeill, op. cit., pp. 678–9.

[3] 420 H.C. Deb. col. 239 (5 March 1946).

himself saw the White Paper as a 'stop-gap'. Defence policy, he noted optimistically, would be dependent on the United Nations. The wartime defence establishment was to be run down, and existing equipment used to satisfy military requirements. Releasable manpower and resources could be better utilized in the Labour government's new social experiment. The 1947 White Paper, published during the unusually severe winter of 1946–7, said that:

Developments in recent months have stressed the urgent need of restoring a balanced peace economy at the earliest moment and by all practicable measures. Defence policy must be compatible with this national need . . . a successful defence policy must find its roots in healthy social and economic conditions. It is both inevitable and right that the rehabilitation of the civil economy should increasingly absorb the country's efforts and resources, to the diminution of activities in the defence field.[1]

As a corollary the Government adopted in 1946 a Ten-Year Rule by which the military were to plan on the official assumption that there would be no major war for a decade. There was a precedent: a similar ten-year rule had been set forth in 1919.[2]

British military thought on the significance of the atomic age for defence policy developed only slowly. The services were preoccupied with demobilization, with the task of meeting their varied overseas commitments with their reduced force structure, and with the complexities of decolonization. Prior to the Czech coup and the Berlin blockade in 1948, the Soviet threat to Western Europe was not fully recognized. The B-29 bombers of the United States Strategic Air Command, then the only means of stabilizing a balance of power against Russia in Europe with atomic weapons, were not brought to England until July 1948. The 1946 Defence White Paper did note: 'The great strides made in the realm of science and technology, including the production of atomic bombs, cannot fail to affect the make-up of our forces.' But it then added: 'Time is wanted for the full effects of these startling developments to be assessed.'[3]

What first struck observers was Britain's immense vulnerability in case

---

[1] *Statement Relating to Defence: 1947*, Cmd. 7042, p. 4.

[2] After the signing of the peace terms, Lloyd George cast about for a formula which would reduce service expenditures to a level consistent with his concept of the new world order. The 'Ten-Year Rule' was designed to tighten the Treasury's grip on the Admiralty, War Office, and Air Ministry, and created despondency among the Chiefs of Staff. In 1928, on Churchill's initiative, the rule was altered to slide forward from one month to the next so that the decade would run on indefinitely. Only in March 1932, after the Japanese invaded Manchuria and Whitehall came to believe that Singapore was also under threat of attack, did the cabinet agree to abandon the Ten-Year Rule after strong representations by the Chiefs of Staff. See Andrew Boyle, *Trenchard* (London, Collins, 1962), pp. 540, 571, 676.

[3] *Statement Relating to Defence: 1946*, Cmd. 6743, p. 3.

of an atomic attack, even from a Hiroshima-type bomb. Britain's high population density and concentrated industrial and commercial centres, combined with her dependence on trade and ports, appeared to make the tight little islands an ideal target. The special vulnerability of the British Isles became a recurrent theme in writings on the atomic age and has justifiably always been a cause of particular anxiety for the British. Liddell Hart estimated that five to ten thermonuclear bombs would destroy the main centres of industry where half of the population is located.[1]

A 1946 report on 'British Security' by a study group of the Royal Institute of International Affairs was in hindsight notable for what it did *not* address itself to. The concept of nuclear deterrence was almost totally lacking, although the report acknowledged that with atomic weapons the 'civilized world would in fact be found to have produced its ultimate doom if some means were not found of avoiding war.' The atom bomb was seen as having greatly increased the prospects for the success of a surprise attack. Yet nowhere in the report was there discussion of a possible British atomic capability. Nevertheless, it was recognized that 'Britain can no longer count, as she has been able to do in the past, on having time to convert her potential strength into actual strength after the war has broken out.'[2]

Not until the arrival of thermonuclear weapons was the revolutionary nature of the atomic age fully grasped. P. M. S. Blackett has suggested that when an important new weapon is invented, opinion as to its effectiveness often falls into two extremes. The *radical* view is that the new weapon (be it crossbow or atomic bomb) has revolutionized warfare and made all other arms obsolete. It is usually supported by a minority of the military and a majority of amateur strategists. The *conservative* view is that the invention is only one more new weapon which will gradually be absorbed, as innumerable cases in the past, into the practice of the military arts without changing their character. It is often popular in military circles. The truth, according to Blackett, usually lies somewhere between the extremes.[3]

The view of the British military in 1946 may well have been accurately

[1] B. H. Liddell Hart, *Deterrent or Defence* (London, Stevens, 1960), pp. 49–50; see also the report of the Chatham House Study Group that met in 1946–7, *Atomic Energy: Its International Implications* (London, Broadwater Press, 1948), p. 59.

[2] Royal Institute of International Affairs, *British Security: A Report by a Chatham House Study Group* (London, Oxford University Press, 1946). Two subsequent studies by groups of statesmen and scholars are also notable for the absence of a discussion of British atomic weapons. See *Defence in the Cold War,* report by a Chatham House Study Group made under the Chairmanship of Sir Ian Jacob, Royal Institute of International Affairs, 1950; Henry L. Roberts and Paul A. Wilson, *Britain and the United States: Problems in Cooperation,* Council on Foreign Relations (New York, Harper, 1953).

[3] P. M. S. Blackett, *Fear, War and the Bomb: Military and Political Consequences of Atomic Energy* (New York, McGraw-Hill, 1949), pp. 1–2.

reflected by Rear Admiral H. G. Thursfield, editor of *Brassey's Annual*, in his introductory article to that year's issue entitled 'The Lessons of the War'. Rejecting the notion that the atomic bomb was opening a revolutionary new era in military technology, he saw it as nothing but a 'bigger and better bomb' and, writing before the Bikini tests, added that 'it may possibly prove to be capable of sinking any ship that may be within range of its destructive effect when it explodes' but 'even that . . . is mere speculation'.[1] The 1947 issue of *Brassey's* contained an article by 'Eyewitness', an anonymous official British observer at Bikini. He personally had no doubts that with the introduction of atomic weapons the old era had passed, but he was concerned about his colleagues in Whitehall. Referring to Mahan's thesis that changes in tactics come after changes in weapons, but usually after an unduly long interval, he admonished the military services to face up to the new era with energy and imagination.[2] As late as 1954 Marshal of the R.A.F. Sir John Slessor in a lecture on 'Air Power and the Future of War' was impelled to comment: 'to my mind it is utterly nonsensical to suggest, as some do, that the atomic and still more the thermonuclear bomb is just a bigger and better bomb different only in degree but not in character from the blockbuster of 1939–1945.'[3]

The post-war decision to manufacture a British atomic bomb was made by the Defence Sub-committee of the cabinet in early January 1947. It was reached in secret without either an internal Whitehall debate or prior public discussion of the relevant issues. To the ministers, scientists, and civil servants, relatively few in number, who were responsible for the atomic energy matters and knew of the decision, its significance at the time was less clear than it became in later years.[4]

The timing of the decision appears to have been set, quite simply, by

---

[1] *Brassey's Annual* (London, William Clowes, 1946), p. 10.

[2] Ibid. (1947), p. 164.

[3] *Journal of the Royal United Service Institution*, Vol. XCIX, No. 595 (August 1954), p. 349.

[4] The date is based on interviews; the location has been publicly identified by G. R. Strauss, the Minister of Supply who had responsibility for the manufacture of the atomic bomb, in a debate by correspondence with R. H. S. Crossman in the *New Statesman* of 10, 17, 24, 31 May and 7 June 1963. Strauss disputed Crossman's statement in the latter's introduction to a new edition of Walter Bagehot's *The English Constitution* (London, Fontana, 1963) that the decision to build a British bomb 'had been taken by Mr. Attlee without any prior discussion in the cabinet and that he had never revealed it to any but a handful of trusted friends'. Crossman had used this as an example to illustrate his thesis that under the Attlee administration Britain moved from 'cabinet' to 'prime ministerial' government. In the ensuing exchange of letters, Strauss revealed the decision was taken at a meeting of the Defence Sub-committee of the cabinet at which the Prime Minister presided and whose minutes were circulated to members of the cabinet. There is no indication that the full cabinet considered the matter, nor that the decision was the subject of extensive discussion at the sub-committee level.

the momentum of the atomic energy programme: the stage had been reached (almost a year and a half after the end of the war) when the scientists and engineers had to know whether the next step was to be, or not to be, the production of a bomb. As we have seen in Chapter 3, it had always been assumed during the war that atomic energy would be developed in Britain at the war's end. Of this there was little question: Churchill had told Roosevelt, Chadwick had told Groves. Within months after the end of hostilities a large nuclear research establishment was organized and factories were planned to produce fissile materials. In 1946 Parliament passed the Atomic Energy Act giving the Government broad powers to control the use and exploitation of atomic energy. These developments are discussed more fully in Chapter 6. The significant point is that by the time a decision was made to move to the bomb manufacturing stage, a well established and comprehensive atomic energy programme already existed.

Among many of the scientists there had always been the expectation that when it became feasible a bomb would be manufactured. The Tube Alloys Technical Committee had made this assumption in advising Sir John Anderson in 1944. Britain had been a pioneer in atomic energy from the start. Not to have continued its development would have seemed almost unnatural. 'The scientists,' wrote Alfred Goldberg, 'were strongly endowed with the curiosity that provides most of the driving force of science and technology. For the atomic pioneers—Chadwick, Cockcroft, Penney, and others—to permit the programme to lapse would have been a denial of the basic instinct that is the very root of science itself.'[1]

There is no evidence to suggest that within the relatively small scientific community involved there was any disagreement concerning the wisdom of making a British bomb on political, economic, or moral grounds.[2] The costs were not held to be prohibitive and, in any case, there was hope of renewing collaboration with the United States. Moreover, scientific knowledge and skill had long been recognized to be one of Britain's national assets. The atomic energy programme had developed in five years not inconsiderable momentum. The building of a bomb had been implicit in the programme from the beginning. A scientific adviser to defence officials of the period has said that when Britain was 'casting

[1] 'The Atomic Origins of the British Nuclear Deterrent', *International Affairs*, Vol. XL, No. 3 (July 1964), p. 426.
[2] However, P. M. S. Blackett, a member of the Advisory Committee on Atomic Energy, in the preface to *Fear, War and the Bomb*, notes he found his views 'diverging more and more widely from those of my colleagues' (p. v). Blackett favoured a strictly defensive policy aiming towards a negotiated agreement with Russia while the West still had a relatively strong bargaining position. Although he does not address himself to the specific question of British nuclear weapons, the shape of his argument suggests that he may well have been opposed to their development.

about' for a means to assure its security it would have been difficult to find 'a more profitable method than by developing and deploying our own nuclear weapons potential. This was a new scientific field which gave plenty of room for the exploitation of our national scientific genius.'[1]

The provision of a delivery system for the atom bomb was not a matter of particular concern. It was assumed that the bomb would be delivered by an existing type of heavy bomber, as was the case in Japan. It was not yet apparent that complex ballistic missiles would be needed in the future to penetrate enemy air defences. The quicksand of vulnerability and rising costs was not yet visible, nor was the need for extensive warning systems recognized. Thus a delivery capability was not thought to present either a major additional expense or important technical difficulties.

But there were, of course, far broader political implications involved. It is difficult now to recall the atmosphere of European-American relations between the end of the Second World War and the American return to Europe through the Marshall Plan and the signing of the NATO treaty. Britain stood alone. It could count on neither the United States nor Europe nor its overseas dependencies to assure the defence of the British Isles. The 'fraternal association' between America and Britain of which Winston Churchill spoke in his famous speech in Fulton, Missouri, in March 1946 was in no way officially recognized. Some British feared the renewal of American isolationism. Because of the intimate ties that had developed during the war between officials of the two countries on a myriad of activities, the British were especially resentful of the unilateral termination of the 'special relationship'.

Nowhere was this more true than in the field of atomic energy. The reasons for the rapid breakdown of collaboration on atomic matters are discussed more extensively in Chapter 6. Its effect on the decision to build British nuclear weapons cannot be underrated. Attlee had gone to great lengths in his personal correspondence with Truman to explain why the British felt entitled to continue to receive information from the United States on atomic energy. Quite apart from the specific provisions of the Quebec Agreement and the Hyde Park Aide-Mémoire, there was a simple question of equity. Britain had made the fullest possible contribution to the Manhattan Project, a contribution which was believed to have been of major importance. In doing so, she had voluntarily desisted from undertaking further development of atomic energy at home in order to achieve the earliest possible realization of the American bomb. This was on the assumption that she could rely on the provisions of the wartime agreements and the 'special relationship' to ensure that she would receive full

---

[1] Sir Frederick Brundrett, 'Rockets, Satellites and Military Thinking', *Journal of the Royal United Service Institution*, Vol. CV (August 1960), p. 337.

access to information on all sections of the project when she returned her scientists to her own endeavour. To Attlee, the provisions of the McMahon Act which would rule out exchange of information with Britain seemed a 'breach of faith'.[1]

A deep-felt sense of betrayal by the United States in cutting off the exchange of nuclear information developed in Whitehall in the year *prior* to the decision to manufacture nuclear weapons. (Right or wrong, this sense of having been betrayed has become part of history: at the Nassau Conference of 1962—sixteen years later—Prime Minister Macmillan recalled it for President Kennedy in the context of the discussions on the unilateral cancellation of Skybolt.) The McMahon Act, the end of lend-lease, the termination of the combined boards, the general rupture of the wartime relationship—these seemed to suggest a maxim for future British policy: the nation's security inasmuch as possible should not be allowed to become totally dependent upon the United States.

American policy, as seen in London, contained strains of immaturity, if not instability. The return of the United States to isolationism was something to insure against; ten years later, the withdrawal of the American nuclear guarantee was also something to insure against. In both cases, national nuclear weapons were seen as the insurance policy. By the end of 1946 several other aspects of post-war international relations had become clearer, perhaps more so in London than Washington. The achievement of international control of atomic energy under United Nations' auspices was going to be a long-term task. The euphoria of peace was giving way to recognition of the deteriorating relations between former allies, especially between the Soviet Union and the West. Military strength was going to remain an important factor in world politics.

For a nation that thought of itself as a Great Power, that was a member of the Security Council and the 'Big Three', acquiring the best military weapons available was a natural thing to do. The scientific and economic resources necessary were thought to exist. France had set up its Commissariat à l'Énergie Atomique in 1945, and after the uncovering of the spying activities of Alan Nunn May the next year there could be little doubt of Soviet intentions. 'Failure to accept the challenge of atomic energy would have been interpreted as a retreat from greatness, an abandonment of power.'[2]

Yet the case of Canada is both instructive and disquieting.[3] Canada had been involved in the Manhattan Project and after the war went on

[1] Williams, op. cit., p. 109.

[2] Goldberg, 'The Atomic Origins of the British Nuclear Deterrent', p. 427.

[3] See Leonard Beaton and John Maddox, *The Spread of Nuclear Weapons* (London, Chatto and Windus, 1962), chap. V.; Jon B. McLin, *Canada's Changing Defense Policy, 1957–1963* (Baltimore, Johns Hopkins, 1967), pp. 123–4.

developing atomic energy at Chalk River. Britain and Canada, with roughly equal atomic facilities and capabilities, and at approximately the same time, made opposite decisions on manufacturing nuclear weapons. The differential factor which appears to have led them to their respective responses was their comparative sense of security. For the Canadians' security was guaranteed by their geographical location next to the United States. An attack on Canada, it was felt, would assuredly activate American retaliation, as all of North America was within the sphere of the vital interests of the United States.

In contrast to Canada, the British sense of security was minimal. As Attlee explained many years later:

At that time we had to bear in mind that there was always the possibility of their withdrawing and becoming isolationist once again. The manufacture of a British atom bomb was therefore at that stage essential to our defence.

You must remember this was all prior to NATO. NATO has altered things. But at that time, although we were doing our best to make the Americans understand the realities of the European situation—the world situation—we couldn't be sure we'd succeed. In the end we did. But we couldn't take risks with British security in the meantime. We had worked from the start for international control of the bomb. We wanted it completely under the United Nations. That was the best way. But it was obviously going to take a long time. Meanwhile we had to face the world as it was. We had to look to our defence—and to our industrial future. We could not agree that only America should have atomic energy.[1]

This suggests that if America had not ruptured the special relationship, if the restrictive provisions of the McMahon Act had excluded Britain from their application, if British security had been guaranteed then as it came to be in the NATO treaty two years later, the decision of 1947 to start on an independent nuclear weapons capability may have been different.

As it was, the British bomb programme came to be viewed as a means of reviving the lost partnership with the United States. Nuclear weapons would help offset the weakening of Britain's favoured position and enhance her influence in Washington. As an unusually perceptive British observer of Washington has noted, the McMahon Act was 'more galling to Britain than any other ally'. In contrast to the war years, when British officials freely participated in the decision-making process, they 'were only too often politely shown the door. Almost all officials and most politicians outside the pacifist wing of the labour party sincerely believed that Britain would never be able to look the United States in the eye, would never be treated as more than a useful or elderly relation until it became a member of the nuclear club.'[2]

[1] Williams, op. cit., p. 119.
[2] Alastair Buchan, 'Britain and the Bomb', *Reporter*, Vol. XX (19 March 1959), p. 23.

The fact that nuclear weapons were being developed was not publicly recognized until Winston Churchill announced in February 1952 plans for testing the first British-made atomic bomb at the Monte Bello Islands off Australia. Throughout its time in office the Attlee government maintained a policy of secrecy, around which there existed a curious air of unreality. There was little discussion—in America there was much—of the future uses of atomic energy and the press was discouraged from visiting the Research Establishment at Harwell. Questions in the Commons, mainly from Government backbenchers, about expenditures, number of personnel, the objectives of research, etc., were shunted aside. One pacifist M.P. was driven to comment: 'When we ask questions in this House about it, one would almost think that an atomic bomb had been dropped. When an Hon. Member asks the Prime Minister about the atomic bomb, he looks at him as if he had been asked something indecent.'[1]

Yet the Government wished that the decision to manufacture an atomic bomb be 'on the record'. The Defence Sub-committee of the cabinet chose a method which released the information while ensuring that the least possible attention be drawn to it. An innocuous phrase about atomic weapons being developed was inserted into an answer the Minister of Defence gave in a question period of the Commons on 12 May 1948. The following day the question and answer as it appeared in Hansard was buried in the parliamentary news of *The Times* without any comment. The press, it appears, had been alerted to the Government's wishes and had given its co-operation. Two days later no mention of it was made in a debate on the international control of atomic energy. In the following years, debates in the Commons continued as if the announcement of atomic weapons being manufactured had never been made. It has since become accepted that Labour developed the atomic bomb 'in secret'. According to Emanuel Shinwell, Secretary of State for War and later the Minister of Defence in the Attlee government, Churchill's announcement in 1952 revealed what even few Labour ministers had been aware of.[2]

---

[1] 448 H.C. Deb. col. 574 (4 March 1948).

[2] This curious episode should be of interest to students of parliamentary democracy, as well as to those of nuclear affairs. The full quotation from Hansard is as follows:

'Mr. George Jeger asked the Minister of Defence whether he is satisfied that adequate progress is being made in the development of the most modern types of weapon.

'The Minister of Defence (Mr. A. V. Alexander): "Yes, Sir. As was made clear in the Statement Relating to Defence, 1948 (Command 7327), research and development continue to receive the highest priority in the defence field, and all types of modern weapons, *including atomic weapons*, are being developed." (Italics mine.)

'Mr. Jeger: "Can the Minister give any further information on the development of atomic weapons?"

'Mr. Alexander: "No, I do not think it would be in the public interest to do that." '

450 H.C. Deb. col. 2117 (12 May 1948).

Richard Crossman has written that 'this is the kind of question which is put to enable a

In a sense, the defence of Britain first came to be based on a strategy of deterrence with the arrival of sixty American B-29 bombers in East Anglia in July 1948. Initially, this probably made Britain more rather than less vulnerable to Soviet attack, for it measurably increased the incentive for making it a prime Soviet target, the B-29's in Britain being the first bombers capable of carrying atomic bombs into the Russian mainland. A comment in a Soviet publication, often repeated by Churchill, that the 'British Isles had now become an aircraft carrier' increased public awareness that Britain had put herself at the forefront of Western defence. The quick and uncomplicated acceptance of the American bombers during the Berlin crisis came as somewhat of a surprise to Secretary of Defense Forrestal and Under-Secretary of State Lovett, so much so that Bevin was asked by Secretary of State Marshall whether he had fully considered its implications.[1]

The establishment of Strategic Air Command bases in Britain marked a shift towards recognition of dependence upon the American nuclear deterrent. By 1950, the Defence White Paper asserted that 'Defence policy is based on the assumption that we should not stand alone in resisting aggression.'[2] Of course, by then NATO had been formed, but one of the most sophisticated students of the Anglo-American alliance dates its revival, or the beginning of its post-war phase, in 1948 with the commencement of the 'Airstrip One' relationship.[3] From then to this day Britain and America have had a special relationship in strategic nuclear weapons.

Minister to conceal the true situation while being on record as having made an announcement . . . the Premier not only concealed a major decision from parliament, and from most of his cabinet colleagues, but went one better by theoretically informing them while actually ensuring their ignorance of the facts.' Letter to the *New Statesman*, 17 May 1963. Secretary of Defense James Forrestal was informed six weeks earlier on 31 March 1948 by Admiral Sir Henry Moore on behalf of Lord Portal that a statement would be made in the House about the construction of modern weapons, including guided missiles and atomic weapons, and that the 'press will be alerted by what they call a "D" notice some days prior to the announcement and will be asked not to emphasize the atomic part of it, and as always, they expect to get full cooperation from the press.' Walter Millis (ed.), *Forrestal Diaries* (New York, Viking, 1951), p. 407. According to Anthony Eden, the Labour government 'made the bomb in secret, ingeniously concealing the large sums expended from public and parliamentary gaze. They were certainly right to make the bomb and they may have been wise to conceal the fact from their followers.' *Full Circle* (London, Cassell, 1960), p. 368.

The Department of State was officially informed by none other than Donald MacLean, future defector, who then was dealing with atomic affairs at the British Embassy!

[1] It is interesting to note part of Forrestal's reasoning, as written in his diary on 15 July 1948: 'We have the opportunity *now* (Forrestal's italics) of sending these planes, and once sent they would become somewhat of an accepted fixture, whereas a deterioration of the situation in Europe might lead to a condition of mind under which the British would be compelled to reverse their present attitude.' Millis (ed.), op. cit., p. 457.

[2] *Statement on Defence: 1950*, Cmd. 7895, p. 2.

[3] Coral Bell, *The Debatable Alliance: An Essay in Anglo-American Relations* (London, Oxford University Press for Royal Institute of International Affairs, 1964), p. 8.

3. Political Attitudes and the Atom Bomb

Labour's decision to develop the bomb, if widely known in both parties, would have had greater support among Conservatives than among the Government's backbenches. Certainly this is one reason for Attlee's policy of secrecy on the programme and for keeping public interest in the entire field of atomic energy as low as possible. There were additional considerations related to security. In the years prior to the first atomic detonation, the programme was almost wholly devoted to military purposes. Government spokesmen could and did justify their silence on reasons of security.[1] Furthermore, American concern regarding British security precautions had become a factor in negotiations to renew collaboration, especially after the Fuchs espionage case was uncovered.

But when Churchill as Prime Minister did reveal the atomic bomb programme he took impish delight in observing that 'some of the late Government's followers hardly relished their success in this sphere.' 'I notice, indeed,' he told the House, 'a certain sense of disappointment with the statement that the achievement which has been made could not be wholly attributed to us.' Attlee, said Churchill, borrowing from Alexander Pope, was in the position of one who ' "did good by stealth and blushed to find it fame" . . . Before the whole story passes from life into history, he will have to do a good deal of blushing in the explanations which he will have to make to some of his followers.'[2]

Throughout its time in office, the Attlee government was bedevilled by the search of its Left wing for a 'socialist foreign policy'. Several strands of thought could be found on the Left, not all of which held together neatly. The pacifists opposed peacetime conscription; were unhappy with British participation in NATO; and argued that whatever be the level of defence expenditure the Government had set as necessary it was too high. The Korean rearmament programme, a courageous endeavour which as much as anything contributed to Labour's defeat in the General Election of 1951, was unpalatable because of the sacrifices it entailed in the social services. The Minister of Defence, as Emanuel Shinwell has noted, is in the Labour party 'a most unpopular post'.[3]

Another strand, which had greater influence on the development of the bomb, was the concept of the 'Third Force'. This was to be an alternative

---

[1] See, for example, the statement by Minister of State, Kenneth Younger, 485 H.C. Deb. col. 2761 (22 March 1951).

[2] 496 H.C. Deb. col. 965–6 (26 February 1952).

[3] Shinwell, *The Labour Story*, p. 194; see also his *Conflict Without Malice* (London, Odhams, 1955), p. 196.

to the Anglo-American alliance and assumed that Britian had sufficient strength to be a separate, independent actor in world politics. The objective of the 'Third Force' was to achieve ideological independence of both capitalism and communism, diplomatic independence of both American and Soviet power. 'The first aim of Britain's economic policy must be to achieve independence of aid from abroad at the earliest moment. Without that freedom there is no independent foreign policy for, more and more, American aid is being voted on conditions which involve British acceptance of American strategic decisions and control not even by Congress, but by the Pentagon, headquarters of the United States Chiefs of Staff'—Harold Wilson in 1952.[1]

If Britain was to be an independent 'Third Force', were not its own nuclear weapons one way of achieving that status? Ironically then, the logic of the 'Third Force' advocates, many of whom were also pacifists, inadvertently and unknowingly supported the Labour government's atomic policy. In 1946–7 it could be said that Britain needed an independent nuclear capability because there was no other guarantee of its security. But several years later so overpowering were the changes brought about by the revival of the Anglo-American alliance, the formation of NATO, and the recognition of dependence upon the American nuclear deterrent, that the argument shifted to developing the bomb to assure British independence *from* America. 'I do not believe it is right that this country should be absolutely dependent on the United States of America,' Attlee told the House in March 1952, 'that is one very good reason for going ahead with our own work on the atomic bomb.'[2]

Finally, an attitude shared with the Left wing by many of the less radical members of the Labour party endowed Britain with a unique role of moral leadership. Britain should set an example in the family of nations. Her moral influence in Washington was seen as imposing a restraint on the extremism of America's leaders. Thus it was widely accepted that it was Attlee's urgent flight to Washington in December 1950 that persuaded President Truman not to use nuclear weapons in the Korean war. In the self-image of Britain as a Great Power, military decline came to be offset by moral ascendancy.[3]

The Conservative brand of nationalism, in contrast to Labour's brand, has traditionally been somewhat less moralistic and more militaristic.

[1] Harold Wilson, *In Place of Dollars*, Tribune pamphlet, London, 1952, quoted in Epstein, *Britain—Uneasy Ally*, p. 55.

[2] 497 H.C. Deb. col. 537 (5 March 1952).

[3] Aneurin Bevan: 'There is only one hope for mankind and that hope still remains in this little island.' Quoted in Bell, op. cit., p. 2. Ernest Bevin, prior to a trip to Washington, told the House that 'however much we may disagree on whether we have enough houses or fried fish shops, we seem to agree on the imperative necessity of Britain retaining her moral lead in the world.' 415 H.C. Deb. col. 1333 (7 November 1945).

The Tories have had a more pragmatic approach to the use of force. Differences in ideology and outlook certainly did exist within the party but they were likely to be less profound than in the Labour party. Diplomacy supported by military strength was accepted as the natural instrument for the pursuit of the national interest. The Conservative opposition supported Attlee's and Bevin's response to the Communist threat and their adherence to the Atlantic pact more fully than did the Government's own followers. Indeed, the main lines of Labour's foreign and defence policy could aptly be termed 'Churchillian'.

There can be little doubt that the Conservatives would have agreed with Attlee's secret decision to manufacture nuclear weapons; returned to office, they congratulated him for it. The Tory spokesman on atomic energy throughout their time in opposition was Churchill himself. His was a proprietary interest—when Attlee became Prime Minister in July 1945 he barely knew of the existence of the Manhattan Project, despite his participation in the War Cabinet as Deputy Prime Minister. For Churchill, from the start, the atomic bomb had a special fascination because of the power it bestowed. When, at the Potsdam conference, news arrived of the first atomic test in New Mexico, Alanbrooke recorded that Churchill:

Let himself be carried away by the very first and rather scanty reports of the first atomic explosion. He was already seeing himself capable of eliminating all the Russian centres of industry without taking into account any of the connected problems, such as delivery of the bombs, production of the bombs, possibility of Russians also possessing such bombs, etc. He had at once painted a wonderful picture of himself as the sole possessor of these bombs and capable of dumping them where he wished, thus all-powerful and capable of dictating to Stalin.[1]

Churchill, more than most European statesmen, believed that it was America's capacity to strike at the heart of Russia with the atomic bomb which deterred the Soviets from large-scale military aggression. In 1948 he told the Conservative party conference that 'nothing stands between Europe today and complete subjugation to Communist tyranny but the atomic bomb in American possession.'[2] The next year at a convocation at the Massachusetts Institute of Technology he said, 'It is certain that Europe would have been communized like Czechoslovakia, and London would have been under bombardment some time ago, but for the deterrent

---

[1] Arthur Bryant, *Triumph in the West: A History of the War Years based on the Diaries of Field-Marshal Lord Alanbrooke, Chief of the Imperial General Staff* (London, Collins, 1959), p. 478. See also Herbert Feis, *Between War and Peace: The Potsdam Conference* (Princeton, Princeton University Press, 1960), p. 172; James F. Byrnes, *Speaking Frankly* (New York, Harper, 1947), p. 262.

[2] *Sixty-Ninth Annual Report of the National Union of Conservative and Unionist Associations*, London, 1948, p. 151.

of the atomic bomb in the hands of the United States.'[1] More than the Labour government, according to Denis Healey, Churchill saw NATO as a 'political instrument for tying SAC to automatic retaliation if Europe were attacked'.[2]

While in opposition, the Conservative spokesmen on foreign affairs and defence, Churchill, Eden, and Macmillan, called for a policy of firmness and strength for the West and specifically for Britain. The stronger the nation, the greater her influence in international politics and the more conciliatory the Russians would be. Churchill's phrase—'we arm to parley' —summed it up neatly. The Tories supported the defence measures Labour proposed and Macmillan, as shadow Air Minister, maintained steady pressure on the Government to expand the R.A.F., especially by creating a strategic bomber force.

After the detection of the first Soviet atomic explosion in August 1949, Churchill began publicly to criticize the Government's nuclear programme. The rapidity of Soviet atomic development had come as a surprise in London as in Washington,[3] but it was particularly disquieting to the British for two reasons. First, it had to be assumed that Britain was now under a major threat of nuclear attack in a way that the United States was not to be until the development of Soviet intercontinental ballistic missiles. Second, Britain had evidently fallen behind since 1945 when it was as-sumed that Britain knew a great deal more than the Soviets about the atomic bomb. On the first parliamentary occasion after the announcement of the Soviet explosion, Churchill supported a backbencher's request for a review of the atomic energy programme in view of the fact that 'we have been outstripped by the Russians.'[4]

During the General Election campaign of 1950 Churchill played up the importance of the Soviet bomb—to the charge of warmongering from Labour—and proposed 'atomic talks' at the summit. In a speech at Edinburgh he asked why it was that after having made so much progress on atomic research during the war, Britain should have fallen so far behind and not have a bomb of its own. Churchill viewed this as 'one of the most extraordinary administrative lapses that have ever taken place.'[5] From the time of the Soviet explosion until his return to power in October 1951,

---

[1] *The New York Times*, 1 April 1949.

[2] Denis Healey, 'Britain and NATO,' in *NATO and American Security*, Klaus Knorr (ed (Princeton, Princeton University Press, 1959), p. 214.

[3] See P. M. S. Blackett, *Atomic Weapons and East-West Relations* (Cambridge, Cambridge University Press, 1956), p. 42; Shinwell, *The Labour Story*, p. 187; Warner R. Schilling, 'The H-Bomb Decision: How to Decide Without Actually Choosing', *Political Science Quarterly*, Vol. LXXVI (March 1961), p. 25.

[4] 468 H. C. Deb. col. 1 (27 September 1949).

[5] *The Times*, 15 February 1950. See also Herbert G. Nicholas, *The British General Election of 1950* (London, Macmillan, 1951), pp. 101, 162, 194–203.

Churchill kept up a steady barrage of criticisms of the Labour government's failure to produce an atomic bomb for Britain.[1] Undoubtedly, his motives were mixed. Churchill often repeated his belief that the Soviet bomb had worsened the West's position. 'Time and patience, those powerful though not infallible solvents of human difficulties, are not necessarily on our side,'[2] he warned. He also knew that he was on solid ground politically. No one questioned his authority on atomic matters, although there are indications that he deliberately kept himself uninformed on the true progress of the atomic programme in order to be free to criticize it. The clear implication was that if he were Prime Minister, Britain would have had the bomb and collaboration would have been maintained with the United States. The Labour government, restrained by its self-imposed policy of silence, could do little more than suggest that Churchill was talking recklessly, and give vague hints that greater progress had been made in developing atomic weapons than was generally assumed.[3]

Returned to power, Churchill indicated surprise in finding that the atomic energy programme had developed as far as it had in producing fissile materials and in manufacturing atomic weapons. 'Considerable, if slow progress had been made,'[4] he admitted in the Commons. Churchill congratulated the Attlee government for its decision but as an 'old Parliamentarian' expressed his astonishment that a 'full and clear' statement of policy had not been made to Parliament, especially in view of the large sums of money which had been voted by the House without its knowledge. (In the debate on the White Paper of 1962, Nigel Birch revealed that the money had been concealed in the Civil Contingencies Fund under the subhead of 'Public Buildings in Great Britain'.)[5] 'The Conservative opposition', said Churchill, 'would certainly have supported the Government, as we did on so many other of their measures of defence, and their majority would no doubt have been overwhelming. Nevertheless, they preferred to conceal this vast operation and its finances from the scrutiny of the House, not even obtaining a vote on the principle involved.'[6]

[1] In the debate on the 1951 White Paper he observed that 'Another subject of grave complaint is the inability of the government to produce any atomic bombs of our own in the five and a half years which have passed since the war. When we remember how far we were ahead, and how we were able to deal on equal terms with the United States, it is indeed depressing to feel that we have been outstripped by the Soviets in this field . . . I say the total failure of the government to hold its own.' 484 H.C. Deb. col. 630 (15 February 1951).

[2] 473 H.C. Deb. col. 200 (28 March 1950).

[3] Minister of State Kenneth Younger rebutted, 'We have advanced further than the country has been led to believe by certain statements that have been made.' 485 H.C. Deb. col. 2670 (22 March 1951).

[4] 494 H.C. Deb. col. 2607 (6 December 1951).

[5] 655 H.C. Deb. col. 262 (6 March 1962).

[6] 496 H.C. Deb. col. 965 (26 February 1952).

Although Churchill's point was appreciated by those involved in the banter of politics, in truth there was remarkably little public interest in the subject of British atomic weapons, certainly as compared with a decade later. The Downing Street announcement of the forthcoming atomic test in Australia received only passing attention from the press, a total of twenty-four lines in *The Times*. The British bomb was still viewed by the general public as essentially a scientific venture, divorced from foreign policy and the great issues of international politics. The one issue the press did note was that the test might unseal the lips of the Americans and avoid further unnecessary duplication.[1]

The first British nuclear device was exploded on board a ship off the Monte Bello Islands on 3 October 1952, slightly over seven years after the first atomic test in Alamogordo, New Mexico. The test was directed by Dr. William Penney, a veteran of Los Alamos and a witness of the Nagasaki mushroom. No American observer had been invited, due to the almost complete cessation in exchange of nuclear information at that time. Having achieved full membership of the club, Britain was in the next years to develop a rationale for her membership. As *The Economist* commented, the Prime Minister could now expound more convincingly his views on strategy, and the military officers could 'start thinking for themselves'.[2]

[1] *The Times, Daily Telegraph, Manchester Guardian,* 18 February 1952.
[2] 11 October 1952.

5 | Defence Policy: Evolution of the Concept of the 'Independent Nuclear Deterrent'

1. Churchill, the H-Bomb, and the British Deterrent

The belief that Britain should have its own independently controlled means of deterrence with nuclear weapons was first officially expressed at the same time as the decision was announced in 1955 to produce thermonuclear bombs.[1] Although the need to prevent war by the deterrence of aggression was recognized as early as the 1946 White Paper, the Attlee government did not attempt to base its defence policy on nuclear deterrence. Looking back in 1955 at Labour's development of the bomb, former Minister of Defence Emanuel Shinwell observed 'we were not speaking in terms of atomic deterrents at the time . . . we did not believe the atomic bomb in itself would prove an effective deterrent.'[2]

The concept of the independent British nuclear deterrent was born in the early 1950s and was to remain at the centre of the defence policies of successive governments for over a decade. Its genesis was due to a number of economic and strategic considerations in 1951–4 which led the Churchill government to increase its reliance on nuclear weapons.

Among the considerations was the strain on the economy caused by the Korean War rearmament programme. At the outbreak of the Korean conflict, the chiefs of staff revised the 'ten year-no-war' planning estimate to a new estimate which envisaged the possibility of a major war in two to three years. The Attlee government in September 1950 announced a three year defence programme of £3,600 million which early in 1951, as a result of American pressure and promises of aid, was revised upwards to £4,700 million, the largest rearmament effort it was believed Britain could undertake without imposing the drastic restrictions of a wartime economy. But the rearmament programme ran into one of the classic dilemmas of the post-war British economy: a high proportion of defence production consists of the products of the metal-using and engineering industries, which in turn are essential to the export trade and the balance of payments. The incompatability under conditions of full employment of increasing defence production while maintaining exports at a steady level led to a serious deterioration in the economy and a severe worsening in the

---

[1] An important distinction must be drawn between independent *control* which permits national targeting and firing, and independent *manufacturing capability* which provides national self-sufficiency. The distinction did not become fully apparent in Britain until the United States provided assistance with delivery systems.

[2] 537 H.C. Deb. col. 1914 (1 March 1955).

balance of payments position. Inheriting this situation the new Conservative government devised the concept of the 'long haul' by which the rearmament programme was to be slowed down and stretched out over a longer period. Churchill noted that it was a 'curious commentary on British politics' that it should fall on a Conservative government in the face of dire financial stress to have to curtail a military defence programme to which a 'Socialist' government had committed the nation.[1] Forced to balance the increase of defence capabilities with the lowering of exports, the Government set the point beyond which it made no sense to purchase an added measure of military security at the price of financial solvency.

Out of the Korean rearmament experience, the conclusion was drawn that the continuation of large, balanced, and well-equipped conventional forces was not compatible with the requirements of a healthy economy, a sound trade position, and the maintenance of an adequate level of social welfare in the British Isles. Furthermore, it was not certain that in the evolving patterns of warfare the West needed to match the Communist bloc in every category of military armaments. Churchill became convinced of the need for a 'new assessment'. He directed the three British Chiefs of Staff in the spring of 1952 to make a fundamental strategic review taking into account the state of the economy, the role of nuclear weapons, and the NATO force goals of ninety-six divisions which had been unrealistically set that February at the Lisbon meeting. In the quiet seclusion of a military college in recess, and without their staffs, the Chiefs overcame initial differences and hammered out a 'Global Strategy Paper' which should rank as a classic among military documents.

The 'Global Strategy Paper' in due course strongly influenced the evolution of strategic doctrine in the West. It eventually led Britain to become the first nation to base its national security planning almost entirely upon a declaratory policy of nuclear deterrence. In the United States it helped originate the 'New Look' military policy of the Eisenhower years. The central thesis of the 'Global Strategy Paper' was that nuclear weapons had revolutionized the character of war. The most effective deterrent would be recognition by the Soviet Union that aggression on its part would bring an instantaneous atomic reprisal. The paper therefore recommended that the Western powers openly declare that Soviet aggression would be met not only at the local point of conflict, but would be punished by nuclear retaliation at the Russian heartland. Reliance on such a strategy of nuclear deterrence would permit a reduction in conventional ground forces.[2]

---

[1] 497 H.C. Deb. col. 447 (5 March 1952).

[2] Charles J. V. Murphy, 'A New Strategy for NATO', *Fortune*, Vol. XLVII (January 1953), pp. 80–5; Alastair Buchan, 'Their Bomb and Ours: Some Concluding Remarks on the Nuclear

Churchill sent Sir John Slessor, the R.A.F. Chief of Staff, to Washington to present the 'Global Strategy Paper' and to argue the case for a reduction in the NATO force level goals. Reservations were voiced by General Omar Bradley, Chairman of the United States Joint Chiefs of Staff, about the effect which the emphasis on nuclear deterrence would have upon NATO's mission. But in December 1952 the NATO Council approved a major reduction in the force goals which had been formally agreed upon at Lisbon only ten months earlier. The following year much of the British thinking was incorporated in the 'New Look' of the Eisenhower Administration. Samuel P. Huntington has written that:

Changes in American military policy often came two or three years after changes in British military policy. The New Look originated with Churchill and the British Chiefs of Staff in 1951 and 1952; it became American policy in 1953 and 1954. . . . While the wealthier country was able to develop new weapons earlier than the poorer one, nonetheless, the poorer one, largely because of its more limited resources often was first in adjusting its military policy to the new technological developments.[1]

Subsequently British and American views on defence strategy evolved in a parallel manner in the first half of the 1950s and undoubtedly reinforced each other. The new Eisenhower administration read essentially the same lesson as the British from the Korean war. A cheaper strategy was needed to reduce the swollen defence budget; real military power was dependent upon a stable economy and a balanced budget; increased reliance upon nuclear striking power was the way to reduce expenditures while enhancing security. When Dulles spoke of the decision to depend primarily upon massive retaliatory power and the capacity to retaliate by means and at places of America's choosing, he justified it by the overriding need to find a 'maximum deterrent at a bearable cost'.[2]

For Churchill, the new emphasis upon nuclear weapons had merely confirmed his long-held view that only their deterrent character had

Paradox', *Encounter*, Vol. XII, No. 1 (January 1959), pp. 11–18; Richard N. Rosecrance, *Defense of the Realm: British Strategy in the Nuclear Epoch* (New York, Columbia University Press, 1968), pp. 159–81.

[1] *The Common Defense* (New York, Columbia University Press, 1961), p. 118. According to Rosecrance, op. cit., 'While the United States talked of deterrence through balanced military capabilities and the Soviets of "constantly operating factors", the United Kingdom was already formulating the world's first doctrine of nuclear deterrence,' p. 20. He observes that 'The Global Strategy Paper respresented an important innovation in military thought. It anticipated changes in American strategy and helped to bring them about. It also provided the basis for a fundamental change in NATO doctrine and force postures,' pp. 171–2; see also Glenn H. Snyder, 'The "New Look" of 1953', in Warner R. Schilling, Paul Y. Hammond, and Glenn H. Snyder, *Strategy, Politics and Defense Budgets* (New York, Columbia University Press, 1962), pp. 388–9.

[2] 'The Evolution of Foreign Policy', *Department of State Bulletin,* Vol. XXX, No. 761, 25 January 1954.

avoided a third world war (an assumption that the Labour government had not fully accepted), and that the long-range bomber had become the supreme expression of military power. (Any doubts he may have had were probably dispelled when shortly before his return to office he was given a briefing by the United States Air Force on the nuclear offensive power of SAC.) Slessor believed that the coming of atomic and hydrogen bombs coupled with the jet bomber had created a revolution in strategy and that 'total war had abolished itself'. Air defence against nuclear weapons was not practical, for even if an effective over-all air defence system should become technically feasible the costs would be prohibitive. Recognizing that Britain could not afford to superimpose a nuclear air strategy upon a conventional land strategy, Slessor recommended first priority for the 'great deterrent'.[1] The Churchill government, shortly after the formulation of the 'Global Strategy Paper', made the decision to obtain the V-bombers in quantity and officially gave their production a 'super priority' rating.

The equipping of NATO forces with American tactical nuclear weapons in early 1954 could not fail but add to the case for a British nuclear deterrent. This attempt to compensate for the insufficiency of conventional forces by atomic weapons seemed to imply acceptance by the alliance that nuclear weapons were 'cheaper' and were an adequate means of offsetting the superiority in manpower of the Communist armies. In a widely noted lecture at the Royal United Service Institute in London, Field Marshal Montgomery, then Deputy Supreme Commander of SHAPE, made it clear that SHAPE's operational planning called for the use of nuclear weapons if attacked. He explained:

the reason for this action is that we cannot match the strength that could be brought against us unless we use nuclear weapons; and our political chiefs have never shown any great enthusiasm in giving us the numbers to be able to do without using such weapons.[2]

If NATO and the United States were to rely increasingly upon the deterrent effect of nuclear weapons, why should Britain not follow suit? The coming of the American and Russian hydrogen bomb profoundly

[1] One must assume that the views Sir John Slessor expressed shortly after retirement, and which received great attention, are indicative of the advice he gave in his official capacity. See his 'The Revolution in Strategy', *The Listener*, Vol. LI, No. 1302 (11 February 1954), pp. 243–4; ibid., No. 1303 (18 February 1954), pp. 283–5; 'Air Power and the Future of War', *Journal of the Royal United Service Institution*, Vol. XCIX, No. 595 (August 1954), pp. 343–58; *Strategy for the West* (London, Cassell, 1954).

[2] Field-Marshal the Viscount Montgomery of Alamein, 'A Look Through a Window at World War III', *Journal of the Royal United Service Institution*, Vol. XCIX, No. 596 (November 1954), p. 508. See also *The Memoirs of Field-Marshal the Viscount Montgomery of Alamein* (London, Collins, 1958), pp. 516–17.

influenced defence thinking in Britain. The belated release of details of America's first thermonuclear explosion by Sterling Cole, Chairman of the Joint Congressional Committee on Atomic Energy, in February 1954, awoke the British public, more than anything else, to its vulnerability. Churchill later told the House he had been 'astounded' by the revelations of the destructive effect of the H-bomb, especially 'considering what immense differences the facts disclosed made to our whole outlook for defence'.[1] On another occasion he declared that 'the advance of the hydrogen bomb has fundamentally altered the entire problem of defence, and considerations founded even upon the atom bomb have become obsolescent, almost old fashioned.'[2] Churchill appears to have been rankled by his lack of access to early and full information on the H-bomb tests (the Eniwetok Atoll tests had occurred fifteen months before their disclosure) and he went to Washington to press once more for an enlarged exchange between the two countries of nuclear data.

The hydrogen bomb removed any remaining doubts about the revolution that had taken place in warfare. But two disparate conclusions were drawn in Britain. On the one hand it no longer seemed reasonable to assume, as some had, that damage from nuclear weapons could be limited and that such weapons would not necessarily be decisive. Clearly the small isles of Britain were now totally vulnerable. On the other hand, the H-bomb was seen as an 'equalizer' or 'leveller' which put a smaller nation possessing thermonuclear weapons at less of a disadvantage compared with a superpower. As Foreign Secretary Anthony Eden wrote:

One consequence of the evolution from the atomic to the hydrogen bomb was to diminish the advantage of physically larger countries. All became equally vulnerable. I had been acutely conscious in the atomic age of our unenviable position in a small and crowded island, but if continents, and not merely small islands were doomed to destruction, all was equal in the grim reckoning.[3]

Britain's decision to manufacture her own thermonuclear bomb, which was formalized in 1954 on the basis of prior research decisions reached in 1952, seemed a natural step given the capability to do so. The scientific and industrial capacity had been developed in the atomic bomb programme; the V-bombers which were on the way could readily be adapted to carry hydrogen as well as atomic bombs. Indeed, it was thought that thermonuclear bombs would require fewer bombers and necessitate less accurate delivery. The very availability of the H-bomb and its means of transport argued for its acquisition.

[1] 530 H.C. Deb. col. 34 (12 July 1954).   [2] 535 H.C. Deb. col. 176 (1 December 1954).
[3] Eden, *Full Circle*, p. 368.

With one important exception, hitherto not publicly known, there was no debate within the Churchill government regarding the wisdom of independent manufacture of thermonuclear weapons. There was no equivalent to the great debate triggered by the H-bomb among the scientists in the United States. The exception took the form of a paper written by Nigel Birch, then Parliamentary Secretary to the Minister of Defence, suggesting that a British hydrogen bomb might complicate disarmament efforts and encourage the development of nuclear weapons by other nations. Birch showed the paper to Harold Macmillan, then Minister of Defence, and to Selwyn Lloyd, the Foreign Secretary, but upon finding that his thesis was not falling on receptive ears he decided not to pursue the matter.[1]

The decision to build a British H-bomb was made without much thought given to the reasons for not duplicating the American H-bomb and SAC. This was not only because the problems of cost and vulnerability had not been foreseen; or because little thought had been given in official circles to the lead Britain might take in what came to be known as 'non-proliferation'; or because of the simplistic notion that Churchill did in fact entertain, that whatever the Americans and Russians possessed, Britain as a Great Power must have also. These are partial explanations, but more fundamentally, strategic doctrine as it had been evolving in Britain supported the H-bomb as the apex of an independent nuclear deterrent.

It was thought that the nature of the next large-scale war would be nuclear and catalytic. The 1954 Defence White Paper said:

It must be assumed that atomic weapons would be employed by both sides. In this event it seems likely that such a war would begin with a period of intense atomic attacks lasting a relatively short time but inflicting great destruction and damage.[2]

Churchill told the House in December 1954 that in spite of the Soviet superiority in armed manpower he did not believe that a surprise attack with conventional weapons would be made against the NATO countries. Because in nuclear arms the Soviets were the weaker power, they would hold back their ground forces in order not to compromise the advantage of a surprise attack by nuclear weapons.[3]

Defence policy therefore had to be based upon the prevention of war. Strategic air power combined with nuclear weapons was to be the deterrent. The 1954 White Paper in talking of a period of 'broken-back' warfare following the initial nuclear exchange attempted to combine the

[1] Interview.   [2] *Statement on Defence 1954*, Cmd. 9075, p. 5.
[3] 535 H.C. Deb. col. 177 (1 December 1954).

expectation of atomic warfare with a continued requirement for large conventional forces. By the following year the phrase had passed from official usage. The 1955 Defence White Paper stated that:

The free nations must base their plans and preparations on the assumption that if a major war were precipitated by an attack upon them they would have to use all the weapons at their disposal in their defence.

Given the size of Soviet and satellite land forces, the:

Use of nuclear weapons is the only means by which this massive preponderance can be countered. . . . If we do not use the full weight of our nuclear power, Europe can hardly be protected from invasion and occupation . . . with all that this implies both for Europe and the United Kingdom.[1]

In the early years after it became known that Britain was the first junior member of an alliance to develop nuclear weapons independently of its senior partner, there was no talk of an independent British force. By 1954 the trend towards what might be termed an independent deterrent role could be read between the lines of that year's Defence White Paper:

The primary deterrent remains the atomic bomb and the ability of the highly organized and trained United States strategic air power to use it. From our past experience and current knowledge we have a significant contribution to make both to the technical and to the tactical development of strategic air power. We intend as soon as possible to build up in the Royal Air Force a force of modern bombers capable of using the atomic weapons to the fullest effect.[2]

The 1955 Defence White Paper, which officially announced the decision to manufacture the hydrogen bomb, confirmed the intention to build an independent nuclear force. A section titled 'The Tasks Before Us' concluded:

We must therefore contribute to the deterrent and to our own defence by building up our own stock of nuclear weapons of all types and by developing the most up to date means of delivery . . . we must, in our allocation of resources, assign even higher priority to the primary deterrent. . . .[3]

The justifications for the independent British force were first openly discussed in the parliamentary debates, which by their nature were less likely than official white papers to cause offence abroad. The military rationale was set on the assumption that America and Britain might have a different order of priorities in the selection of targets and that Britain should have the capability of first hitting targets vital to its own security

[1] *Statement on Defence: 1955*, Cmd. 9391, p. 7.
[2] Ibid., *1954*, Cmd. 9075, pp. 4–5.
[3] Ibid., *1955*, Cmd. 9391, pp. 8–9

but which might be less vital to the alliance's strategic plan as a whole. This argument was supported by the experience of World War II, when differences of opinion had arisen between the R.A.F. and the U.S.A.F. as to the relative priority of bombing the V-1 and V-2 sites in Northern Europe during the closing stages of the war. Whereas the rocket sites added little to the German war potential, the destruction of which was the primary goal of the U.S.A.F. in selecting bombing targets, the sites were somewhat less irrelevant to the concerns of the inhabitants of southern England. Thus Churchill reasoned that:

Unless we can make a contribution of our own . . . we cannot be sure that in an emergency the resources of other powers would be planned exactly as we would wish, or that the targets which would threaten us most would be given what we consider the necessary priority in the first few hours. These targets might be of such cardinal importance that it could really be a matter of life and death for us.[1]

He may also have had in mind evidence of spectacular growth of the Soviet bomber force. The May Day parade of 1954 had demonstrated that Russia possessed long- and medium-range bombers then capable of reaching Britain and which might one day make America vulnerable as well.

But it was the need for political influence and independence vis-à-vis the United States, not the Soviet Union, that was at the heart of the Government's case for an independent deterrent. In the debate on the 1955 Defence White Paper, Minister of Defence Macmillan rejected without difficulty the view (then held by a few) that because of the American deterrent there need not be a British nuclear role:

I think this is a very dangerous doctrine. . . . Politically it surrenders our power to influence American policy and then, strategically and tactically it equally deprives us of any influence over the selection of targets and the use of our vital striking forces. The one, therefore, weakens our prestige and our influence in the world, and the other might imperil our safety.[2]

Churchill also felt that the British contribution to the alliance should be more substantial than mere criticism of any 'unwise policy' into which the United States might 'drift or plunge':

Personally, I cannot feel that we should have much influence over their policy or action, wise or unwise, while we are largely dependent as we are today upon their protection. We too must possess substantial deterrent power of our own.[3]

[1] 537 H.C. Deb. col. 1897 (1 March 1955).
[2] Ibid., col. 2182 (2 March 1955).
[3] Ibid., col. 1905 (1 March 1955).

One assumption implicit in these statements, although not publicly explained or examined at the time, was that British nuclear weapons could constitute an effective deterrent. Another was that nuclear weapons, through an equality of vulnerability, would lead to stable, mutual deterrence. In Churchill's famous words:

Then it may be that we shall, by a process of sublime irony, have reached a stage in this story where safety will be the sturdy child of terror, and survival the twin brother of annihilation.[1]

This assumption went beyond parliamentary rhetoric. According to Anthony Eden, he found himself at the Geneva conference on Indochina in 1954 conscious and grateful for the deterrent effect of the hydrogen bomb, and did not believe that a major war could have been avoided without it.[2] The 1955 Defence White Paper confidently predicted that 'the existence of the nuclear weapon may discourage overt armed intervention by the Communist powers such as occurred in Korea.'[3] 'The advent of the hydrogen bomb', stated the 1956 Defence White Paper, 'has enormously strengthened the power of the deterrent and, provided the deterrent is maintained, the likelihood of global war has decreased.'[4]

British thermonuclear weapons would also help preserve the nation's standing as a Great Power. Eden saw the H-bomb as giving Britain the 'quills of the porcupine' which would be 'deadly against any power'.[5] The 1956 Defence White Paper stated that British forces must make a contribution to the Allied deterrent 'commensurate with our standing as a world power'.[6] Some on the chauvinistic wing of the Conservative party hoped that British H-bombs would serve to recoup the lost prestige of past years. As Julian Amery saw it:

It would seem that the hydrogen bomb, when we have it, will make us a world power again. The atom bomb rather put us out of the race because only big territorial expanses like the United States or the Soviet Union could stand up to atom-bombing and hope to survive. We should have been obliterated very quickly. But the hydrogen bomb is a great leveller. It cancels out the disparity between population and the big areas of territory and smaller ones. It would be just as dangerous for the Soviet Union, or the United States to incur thermonuclear bombardment as it would be for us.[7]

The hydrogen bomb, as the centrepiece of the nuclear force, would keep Britain in the rank of the Great Powers. For some, such as Julian Amery, it would even restore superpower status.

---

[1] 537 H.C. Deb. col. 1899 (1 March 1955).   [2] Eden, *Full Circle*, pp. 123, 369.
[3] *Statement on Defence: 1955*, Cmd. 9391, p. 6.
[4] Ibid., *1956*, Cmd. 9691, p. 8.   [5] Eden, *Full Circle*, p. 368.
[6] *Statement on Defence: 1956*, Cmd. 9691, p. 4.
[7] 549 H.C. Deb. col. 1091–2 (28 February 1956).

2. Suez, Sandys, and the 1957 White Paper

In the great debate of 1957–64 on the independent nuclear deterrent critics usually identified the original villain as Duncan Sandys, Suez as the backdrop, and the 1957 Defence White Paper as the beginning of the concept. Harold Wilson in the parliamentary debate on the Nassau Agreement characterized the 1957 statement as the Macmillan government's reaction to Suez, a conscious decision by a new Prime Minister to undertake a swing towards reliance on nuclear weapons;[1] Denis Healey in the debate on the 1963 Defence White Paper said the Government of the day had wanted 'a virility symbol to compensate for the exposure of its military impotence at Suez';[2] according to Richard Crossman 'it was not until 1957 that the New Look strategy was adopted in London.'[3]

Part of the reason for the subsequent notoriety of the 1957 White Paper was the new Macmillan government's attempt to bestow upon it an aura of novelty. The statement was two months late, after an appropriately dramatic staging of preliminaries. It spoke of the time having come to revise 'not merely the size but the whole character of the defence plan'. This was not to be an ordinary defence white paper but was billed as an original 'outline of future policy' for the next five years, blandly overlooking a less publicized statement in the 1956 Defence White Paper that that year's statement was based on probable developments over the next seven years.

In truth, the deterrent strategy enunciated in the 1957 Defence White Paper was in its broad fundamentals virtually the same as that proposed by the Chiefs of Staff in 1952 in the Global Strategy Paper and written into every defence statement since 1954. As to the independent British capability, the statement which Macmillan as Prime Minister approved in 1957 ('There is a wide measure of agreement that she [Britain] must possess an appreciable element of nuclear deterrent power of her own')[4] was essentially identical to that which he as Minister of Defence was said to have personally written in 1955 ('We must therefore contribute to the deterrent and to our own defence by building up our own stock of nuclear weapons of all types and by developing the most up to date means of delivery').[5]

Contrary to much popular opinion, therefore, the 1957 White Paper did not introduce a revolutionary new deterrent policy but consolidated

[1] 670 H.C. Deb. col. 1237 (3 January 1963).
[2] 673 H.C. Deb. col. 49 (4 March 1963).
[3] R. H. S. Crossman, 'The Nuclear Obsession', *Encounter*, Vol. XI, No. 1 (July 1958), p. 6.
[4] *Defence: Outline of Future Policy: 1957*, Cmnd. 124, p. 3.
[5] *Statement on Defence: 1955*, Cmd. 9391, p. 8.

existing trends of the previous years. Its significance in the history of post-war defence policy lies in the practical conclusions for the military services and the economy which were drawn from its strategic assumptions. The announced intentions to end national service, to reduce the size of the armed forces from 690,000 to 375,000 by 1962, to scale down the forces in Europe from 77,000 to 64,000 within a year, to cancel the development of a supersonic manned bomber, to rely in the future on ballistic missiles for long-range delivery, and the subsequent increased influence over military policy-making by the political leadership of the Government were what gave the 1957 statement its cutting edge.

Undoubtedly, the abortive Suez episode increased the psychological desire for independence of action while at the same time brutally demonstrating Britain's diminished capabilities. The Suez adventure can be seen as a response to the widespread resentment of Britain's loss of empire and stature. The refusal of the United States to support the Anglo-French action led to a wave of anti-Americanism in the winter of 1956–7. For the Right wing of the Conservative party, the United States was regarded as the 'general enemy of British imperial interests'.[1] Frustrated, many Conservatives yearned for the renewal of independent British power unhampered by the United States or the United Nations.

The sting of Suez probably did increase the desire of the Conservative leaders for an independent nuclear deterrent. Two years later Randolph Churchill told the American Chamber of Commerce in London:

Britain can knock down twelve cities in the region of Stalingrad and Moscow from bases in Britain and another dozen in the Crimea from bases in Cyprus. We did not have that power at the time of Suez. We are a major power again.[2]

But the lesson drawn from the Suez experience with respect to the relevance of nuclear weapons might, or perhaps should, have been different. In November 1956 the R.A.F. was equipped with atomic bombs and a means of delivery. But since they did not constitute an effective deterrent against the Soviet Union, the possession of nuclear weapons did little to strengthen British resolve against the threat of Russian rockets. The British and French halted operations in Suez within hours after receiving Bulganin's threatening message at a time when the immediate military objectives of the intervention were within reach, according to the judgement of British officers on the scene.[3] There were a number of considera-

[1] Leon Epstein, *British Politics in the Suez Crisis* (Urbana, University of Illinois Press, 1964), p. 55. The author found a 'very large segment of the Conservative party essentially unreconciled to a second place in an American alliance or to internationalism in general', p. 57.

[2] *The Times*, 14 November 1958.

[3] Hans Speier, 'Soviet Atomic Blackmail and the North Atlantic Alliance', *World Politics*, Vol. IX (April 1957), p. 324.

tions—such as the deep cleavage in British public opinion, the split with the United States, the pressures at the United Nations, the protests from the Commonwealth, and the weakness of sterling—which may have had a far greater impact on altering the Government's plans than the Soviet rocket threat. Yet the vulnerability of the British Isles in a nuclear exchange and the inadequacy of the deterrent capability of British nuclear weapons could not have been overlooked in Downing Street. Neither did nuclear weapons seem relevant to the problem of dealing with Nasser. A Western government is not likely to initiate the use of nuclear weapons against a non-nuclear country, especially in defence of its overseas interests. Finally, they had no impact on the possibility of sanctions from the United Nations or on the openly hostile policy of Britain's principal ally. Thus the possession of nuclear weapons was seemingly irrelevant to British objectives and interests at the time of Suez.

Suez also exposed the weakness of the over-extended defence establishment and its precarious dependence upon the nation's finances. The strain put on the monetary reserves by the military operations and the run on the pound was so great that some later thought the intervention could not have continued for another week without financial disaster in the form of the collapse of sterling. The Suez experience therefore reinforced the Government's earlier intention of undertaking a major review of defence commitments and expenditures. In July 1956, after Eden had been informed that defence costs would rise from £1527 million in 1955 to £1929 million in 1959 unless existing programmes were revised, he set up a sub-committee of the cabinet to examine future defence roles and requirements. The accepted premises under which it deliberated were that since 1945 Britain had been attempting to do too much in too many spheres of defence; that this contributed to the continuous economic crisis; and that thermonuclear weapons could now be relied upon not only to deter aggression but to deal with it should it occur.[1]

Thus the economic incentive was as strong as any in shaping the 1957 Defence White Paper. Macmillan told the House in January 1957 that he was entrusting his Minister of Defence 'with the task of formulating in the light of present strategic needs a defence policy which will secure a substantial reduction in expenditure and manpower and to prepare a plan for reshaping and reorganizing the Armed forces in accordance therewith'.[2] As Chancellor of the Exchequer he had spoken of his 'pipe dream' of cutting defence expenditures by half: if only fifty per cent of the savings were shifted into exports, it could eliminate the foreign exchange problem and lead to a reduction in taxes. Macmillan believed that Britain was carrying 'two rifles', for compared to the continental European

[1] Eden, *Full Circle*, pp. 370–3.   [2] 563 H.C. Deb. col. 396 (24 January 1957).

members of the alliance she was devoting nearly twice as large a share of her resources to defence.[1] An economic ceiling on defence was therefore clearly written into the White Paper:

Britain's influence in the world depends first and foremost on the health of her internal economy and the success of her export trade. Without these, military power cannot in the long run be supported. It is therefore in the true interest of defence that the claims of military expenditure should be considered in conjunction with the need to maintain the country's financial and economic strength.[2]

Defence in the past five years had absorbed 9 per cent of Britain's G.N.P. The high demands of the defence industries for skilled personnel had created a technological manpower shortage in the civil industries, especially the metal-using industries upon which the export trade so largely depended. Altogether defence consumed 7 per cent of the working population and 12 per cent of the output of the metal-using industry. The defence plan was partially designed to release skilled manpower, especially scientists, technicians, and engineers for the civil sector of the economy.[3] The White Paper noted that 'an undue proportion of qualified scientists and engineers are engaged on military work.' Apparently little weight was given to the benefits to the civil sector from the 'spill-over' of military research and development.

The Government's contention that the choice lay between the strength of the economy and the maintenance of the military programme at existing levels was, however, over-simplified and misleading. Both of these priorities could have been attained through a cut in the growth of consumption or investment. The British people, however, were coming out of sixteen years of austerity and economic controls later than in most of the European nations. The public was in a mood for spending. Macmillan was to tell it that 'you never had it so good' and this theme was to become a central Tory plank in the 1959 General Election. The alternatives of reducing the share of the G.N.P. devoted to investment or consumer spending were unacceptable, for the first would have imperilled an already inadequate rate of economic expansion and modernization, and the second was politically unpopular. Implicit though unstated in the 1957 assumption that the military budget must be reduced was the decision to give defence

---

[1] Speech before the Foreign Press Association in London, *Manchester Guardian*, 17 May 1956. From the start of the Korean War in June 1950 to 1957 defence expenditures had almost doubled. See Table 1.

[2] *Defence: Outline of Future Policy, 1957*, Cmnd. 124, p. 1.

[3] See George L. Payne, *Britain's Scientific and Technological Manpower* (Stanford, Stanford University Press, 1960), p. 389.

a smaller place in the nation's rank of priorities and to increase the non-military share of the allocation of resources.[1]

It was the decision to end national service in 1960—rather than the emphasis on nuclear deterrence—that attracted most attention to the 1957 Defence White Paper at the time. Desirous in the post-Suez atmosphere of restoring confidence in the Conservative government, Macmillan is reported to have decided upon this politically popular step shortly after becoming Prime Minister.[2] With the easing of the cold war tensions after the Korean war, politicians in both parties had begun to question the need for continued conscription. Reductions in the size of the services in 1955–6 served only to increase public dissatisfaction, for the very equity of national service created a surplus of manpower and a burdensome system of call-up. The intention to end conscription was not criticized by the Labour party, for many of its supporters had been unhappy with it for some time. Indeed, Labour politicians regretted having lost the electoral advantage which it was acknowledged would now be given to the Government. Within the military services the end of national service was not unwelcome, for it would allow for more professional military services without the burden of training large numbers of personnel with rapid turnover.

As presented to the public and in the parliamentary debates, the end of national service was made possible by the availability of an independent nuclear force. Nuclear weapons would effectively replace the reductions in conventional strength; without greater reliance on the nuclear force, national service could not be terminated. Iain Macleod, then Minister of Labour and National Service, admitted to the House: 'If we refuse to rely on the deterrent we cannot at the same time urge the abolition of National Service.'[3] Although the nuclear deterrent was not then an issue, Macmillan stated the alternatives as follows:

The fundamental question which the House must face . . . is whether or not the nuclear deterrent is to form the basis of British defence planning. If this is not faced, no one except perhaps a genuine pacifist has the right to urge the ending of national service. There can be no doubt about this . . . *the end of conscription must depend upon the acceptance of nuclear weapons.*[4] (Italics mine.)

The termination of national service rested on the assumption that large conventional forces would not be required for a future war. Russian conventional strength in manpower was then thought to be so great that

[1] See A. C. L. Day, 'The Economics of Defence', *Political Quarterly*, Vol. XXXI, No. 1 (January–March 1960), pp. 57–65.
[2] 'Macmillan Faces Defence Split', *Observer*, 28 July 1957.
[3] 568 H.C. Deb. col. 1958 (17 April 1957).
[4] Ibid., col. 2040 (17 April 1957).

it could not be matched in peacetime by any effort that Britain and her NATO allies could or would tolerate and afford. If the enemy was given no reason to doubt that the West would retaliate against a major aggression with nuclear weapons, then he would not risk the attack; if he was given such a reason, then the danger was real but no level of conventional forces acceptable in peacetime would eliminate it. Such reasoning virtually omitted limited wars of the Korean type from the calculation.

The net result of the defence strategy and structure detailed by Duncan Sandys was to emphasize the effectiveness and cheapness of a deterrent based on nuclear weapons in contrast to the costs of conventional forces. This was the same formula which had beguiled the Eisenhower administration in 1954. Both 'new looks' were motivated primarily by the perceived need for economy, were accepted more readily at the political than the professional military level, and were presented to their respective publics as fresh and original concepts. However, at the very time official British defence doctrine was coming to rely more heavily than ever upon massive retaliation, American thinking was edging towards a policy of graduated response in Europe.[1] Britain was following America's past lead though not its present advice. Publicly, Sandys and Macmillan returning from separate meetings with their counterparts in the spring of 1957 spoke of the sympathetic reception given in the United States to their new defence policy and the post-Suez revival of Anglo-American relations; privately, they rebuffed Eisenhower's attempt to forestall the reduction of their NATO forces.[2]

On the one hand there was increasing recognition of the need for *interdependence* with the United States, particularly in research and development of guided missiles and other weapons systems. On the other, there was a continuing desire for *independence* from America. The military and strategic argument for an independent nuclear force shifted for the first time in the debate on the 1957 Defence White Paper from the need for separate targeting to a substitute for the American deterrent because of the growing incredibility of its guarantee with the growth of Soviet nuclear missile power. As Sandys asked:

So long as large American forces remain in Europe, and American bombers are based in Britain, it might conceivably be thought safe—I am not saying that it would—to leave to the United States the sole responsibility for providing the nuclear deterrent. But, when they have developed the 5,000 mile intercontinental

---

[1] See John Foster Dulles, 'Challenge and Response in United States Policy', *Foreign Affairs*, Vol. XXXVI, No. 1 (October 1957), p. 31.

[2] Macmillan told Eisenhower that the condition of the British Exchequer made immediate force cuts necessary. Dwight D. Eisenhower, *Waging Peace* (New York, Doubleday, 1965), p. 121.

ballistic rocket, can we really be sure that every American administration will go on looking at things in quite the same way?[1]

With the launching of Sputnik half a year later, a new chapter was to begin in the argument for nuclear independence.

3. The Response: Labour Party, Commentators and Press, Public Opinion, and Allies

In discussing the response to the evolution of the concept of the independent nuclear deterrent, one must distinguish between the reactions to (a) the development of the British nuclear force, (b) the adoption of a declaratory policy of massive retaliation, and (c) the changes in the structure and commitment of the military services. It was possible for some to approve of (a) and (c) while rejecting (b).

The front bench of the parliamentary Labour party supported the Conservative government's development of an independent nuclear force until the cancellation of the Blue Streak missile in the spring of 1960. Throughout most of the 1950s many of the justifications cited by Labour spokesmen for a British nuclear deterrent were essentially identical to those of the Government. There was often more disagreement between the Left wing of the Labour party and its front bench leaders than between the Government and the opposition. The decision to manufacture British thermonuclear weapons was accepted without open opposition. The National Executive Committee of the Labour party in its resolution of 30 March 1955 on the hydrogen bomb adopted much of Churchill's logic:

Hitherto only the U.SA. and the U.S.S.R. have possessed the Hydrogen bomb. Labour believes that it is undesirable that Britain should be dependent on another country for this vital weapon. If we were, our influence for peace would be lessened in the councils of the world. It was for that reason that the Labour Government decided on the manufacture of the atomic bomb and that we support the production of the hydrogen bomb in this country.[2]

Within the party, however, support for the British nuclear force was not as solid and unrestrained as the above resolution made it appear. Before the release of the 1955 Defence White Paper, announcing the decision to build the hydrogen bomb, Attlee, with the assistance of an advance notice from Churchill, privately told Labour parliamentarians that the

---

[1] 568 H.C. Deb. col. 1760–1 (16 April 1957).
[2] *Report of the Fifty-Fourth Annual Conference of the Labour Party* (London, Transport House, 1955), p. 25.

H-bomb was necessary, thus stealing the march on the critics. *The Economist* noted that Labour had taken the decision to manufacture the bomb surprisingly calmly and that because of Attlee's softening of his party 'an announcement that might otherwise have touched off an emotional storm has been accepted with almost tame resignation.'[1] But looking back approvingly two years later, John Strachey observed that Labour 'came to that decision . . . with great difficulty, with great heart searching and with some division of opinion in our ranks.'[2]

In the Commons there was little criticism of the H-bomb decision, nor were the justifications for it advanced by Churchill and Macmillan challenged. Most of the opponents were pacifist and even they staked their position on a different issue. Aneurin Bevan's revolt of March 1955, in which he and sixty-one other Labour backbenchers abstained from voting for the Labour amendment, was based not on the front-bench support of the manufacture of hydrogen bombs, but on the amendment's failure to call for a 'no first use' policy by stipulating that nuclear weapons should only be used to retaliate against an attack using nuclear weapons.[3] The Government's decision was not an issue two months later in the General Election of 1955.[4] The most cogent criticism of it was to be found in the liberal section of the press. The defence correspondent of the *Observer* wrote that the British H-bomb would add little to the security of the West. Britain, with her limited resources and no prospect of having to fight alone, would gain more influence in Washington and would make a more effective contribution to the West's deterrent with bases and with weapons such as missiles and atomic cannons. The *Manchester Guardian* also found the attempt to duplicate the SAC an 'unhappy basis for an alliance in the middle of the twentieth century'. *The Times,* however, saw the Government's resolve to be strong as the 'price of peace'.[5]

The Labour opposition spoke with slightly less enthusiasm of the British nuclear force than the Government, but supported it with the same arguments. When it reminded the Government that Britain did not yet have a deterrent, the intended embarrassment was designed to speed, rather than delay, its development. In 1956 a front-bench spokesman on defence called for quick development of the H-bomb so that Britain would become the equal to the United States and the Soviet Union in disarma-

---

[1] 'Labour and Defence', 26 February 1955.

[2] 564 H.C. Deb. col. 1377 (13 February 1957).

[3] For an analysis of the events which led to the withdrawal of the whip from Bevan, see Leon Epstein, 'Cohesion of British Parliamentary Parties', *American Political Science Review*, Vol. L (June 1956), pp. 372–3.

[4] David E. Butler, *The British General Election of 1955* (London, Macmillan, 1955), p. 30.

[5] 'Britain's Share', *Observer*, 20 February 1955; *Manchester Guardian*, 2 March 1955; 'The Price of Peace', *The Times*, 18 February 1955.

ment talks. The following year George Brown, then a front-bench spokes-man on defence, observed that:

The more we look at it, the less attractive it becomes . . . but if we still have visions of retaining influence in the world, if we still have visions of our-selves as the centre, if no longer the mother of a great commonwealth of nations, and if we see ourselves influencing the circumstances in which the deterrent might be used, I do not see how we can do without it.[1]

With the authority of a former Prime Minister, Attlee supported the view that nuclear weapons give influence:

I think we have influence in the world. That influence does not depend solely upon the possession of weapons, although I have found in practical conversation that the fact that we do possess these weapons does have an effect upon the rulers of other countries. It is quite an illusion to think that it does not have an effect.[2]

Who was to be influenced? Most statements suggested the desired locale of influence to be Washington, more than Moscow. In rejecting unilateral British renunciation of nuclear weapons John Strachey told the Labour Party Conference of 1957 that its effect would be:

To make Britain the wholly dependent satellite of the United States . . . it would make a future Labour Foreign Secretary unable even to consider policies which were not approved by the State Department in Washington.[3]

Influence could also make Britain an intermediary. To the dismay of his former Left wing supporters, Aneurin Bevan upon entering the shadow cabinet changed his attitude towards nuclear armaments. As shadow foreign secretary he feared that unilateral renunciation would 'send a British Foreign Secretary, whoever he may be, naked into the conference table'. It would reduce British influence and drive her into a 'diplomatic purdah'. Harking back to the Left wing's 'Third Force' concept of a decade earlier, Bevan argued that British nuclear weapons offset American-Soviet bipolarity:

It is against that deadly, dangerous negative polarization that we have been fighting for years. We want to have the opportunity of interposing between these two giants, modifying, moderating and mitigating influences.[4]

[1] 564 H.C. Deb. col. 1293 (13 February 1957).
[2] 537 H.C. Deb. col. 2175 (2 March 1955).
[3] *Report of the Fifty-Sixth Annual Conference of the Labour Party* (London, Transport House, 1957), p. 177.
[4] Ibid., pp. 181–2.

Labour leaders also agreed with the Sandys thesis that because Britain's vital interests might not always be the same as America's, she should not be totally dependent upon the American deterrent and the willingness of the President to risk attack by Soviet missiles in order to come to Britain's aid. As Gaitskell explained in 1957:

We felt that a situation might conceivably arise in which Soviet Russia might threaten us in some way or other and in which we then, faced with this threat, had to turn to some future American President and Congress who might . . . not be too well disposed to us. We might have to say to them, 'Will you please threaten to use the ultimate deterrent? We have not got it.' Could we be sure in those circumstances that the American President and Congress would be prepared to risk the wholesale destruction of American cities merely to meet our point of view?[1]

There were two essential characteristics of the arguments for an independent nuclear deterrent advanced by Conservative and Labour front-bench spokesmen. First, they assumed the alternatives were either a British deterrent or unilateral disarmament. The more sophisticated arguments favouring reliance on the American or a NATO deterrent but rejecting a national British nuclear force came initially only from a few backbenchers and defence commentators. Some of the more extreme statements supporting the independent deterrent made in the mid-1950s by such persons as John Strachey must be seen in the context of rejecting the alternative of unilateral renunciation of the entire deterrence concept. Second, the justifications put forth were essentially national in character.[2] They rested on a conception of Britain's separate need rather than the requirements of a NATO, European, or Anglo-American deterrent. Asked on a radio broadcast in 1957, 'Why does Britain need a hydrogen bomb in the opinion of the Labour party?', George Brown replied: 'I want us to have our own foreign policy, and that means having the means to carry it out.'[3] The independent deterrent commanded support in both political parties because it fostered the belief that it would permit Britain, if the need arose, to pursue a foreign policy independent of the United States.

[1] 568 H.C. Deb. col. 71 (1 April 1957).

[2] For a view that the separate national concerns put forth in the argument failed to confirm an Anglo-American version of Karl Deutsch's concept of a 'pluralistic security-community', see Leon Epstein 'Britain and the H-bomb, 1955–1958', *The Review of Politics*, Vol. XXI (August 1959), pp. 511–29. Bruce H. Russet came to a contrary conclusion in his systematic survey of Anglo-American relations since 1890, citing the fact that problems are handled, or are expected to be handled, without resort to violence. See his *Community and Contention: Britain and America in the Twentieth Century* (Cambridge, Massachusetts Institute of Technology Press, 1963).

[3] Quoted in 622 H.C. Deb. col. 276 (27 April 1960).

The principal early non-pacifist critics of the assumptions regarding British nuclear independence that were firmly held by both parties were Richard Crossman and Denis Healey as backbenchers, and Alastair Buchan, writing in the *Observer*. They were the true intellectual architects of the mass of criticism which Sputnik later unleashed (P. M. S. Blackett and Liddell Hart concentrated most of their criticisms on the strategy of massive retaliation). In the 1954 debate on the Air Estimates, Crossman opposed Labour's support, announced by John Strachey, for the Government's newly announced policy of developing a strategic bomber force. Crossman contended that this would continue the pretension of being a Great Power. In the following three years the critics raised germinal questions concerning the economic costs, military rationale, and political purpose of an independent nuclear deterrent. They agreed with the Government's assertions that Britain could not afford to prepare for every conceivable type of war by maintaining both a growing nuclear force and large-scale conventional forces, but argued that the wrong conclusion had been drawn in increasing nuclear striking power and reducing the capacity to respond to local aggression. Furthermore, they were sceptical as to Britain's ability to meet the costs of a nuclear force as the transition from bombers to missiles brought with it the increasing complexity and rapid obsolescence of weapons systems. As far back as 1955, Healey—while going along with his party on the British deterrent because of the 'extra means of security' it provided—called for national specialization in arms production through some type of European arms pool, possibly within the Western European Union.[1]

Most of the critics argued that there was no military need for the British deterrent since it would not add measurably to the nation's security, not only because of the irrationality of a massive retaliation strategy but because it was inconceivable that Britain would use her nuclear weapons except in conjunction with the far more powerful American nuclear force. As Crossman put it: 'By just adding a few bombs marked "B for Britain" to the bombs marked "A for America" we do not alter in any way the balance of power.'[2] Crossman also was the first to tie British nuclear policy to the then hardly visible problem of the spread of nuclear weapons. Starting with the debate on the 1957 White Paper, he argued that Britain's example in developing an independent nuclear force for political reasons would encourage France and Germany to do likewise for the same reason. If Britain was publicly announcing that it could not trust America to come to its defence, would not other nations do the same? He correctly foresaw that the nuclear issue would weaken NATO and urged Britain to give an

[1] 537 H.C. Deb. col. 1935–7 (1 March 1955).
[2] 549 H.C. Deb. col. 1285 (29 February 1956).

example to the still non-nuclear nations by renouncing what he judged to be her comparatively insignificant addition to the American nuclear stockpile.[1]

The most subtle criticism by the critics of the views shared by the leaders of both political parties was of their assumption that nuclear weapons bestowed political influence and independence. British influence, it was argued, would depend more on the nation's ability to forestall trouble and maintain order and confidence in South East Asia and Africa, and to contribute to the conventional defence of Western Europe, than on duplicating SAC in minute scale. There was no evidence that Britain's nuclear capacity enabled her to restrain American intervention or impetuosity. Whatever influence Britain had exercised in limiting the war in Korea was two years before her first atomic explosion. Nor had her nuclear weapons influenced Dulles on Suez. In laying stress upon the independent deterrent the Government was therefore being led by false conceptions of prestige and influence and was misrepresenting the true source of British influence in Washington. Furthermore, it was becoming increasingly evident that defence was no longer possible on a purely national basis. Technologically, Britain was becoming ever more dependent upon American research and development. Strategically, her own nuclear force was not making her independent in defence, for it was improbable that Britain would need to use her force separately unless NATO collapsed, in which case it was unlikely that under the circumstances of fighting a war alone she would initiate the use of nuclear weapons. Pursuing the independent deterrent, it was argued, was chasing a 'will-o'-the-wisp'.[2]

Although the development of the nuclear force had widespread support in Britain, the strategic doctrine with which the Government accompanied it was subject to greater criticism. Successive Defence White Papers from 1955 on assumed that any major aggression would be met with nuclear

[1] 568 H.C. Deb. col. 1975–87 (17 April 1957); 574 H.C. Deb. col. 1376–8 (31 July 1957). Crossman's back-bench speeches often presaged the views of progressive thinkers sometime later, but he was not always consistent. After stating his opposition to a British nuclear force in 1954, in a joint article with George Wigg in 1955 he fully reversed himself. Perhaps at the time he was influenced by Attlee's rallying of Labour party support for the British H-bomb. In 1956 he reverted to his views of two years earlier. Labour critics of Alec Douglas-Home's view of the independent deterrent as a 'ticket to the top table' should have taken note of Crossman and Wigg in 1955: 'A Labour government bent on high level disarmament talks will probably carry more weight in the Kremlin if it possesses the H-bomb.' 'The Dilemma of the H-bomb', New Statesman, 26 February 1955.

[2] See Alastair Buchan, 'The Only Way', Observer, 27 January 1957; 'Prestige', Observer, 14 July 1957; Denis Healey, News Chronicle, 16 April 1957; Manchester Guardian, leader, 15 April 1956.

weapons. Given Britain's total vulnerability, it was not unnatural that there should be concern lest Britain unnecessarily initiate the use of nuclear weapons in response to a localized conventional attack, thereby risking the annihilation of the British Isles. Government spokesmen, caught between the conflicting objectives of calming the British public but not reducing the credibility of the deterrent in Russian eyes, were unwilling to specify the precise circumstances which would activate the nuclear deterrent despite repeated efforts by Labour M.P.s to force the Government to commit itself.[1] Presumably to do so would communicate to the enemy in advance how far he could safely go.

The first-strike strategy magnified Britain's dependence upon the doctrine of massive retaliation—a growing dependency as conventional capabilities were gradually cut back in the 1950s. Yet for Britain, more than the United States prior to the arrival of the inter-continental ballistic missile, a strategy of massive retaliation against the Soviet Union was self-defeating. Because of the high population density of the United Kingdom, a two-way thermonuclear exchange would be tantamount to total destruction. The adopted declaratory strategy, by limiting the intermediate alternatives, either inhibited retaliatory action or led to national suicide. John Strachey in discussing the limitations of a nuclear strategy for Britain likened her position to that of the bee: 'The bee has a sting, but if it uses that sting it dies; it is quite certain, therefore, that the bee will never use the sting except in the ultimate necessity.'[2]

Some doubted that a British government would ever be the first to use nuclear weapons. In an early critique (1954) of Britain's first-strike deterrent strategy, P. M. S. Blackett concluded that at the critical moment it would be found to be a bluff. Blackett observed that when the Soviets acquired thermonuclear bombs, the West lost the decisive military superiority which had made deterrent policy credible in Europe since World War II. The credibility of British policy was now dependent upon the ability to stop almost all enemy bombers from getting through. He did not think that a really effective defence system, even if feasible, would be found practicable because of its unacceptable cost in money and manpower. Blackett thought that wisdom would have British strategy based on the realities of her defensive strength rather than on an assumed offensive power.[3] In his *Atomic Weapons and East-West Relations*, published in 1956, Blackett argued that Britain did not have an acceptable theory of nuclear strategy, given the Government's disinclination to admit to any

---

[1] See, for example, Denis Healey's complaint of the 'appalling ambiguity' of the 1955 White Paper on whether thermonuclear war would be the inevitable consequence of a conventional attack. 537 H.C. Deb. col. 1931–2 (1 March 1955).

[2] 537 H.C. Deb. col. 2069 (2 March 1955).

[3] 'British Policy and the H-bomb', *New Statesman*, 14, 21, 28 August 1954.

restraint on the defensive use of strategic nuclear weapons. Defence white papers since the adoption of the 'New Look' strategy, he suggested, read more as if they were intended for the moral and political exhortation of the public than to be a serious analysis of strategy.[1]

In 1955–6, a number of defence experts and Labour M.P.s attempted to hammer out a strategy which would be non-suicidal and which would provide a way to deal with limited aggression without invoking a full thermonuclear response. Thus came the proposal for 'graduated deterrence', an attempt to make the punishment fit the crime. Starting with the proposition that the massive retaliation strategy ran counter to the basic military doctrine of using the minimum force necessary to achieve a given end, the proposal suggested that a distinction be publicly made between strategic and tactical nuclear weapons. A tacit understanding would then be reached between the West and East as to agreed limitations in types of weapons and targets in a future war, thus minimizing the danger of its spread into a total war.[2]

Like the later strategy of 'flexible response', 'graduated deterrence' sought to make the retaliation proportionate to the issues at stake. But it differed from the American strategy of the 1960s in that some type of nuclear weapon was still assumed to be essential to counter the Communist superiority in land forces. The British government's view that the uncertainty of nuclear response increased the deterrent was thought to be an illusion. 'Graduated deterrence' was also designed to provide a theory for the tactical atomic weapons which had been placed in Europe since 1954. For Britain it made more attractive a less costly and more specialized contribution to the Western deterrent in the form of small nuclear arms.

Whitehall defence planners, however, believed that 'graduated deterrence' raised complex questions of feasibility which made its adoption impractical and unwise. They thought it was impossible to make a useful distinction between the tactical and strategic use of nuclear weapons, and that any attempt to confine nuclear weapons to tactical purposes would inevitably escalate into total nuclear war. Ministers were unconvinced that limiting the risk of massive retaliation would not reduce the credibility

---

[1] (Cambridge, Cambridge University Press, 1956), pp. 22–6.

[2] The most authoritative expositions of graduated deterrence are: *On Limiting Atomic War*, Study Group of the Royal Institute of International Affairs, London, 1956; Rear Admiral Sir Anthony W. Buzzard, 'The H Bomb: Massive Retaliation or Graduated Deterrence?' *International Affairs*, Vol. XXXII, No. 2 (April 1956), pp. 148–58; Buzzard, 'Massive Retaliation or Graduated Deterrence', *World Politics*, Vol. VIII (January 1956), pp. 228–37. A senior defence scientist in the Ministry of Supply suggested that a 'tacit bomb line' be drawn to demarcate the area outside of which aggression would not be met by a full thermonuclear riposte. This differed from other proposals for graduated deterrence in that it introduced a geographical distinction, rather than one based on types of weapons or targets. See R. Cockburn, 'Science and War', *Journal of the Royal United Service Institution*, Vol. CI, No. 601 (February 1956), pp. 23–35.

of the deterrent, thereby making aggression more likely. Labour party spokesmen were critical of the Government's lack of precision on the use of tactical nuclear weapons but they themselves were unsure that, as John Strachey put it, Queensberry rules for atomic war could be devised.[1] As in the United States, the consensus of private and official opinion by 1959 ran counter to a doctrine of 'graduated deterrence' using tactical nuclear weapons.[2]

When the 1957 White Paper was published, the initial response in Britain was favourable. The deterrent strategy it postulated aroused relatively little interest or opposition. Most attention was drawn to the promised end of national service, the economies in defence expenditure, and the streamlining of the military services. The statement's frank recognition that it was no longer possible to maintain the forces necessary to meet all possible contingencies was praised as realistic. On 5 April 1957 the press comment ran as follows: *Times*—'courageous' and 'clear thinking'; *Manchester Guardian*—'realistic' and 'sensible'; *Daily Telegraph*—'clear' and 'ruthless'. Even the *Observer* two days later found the new defence plan 'bold' and 'workmanlike'.

Hardly noticed at the time was the return to massive retaliation, the sparsity of planned conventional forces for limited war action, the unilateral nature of Britain's decisions within the NATO alliance and the mounting evidence of rapid Soviet missile progress.

It was often conveniently forgotten later that many of the decisions announced in the 1957 statement accepted Labour's proposals and criticisms of the previous three years. Labour spokesmen had been calling for a more coherent policy of priorities; a reappraisal of the role, size, and shape of the military services; the abandonment of unnecessary commitments and bases; more centralized planning and control in the Ministry of Defence; and a more rapid and efficient military aircraft production programme. While taking pains not to appear 'irresponsible', Labour leaders had been suggesting that national service should not continue. Since defence strategy was to be based on the nuclear deterrent, the nation could not afford nor did it need all the traditional forces and armaments of a Great Power, but rather smaller and more efficient forces. Although, as George Brown said, Labour thought the 1957 Defence White Paper was 'being sold a wee bit highly'[3] many of the policies Labour had advocated were indeed similar to those adopted by Duncan Sandys.[4]

[1] 568 H.C. Deb. col. 2025 (17 April 1957).

[2] B. H. Liddell Hart provided a consistent criticism of the use of tactical atomic weapons in NATO. See his letter to *The Times*, 3 January 1955 and *Deterrent or Defence, passim*.

[3] 568 H.C. Deb. col. 1777 (16 April 1957).

[4] In their widely noted joint article of 1955, Richard Crossman and George Wigg criticized the Government, not for making the H-bomb, but for merely adding it to traditional service roles without a drastic revision of defence policy and force structure: 'The one fatal thing is to

Public opinion favoured the development of nuclear weapons and the strategic force by the Labour and Conservative governments, according to polls taken by the British Institute of Public Opinion. When the manufacture by Britain of its own atomic bomb became known in 1952, 60 per cent 'approved' ('disapprove'—22 per cent, 'don't know'—18 per cent). In November 1945, 59 per cent thought the United States should share atomic information with others ('should not'—25 per cent, 'don't know'—16 per cent). By December 1953, 65 per cent thought there should be a complete exchange of atomic information between America and Britain ('should not'—16 per cent, 'don't know'—19 per cent). Support for the making of the fusion bomb was less than for the fission bomb, but still substantial: 54 per cent thought in March 1955 that Britain should make the hydrogen bomb ('should not'—32 per cent, 'don't know'—14 per cent).

The British public accepted the view that nuclear weapons increased the chances for peace, at least when they were in Western hands. In August 1945, 52 per cent thought the atomic bomb made war less likely ('more likely'—12 per cent, 'no difference'—21 per cent, 'don't know'—15 per cent). Ten years later 53 per cent thought the H-bomb made another war less likely ('more likely'—22 per cent, 'don't know'—25 per cent). But as for the Russian atomic bomb, a plurality in 1949 of 35 per cent thought it made war *more* likely ('less likely'—22 per cent, 'same'—25 per cent, 'don't know'—18 per cent). The Sandys-Macmillan defence strategy was strongly approved in December 1957. To the question, 'Which do you think is more important for Britain to concentrate on: building up strength in atomic weapons and missiles, or building up strength in conventional weapons like troops, tanks and bombers?', 52 per cent answered atomic weapons and missiles; 8 per cent conventional weapons; 22 per cent neither—should disarm; 18 per cent don't know.[1] Although it is true that public opinion in Britain generally follows the official policy on foreign and defence matters, successive Governments up to 1957 were obviously assured of public support for their nuclear programme and strategy.

It was from abroad that the first large swell of critical comment came. In Western Europe the decisions to end conscription, cut the size of the British Army of the Rhine, reduce the contribution to NATO naval

believe, as Mr. Macmillan seems to, that Britain can have nuclear weapons, a strategic air force, rockets, guided missiles, day and night fighters, a traditional army equipped with modern weapons and the third largest navy in the world, as well as civil defence. That way lies certain failure. . . . By attempting to maintain the army, navy and air force of a Great Power, we have overstrained our resources and achieved, not strength, but a military weakness far worse than that which Sir Winston exposed in the 1930's when he was campaigning against Neville Chamberlain.' 'The Dilemma of the H-bomb', *New Statesman*, 26 February 1955.

[1] I am greatly indebted to the British Institute of Public Opinion, and especially to its director, Dr. Henry Durant, for permission to cull this data from its files.

forces, and reduce the size of the tactical air force in Germany, were interpreted as a weakening of Britain's commitment to the alliance. This, it must be remembered, came at a time when conscription was being instituted for the Bundeswehr and when France had 1,500,000 soldiers in Algeria. In Washington, the 1957 Defence White Paper was seen sadly as a resignation by Britain from her world role, thereby further overloading the American basket of global tasks.

The increased reliance on a strategy of independent nuclear deterrence created a sense of uneasiness among the allies, not only because of the policy itself, but because of Britain's unilateral assertion of strategy and the by-passing of the alliance, in spirit as well as in fact. The White Paper had been written with hardly any consultation with the Foreign Office, whose representatives later had to defend its unpopular implications in European capitals. The revival of massive retaliation was harmful to General Norstad's attempts to bring greater flexibility to NATO strategy. It had a divisive effect among NATO members. Britain's turn to America for assistance in developing long-range missiles and her emphasis on the political necessity of nuclear independence did not pass unnoticed, as we shall see in later chapters, in either Bonn or Paris.

6 | Developing the Nuclear Capability

1. The Breakdown of Anglo-American Collaboration

Over the years it has become commonplace to lay the blame for the termination of nuclear co-operation between Britain and America at the feet of the Congress in myopically legislating certain restrictive provisions in the Atomic Energy Act of 1946. In actuality, the passage of the McMahon Act in August 1946 gave legal form to a policy which as we have seen had first been considered in 1942 and which became the officially accepted doctrine shortly after the close of the war. In 1945 the British had the scientific and theoretical knowledge necessary for producing fissile materials; but they did not have complete information on the engineering design of an atomic bomb or on the construction and operation of atomic energy plant facilities. Because of this, and in order to avoid the cost of unnecessary duplication, the British quite naturally desired to obtain as much information and assistance as possible from the United States for their own atomic energy programme. On the basis of the wartime collaboration, and in particular the Quebec Agreement and the Hyde Park Aide-Mémoire, they had no doubt as to the legitimacy of their claim for the continued exchange of information. Throughout the development of the British atomic and thermonuclear bombs, the collapse of collaboration and the continuing desire to restore the nuclear relationship with America played an important role.

Almost immediately after the end of the war the British representatives on the Combined Policy Committee, that had been set up by the Quebec Agreement to co-ordinate nuclear policy between the two countries, were given the impression that the exchange of information would be limited pending the conclusion of some new arrangements. An ominous note was struck by President Truman when he told an informal press gathering at Reelfoot Lake, Tennessee, that the United States 'would not give away its engineering know-how which produced the atomic bomb to any nation ... only the United States had the combination of industrial capacity and resources necessary to produce the bomb ... although Britain and Canada had the blueprint of the atomic bomb secret, they would be unable to apply the knowledge for lack of plant facilities.'[1] By October 1945 Lord Alanbrooke, Chief of the Imperial General Staff, and a member of the Advisory Committee on Atomic Energy, noted that there was anxiety in London about Britain being 'frozen out of the atomic bomb by our American friends'.[2]

[1] *The New York Times,* 9 October 1945.   [2] Bryant, op. cit., p. 488.

Attlee thus proposed a meeting with President Truman to discuss the novel issues which atomic energy was raising in post-war international relations. His letter to the President was couched mainly in terms of the need to devise an effective system of international control of the new scientific discovery, but equally on the minds of some in his administration was the need to confirm and extend the bilateral ties between the two countries in the atomic field.[1] To the British the two objectives did not appear incompatible. The steps on the road to international control ought not, they thought, to block the continued exchange of scientific and technical data between the two countries.

When Attlee, Truman, and Mackenzie King of Canada met in Washington between 10–16 November 1945 they came to an agreement on a proposed commission under United Nations' auspices, the purposes of which would be to control atomic energy by ensuring its development for peaceful uses only, to eliminate atomic weapons, and to provide effective safeguards through an inspection system. Meanwhile, upon the instigation of the British and without publicity, the officials most directly concerned with atomic matters were also charged with the task of working out a basis for future co-operation. Sir John Anderson told the Americans that the British hoped to build pilot plants soon and needed to know where they stood. Both sides agreed that it would be desirable to terminate the Quebec Agreement of 1943 and replace it with a fresh arrangement more suitable to the post-war situation.[2] Under the pressure of time, however, they were forced to settle for a brief directive which was signed on 16 November by the President and the two Prime Ministers providing for continued co-operation in the post-war era. In it they agreed that:

1. We desire that there should be full and effective cooperation in the field of atomic energy between the United States, the United Kingdom and Canada.
2. We agree that the Combined Policy Committee and the Combined Development Trust should be continued in a suitable form.
3. We request the Combined Policy Committee to consider and recommend to us appropriate arrangements for this purpose.[3]

To accompany this statement a more detailed 'Memorandum of Intention' was drawn up by Anderson and General Groves to serve as a guideline for the Combined Policy Committee (C.P.C.) in its drafting of a document to replace the Quebec Agreement. The paragraph of the Groves-Anderson memorandum relating to the exchange of information was essentially the same in content as the related provisions of the Quebec

[1] Williams, op. cit., pp. 97–104.
[2] Hewlett and Anderson, Jr., op. cit., p. 466.
[3] Harry S. Truman, *Memoirs*, Vol. I, *Year of Decision* (New York, Doubleday, 1955), p. 544.

Agreement. It provided for full and effective co-operation in the field of basic scientific research, but once again as in the earlier agreement it imposed a qualification on the development, design, construction, and operation of plants. Such co-operation, while recognized as desirable in principle, was to be regulated by such *ad hoc* arrangements as might be considered by the C.P.C. to be mutually advantageous.[1]

On leaving Washington Attlee and Anderson were satisfied with the results of their mission.[2] Within six months Anglo-American nuclear co-operation was to collapse and the British were to feel that they had been deceived. On 4 December the C.P.C. met according to the Truman-Attlee-King directive and appointed a sub-committee consisting of General Groves (U.S.A.), Roger Makins (U.K.), and Lester Pearson (Canada) to draft a successor to the Quebec Agreement, using as a guide the Memorandum of Intention. They recommended altering the second clause of the 1943 agreement regarding not using the atomic bomb without each other's *consent* to requiring prior *consultation*. The United States was to waive the fourth clause's restriction on Britain's development of atomic energy for industrial or commercial purposes. Excluded from the Quebec Agreement, Canada was to be a signatory. The three Governments were to continue their co-operation in raw materials allocation, especially in uranium and thorium, through the Combined Development Trust. With respect to exchange of information, they recommended a sweeping provision for full and effective exchange to meet the requirements of their respective national programmes.[3]

Although Groves consented to presenting these recommendations to the full C.P.C., he had strong reservations with respect to the provision for exchange of information. He advised Secretary of State Byrnes, the ranking American on the C.P.C., that it was tantamount to a military alliance based on the single most important weapon in existence. Groves correctly expected the British to ask for information which would help them build a large-scale plant for producing fissionable materials and evidently he was personally opposed to such assistance. Furthermore, Groves argued that under Article 102 of the United Nations Charter a new agreement would need to be registered with the Secretariat and published. Such an agreement on nuclear co-operation would reflect badly on the sincerity of the forthcoming American proposal for international control. Thus when Byrnes, agreeing with Groves, brought up the requirements of Article 102 at the next meeting of C.P.C. on 15 February 1946, the first major impasse was reached.

[1] Groves, op. cit., p. 404; Hewlett and Anderson, Jr., op. cit., p. 468.
[2] Wheeler-Bennett, op. cit., pp. 332–6.
[3] Hewlett and Anderson, op. cit., pp. 477–80; Groves, op. cit., pp. 403–6.

As the legislation which was to lead to the McMahon Act gained ground in the early spring of 1946, the British became increasingly apprehensive. Attlee told the American Ambassador in London, Averell Harriman, that if congressional action restricted further co-operation Britain would independently build her own plants for the production of fissile materials for peaceful and military purposes. He also instructed the British Ambassador in Washington, Lord Halifax, to request detailed information on the construction and operation of atomic energy plants in the United States at the next meeting of the C.P.C.[1]

The British request met with a blank refusal when the C.P.C. met again on 15 April. Of still greater significance was the inability of the conferees to agree on a basis for future co-operation. The Americans, Byrnes, Vannevar Bush, and Secretary of War Robert Patterson, refused to endorse the C.P.C. sub-committee's recommendations on a new agreement. They also rejected a suggestion made by Lord Halifax that co-operation simply be continued under the Quebec Agreement, making such amendments as became necessary by administrative action. The Americans cited the opinion of their legal advisers that neither option overcame the difficulties of Article 102 of the United Nations Charter. The British protested that this left the Truman-Attlee-King directive of 16 November pledging 'full and effective co-operation' a dead letter. Byrnes could only reply that nothing should be done which could in any way compromise the success of discussions on atomic energy within the United Nations.

The following day Attlee sent a strongly worded personal message to Truman. He was 'gravely disturbed' by the turn of events in the C.P.C. and its inability to implement the 16 November tripartite directive calling for 'full and effective co-operation'. This directive, he wrote, 'cannot mean less than the full interchange of information and a fair division of the material'.[2] Attlee urged that if the C.P.C. continued to fail to agree on a satisfactory basis for co-operation, Truman, King, and he, himself, should issue instructions within their respective bureaucracies to assure the interchange of information. He probably had in mind Churchill's successful advocacy with Roosevelt at the time of the Quebec Agreement and the tactics thereupon used by the President to overcome the objections of his professional advisers.

Truman's reply on 20 April indicated that he was placing a wholly different interpretation on 'full and effective co-operation'. Secretary Byrnes had advised him that this phrase was very general; it was not intended to oblige the United States to furnish the engineering and operational assistance necessary for the construction of an atomic energy

---

[1] Williams, op. cit., p. 110.   [2] Ibid.

plant. That such an obligation was not intended at the time was indicated by the Groves-Anderson Memorandum of Intention, in which the words 'full and effective co-operation' applied only to the field of basic scientific information, whereas information on plant design and operations was to be regulated by special *ad hoc* arrangements. Truman thought it would be 'exceedingly unwise' for the United States to enter into an agreement with Britain at this time to assist in building an atomic energy plant. At the Washington conference, Britain, Canada, and the United States—on the day prior to the signing of the directive for continued co-operation among the three—had issued jointly a declaration of their intention to request the United Nations to establish a commission to control the production of atomic energy so as to prevent its use for military purposes. 'I would not want to have it said', the President wrote to Attlee, 'that on the morning following the issuance of our declaration to bring about international control, we entered into a new agreement the purpose of which was to have the United States furnish the information as to the construction and operation of plants which would enable the United Kingdom to construct another atomic energy plant.'[1]

Attlee delayed his reply until 6 June in order to discuss it with Halifax and Mackenzie King. He then sent a lengthy telegram tracing the entire history of Anglo-American co-operation in atomic energy. Attlee noted that in 1940 British scientists had recognized the enormous military possibilities of atomic energy. The United Kingdom had the resources and the scientific and technical skill necessary to embark on an atomic energy project in Britain, but to do so would have meant the diversion of resources and the reduction of essential wartime efforts in other fields. Fortunately, this had become unnecessary as the two countries pooled their resources and divided their wartime efforts through a system of reciprocal aid. In the latter days of the war the Government had more than once considered undertaking more active development of atomic energy in Britain in order not to fall further behind in a field in which the nation had once been in the forefront, but on each occasion had decided that as long as British scientists could make a contribution to the Manhattan Project they should not be withdrawn.[2] This was in keeping with the Quebec Agreement's first priority of achieving the earliest possible realization of the project, before consideration of any separate national advantages. Britain felt

[1] Harry S. Truman, *Memoirs*, Vol. II, *Years of Trial and Hope* (New York, Doubleday, 1956), pp. 13–14.

[2] In Chapter 3 it is suggested that more important factors in Whitehall's decision not to begin a separate British project before the end of the war included the fact that British scientists were acquiring data of considerable value in the United States at the time and wished to continue doing so, and the general political desire to retain as close a relationship with the Americans as possible.

that it could rely on the provisions of the Quebec Agreement to ensure that her interests would not suffer and expected at the end of the war to be given full access at the highest level to the knowledge which had been developed up to that point in all sections of the joint project. Turning to the current deadlock, Attlee noted the unwillingness of the American members of the C.P.C. to enter into any new agreement as called for in the 16 November head-of-state directive. 'I cannot agree with the argument', Attlee wrote, 'that to continue such co-operation would be inconsistent with the public declaration on the control of atomic energy which you and Mackenzie King and I issued in November. That our three governments stand in a special relationship to one another in this field is a matter of record and was, in fact, the reason why we took the initiative in issuing the declaration. It is surely not inconsistent with its purpose that the co-operation begun during the war should continue during the peace unless and until it can be replaced by a wider system.'[1]

This forceful message was never answered. Truman felt that pending the outcome of legislation regulating atomic energy then in the Congress, it was not possible to make any new statement on policy, especially since it was already clear that the new law would seriously hamper and restrict future co-operation with Britain.[2] The passage of the McMahon Act in July 1946 seemed to settle the issue. Exchange of information between the nuclear scientists of the two countries had been withering away in past months, although Dr. William Penney had witnessed the American tests at Bikini. After the President's signature of the McMahon Act on 1 August practically all co-operation came to a halt except in the allocation and control of raw materials.

The congressional draftsmen of the McMahon Act had been totally unaware, it seems, of the existence of the Quebec Agreement and the Hyde Park Aide-Mémoire. The public and legislative debate on the bill had been focused on the issue of civilian versus military control of the atomic energy programme. President Roosevelt had not informed any members of Congress at the time he had made the two accords with the British, and the Truman administration continued the policy of severely restricting knowledge of their existence. Members of the executive branch of the Government discussed various aspects of national and international control of atomic energy with the Congress without mentioning the agreements with the British. According to Dean Acheson, then a member of the administration, the 'somewhat incredible truth' was that very few knew about it, in part because there had been so many changes in the higher echelons of the Government.[3] The members of the Senate Foreign

---

[1] Williams, op. cit., p. 116.　　[2] Truman, *Memoirs*, Vol. II, p. 15.
[3] Dean Acheson, *Present at the Creation* (New York, W. W. Norton, 1969), p. 167.

Relations Committee and the Joint Committee on Atomic Energy (J.C.A.E.) first heard of the wartime agreements in 1947.[1] Even Secretary of Defense Forrestal professed to have been in the dark until he heard of the Quebec Agreement from Senator Hickenlooper in July 1947.[2] At the time of the announcement of preparations for the first British atomic test in 1952, Senator McMahon as chairman of the J.C.A.E. commented:

This event is likely to raise in still sharper focus the problem of atomic co-operation between ourselves and Great Britain. The British contributed heavily to our own wartime atomic project. *But due to a series of unfortunate circumstances the nature of the agreements which made this contribution possible was not disclosed to me and my colleagues on the Senate Special Atomic Energy Committee at the time we framed the law in 1946.*[3] (Italics mine.)

To blame the end of nuclear co-operation on the simple failure of the Truman administration to inform Congress of the existence of the two bilateral agreements is to misinterpret the political atmosphere of the time. In later years this was the tendency, particularly in Britain. According to Churchill, McMahon had told him in 1952 that if he had known of the Quebec and Hyde Park Agreements 'there would have been no McMahon Act',[4] by which he must have meant to say that it would have been enacted in a somewhat different form. This tendency was supported by the inclination of American officials in the first post-war decade to cite the restrictive section 10(a) of the atomic energy legislation as the basis of their inability to renew co-operation. In 1945–6, however, the McMahon Act probably accurately reflected the predominant sentiment in the executive branch as well as in the Congress.

The American attitude was a curious mixture of monopolism, insecurity, and idealism. Through a tremendous expenditure of money and effort American ingenuity had discovered 'the secret'—few had given much thought to the British participation. The omnipotence of America's immediate post-war situation produced a smokescreen through which the legitimate and inevitable desire for security on the part of less powerful nations remained unseen. Since it was begrudgingly recognized that the theory of atomic energy was available to the world, and that others could

[1] According to two members of the Atomic Energy Commission: David E. Lilienthal, *The Journals of David E. Lilienthal*, Vol. II, *The Atomic Energy Years, 1945–1950* (New York, Harper and Row, 1964), pp. 175–6; Strauss, op, cit., p. 370. Lilienthal noted on 20 January 1946 that the special committee of the Senate on atomic energy was refused information on dealings with other nations involving uranium materials and that this information was unknown also to the State Department (p. 12).

[2] Millis (ed.), op. cit., p. 338.

[3] *The Times*, 18 February 1952.

[4] 526 H.C. Deb. col. 52 (5 April 1954).

in time develop the technical knowledge necessary to build weapons of mass destruction, it seemed desirable to prevent or delay the achievement of a nuclear capability by others as long as possible. This attitude was strongly represented in the Congress, whose leaders regularly admonished the President not to give away American 'know-how'. As Senator Vandenberg wrote on 13 November 1945:

If it were possible to keep this secret in our own possession indefinitely, this would be my first and emphatic choice because we know that America will not use this devastating weapon for aggressive purposes.[1]

Those who possess a monopoly rarely see a disadvantage in it.

The reason the Congress was not informed of the two wartime agreements by the President was probably related to this monopolistic instinct. The provision of the Quebec Agreement whereby the two countries agreed not to use the atomic bomb without each other's consent could be interpreted as an incursion into the national sovereignty. That this veto might prove politically embarrassing to the Democratic administration was borne out by the vehemence with which Republican leaders insisted it be negotiated away as soon as they were apprised of it in 1947. The 'special relationship' with the British had already been a source of political tension for the administration. Senators Connally and Vandenberg had strongly resented the failure of the President to consult with them at the time of the Truman-Attlee-King conference.[2]

From the earliest days of the Manhattan Project the American military authorities and some of the scientists had never extended to the British the same trust as that they did to their fellow-countrymen. Prior to the Quebec Agreement it had been argued by some that the British were primarily interested in participating in the bomb's development in order to reap the industrial and commercial advantages of atomic energy after the war at the American taxpayer's expense. In 1944 there was concern regarding information passed on to Joliot-Curie after the liberation of France by French scientists associated with the British research team in Canada. Groves believed that the British had violated the Quebec Agreement's clause forbidding the dissemination of information to third parties except by mutual consent, had not been forthright in telling the Americans the details of their liaison with the French, and had permitted top secret American information to pass on to the French.[3] In May 1945 General de Gaulle asked Joliot-Curie, then an acknowledged Communist sympathizer, to direct the newly established Commissariat à l'Énergie

[1] Arthur H. Vandenberg, Jr. (ed.), *The Private Papers of Senator Vandenberg* (Boston, Houghton Mifflin, 1952), p. 124.
[2] Ibid., pp. 226–7.
[3] Groves, op. cit., pp. 224–9.

Atomique. Distrust of the effectiveness of British security precautions was further increased by the revelation in February 1946 of the Gouzenko spy ring. Alan Nunn May, a British nuclear physicist assigned to the Montreal project, had admitted giving to Soviet agents some information known to him about American atomic energy research. The mounting evidence of Soviet espionage confirmed for many the inherent risk to the national security of the exchange of classified atomic data.

The rationale most often articulated for not assisting Britain to be an equal atomic partner was that first priority must be given to the establishment of a system of international control of atomic energy. To start the Soviets down the path of nuclear co-operation was becoming a major objective of American diplomacy. Sharing information with any nation, even Britain, was likely to make achievement of international control that much more difficult. The Baruch plan was the first effort to halt the proliferation of nuclear weapons. Vannevar Bush and others who had worked with the British during the war were advising the President that the wartime tie with the United Kingdom should not be allowed to jeopardize the search for a broader international arrangement.

From the viewpoint of America's national interest, there was no visible incentive for maintaining the special relationship on nuclear matters with Britain or in any way encouraging her separate development of atomic energy. Little scientific knowledge that could not be developed in the United States would be derived from it. In the world of 1946, allies were seen by some, especially in the Congress, as more of a nuisance than a help, and certainly no one was thinking in those days of cementing alliances with science and technology. Britain counted for much less in Washington than her former colony did in London. Furthermore, inexplicably to many Americans, there was a new 'socialist' régime in Britain. That Attlee's government should merit the same trust as Winston Churchill's had yet to be proven.

To the British, their wilful exclusion from the benefits of the common wartime endeavour seemed manifestly unfair. It was a violation of the spirit if not the letter of the Quebec Agreement and the Hyde Park Aide-Mémoire. However informal the latter may have been, it did stipulate that full collaboration 'should continue after the defeat of Japan unless and until terminated by joint agreement'. The British had never hidden their intention to produce their own atomic energy facilities. Assistance from the United States, to which they felt they had a valid claim, could save time and money. The great sense of betrayal which grew after the breakdown of nuclear co-operation fostered a distrust of the United States which strongly influenced British politicians and civil servants during the quest for an independent deterrent.

2. Priorities of the Atomic Energy Programme, Military and Civil

Significantly the decision to make a British atomic bomb, which as we have seen in Chapter 4 was made by the Defence Sub-committee of the cabinet in January 1947, was made within months after the legislation of the McMahon Act and the total collapse of Anglo-American nuclear co-operation. By that time it had also become apparent that the international control of atomic energy under the United Nations was not going to be achieved in the foreseeable future. The decision was not made, it should be noted, until one and a half years after the end of the Second World War.

No time had been lost, however, in establishing a comprehensive atomic energy programme. On 21 August 1945—two weeks after the surrender of Japan—Attlee announced the formation of an Advisory Committee on Atomic Energy, with Sir John Anderson as chairman, to deal with the 'many far reaching questions' raised by the discovery of atomic energy with respect to both international control and its development in Britain 'whether for industrial or military purposes'.[1] It became the successor to the wartime Tube Alloys Consultative Council and continuity was provided by a number of scientists and administrators in addition to Anderson who were members of both committees.[2] Only two months later, on 29 October, Attlee told the Commons that a research and experimental establishment was to be set up at Harwell to engage in research on all aspects of atomic energy. The financially pressed Labour government was willing to devote considerable resources to the programme. The Prime Minister said in November that the initial cost of Harwell was estimated at £1,000 million and that annual operating costs would be about £500 million, adding prophetically that there are 'other important developments on which substantial expenditure is likely to arise in the future'.[3] Professor John Cockcroft, who was in charge of the Montreal and Chalk River Laboratories, was chosen as the first director of Harwell. In Canada, British scientists had gained valuable experience in running an atomic energy establishment and many of them eventually joined Cockcroft in the post-war project.[4]

[1] 413 H.C. Deb. col. 442–3 (21 August 1945).
[2] The membership of the Advisory Committee included, among others, Sir James Chadwick, Sir George Thomson, Professor P. M. S. Blackett, Sir Henry Dale, Lord Alanbrooke, Sir Edward Appleton, and Sir John Anderson. Others who attended some meetings included Sir Roger Makins, Lord Tedder, Sir Oliver Franks, and Sir Henry Tizard.
[3] 416 H.C. Deb. col. 1529 (29 November 1945).
[4] See United Kingdom, Ministry of Supply and the Central Office of Information, *Harwell: The British Atomic Energy Research Establishment 1946–1951* (London, H.M.S.O., 1952).

From the start there was no intention to limit the programme to pure research. A full-scale atomic energy project necessitated plants to produce fissile materials. Attlee announced on 29 January 1946 the formation of a production organization at Risley to manufacture fissile materials as speedily as possible in sufficient quantity 'as circumstances may require'.[1] This part of the atomic energy programme was placed under the Ministry of Supply, the munitions provider of the services. Lord Portal of Hungerford, a former Chief of the Air Staff who during World War II had for a time headed the Bomber Command, was appointed Controller of Atomic Energy in the Ministry of Supply.

At this time the British had little knowledge of the details of construction and operation of large production facilities. As a result of their own research and their wartime collaboration in the United States they had much information on the methods and processes of uranium separation, but far less on the technology of pile design and the engineering of bomb construction.[2] Thus Sir Christopher Hinton, the man chosen to design, construct, and operate the factories of Lord Portal's organization, was faced with a formidable task. There were hardly any engineers in Britain with any knowledge of atomic energy. Hinton, an engineer himself, had been in charge of the building and operation of Royal Ordnance factories during the war. Of the initial group at Risley, only one person who had been at Chalk River knew anything about the engineering aspects of atomic energy. Between 1946 and 1952 the production organization built a series of 'atomic factories' for the manufacture and processing of nuclear fuels, probably the largest engineering effort undertaken in Britain during the first post-war decade.[3]

The specific task given to the Risley organization was the production of plutonium for military purposes. The Advisory Committee decided that fissile materials could be obtained more cheaply and easily through producing plutonium by way of a reactor and chemical separation plant than by the alternative route of separating U-235 from U-238 in a diffusion plant. In the Manhattan Project plutonium had been produced in a water-cooled, graphite-moderated pile at Hanford. But the British knew very little about the American large-scale production piles because Hanford was the one centre their scientists had not worked in or visited. As the exchange of nuclear information had dried up by the time the plutonium method was chosen, British scientists in the production organization began from scratch with little more knowledge about the manufacture of

[1] 418 H.C. Deb. col. 683 (29 January 1946).

[2] Blackett, *Atomic Weapons and East-West Relations*, p. 41.

[3] K. E. B. Jay, Division of Atomic Energy, Ministry of Supply, *Britain's Atomic Factories* London, H.M.S.O., 1954), pp. 5–7.

plutonium than that obtainable in the Smyth Report.[1] Some delay was encountered when it was ascertained that because of safety precautions there was no site suitable in the United Kingdom for a water-cooled reactor, and it became necessary to design a gas-cooled reactor. The first plutonium-producing pile went critical at Windscale in July 1950, three and a half years after the site was chosen.

The military use of atomic energy and in particular the development of the British atomic bomb had clear priority in the first eight years of the atomic project. All of those involved in the project believed that the civil use of nuclear energy would be of special importance to Britain given its limited fuel resources, but this was for the medium-range future after the first need of atomic weapons had been met. Up to 1954 military requirements accounted for 90 per cent of the atomic programme's activities and were the only concrete objective.

After the Defence Sub-committee of the cabinet decided in early 1947 to make an atomic bomb, the Advisory Committee on Atomic Energy drew up a programme whereby the first plutonium should be produced by the Windscale pile in the first quarter of 1952.[2] Attlee placed the atomic bomb on his list of top priorities and throughout his term in office maintained a personal interest in the project, retaining a supervisory role for himself.[3] The 1952 date at which time a quantity of plutonium was to be available for the testing of a bomb became an immutable deadline around which the whole atomic energy programme revolved.[4] To some of the engineers and technologists it appeared to be an arbitrarily fixed date set by political considerations. The fact is that when it was set in 1947 it had not been determined by what date a Soviet bomb might be expected or any similar consideration,[5] though in hindsight it is surprising that such politico-military factors were not taken into account. It was based essentially on the Advisory Committee's and Hinton's technological estimate as to the time it would take to construct the plants. The deadline was met with remarkable accuracy: when Churchill told Parliament in February 1952 of plans to test an atomic weapon at Monte Bello in October, the plutonium was still not ready; but it was ready in time for the test to be run as scheduled in the fall.

[1] Sir Leonard Owen, 'Nuclear Engineering in the United Kingdom—The First Ten Years', *Journal of the British Nuclear Energy Society*, Vol. II, No. 1 (January 1963).

[2] Sir Christopher Hinton, 'The Chairman's Inauguration of the Conference', *The Journal of the British Nuclear Energy Conference*, Vol. I, No. 1 (January 1956); Wheeler-Bennett, op. cit., p. 339; British Information Service, *Nuclear Energy in Britain* (London, H.M.S.O., 1962), pp. 8–9.

[3] The Principal Parliamentary Secretary to the Minister of Supply, Mr. Arthur Woodburn, told the Commons on 24 July 1947 that atomic energy had one of the six priorities given by the Government in the allocation of materials, metals, and labour noting that 'It could not have a higher priority.' 440 H.C. Deb. col. 1718 (24 July 1947).

[4] Bertin, op. cit., pp. 115, 124–5.   [5] Interviews.

The first British bomb was developed steadily and rapidly but without the same sense of urgency that characterized the Manhattan Project.[1] The unexpected detection of a Soviet explosion in 1949 did not result in an acceleration of the programme. The operations at Harwell, Risley, and Aldermaston, where an Atomic Weapons Research Establishment was organized in 1949, were never hampered for lack of funds. The costs were manageable though it was recognized that they could be reduced if a way could be found to obtain information from the Americans. The chief limitation in fact was the shortage of scientists and design engineers.[2] The atomic energy project, unlike the post-war American nuclear organization, carried out most of its own research, construction, and operation of plants rather than relying upon contractors. Consequently, the project had to compete for scarce manpower and materials with British industry, which after six years of war was anxious to return to peacetime work and the promotion of exports. In the post-war atmosphere it was difficult to persuade industrial firms to release valuable engineers and scientists, and to divert manufacturing resources for the unique needs of Risley and Harwell.

Although the number and types of nuclear warheads has never been published, a well-informed observer once estimated that there were between 1,000 and 1,500 nuclear weapons in the British stockpile in 1964.[3] Eight nuclear reactors were constructed at Chapelcross and Calder Hall in the mid-1950s, which are estimated to have been capable of producing enough plutonium for 200 bombs a year. A gaseous diffusion plant, which it can be assumed has produced U-235 of weapons grade for hydrogen warheads, went into production in 1957 at Capenhurst. In the 1964 Defence White Paper the Government announced that the production of plutonium for military purposes was gradually being brought to an end and that the output of enriched uranium at Capenhurst was being reduced to the minimum level necessary to keep the plant in production. This was possible because 'we have now reached a point where supplies of fissile material already available or assured will be sufficient to maintain our independent nuclear deterrent and to meet all defence requirements for the foreseeable future.'[4] It is also known that in recent years enriched

---

[1] See Sir Christopher Hinton, 'British Developments in Atomic Energy', *Nucleonics*, Vol. XII (12 January 1954), pp. 6–8.

[2] Britain has perhaps had a higher per capita quota of eminent scientists than any other nation; nevertheless, Sir Henry Tizard, then chairman of the Defence Research Policy Committee and the Advisory Council on Scientific Policy, was concerned about the level of scientific manpower, which he considered more important than any other single factor in a future world war: 'It is no good breeding Winston Churchills unless we also breed Rutherfords.' Quoted in Clark, *Tizard*, p. 380.

[3] Leonard Beaton, *Would Labour Give Up the Bomb? Sunday Telegraph* pamphlet, 1964, p. 5.

[4] *Statement on Defence: 1964*, Cmnd. 2270, p. 10.

uranium from the United States has been exchanged for British plutonium which is not used for weapons purposes. Britain in the early 1970s has a more complete and balanced nuclear stockpile than any nation other than the United States and the Soviet Union and has the capacity to keep this lead for some years.

The 'peaceful uses' of atomic energy did not receive major attention until after the first atomic bomb was tested. In part this was due to the fact that in the first two stages of the production of plutonium, facilities are created which can be used for both military and civil needs. The Government, however, clearly put the development of the industrial use of atomic energy at a lower level of priority. The first civil reactor programme was not approved until June 1952. The Monte Bello test served as a watershed after which considerably more attention was given to the civil benefits of the atom. In April 1953 Churchill appointed a Committee headed by Lord Waverly, the former Sir John Anderson, to devise a plan for transferring responsibility for atomic energy from the Ministry of Supply, which was part of the defence establishment, to a new organization. The Waverly Committee's recommendations[1] led to the establishment in 1954 of the United Kingdom Atomic Energy Authority.[2] In the parliamentary debates on the enabling statute, government spokesmen indicated that programmes for the industrial application of atomic energy would now be expanded. The new 'non-departmental' Atomic Energy Authority was devised as a way to provide a better mechanism for assessing the best allocation of resources between military and civil uses and in order to ensure that full advantage was taken of the prospects for the latter.[3]

The potential economic benefits of nuclear energy had been recognized since before World War II. They were expected to be of special significance for Britain because of her limited resources for fuel and power. Britain's coal supply is substantial enough to last several centuries, but it is in seams located far below the surface and therefore difficult to extract. The progressively increasing cost of the extraction of coal, rather than the exhaustion of the coal supply commonly cited as the cause, was thought to be making coal an uneconomical source of power. Dependence on oil imports has the double disadvantage of being a drain on the balance of payments and an uncertain source of supply, as the two Suez episodes, of 1956 and 1967, have shown. The generation of electricity with water has

[1] *The Future Organization of the United Kingdom Atomic Energy Project*, Cmd. 8986.
[2] Not without a major Whitehall battle between Duncan Sandys, the Minister of Supply, and Lord Cherwell, still Churchill's scientific adviser. See Earl of Birkenhead, op. cit., pp. 295–315.
[3] 521 H.C. Deb. col. 2286–324 (10 December 1953); 524 H.C. Deb. col. 844–966 (1 March 1954).

never been very suitable for Britain. So it was that some members of Parliament as early as the fall of 1945 urged the Government to undertake a broad programme for the industrial development of nuclear energy because, as one backbencher put it, for Britain to be left behind would be the equivalent to living in the Stone Age while other nations moved on to Bronze and Iron.[1] The scientists generally gave their support to this view. Sir John Cockcroft in 1947 felt that the possibilities for the peaceful uses of atomic energy were sufficiently large to justify Britain's making a determined effort,[2] while for Sir George Thomson the discovery of nuclear energy and its potential use for power on a large scale had 'come like the answer to a prayer'.[3]

It was not until the mid-1950s, after the atomic bomb had entered the military inventory and the hydrogen bomb was on its way, that the nuclear power programme came into its own. The Atomic Energy Authority in 1955 developed a plan which called for 40 per cent of Britain's electrical power to be produced with nuclear energy by 1975.[4] Ironically, the Suez episode had a stimulative effect on the civil programme similar to its effect on the strategic nuclear force. As a result of the stoppage of the flow of oil, the 1955 goals were revised substantially upwards in order to provide a source of power which was less subject to the political environment and more easily transportable. The early expectation of atomic energy rapidly becoming a comparatively cheap source of power has not yet been realized, however, in part because the fears of coal scarcity and high prices for oil have proved unfounded. Moreover, the centralized management of atomic energy in Britain has become subject to criticism for failing to exploit the promise of nuclear energy efficiently, either at home or in the sale abroad of reactors.[5]

Nevertheless, Britain today has by far the most advanced atomic energy programme, civil and military, of any middle power. Perhaps this was the 'silver lining' in the collapse of Anglo-American nuclear collaboration, for the British were then forced to undertake a broad development programme of their own.[6] The domestic benefits of the atom as a source of energy may be achieved earlier and more widely in the United Kingdom

[1] 415 H.C. Deb. col. 1316 (7 November 1945).

[2] 'The Peaceful Uses of Atomic Energy', *Atomic Energy: Its International Implications*, Chatham House Study Group (London, Broadwater Press, 1948), pp. 61–6.

[3] 'Britain's Drive for Atomic Power', *Foreign Affairs*, Vol. XXXV, No. 1 (October 1956), p. 96.

[4] United Kingdom, *Programme of Nuclear Power: 1955*, Cmd. 9389.

[5] See, for example, Duncan Burn, *The Political Economy of Nuclear Energy* (London, The Institute of Economic Affairs, 1967).

[6] Sir Leonard Owen, Hinton's deputy at Risley, has commented: 'Looking back, the McMahon Act was probably one of the best things that happened to the technologists of the British Atomic Energy Project as it made us work and think for ourselves along independent lines.' Op. cit.

than in any other nation, except the United States. The nuclear reactor at
Calder Hall became in October 1956 the first in any country to deliver
electricity for commercial purposes to a national grid system. More than
one thousand industrial firms are in the nuclear field, and many are
assisting other nations to establish programmes for peaceful uses. By 1967
Britain had generated more electricity by nuclear means than the rest of
the world, including the United States, put together; she had a greater
installed capacity for nuclear power than any nation.[1] With the lead held
in fast-breeder nuclear reactors in 1970, Britain can expect to make sizeable
profits in commercial nuclear power reactors throughout the coming
decade. Thus the atom has become more than a compensation for the
British Isles' lack of resources; it has become an important sector of the
economy.[2]

3. The Pre-Detonation Period: The *Modus Vivendi* and the 1949 Negotiations

Britain hardly ever ceased pressing for the resumption of Anglo-American
nuclear co-operation from the time when it had almost completely ceased
following the McMahon Act to the time of the 1958 amendments of the
United States atomic energy legislation. The latter were designed to discriminate in favour of Britain and thus marked the renewal of full collaboration. There were two reasons for this pressure. The resumption of the
exchange of information would reduce the cost and increase the speed of
the British programme by making unnecessary the duplication of research
already undertaken in the United States. But there was always another consideration: the principal interest in the renewal of the nuclear partnership
was to provide a channel for Britain to influence American strategy and
politics in the nuclear age. British statesmen, having recognized that they
were no longer able to follow a fully independent foreign policy, felt that
they could maximize their national security and their influence around the
world by having a special role and voice in Washington. There was no
better mechanism for this than a unique relationship with America on
nuclear matters. This was an area in which Britain had a special claim and
a valuable contribution to make, to which the Americans attached the

[1] 'London's Last Chimneys', *The Economist*, 23 September 1967; *Fuel Policy*, Cmnd. 3438;
Sir William Penney, 'British Nuclear Power', The *Guardian*, 8 December 1966.

[2] In December 1969 Britain, together with the Netherlands and West Germany, approved an
agreement to collaborate on the new gas centrifuge process of enriching uranium. One of the
two enrichment plants will be located in the United Kingdom as will be the headquarters
organization. This new process, it is hoped, will satisfy the rapidly growing demand in Western
Europe for enriched uranium for nuclear power stations and will reduce the present dependency
on the United States.

highest importance and priority, and on which it was thought the peace of the world depended.

The British were on the whole unsuccessful in restoring co-operation in the period prior to the testing of their first atomic bomb. After the Monte Bello test—when there was no denying that they had joined the nuclear club—the hallowed doors of nuclear co-operation gradually opened up. In this there may be a lesson for future nations that go down the nuclear path.

The first break in the post-McMahon Act deep freeze were the negotiations that led to the signing of the *Modus Vivendi* of 8 January 1948. This agreement provided for:

1) Britain to receive nuclear information in nine specific areas having to do with health, safety, and certain other subjects not related in any way to military weapons.

2) The United States to receive a larger share of uranium ore from the British Empire, especially South Africa, and to receive the entire allocation of uranium ore produced in the Belgian Congo in 1948–9.

3) The United States—*vide* clause four of the Quebec Agreement—to give up control over Britain's development of atomic energy for industrial purposes.

4) Britain—*vide* clause two of the Quebec Agreement—to give up the right to veto the use of the atomic bomb against third parties without each other's consent.[1]

The two *quid pro quo* had their origins in particular circumstances which help explain the relative ease, compared to later attempts, with which agreement was reached. Within the executive branch of the American government there was a desire to work out an arrangement with the British whereby the United States would receive larger quantities of uranium ore which were badly needed. Since the establishment of the Combined Development Trust in 1944 to seek on a joint basis the control of accessible supplies of uranium, the British and Americans had jointly allocated this raw material so crucial to atomic energy. Surprisingly, co-operation in the Combined Development Trust had been sufficiently valuable to both parties to survive the McMahon Act. But as the United States started producing atomic bombs in large numbers after it used its second and last wartime-made bomb at Nagasaki, its needs for uranium ore increased measurably and were not met by its allocation in the Combined Development Trust or by available deposits in North America.

---

[1] See Richard G. Hewlett and Francis Duncan, *Atomic Shield 1947–1952*, Vol. II, *A History of the United States Atomic Energy Commission* (University Park, The Pennsylvania State University Press, 1969), pp. 273–84.

Since Britain had an option on half the deposits in the Belgian Congo and controlled sources elsewhere there was a strong incentive to work out a more favourable arrangement.[1]

Within the Congress the primary concern was of a different nature. The discovery in the spring of 1947 that President Roosevelt had made secret wartime agreements with the British on atomic matters was bad enough news for some of the key Republican Senators who then controlled the Foreign Affairs and Atomic Energy Committees. Worse still was the shocking fact that the Quebec Agreement gave the British a 'veto' over a decision to use the atomic bomb in the provision that required mutual consent. Vandenberg thought the two wartime agreements were 'astounding' and 'unthinkable'. Failure to revamp them, he suggested, would have a disastrous effect on congressional consideration of the Marshall Plan, at that time in a formative stage. Vandenberg discussed the problem with Truman, Marshall, and Forrestal; and Hickenlooper wrote to Marshall that he would be unable to support American economic aid to Britain unless the situation was rectified at once.[2]

At a meeting at Blair House on 26 November 1947, administration officials (Lilienthal and Carroll Wilson of the A.E.C., Forrestal, and Bush) were pleasantly surprised to hear from Vandenberg and Hickenlooper that they had no objections to the giving of limited technical information to the British. On 5 December Lilienthal met with the full Joint Committee on Atomic Energy. The committee members agreed to the State Department's entering into negotiations with the British and after discussion accepted in principle the view that there should be no explicit tie between the negotiations on atomic energy and the granting of economic aid to Britain, though 'the two cannot be wholly separated in reality'. To Lilienthal it seemed clear that Vandenberg approved the exchange of non-military information with Britain as a way of getting rid of the veto in the Quebec Agreement, which he thought could be a 'source of desperate embarrassment'.[3]

For the British their ostensible right to 'veto' an American decision to use the bomb must have seemed fairly ineffective at the time, given the way their former partner had failed in their view to live up to the other provisions of the wartime agreements. Furthermore, would not the veto, if retained, also apply to *their* bomb once it was ready? It would be even more difficult to justify an American veto over a British bomb which had been independently developed. There is no indication that the British

[1] Lilienthal, *Journals*, Vol. II, pp. 175, 182, 218, 282; Truman, *Memoirs*, Vol. II, p. 298. See also the testimony of George Kennan, then Director of the Policy Planning Staff of the State Department, U.S. Atomic Energy Commission, *In the Matter of J. Robert Oppenheimer*, pp. 355–6.
[2] Vandenberg, Jr. (ed.), op. cit., pp. 359–61; Millis (ed.), op. cit., pp. 337–9.
[3] Lilienthal, *Journals*, Vol. II, pp. 260, 265–8.

were particularly unhappy to give up the veto provision which bothered the Senators so greatly, or that this was a sticky issue in the negotiations. When the Quebec Agreement was first made public in 1954, Churchill in a rowdy Commons debate tried to make much of the fact that 'the abandonment of our claim to be consulted and informed as an equal was the act of the Socialist Administration.'[1] But this was really in the context of an attempt to embarrass Attlee and the other Labour party leaders, whose backbenchers were bemoaning the inability of Britain to stop the Americans from testing the hydrogen bomb.

Thus when the British made a request for limited information in 1947 they received a favourable response. But this was deceptive if interpreted as indicating the likelihood of greater co-operation in the future. In the executive branch there was a desire to set United States-United Kingdom nuclear relations on a firmer footing as there developed a growing awareness of the value of Britain as an ally, of the failure of attempts to work out a system of international control, and given the need for British controlled raw materials. But in the Congress—and on few subjects is the American government as bifurcated as on atomic energy[2]—once the limited but all important aim of eliminating the British 'veto' had been achieved, the incentive for further nuclear co-operation was measurably reduced. In the clearly differing rationales for supporting the *Modus Vivendi* which were to be found at the two ends of Pennsylvania Avenue lay the seeds of future difficulties.

The *Modus Vivendi*, which in effect supplanted the Quebec Agreement, was intended to set the terms of co-operation for two years, until the end of 1949. During this time, as the British atomic bomb project gathered momentum, its financial costs were becoming clearer. Although the costs were considered manageable and in no way prohibitive for the continuation of the project, they were mounting higher than anticipated. A decision was pending on the construction of a large and expensive high-separation gaseous diffusion plant at Capenhurst to make enriched uranium. The pound sterling was under pressure which pointed towards devaluation. There were strong economic arguments to be made for renewed efforts to collaborate with the United States in order to avoid duplication.

The British were therefore willing in 1949 to merge their undertaking with the Americans', and possibly forgo the separate manufacture of atomic bombs, if a suitable arrangement could be made. The formation of NATO

---

[1] 526 H.C. Deb. col. 51 (5 April 1954).
[2] See Harold P. Green and Alan Rosenthal, *Government of the Atom: The Integration of Power* (New York, Atherton Press, 1963).

that year seemed to augment British security; the case for an independent nuclear force had not yet completely crystallized.

In Washington, also, a joint project was becoming more attractive though not altogether for the same reasons. The *Modus Vivendi* had led to friction since it had been impossible to fit nuclear data neatly into the categories of the agreement. It was recognized that the British had cause for general complaint regarding the way they had been treated since 1945 on atomic energy and that it was in the political interest of the United States to relieve some of the irritation. In addition, it was reasoned that since the policy of restricting the exchange of information had failed to thwart the development of a British bomb, the best way to control the British would be to bring their entire project to the United States. This was really an inversion of the arguments of the 'monopolists' of 1945–6.

A sub-committee of the National Security Council, asked by President Truman to plan relations on atomic matters with Britain and Canada for the period after the *Modus Vivendi* was due to expire, recommended on 2 March 1949 that the United States make a new approach 'so as to bring as much atomic material and production as possible to the North American continent'.[1] British scientists and engineers would be brought to the United States as would all available uranium for processing and storage, in what was acknowledged to be a return to the World War II type of collaboration. Part of the thinking behind this, apparently, was concern that the British Isles, located closer to the Soviet Union than the United States, was an 'unsafe' place to have atomic bombs. Truman told Lilienthal in February 1949 that 'we certainly must try to see that the British do not have information with which to build those atomic weapons in England because they might be captured.'[2] The administration, however, was generally sympathetic to the British request for collaboration. The Labour cabinet had shown Washington since 1945 that it provided as responsible an ally as Churchill's cabinet. The General Advisory Committee to the A.E.C. frequently pointed out that closer collaboration would bring technical benefits to the United States.[3] Furthermore, the United States was still dependent on Britain for the procurement of uranium ore. The State Department and the A.E.C., with the dissenting voice of A.E.C. Commissioner Lewis Strauss, favoured a new and more enlightened approach.

The Truman administration's proposal for broader co-operation with Britain and Canada was presented to Congressional leaders at Blair House on 14 July 1949 and to the Joint Committee on Atomic Energy on 20 July, before the opening of formal negotiations with the British. There was to be full co-operation with Britain, including exchange on all aspects of nuclear

---

[1] Truman, *Memoirs*, Vol. II, p. 302.   [2] Lilienthal, *Journals*, Vol. II, p. 465.
[3] *In the Matter of J. Robert Oppenheimer*, p. 18.

weapons. Strategic considerations suggested that production plants and stockpiles should be located in North America to the fullest extent possible.

At these meetings a large number of objections were raised, chiefly by the Republican senators, which eventually frustrated the attempt to renew collaboration. The objections covered a wide range and were characterized by the belief that the United States had a monopoly on atomic energy and must hold on to its 'secret': the American people would not stand for giving away its know-how to the British, to whom too much had been given already; even if Britain had the knowledge of the bomb, few knew it, so that the American monopoly was a psychological fact—thus Vandenberg told Acheson that an American Secretary of State would lose his influence at international conferences if he had a partner there in his secret; British security arrangements were unreliable; the President did not have the legal authority to enter into such an agreement without congressional approval because of the Atomic Energy Act of 1946. The many comments that the public would react violently to a collaboration led Lilienthal to detect a 'nice, juicy, resounding political issue against Truman: he gave away the Secret'.[1]

The President was thus forced to weigh the benefits which might accrue from increased co-operation with Britain against the political costs of antagonizing influential congressmen on this issue. Although he had little doubt as to his constitutional authority, he was also given the impression that many legislators 'would refuse to go along'. At the time Lilienthal was under strong attack from Hickenlooper for mismanagement of the A.E.C., and particularly for laxity on security matters,[2] and the British question tended to become enmeshed with this issue. The administration needed large amounts of political capital for congressional approval of E.C.A. funds and military assistance to European nations, including Britain. Truman, therefore, decided to instruct the State Department to work out an arrangement with the British which would not include the complete sharing of weapons and data. As he later explained: 'It seemed to me more important to maintain bi-partisan support for the atomic program than to insist on a program which was opposed by strong elements in Congress.'[3] Nuclear partnership with Britain had a lower priority for the administration than some other issues.

Exploratory negotiations nevertheless began in the Combined Policy

---

[1] Lilienthal, *Journals*, Vol. II. pp. 543–52, 565, 574–5. After testifying at the J.C.A.E. hearing, Eisenhower, then President of Columbia University, was driven to remark: 'I never realized what a lot of cross-currents there are—I just don't know what that sort of thing is about.' Ibid., p. 552; Acheson, op. cit., pp. 316–18.

[2] See Harold L. Nieburg, *Nuclear Secrecy and Foreign Policy* (Washington, Public Affairs Press, 1964), pp. 39–40.

[3] Truman, *Memoirs*, Vol. II, p. 304.

Committee in September 1949 and ran on some time, during which a number of far reaching proposals were made. They provided for close collaboration in most aspects of atomic energy, including weapons, research, production of fissionable materials, and peaceful applications. The United States in essence wanted the British to give up the separate manufacture of an atomic bomb. This the British were perhaps willing to do, but only if in return the United States supplied 'X' number of atomic bombs to be stored in the United Kingdom under British custody and more to be held in Canada at the disposal of Britain. American officials were hesitant but willing to consider this if atomic bombs were only to be used in accordance with common war plans. Another proposal was that the British atomic project be transferred to the United States and Canada. The British, however, did not just want independent control of atomic bombs. They felt their standing as a major industrial nation warranted, perhaps even depended upon, the development of all aspects of atomic energy in Britain. Although they were willing to send a large number of their scientists and technicians to North America, they insisted upon the retention of a small but complete programme in Britain, including some fissile material production plants, and facilities and personnel for work on atomic weapons. This was to prove unacceptable to the Americans as a basis for collaboration or for the broadening of the exchange of information. The British, mindful of the way they had been excluded in 1946 in spite of the wartime agreements, were not willing to give up totally their projected independent nuclear capability.[1]

The Americans talked to the British with one eye on the J.C.A.E., given the President's decision not to support an arrangement which would present major difficulties in the Congress.[2] The negotiations broke down when it became evident that any programme for collaboration that was satisfactory to the British would be unacceptable to the J.C.A.E.[3] Lilienthal was critical of the ability of some members of one specialized congressional committee to impose its will on a major foreign policy issue (the Foreign Affairs and Armed Forces Committees were not consulted) and blamed the failure of the negotiations in part on American insensitivity and failure of judgement:

[1] Interviews; also Hewlett and Duncan, op. cit., pp. 305–12.

[2] William T. R. Fox and Annette Baker Fox have observed that 'JCAE members are highly conscientious, non-partisan, and strongly loyal to their own committee, but they are short on international experience. They have a narrow conception of national security, and during much of its life the committee has been more interested in building up and protecting American nuclear development than in gearing such development into foreign affairs.' *NATO and the Range of American Choice* (New York, Columbia University Press, 1967), p. 235.

[3] Acting Secretary of State James Webb reported to the President that the talks had failed because what the United Kingdom proposed was something some members of the J.C.A.E. 'would not take'. Lilienthal, *Journals*, Vol. II, p. 574.

If we take the course of the hard-boiled banker, or try to blackjack the British, or deprecate them, they will respond as almost any human being would respond, by also being difficult, by insisting on doing things atomically that would not be the most economic division of labors and of materials between real partners, but just to assert their pride and place in the world. This is what Hickenlooper and Strauss and others have accomplished with their pecking away at technical cooperation, and the kind of things that were said at the time of the Blair House meeting. It is a shameful record of the tyranny of a tiny minority.[1]

After the collapse of the 1949 negotiations Anglo-American nuclear relations were not significantly improved until the changes made in 1954 in the United States atomic energy legislation. Several events in 1950 supported those who looked unfavourably upon expanding co-operation with the United Kingdom and served to harden congressional opposition. The loss of the American monopoly with the announcement in September 1949 of the detection of the explosion of a Soviet atomic device came as a shock and measurably increased awareness of the stakes in the atomic race. Then in February 1950 Dr. Klaus Fuchs, Chief of the Theoretical Physics Division at Harwell, was arrested on charges that he had deliberately passed on highly classified data to Soviet agents. Fuchs had been at Los Alamos during the war and had a thorough knowledge of the gaseous diffusion process and possibly plutonium production. Some American scientists believed that he may have transmitted valuable information which helped account for the Soviets having developed their atomic bomb earlier than expected. In October 1950 Bruno Pontecorvo, an Italian-born physicist who had also participated in the Manhattan Project and later had worked at Chalk River and Harwell, suddenly flew to Helsinki and disappeared behind the Iron Curtain. These events, together with the Alan Nunn May case of 1946, led to serious distrust in Washington of British security procedures—all the more so since Fuchs, a German refugee, had been known to have had communist sympathies prior to the Hitler era but had received British clearance none the less. The Fuchs and Pontecorvo cases contributed to the failure to renew collaboration with the British but were not the principal cause as is sometimes alleged. Nevertheless, taken together with the views of the Joint Committee, the impact of the Soviet bomb, and the wave of McCarthyism that swept the United States in the early 1950s, they argued poorly for an early resumption of the nuclear partnership.[2]

[1] Lilienthal, *Journals,* Vol. II, p. 575; see also David E. Lilienthal, *Change, Hope and the Bomb* (Princeton, Princeton University Press, 1963), pp. 119–21.

[2] A commissioner of the A.E.C. from 1950 to 1957 has written: 'One reason for our delay in reaching an understanding with the British was our knowledge that British security standards were not comparable with our own. Numerous F.B.I. studies of the UK's security system showed clearly that it was not as reliable as ours and not even as good as Canada's . . . each

Consideration was intermittently given by the British to collaborating with the French but there were a number of inhibiting factors. Not only was Joliot-Curie, the High Commissioner until April 1950 of the Commissariat à l'Énergie Atomique, a member of the Communist Party but so were a number of other scientists in key positions in the French programme. The Governments of the Fourth Republic were considered politically unstable and their ministries subject to communist infiltration. Collaboration with France was all the more difficult because of the history of past collaboration with the United States. It was almost impossible to unravel what information had been acquired completely independently of World War II collaboration or the *Modus Vivendi*, and thus did not require American permission before it could be transmitted to the French. [1] Furthermore, there was always the hope that American policy would change and therefore the desire not to decrease the chances for this, or complicate it, by entering into a special relationship with France.

The failure of the 1949 negotiations did not lead to a major review in Whitehall of the decision to make the bomb. Although the increasing financial costs of continuing alone were regrettable, they were not considered to be prohibitive. The scientists and administrators dealing with atomic energy assumed that the bomb would be deliverable by long-range aircraft and neglected to give much further thought to the delivery aspect. It was recognized that France and perhaps others might some day—in the long-term future—be capable of making an atomic bomb, but this did not seem to be something to worry about. The outbreak of the Korean War in June 1950 seemed to confirm the wisdom of British policy. The danger of its escalating into a world war created great anxiety in Britain and supported the necessity of military preparedness. The uneasiness regarding America's conduct of the war, especially the fear that General MacArthur would initiate the use of nuclear weapons, underscored the value of a defence policy which permitted a degree of disassociation from the United States and which was not dependent upon an ally for the major weapons system.

succeeding press revelation of espionage and treason cases involving such scientists and officials as Fuchs, Pontecorvo, May, Burgess, and MacLean served only to confirm our analysis.' Thomas E. Murray, *Nuclear Policy for War and Peace* (Cleveland, World Publishing Co., 1960), p. 166.

[1] In 1955 the Commissariat à l'Énergie Atomique negotiated with the United Kingdom Atomic Energy Authority for the construction of a gaseous diffusion plant in France. The British were very anxious to enter into such a financially attractive enterprise but were forced to give up the opportunity because of past arrangements with the United States. Bertrand Goldschmidt, *L'Aventure atomique* (Paris, Fayard, 1962), pp. 118–19. See also Goldschmidt, *Les Rivalités atomiques, 1939–1966*, pp. 225–7.

4. The Post-Detonation Period: Return of Collaboration

Following the demonstration of Britain's independently achieved atomic and hydrogen weapons capability, the doors of collaboration were gradually opened by the United States. The relaxation of America's policy of nuclear secrecy and the open discrimination in favour of Britain were no doubt in a large measure the result of the success of Britain's nuclear programme. A number of additional factors, ranging from the coming to office of new statesmen and advisers in both countries, to changes in NATO strategy, and to Soviet nuclear progress, also made their contribution.

One of the principal aims Winston Churchill set for himself upon his return to power in October 1951 was that Britain should 'play her full role' and that there should be a 'revival of her former influence and initiative among the allied powers'.[1] Churchill no doubt wished to return to his Second World War conception of 'grand strategy' as something to be decided at the Summit. Within this context atomic weapons had a special place for they had become the distinctive feature of American military power and they were the one item on which Britain, and he personally, had a special claim. Churchill thus made a determined effort to return nuclear collaboration to its 1945 level. Perhaps more so than Attlee, he was acutely conscious of the *political* dividends of a nuclear partnership.[2]

Prior to the detonation of the first British atomic device Churchill was no more successful than Attlee had been in persuading the Americans to share their information. Before travelling to Washington in January 1952, he publicly reminded American officials of the 'peculiar risks' of nuclear attack Britain had undertaken in becoming an 'aircraft carrier' by providing bases in East Anglia for the atomic bomb carrying planes of the U.S.A.F. He deduced from this the right to special consideration for the British point of view. Although Churchill received in writing a previously verbal understanding that U.S.A.F. bombers would not start a nuclear reprisal from the East Anglia bases without British consent when circumstances permitted,[3] he returned empty-handed with respect to the exchange of nuclear data.[4]

[1] See his Guildhall speech, *The Times*, 10 November 1951.

[2] According to a commissioner of the A.E.C. at the time, 'British appeals for a resumption of nuclear cooperation became particularly insistent after Mr. Churchill's return to power in 1951.' Murray, op. cit., p. 168.

[3] Since 1948 there has been an informal 'Gentleman's Agreement', peculiar to the intimate Anglo-American relationship on defence matters, concerning consultation prior to the use of nuclear weapons. Initially this arrangement was specifically related to American air bases in Britain and it was reconfirmed by successive new heads of state. In 1962 Kennedy and Macmillan gave it world-wide applicability. See 661 H.C. Deb. col. 958 (26 June 1962) and 'U.S. Bases in Britain', *The World Today*, Vol. XVI, No. 8 (August 1960), pp. 319–25.

[4] For a review of his efforts, see Hewlett and Duncan, op. cit., pp. 573–5. Washington officials urged Churchill to tighten British security measures.

Churchill expected that the first British atomic test off Australia would have a major impact across the Atlantic. On his trip to the United States in January 1952, before the test, he found that the plans for testing were 'certainly a real advantage to us and when I informed the Americans in Washington of the position which had been reached quite a new atmosphere was created on this subject.' He read to the Commons Senator McMahon's statement that 'the achievement of an atomic explosion by Great Britain, when an accomplished fact, will contribute to the keeping of the peace because it will add to the free world's total deterring power', which included the comment by the chairman of the J.C.A.E. that with regard to atomic co-operation 'now we may consider rethinking the entire situation with all the facts in front of us.'[1] The British made a point of conducting the Monte Bello test quite independently; no American observers were invited to witness the explosion. After the test Churchill gave voice to his expectation:

We have conducted the operation ourselves, and I do not doubt that it will lead to a much closer American interchange of information than has hitherto taken place. . . . There are a very large number of important people in the United States concerned with this matter who have been most anxious for a long time that Britain should be kept better informed. This event will greatly facilitate and support the task which these gentlemen have set themselves.[2]

Within weeks of the British test General Eisenhower was elected President. Shortly after his inauguration, according to the new chairman of the A.E.C., Churchill began to press the President for a restoration of the nuclear relationship which had existed when they were comrades in arms. Eisenhower sympathized with the Prime Minister's point of view for his professional military instinct led him to believe that it was unrealistic to expect the British to be satisfied with weapons less effective than those of her principal ally. As he told Strauss, 'If we are forced to do battle with an enemy equipped with modern weapons, it could not make much sense to expect allies covering our flanks to be limited to the use of bows and arrows.'[3] Moreover, Eisenhower seems to have felt that the British were not treated fairly after the war with respect to the exchange of information and that the two countries which 'believed in the Bill of Rights ought to stick together'.[4]

In October 1953, Lord Cherwell, Makins, Cockcroft, and Hinton conferred with American officials about obtaining a more liberal interpretation of the areas in which information was being exchanged. Makins, the

---

[1] 496 H.C. Deb. col. 964 (26 February 1952).
[2] 505 H.C. Deb. col. 1270–1 (23 October 1952).   [3] Strauss, op. cit., pp. 371–2.
[4] Quoted in Lilienthal, *Journals*, Vol. II, p. 219.

Foreign Office official most familiar with the tangled history of the nuclear negotiations, had been wisely appointed Ambassador in Washington. Cherwell was an old friend of Strauss and their personal friendship has been credited with easing the stringency of American nuclear policy.[1] The British obtained little more than a promised exchange of data regarding the effects of blast, heat, and radiation resulting from atomic explosions, but the way was cleared for the Prime Minister to discuss nuclear matters with the President at Bermuda in December 1953. To this meeting Churchill brought as a reminder of past injustice a photograph of the original Hyde Park Aide-Mémoire. He left with a promise from Eisenhower to seek in the next session of Congress changes in the United States atomic energy legislation which would permit a greater sharing of information and equipment with Britain. In return, Churchill warmly endorsed the President's new 'Atoms for Peace' proposal (which because of the incentive it gave to the spread of nuclear technology was to give a strong boost to non-peaceful possibilities). On 17 February 1954 Eisenhower sent a message to the Congress requesting amendments to the McMahon Act. Subsequently Churchill revealed for the first time the text of the Quebec Agreement of 1943 with the explanation that its release was 'in the national interest and can do nothing but good on both sides of the Atlantic'. Referring to the increased latitude the President was seeking he commented: 'I trust that nothing will be said in the House today which will arouse needless antagonism in Congress and throughout America.'[2]

The British during this period based their case less on past commitments than on the utilitarian principle that the sharing of information would benefit the American programme as well as their own. They contended that because of the high level of knowledge that had already been reached independently their scientists sooner or later would know as much as there was to be known regarding nuclear energy. Therefore, it was in America's self-interest to take advantage of British scientific and technological skill by pooling the resources of the two countries. Furthermore, they argued that exchange would not be a one-way street and that they could offer data which would be of value to American scientists. The political side of their argument was that only a common means of defence made sense against the mutual enemy.

---

[1] Strauss had been actively opposed to co-operation with the British in 1948–9 and had been very upset to learn that the British were making a bomb, in part because the Labour government in his opinion was 'Leftist' and untrustworthy (Lilienthal, *Journals*, Vol. II, pp. 383–5, 477, 551). When he became chairman of A.E.C. the Tories took special care to cultivate him. Cherwell's biographer believes that their close friendship contributed greatly to the relaxation of the McMahon Act. Earl of Birkenhead, op. cit., p. 297.

[2] 526 H.C. Deb. col. 56 (5 April 1954).

The Atomic Energy Act of 1954 permitted sharing data on the external characteristics of nuclear weapons (size, weight, shape, yield, and effects) but withheld information on the design and fabrication of the nuclear components.[1] To many in Whitehall this modest improvement was interpreted as a result of the demonstration at Monte Bello that Britain had the capability to make the atomic bomb and would so do. An additional factor, however, was the Soviet thermonuclear bomb explosions in August 1953 which had further shattered any remaining semblance of an American monopoly. After 1954 the British continued to receive preferred treatment. This was made easier by a quiet but vigorous tightening up of British security procedures after the Fuchs case. But the Eisenhower administration's motive in seeking the new law was not limited to assisting Britain. The testimony given by Secretary of State Dulles before the J.C.A.E. suggests that the primary interest was to facilitate the training of allies with tactical nuclear weapons.[2] After the passage of the Atomic Energy Act, Dulles persuaded the NATO Council of Ministers in December 1954 to adopt a strategy calling for the initiation of the use of tactical nuclear weapons against conventional attacks as a way to compensate for the manpower deficiencies of the alliance.

As a result of the 1954 Act, two bilateral agreements were signed on 15 June 1955. One provided for the exchange of information on military aspects of atomic energy including defence planning and training in the use of nuclear weapons but specifically excluded warhead design and fabrication.[3] The second agreed to the exchange of information on civil uses of atomic energy, including the transfer of fissile materials and equipment.[4] The following year the British asked for assistance in order to help in the development of an atomic submarine. The Department of Defense supported the British request as it would increase the total submarine force strength of the West. In June 1956 in spite of objections from the A.E.C. and J.C.A.E., the Defense Department with White House and Department of State support used a legal technicality to conclude an agreement to give the British data on the nuclear submarine *Nautilus*, including information on nuclear ship propulsion reactors.[5] Collaboration between the nuclear scientists of the two nations in research on the control of thermonuclear reactions began in October 1956. The break in the log-jam in 1954 whetted the appetite for further co-operation

---

[1] *Public Law 703*, 83rd Congress, 2nd session.

[2] Joint Committee on Atomic Energy, *Hearings to Amend the Atomic Energy Act of 1946*, 83rd Congress, 2nd session, p. 686.

[3] *Agreement for Co-operation Regarding Atomic Information for Mutual Defence Purposes*, Cmd. 9555.

[4] *Agreement for Co-operation on the Peaceful Uses of Atomic Energy*, Cmd. 9560.

[5] Nieburg, op. cit., p. 67.

and this came about by degrees as the areas of exchange of information were gradually extended.

Suez, ironically, became a milestone in the return to collaboration. As we have seen in the last chapter, the Suez episode fed the desire for nuclear independence; but in its aftermath Suez also led to greater 'interdependence'. When Harold Macmillan came into office in January 1957 one of the major tasks he set for himself was to restore Anglo-American relations after the rupture of Suez. He travelled to Bermuda in March and to Washington in October to confer with Eisenhower, and out of these meetings there originated a number of new accords on defence matters which can truly be characterized as a 'partnership'.

One of these provided for the installation in eastern Britain of sixty 'Thor' liquid fuel Intermediate Range Ballistic Missiles under a 'two-key' system. The missiles and warheads were provided by the United States and the sites and supporting facilities by Britain under an arrangement whereby an American key activated the warheads and a British key launched the missile, thereby necessitating a joint decision before a missile could be fired. Although the United States, in the wake of Sputnik and the threat of a possible missile 'gap', presented to the NATO Council in December 1957 a plan to disperse IRBMs in Europe, the arrangement was initially agreed upon with the British in March 1957 at the Bermuda conference as a bilateral one outside NATO. All the allies except Turkey and Italy declined to place IRBMs on their territory, a situation which made the prompt and easy British acceptance all the more welcome in Washington.[1] Eisenhower considered the meeting when the Thors were decided upon to be 'by far the most successful international conference that I had attended since the close of World War II'.[2]

The intimacy of having agreed to share nuclear weapons systems not unnaturally encouraged further intimacies. Two weeks after the launching of Sputnik on 4 October 1957, which dramatized Soviet military and scientific strength, Macmillan went to Washington to suggest a further pooling of efforts—atomic energy was particularly on his mind.[3] The atmosphere of renewed co-operation that had been created at Bermuda six months earlier was now so intensified that *The Times* reported: 'In terms of the Anglo-American alliance, participants in the talks have known

---

[1] The first squadron of Thor missiles in Britain became operational in June 1959, by which time the liquid fuel, fixed site 'soft' missiles were already vulnerable to Soviet IRBMs. None were installed after 1960 and by 1963 all the Thors were phased out. In Italy and Turkey, Jupiter IRBMs were installed. For the details of the Thor agreement see 'Exchange of Notes Concerning an Agreement for the Supply of Intermediate Range Missiles to the United Kingdom', *Department of State Bulletin*, Vol. XXXVIII, pp. 418–19 (17 March 1958).

[2] Eisenhower, *Waging Peace, 1956–61*, p. 124.

[3] Harold Macmillan, *Riding the Storm 1956–1959* (London, Macmillan, 1971), pp. 321–6.

nothing like them since the wartime conferences at Cairo and Casablanca.'[1] At the conclusion of the talks a 'Declaration of Common Purpose' was issued, clause three of which committed the President to 'request the Congress to amend the Atomic Energy Act as may be necessary and desirable to permit close and fruitful collaboration of scientists and engineers of Great Britain, the United States and other friendly countries'.[2]

The resulting 1958 amendments to the Atomic Energy Act of 1954 brought to a climax Britain's long drive to share nuclear information and to take part in American strategic planning for nuclear war—rights to which she believed she had a claim as a former atomic collaborator and which she sought as a close ally. The new legislation was clearly designed to give Britain even more preferential treatment. The amendments permitted the exchange of information about the design and production of nuclear warheads, and the transfer of fissile materials although they did not allow the actual supply of completed nuclear weapons. Such exchange, however, was only permitted with countries that had already made 'substantial progress in the development of atomic weapons' and where it would improve the existing 'atomic weapon design, development and fabrication capacity' of the recipient country.[3] At the time Britain was the only ally that could qualify and to date it is the only nation to which such assistance has been granted, the 'force de frappe' notwithstanding. On 3 July 1958, the day following the legislation of the 1958 amendments, an 'Agreement for Cooperation on the Uses of Atomic Energy for Mutual Defence Purposes'[4] was signed which permitted Britain to make important technical advances in the design and production of nuclear warheads. This was supplemented by a further agreement signed in May 1959 which contained provisions to enable Britain to buy from the United States component parts of nuclear weapons and weapons systems and to make possible the exchange of British plutonium for American enriched uranium.[5] These agreements led to the sale of a marine

[1] *The Times*, 26 October 1957.

[2] *Department of State Bulletin*, Vol. XXXVII, 11 November 1957, p. 740.

[3] *Public Law No. 85–479*, 85th Congress, 2nd session. The intention to discriminate in favour of Britain was implicit in the report of the J.C.A.E. on the bill, which defined 'substantial progress' in the following manner: 'The cooperating nation must have achieved considerably more than a mere theoretical knowledge of atomic weapons design, or the testing of a limited number of atomic weapons. It is intended that the cooperating nation must have achieved a capability of its own of fabricating a variety of atomic weapons, and constructed and operated the necessary facilities, including weapons research and development laboratories, weapons manufacturing facilities, a weapons testing station, and trained personnel to operate each of these facilities.' Senate Report 1654, House Report 1859, 85th Congress, 2nd session, p. 12.

[4] Cmnd. 537.

[5] *Amendment to Agreement between the Government of the United Kingdom of Great Britain and Northern Ireland and the Government of the United States of America for Cooperation on the Uses of Atomic Energy for Mutual Defence Purposes of July 3, 1958*. Cmnd. 859.

nuclear propulsion plant for the first British nuclear submarine, the *Dreadnought*. The transfer of data on the design of thermonuclear warheads gave Britain valuable information on the design of smaller, more sophisticated warheads to be used for missiles such as Blue Streak and Polaris and also permitted a significant increase in their rate of production in Britain.

What are the factors that account for the resumption of full nuclear co-operation between Britain and America in the late 1950s? First, the need to balance the expansion of Soviet military strength with a stable Western deterrent increasingly called for a variety of contributions by European members of the alliance. The need for co-operation on such matters as the provision of launching sites for IRBMs on the British Isles and the continent, and the equipping of NATO forces with tactical nuclear weapons made it necessary for the United States to begin to give serious thought to the reciprocal nature of a defence alliance. Common defence planning and training, and the equipping of forces with nuclear weapons under the two-key system or in other forms, could take place only if allied commanders knew more about the use of such weapons and had some access to United States intelligence estimates of the Soviet capabilities which might have to be met. Sputnik added a new urgency to the strengthening of NATO and created pressures to increase scientific and technological co-operation within the alliance.

When shortly after Sputnik Eisenhower and Macmillan met—at the conference at which Eisenhower agreed to seek amendments to the atomic energy law—they gave currency to the concept of 'interdependence'. In the communiqué after the talks they agreed that:

The concept of national self-sufficiency is now out of date. The countries of the free world are interdependent and only in genuine partnership, by combining their resources and sharing tasks in many fields, can progress and safety be found. For our part, we have agreed that our two countries will henceforth act in accordance with this principle.[1]

It was natural that Britain and America should be the first to be proclaimed 'interdependent' and it was equally natural from the British viewpoint that nuclear weapons should hold the key. In Britain, Sputnik in combination with the impetus given by the Sandys 'New Look' had the effect of increasing press and parliamentary criticism of the wasteful duplication of defence projects because of the alleged American refusal to engage in genuinely co-operative programmes of research and development. Secre-

[1] *Department of State Bulletin,* Vol. XXXVII, 11 November 1957, p. 740.

tary of State Dulles told the sceptical J.C.A.E. that it had become 'common sense' to reinstate nuclear collaboration in order to make the most efficient use of the resources of the alliance.

Second, it would appear that the British case was more sympathetically heard because Eisenhower was in the White House. Before his election Eisenhower had already concluded that the McMahon Act had treated Britain unfairly and in a manner unbecoming a trusted ally; during the 1949 negotiations he favoured a return to complete collaboration. He had always revered Churchill, but with Macmillan there was a special bond dating back to when Macmillan had served as his political adviser in North Africa. Macmillan throughout his premiership gave the Anglo-American alliance the highest priority and advisers of both leaders credit their relationship of frankness and mutual trust to their World War II days.[1] To Eisenhower the bonds of the alliance were more meaningful than the abstract concern regarding the spread of nuclear capabilities that marked the Truman presidency or the vigorous strategic analysis that later put itself in opposition to independent nuclear deterrents in the Kennedy administration. Thus, as Macmillan recounted in 1963, when early in the days of his premiership he raised with Eisenhower the 'moral obligation' of his administration to reverse the McMahon Act and revert to the principles of co-operation between the two countries, the President fully accepted the point and laid the groundwork for the 1958 amendments.[2] Eisenhower told his officials as they studied the prospects of nuclear co-operation: 'Don't be too lawyer-like. A great alliance requires, above all, faith and trust on both sides.'[3]

The third and most important factor which helps account for the resumption of collaboration was the success of the British programme itself. Through the ironic logic of American policy, Britain's independent achievements became the strongest arguments for persuading the Americans to share their nuclear knowledge. In May 1957 a British thermonuclear bomb was tested at Christmas Island in the Pacific. American officials were subsequently amazed to learn the full extent of Britain's knowledge and expertise. It became evident that Britain was so far advanced that there was little point in continuing to withhold information. There was also less concern in the United States of secret data leaking to the Soviet Union, for the Russians were now known to have mastered the design of thermonuclear warheads. In addition, the British had taken steps to make Washington officials still more confident of the efficiency of their security procedures. Collaboration was not to be a one-way street: in certain areas

[1] See Sherman Adams, *Firsthand Report: The Story of the Eisenhower Administration* (New York, Harper, 1961), p. 287; 'Memoirs of the Earl of Swinton', *Sunday Times*, 17 October 1965.

[2] 670 H.C. Deb. col. 956 (30 January 1963).

[3] Eisenhower, *Waging Peace, 1956–61*, p. 219.

British scientists and engineers were further advanced and had information of considerable value to the United States.[1]

In developing a nuclear weapons capability independently, the British succeeded in overcoming the restrictions of American atomic energy legislation which they believed prevented them from exercising close influence in Washington. The atomic energy amendments of 1958 were clearly designed specifically for the United Kingdom and thus granted the British what they had desired since 1945. As full nuclear partners they acquired a privileged position which no other ally enjoyed in day-to-day discussions of nuclear targeting and war planning. The act of nuclear sharing also created an environment in which American trust in the British government deepened so that American officials discussed a wider range of military and political topics more frankly with their British counterparts than with officials of other friendly nations. The differentiation of the British from other nations was to later have some unfortunate consequences for the NATO alliance.[2] Although there are a number of factors other than the nuclear partnership which account for the 'special relationship', it would appear that without their atomic programme the British would not have received the same preferred treatment on nuclear matters and the same intimate rapport between Governments would not have been achieved. The return to collaboration and the beginning of 'interdependence' might have been thought to weaken the case for an independent nuclear force. But, as we shall see, the acknowledgement of the existence of British nuclear power also tended to strengthen for some the very appeal of nuclear independence.

[1] In the debate on the 1959 Defence White Paper, Aubrey Jones, then Minister of Supply, attributed the falling of the barriers to collaboration to the fact that Britain had something to contribute to the exchange of data. 600 H.C. Deb. col. 1325 (26 February 1959).

[2] As Fox and Fox perceptively note, 'Several problems which later threatened the cohesion of NATO can be traced to this period when the policy of shaping information on a carefully discriminating basis was being implemented.' Op. cit., p. 93.

7 | Developing the Delivery Capability

Having examined the evolution of the concept of independent deterrence and the growth of the nuclear capability, we now turn to the development of the delivery system. Delivery of the nuclear warhead by a reliable and invulnerable weapons system has been Britain's greatest obstacle in the continuing quest for an independent nuclear force. That this would be so was not apparent in the first years after the Second World War when manufacturing the atomic bomb was the overriding objective. At that time, it was somewhat naïvely assumed that the British bomb would be readily conveyable by long-range bombers of the Royal Air Force. As it was, by the time the V-bomber force was fully operational its vulnerability was already a matter of serious concern. The revolution in the technology of aircraft, missiles, and electronics which in two decades magnified out of all former proportions the factors of cost and vulnerability was hardly foreseen in the late 1940s. The tendency of the R.A.F.'s top officers was to look back upon World War II as confirming their long held views on the supremacy of air power and the efficacy of strategic bombing, despite some evidence to the contrary. Defence through nuclear deterrence, which as we have seen was probably first given a governmental *imprimatur* in Britain, was the natural outgrowth of a strategic bombing doctrine formed in the years between the two world wars on the basis of the experience of the First World War. We must very briefly look at the R.A.F. in the pre-atomic years, for it helps to explain much of the military's incentive for an independent nuclear deterrent.

1. Trenchard and the Heritage of Strategic Bombing

The doctrine of strategic bombing—the belief that the decisive factor in future warfare would be the destruction of the enemy's morale and war-making productive capacity by air attack with manned bombers—was a dominant perspective of the R.A.F. since its beginning. Indeed, it was the *raison d'être* of its birth. This historical relationship and the strong influence of Lord Trenchard during his ten years as the first Chief of the Air Staff shaped a generation of military officers who later took the responsibility for the delivery of atomic weapons.

Trenchard was deeply committed to the view that air power provided the key to victory in warfare. Direct strikes at the enemy's heart would destroy the enemy's morale and will to resist, and the production facilities without which he could not continue. Thus available offensive striking power constituted the best policy in the long run for defence of the home-land—a concept not totally unlike that of deterrence. In 1917, after London was bombed by German Gotha aircraft, the Independent Bomber Force was organized under the command of Trenchard to carry out the strategic bombardment of Germany. This became the world's first separate air force. Following the First World War, Trenchard, later known as the 'father' of the R.A.F., fought against the Royal Navy and the Army for the retention of the air force as an independent service. He argued that the capabilities of air power could only be demonstrated and developed to their full potential by a separate service. The struggle for maintenance of its autonomy became an integral part of the Royal Air Force's tradition and esprit and in this contest the requirements of long-range bombing rather than defence by fighters provided the rationale for a specialized new service.[1]

Throughout most of the inter-war period the strategic bombing doctrine dominated the R.A.F. In the successive aircraft armament 'schemes' drawn up by the Air Staff, the production and funding of bombers was consistently given priority over fighters. In the first phase of the Second World War, however, R.A.F. Bomber Command took heavy losses in its attempts at daylight precision bombing without obtaining significant damage of the target areas. The Battle of Britain was won by a relatively small number of Spitfire and Hurricane fighters. Ultimately strategic bombing became a principal weapon in allied strategy but only after methods of navigation, target finding, and damage assessment had been radically altered so as to permit area bombardment by night.[2] Production of heavy bombers for the R.A.F. was steadily expanded to the extent that in 1944 as much labour was devoted to this purpose as to equipping the entire British Army. There is little doubt that the massive bombing of Germany by the R.A.F. and the United States 8th Air Force made a powerful contribution to the winning of the war. Whether it achieved the objectives of destroying the enemy's war-making productive capacity and eroding his civilian morale is debatable. Surveys made after the war found that there was a steady increase in German military production

[1] See David Divine, *The Broken-Wing: A Study in the British Exercise of Air Power* (London, Hutchinson, 1966); Andrew Boyle, *Trenchard* (London, Collins, 1962); Sir John Slessor, 'Trenchard and the Birth of the Royal Air Force', *Journal of the Royal United Service Institution*, Vol. CVII, No. 627 (August 1962), pp. 216–19. Bernard Brodie has noted that the concepts of aerial bombardment attributed to Trenchard are too similar to those of Gulio Douhet, the Italian theorist, not to have come from a common source and implicitly suggests that Trenchard or his staff benefited greatly from giving Douhet a careful reading. See Brodie's *A Review of William W. Kaufmann's The McNamara Strategy*, P-3077 (Santa Monica, Calif.: RAND Corp., March 1965), pp. 7–8. For a rebuttal to Brodie, see Robin Higham, *The Military Intellectuals in Britain: 1918–1939* (New Brunswick, Rutgers University Press, 1966), pp. 257–9.

[2] Basil Collier, *The Defence of the United Kingdom*, History of the Second World War: United Kingdom Military Series (London, H.M.S.O., 1957).

through 1944, the year of maximum allied bombing tonnage. The population's morale had not been broken by bombardment at the time allied troops invaded the continent. Some analysts later thought that a portion of the enormous resources devoted to strategic bombing could have been used more productively in other ways.[1]

Within the Royal Air Force, whatever the doubts of some outside critics, it was thought that the strategic use of air power had reversed the tide of the war. British and American bombers were credited with having sufficiently weakened Germany's war resources and reduced her powers of resistance as to make it possible for the Allied armies to invade her territory. A crucial factor had been the achievement of air superiority. Although the fighter force had protected the homeland successfully (except from the V-rockets against which it was relatively powerless), it was the bomber offensive which forced the enemy to fight the air war over his territory. The R.A.F. believed that by making Germany turn increasingly towards the production of fighters and by forcing her to use the Luftwaffe's best pilots for home defence, strategic bombing had given the British Isles increasing immunity from air attack. Thus the experience of the war was seen as vindicating Trenchard's doctrine and offering a signpost for the future. In a lecture in 1947, Lord Tedder, the Chief of the Air Staff, said:

I am utterly convinced that the outstanding and vital lesson of this last war is that air power is the predominant factor in this modern world and that although the methods of exercising it will change, it will remain the dominant factor so long as power determines the fate of nations.[2]

2. The R.A.F.'s Self-Image in the Nuclear Age

In the first years after the war the lesson drawn from the development of the atom bomb was that it would multiply many times over the effectiveness of air power. During the war the R.A.F. had had little, if any, direct contact with the Manhattan Project. The performance requirements for the first jet bomber had been mapped out by the Air Staff in 1944 without knowledge of the revolutionary new weapon which in later years was to transform the service. After Hiroshima and Nagasaki the long-range manned bomber was quickly seen as having almost overnight acquired a

---

[1] Sir Charles Webster and Noble Frankland, *The Strategic Air Offensive Against Germany, 1939–1945*, History of the Second World War: United Kingdom Military Series (London, H.M.S.O., 1961), Vol. III, pp. 284–311.

[2] The Lord Tedder, Marshal of the R.A.F., *Air Power in War* (London, Hodder & Stoughton, 1947), p. 123.

new misson as the logical carrier of the new atomic weapon. The coupling of the atom bomb and the strategic bomber was natural, there being no alternative means of delivery. Even if one thought that the results of strategic bombing in the Second World War had been disappointing, the atom bomb seemed to give the bomber a new importance.

With the development of the concept of nuclear deterrence, the advocates of air power finally emerged supreme. Air power was seen as having replaced sea power as a natural extension of Britain's nineteenth-century imperial legacy. On 10 March 1953, shortly after his retirement as Chief of the Air Staff, Sir John Slessor in a lecture on 'The Place of the Bomber in British Policy' at the Royal Institute of International Affairs observed:

For a century before 1914 the Pax Britannica rested squarely on the British fleet. Then came thirty-five years of grey twilight when there was nothing to take the place of our sea power. Today I believe the Pax Atlantica depends as surely, and probably more permanently, on Anglo-American air power, of which the decisive expression is the long-range atomic bomber.[1]

The bomber was seen as becoming the main pillar of British defence policy as Western policy turned increasingly towards reliance on 'massive retaliation' and nuclear deterrence.

Here Britain was following America's lead. Although primary reliance on the concept of nuclear deterrence was first adopted as a working policy in Britain, as we have seen in Chapter 5, the creation of the means for such a policy in the form of a strategic nuclear bomber force was first achieved in the United States. The Strategic Air Command served as a model for Bomber Command to follow as it developed the V-bomber force. Relations between the two air forces were excellent and far more intimate than they were between the other respective services of the two countries. This was explainable in part by their common experience in seeking to establish themselves as the 'newest' service (the R.A.F., in fact, was a quarter century older than the U.S.A.F.), and their respective elevation to dominance over the other services in recognition of the new importance of air power (although the R.A.F. never acquired the same share of its national defence budget as did the U.S.A.F.). More important still was the close and excellent working relationship that evolved after SAC bombers were first placed on British bases in 1948. It is interesting and significant to note that the British never used the availability of bases for the use of the U.S.A.F. as a lever with which to gain access to atomic information.

[1] Sir John Slessor, 'The Place of the Bomber in British Policy', *International Affairs*, Vol. XXIX (July 1953), p. 304; on another occasion Slessor said: 'I believe that British and American air power can ensure the peace of the world for another hundred years as British sea power secured it for a hundred years after Trafalgar.' Quoted in 524 H.C. Deb. col. 1470 (4 March 1954).

The British were encouraged by the United States Air Force to build up the strategic nuclear bomber force. The U.S.A.F. and the R.A.F. assisted each other in their respective inter-service disputes and budgetary debates in Whitehall and Washington. As the V-bomber force came into its own it was seen by the United States Air Force as fulfilling a useful complementary role to SAC and adding to the geographical dispersal of the Western deterrent. There was little concern in the U.S.A.F. about unnecessary duplication among allies; few questions were asked as to whether British resources from an alliance viewpoint might not be more efficiently used for other defence purposes, as for example, personnel transport aircraft. The contribution which Bomber Command made was regarded by Pentagon planners as a welcome extra 'bonus'. But it was *not* seen as a contribution which permitted the United States to shift an equivalent amount of resources to some other defence requirement. A more rational division of labour between Britain and the United States had not been encouraged either by the American attitude towards nuclear collaboration, or by the refusal to admit until later British representatives to the nuclear target planning at SAC headquarters. The resulting duplication also reflected the failure of NATO to develop an accepted nuclear doctrine and formula for defence sharing. Bomber Command, like SAC, developed its nuclear bomber capability separately from NATO force structure planning.

Government spokesmen, while admitting that the primary military support for the deterrence strategy rested with America's nuclear power, maintained that a British strategic nuclear force was necessary. The British force, while smaller than that of the United States and the Soviet Union, would be highly efficient and would consist of aircraft whose performance was equal to that of the other nuclear powers. The V-bombers would be capable of striking a target list which might be patterned more closely than that of SAC's to the British order of priorities. Moreover, a long-range force provided a way to fight an 'immaculate' war by reaching the enemy directly without the costs and confusion of the battlefield.[1] Underlying the Government's policy was the belief that Britain could not retain its position of influence as a world power if it did not have a strategic nuclear bomber force of its own. Slessor's remark in a widely noted B.B.C. broadcast correctly reflected the Government's attitude:

The bomber is the primary agent of air mastery. If we want to remain a first class power we cannot possibly leave to an ally, however staunch and loyal,

---

[1] Slessor suggested that in case of war with the Soviet Union, 'we should make it clear to the Russian people at the onset that we have no intention of letting a single allied soldier put a foot on Russian soil.' 'The Place of the Bomber in British Policy', p. 306.

the monopoly of their instrument of such decisive importance in these massive issues of war and peace.[1]

Bomber Command became a symbol of Britain's Great Power status and a relevant extension of her diplomacy. The idea that the provision of strategic nuclear striking power should be left solely to the Americans, who were carrying the main burden in any case, while Britain concentrated on a less costly defence, had little support in the opposition party and certainly none in the R.A.F.[2] Bomber Command had been at the heart of the Royal Air Force since its beginning and assignment to it had always been the most prestigious of R.A.F. postings. Many of the officers who achieved high command had come up through the bomber ranks during World War II. They were in agreement with Slessor that the R.A.F. 'without a long-range bomber force would be like the Royal Navy of Nelson's day without its line of battle'. Britain was seen as having an unrivalled tradition of experience, skill, and knowledge in the bomber business which gave her the ability to make a unique contribution.[3] This was backed up by a long-established aircraft industry with a special aptitude for scientific inventiveness, which possessed some of the world's most capable design teams.

The Labour party gave the Churchill government its support in the development of the V-bomber force. In the debate on the Air Estimates for 1954, the principal parliamentary debate on the creation of the strategic nuclear bomber force, John Strachey as opposition spokesman said he was convinced that the Government's policy was the right one. The atomic bomb coupled with the strategic bomber would play the role of the *Dreadnought* battleship in earlier times and be the 'essential weapon for this island'. While disclaiming to be anti-American, Strachey thought it would not be right for Britain to leave the development of a weapon so crucial to British security to 'any ally'.[4] Arthur Henderson, a respected former Secretary of State for Air, thought that the British force would be expected to serve alongside the United States bomber force, but added that 'I do not think that we should put all our bombing eggs into the copious American basket.'[5] In the following year's Air Estimates debate, the Under Secretary of State for Air, George Ward, observed that the

---

[1] Sir John Slessor, 'The Revolution in Strategy', *The Listener*, Vol. LI, No. 1302 (11 February 1954), p. 244.

[2] For a characteristic R.A.F. attitude see W. M. Yool, 'Changing Patterns of the Royal Air Force', *Brassey's Annual* (London, William Clowes, 1953), pp. 327–33.

[3] See, for example, the statement of George Ward, Under-Secretary of State for Air, in the Air Estimates debate of 1954. 524 H.C. Deb. col. 1362 (4 March 1954).

[4] 524 H.C. Deb. col. 1503 (4 March 1954).

[5] Ibid., col. 1378 (4 March 1954).

need for the strategic nuclear force was 'now fully recognized by the great majority of the House and the public'.[1]

As a result of the priority given to bombers the R.A.F.'s capacity for air transport was woefully neglected for a number of years until Suez exposed its inadequacy. Former Air Vice-Marshal Kingston-McCloughry put the blame for this short-sighted policy on the dominance of the R.A.F. by its bomber enthusiasts, with Transport Command receiving insufficient attention.[2] More important still was the lack of attention given to the potential of guided missiles. During the formative years of the V-bomber force the R.A.F. had little enthusiasm for putting effort into the research and development of this new technology. The resulting slow start partially explains the later failure to produce a viable intermediate range ballistic missile. The Royal Air Force's emphasis on its strategic bomber competence was part of a desire to perpetuate its autonomy and independent role. A predominantly tactical air force would not have given the public and the political leaders the same sense of institutional power and prestige.[3]

3. The Creation of the V-Bomber Force

The actual coming into being of the first delivery system for the 'independent nuclear deterrent' must be dated several years after the announcement of the strategic doctrine. This is partially due to the nature of the British political system whereby 'declaratory' policy tends to run ahead of 'action' policy. The defence area is particularly susceptible to this phenomenon because of the tradition of the annual Defence White Paper. These statements are usually designed to make the party in power appear in the best possible light. Thus they tend to project an optimistic estimate of defence capabilities and planned weapons systems. Although British national security was officially stated to be based on the nuclear deterrence concept in 1955, the first squadron of Victor bombers was not operational until 1958. The first generation of the V-bomber force was not completed and equipped with hydrogen bombs until as late as 1961. By that time the

---

[1] 538 H.C. Deb. col. 630 (10 March 1955).

[2] According to Kingston-McCloughry, the R.A.F.'s leaders 'have always been susceptible to the charm of being bomber barons, and they are therefore inclined to be hypnotised by the bomber striking forces while disregarding other factors. This dearth of realistic thinking is similar to the hypnosis which capital ships exercised over our admirals long after such ships were virtually useless.' E. J. Kingston-McCloughry, *Defence: Policy and Strategy* (London, Stevens, 1960), p. 179.

[3] For a pertinent discussion of the incentives and techniques for the self-perpetuation of organizations see Philip Selznik, *Leadership in Administration* (Evanston, Row, Peterson, 1957), especially pp. 71-2.

R.A.F. was fully engaged in a struggle against the growing vulnerability of the V-bombers, and the Soviet Union and the United States were putting most of their strategic weapon efforts into long-range missiles.

The V-bomber force took longer in coming than the British atomic bombs; it was hardly past the prototype stage at the time the first atomic device was tested in 1952. Long-range nuclear bombers were not developed with the same sense of necessity that characterized the atomic bomb programme, nor did they receive the same priority in the allocation of financial and economic resources in the first years after the war.

The Labour government's adoption in 1946 of the Ten Year Rule, which assumed that there would be no major war for that period of time, set the direction and the limits of military weapons planning. Until the outbreak of the Korean War the R.A.F. was in a condition of 'accelerated rundown'. The manpower level was cut to less than twenty per cent of the wartime high and the service was expected to make maximum use of existing aircraft. Accordingly, Bomber Command had to make do with the wartime propeller-driven Lancaster and its successor, the Lincoln, which had reached the production stage at the end of the war. Neither of these aircraft, however, had a sufficient range to reach targets in the Soviet Union and both would have difficulty surviving against jet fighters.

In the post-war austerity period the Labour government was not inclined to approve the production of major new weapons systems. In order to compensate for this, and also because of the difficulty of predicting the new patterns of warfare in the atomic age, special attention was given to defence research and development. Successive Defence White Papers from 1946 onwards laid great stress on giving high priority to research and development in order that Britain should keep up with the 'state of the art'. Minister of Defence A. V. Alexander spoke in 1947 of a 'long-term' defence plan which assigned first priority to defence research and second to the 'maintenance of the structure' of the R.A.F.[1] Within the sector of defence R & D, a high proportion of expenditure was allocated to aeronautical research and the development of aircraft.[2]

Circumstances thus led the R.A.F. to plan a decade ahead for the equipment of Bomber Command with new strategic aircraft. By being forced through government policy to think almost solely in terms of long-term requirements, the R.A.F. was encouraged to seek a highly advanced and sophisticated long-range jet bomber which would be the best producible and equal to those of any nation. This was not unreasonable, for Britain

[1] 'The third priority is . . . for the most efficient Navy we can get in the circumstances and then we will do the best we can for the Army.' 443 H.C. Deb. col. 652 (27 October 1947). This order of priorities was not left uncontested by the Army. See Montgomery, *Memoirs*, pp. 480–1.

[2] *Statement Relating to Defence: 1948*, Cmd. 7327.

had been a pioneer in jet propulsion technology and its gas turbine engines were of the most advanced design. When the Russians turned to Britain in 1947 and bought the Nene jet engine it was thought by experts that they had thereby acquired considerable new knowledge for the development of their own engines. The British aircraft industry was still a leader in the science of aerodynamics, although its heavy concentration on production during the war had caused some falling behind in this art.

The Air Ministry on 1 January 1946 issued specifications to the aircraft industry for the development of a four-engine jet bomber to be ready by a 1957 target date.[1] It was eventually decided to develop three types of V-bombers—the Valiant, the Vulcan, and the Victor—each by a separate company, Vickers, Avro, and Handley Page respectively. Specifications for the Valiant were revised in July 1947 so as to make it available earlier, but the performance requirements of the delta wing Vulcan and the crescent wing Victor were essentially identical, despite their difference in design. Although the R.A.F. had a natural interest in spreading the development risks of these advanced bombers as a form of insurance against technical uncertainties, informed opinion in Britain looked upon the resulting duplication, especially of the Victor and Vulcan, as due in large measure to pressures from the air lobby: the aircraft industry with the willing co-operation of the Ministry of Aviation and the R.A.F.[2]

The V-bombers were designed to carry the atom bomb and to approximate the B-47, the American medium-range atomic bomber. When the development specifications were issued, however, they did not mention the atom bomb. Very likely the R.A.F. was lobbying for a nuclear role at the time it was drawing up the specifications for the bombers. It is a most interesting historical fact that the Defence Sub-committee of the cabinet made the decision to manufacture the atomic bomb, as discussed earlier, in the same month that the V-bomber specifications were issued. Certainly the link between the two actions must have been in the mind of at least one cabinet minister.

Nevertheless, until the Korean War the Attlee government hesitated to commit itself to the nuclear bomber force. The first production order for a V-bomber—the Valiant—was not placed until early 1951.[3] In the late 1940s a far higher priority was given to the building of a jet fighter force. At that time Labour air and defence ministers tended to emphasize the importance of air defence and indicated their willingness to leave strategic bombing to the United States. This view came under criticism from the

[1] Alfred Goldberg, 'The Military Origins of the British Nuclear Deterrent', *International Affairs*, Vol. XL (October 1964), p. 606.

[2] Richard Worcester, *Roots of British Air Policy* (London, Hodder & Stoughton, 1966), pp. 152–7.

[3] *The Supply of Military Aircraft*, Cmd. 9388.

Conservative opposition, especially the shadow Air Minister, Harold Macmillan. The Tory leaders, with the full support of the R.A.F., pressed the Government to move quickly from the development to the production stage of the V-bombers in order to create a powerful strategic bomber force. When, starting in 1950, Bomber Command received seventy B-29s under the United States Military Assistance Program, some Conservatives, though not Macmillan himself, criticized Labour for turning to the United States instead of manufacturing a fleet of British bombers.[1]

The decision to give priority to the creation of the V-bomber force appears to have coincided with the adoption by the Churchill government of the nuclear deterrent strategy in 1952. The reversal of the 'accelerated rundown' of the R.A.F. began with the Korean rearmament programme initiated by the Labour government. The projected three-year build-up called for the expansion of the R.A.F.'s personnel, the construction of new airfields and facilities, and equipment of the R.A.F. with more jet fighters and tactical bombers. The Labour government did not, however, undertake a major re-equipment of Bomber Command. This fell to the new Conservative government which at the same time decided to scale down the over-ambitious rearmament effort. After the Chiefs of Staff presented Churchill with the 'Global Strategy Paper' discussed in Chapter 5, suggesting reliance on a strategy of nuclear deterrence, a significant new departure was taken in aircraft procurement. A cut-back in the production of jet fighters was announced and existing orders for them were partially cancelled, while the 'super priority' designation officially assigned in early 1952 to Canberra tactical bombers and Valiants was extended in December to the long-range Victors and Vulcans.[2]

As British policy moved towards increased reliance on nuclear deterrence it brought new vigour to the hitherto somewhat lethargic development of the V-bombers. In March 1953 Churchill told the Commons that as a 'result of the Government's strategic review the types and quantities of weapons and ammunition to be produced have been more precisely related to the kind of war or wars which we might have to fight'.[3] The new importance given to long-range bombers was certainly a result of the increased role of nuclear weapons in British defence policy; the

[1] Goldberg, 'The Military Origins of the British Nuclear Deterrent', pp. 608-9; 'Mutual Defence Assistance Agreement Between the United Kingdom and the United States', Cmd. 7849; *Statement on Defence: 1950*, Cmd. 7895.

[2] *Air Estimates for 1951-52*, Cmd. 8162; *Statement on Defence: 1953*, Cmd. 8768; 537 H. C. Deb. col. 1695 (28 February 1955); W. M. Yool, 'The Task of the Royal Air Force', *Brassey's Annual* (London, William Clowes, 1952). Between 1949 and 1954 net expenditures on the R.A.F. rose from under £200 million to over £500 million. See *Air Estimates for 1954-55*, Cmd. 9076.

[3] 512 H.C. Deb. col. 579 (5 March 1953).

reduction in fighter production reflected the view that since complete air defence of the British Isles against nuclear attack was an impossibility it should not be approximated. Churchill's determination to give the R.A.F. the best possible strategic bombers fitted in with his ideas on 'keeping up with' the Americans. Some of the initial doubts which he did entertain as to whether the V-bombers would be worth the expense were dispelled after Sir John Slessor asked the Commander of the Third United States Air Force in Britain to describe for the Prime Minister the capabilities of SAC bombers. As after the earlier Pentagon briefing mentioned in Chapter 5 a fascinated Churchill thought that Britain must have the same.

In spite of the 'super priority' given to the V-bombers in the allocation of materials and technical resources, they were not operational in quantity for Bomber Command by the target date of 1957 which had been set ten years earlier. An exception was the Valiant which was designed as a less advanced aircraft and chosen for more rapid development in order to provide an 'insurance' bomber until the higher performance Victors and Vulcans were available. The first Valiant squadron came into service in 1955, equipped to carry atom bombs. In 1958 some Valiants were converted into tankers and in 1960 others were diverted to reconnaissance and tactical duties in Germany under SACEUR. The first squadron of Vulcans was available in 1957, and the first squadron of Victors became fully operational in the spring of 1958.[1] But it was not until 1960 that Bomber Command had its planned complement of V-bomber squadrons. Ironically, the first R.A.F. atomic bomber was not one of the V-bomber series but the Canberra made by English Electric, a twin-engined light jet bomber which had been conceived in 1944,[2] and had not been designed to carry atomic weapons. Although it could not be considered a strategic bomber because of its limited range, the Canberra bomb bay was adjusted to carry low yield atom bombs when they were first provided to the R.A.F. in 1954.

The V-bomber force took thirteen years to develop from the specifications stage to the completion of Mark I production. The reason for this slow pace—which was to contribute to the force's early vulnerability—lay initially in the Labour government's lack of certainty that a strategic bombing role was essential for Britain. Once the Conservative government adopted the strategy of nuclear deterrence and gave 'super priority' to the V-bombers, the primary causes of delay were attributable more to difficulties in aircraft production than to competing defence requirements.

[1] *Jane's All The World's Aircraft, 1960–61*, pp. 48, 70; J. D. Scott, *Vickers: A History* (London, Weidenfeld & Nicolson, 1962), p. 343.
[2] *The Supply of Military Aircraft*, Cmd. 9388.

The post-war aircraft industry was too widely diversified and too many different projects were being undertaken (many of which were eventually cancelled) for the available supply of technologists and engineers.[1] Thus the V-bombers lagged behind schedule at many stages and without indirect American assistance they might have taken still longer. The United States strengthened the R.A.F. and freed resources which could then be spent on the V-bombers, first by giving to the R.A.F. a number of B-29s, thereby permitting the cancellation of a planned interim bomber, the Short S.A.4, and then by granting substantial amounts of military assistance under the United States Mutual Security Act. Most of this assistance went to the R.A.F. and was in the form of F-86 Sabre jets, anti-submarine aircraft, and helicopters, some of which were purchased in the United Kingdom under 'offshore procurement' provisions.

If one looks back upon the official rhetoric and the public debate in Britain concerning the Government's adoption of a strategy of nuclear deterrence and, in effect, massive retaliation from the 1955 White Paper onwards, it is interesting to note that in 1956 three-quarters of Bomber Command's total strength still consisted of Canberras that were unable to reach the Russian heartland.[2] Indeed, the propeller-driven Lincolns remained in 'first line' squadrons until December 1955. The Valiants, whose development was rushed in order that they become the first strategic atomic carriers, were delivered in quantity to the R.A.F. in 1956, but Bomber Command's squadrons were not fully equipped with the planned complement of longer range Victors and Vulcans until 1960,[3] the year the Blue Streak missile was cancelled. The Victors and Vulcans were not equipped with free falling hydrogen bombs until 1961. Thus one must conclude that Britain's actual capacity for strategic nuclear deterrence, leaving aside the question of effectiveness, lagged several years behind her declaratory policy.

Once the V-bombers were available they did, nevertheless, constitute a formidable offensive force. Capable of flying at over 50,000 feet and of reaching nearly Mach 1, their altitude and speed performances compared favourably with the best Soviet and American bomber aircraft. Though possessing a shorter range, the 180 'first line' V-bombers—this was the

---

[1] In the mid-1950s the slowness of military aircraft production was criticized by the Labour opposition and the press, including the *Daily Telegraph* which usually reflects the opinions dominant in the military establishment. The special White Paper in 1955 on *The Supply of Military Aircraft*, Cmd. 9388, was an attempt by Minister of Defence Harold Macmillan to deal with this criticism. An authority on the British Aircraft industry believes that the scarcity of jet aircraft in actual squadron use by the R.A.F., in contrast to those shown at the annual flight demonstrations at Farnborough, was explained by the fact that the resources for eliminating 'teething' troubles and getting aircraft into production had not kept pace with advances made in design. Sir Roy Fedden, *Britain's Air Survival* (London, Cassell, 1957), p. 7.

[2] Goldberg, 'The Military Origins of the British Nuclear Deterrent', p. 611.

[3] *Jane's All the World's Aircraft, 1960–61*, pp. 22, 48.

maximum strength obtained despite early plans for 250—were capable of reaching the majority of industrial targets in Russia from bases in Britain and Cyprus. The Mark II V-bombers, which Bomber Command received in 1963–4, had a longer range and higher ceiling and carried the Blue Steel 'stand off' bomb, which could be launched at a 200 mile distance from the target thereby penetrating enemy air defences from afar. But even if the danger of Soviet surface-to-air missiles or advanced manned interceptors could be avoided, the V-bomber bases became susceptible to destruction by incoming Soviet intermediate range ballistic missiles. After 1958, when concern regarding the vulnerability of the V-bomber force developed, the R.A.F. began adopting a variety of techniques —dispersal of aircraft, four minute scrambles, low level below-radar flying—to reduce their vulnerability. This was a somewhat melancholy struggle against obsolescence, however, for the simple reason that the V-bomber force did not come fully of age until the era of missiles.[1]

---

[1] The *Statement on Defence: 1963*, Cmnd. 1936, said the V-bomber force was only *then* reaching its peak.

PART THREE
The Great Nuclear Debate
1957–1964

8 | The Issues Emergent

Debate on the merits and disadvantages of the British nuclear force has run parallel to its development ever since the first public awareness of its existence. It was in the years between the 1957 Defence White Paper and the Nassau Conference of December 1962, however, that the principal issues emerged and crystallized. This period has therefore been selected as the most suitable for a subject analysis, discussing the principal issues one by one. One should recognize, however, that many of the questions keenly debated in these years also had some relevance at other times. In the chapter following this one, the issues here discussed are placed within the context of events such as the cancellation of the Skybolt missile, the Nassau Conference, the proposal for a multilateral nuclear force, and the debate over the 'independent nuclear deterrent' in the General Election of 1964.

Several trends and events formed a backdrop to the great nuclear debate. First, the strategic doctrine adopted in the administration of Duncan Sandys served as a watershed in the evolution of British defence policy because of its strong emphasis on nuclear deterrence in providing for the nation's security and the consequent reduction in conventional capabilities. Second, the unexpectedly rapid development of Soviet long-range missile power cast doubt upon the reliability of the American nuclear guarantee—that is, the willingness of the United States to retaliate with nuclear weapons because of Soviet aggression in Europe if the retaliation would lead to an almost certain Soviet nuclear attack upon the North American hemisphere. (One should note that the significance of the rocket thrust capability demonstrated by the launching of Sputnik in October 1957 lay primarily in the expected new vulnerability of the United States. It had been generally assumed in Whitehall since 1955 that the British Isles were within range of Soviet IRBMs, although this was not widely publicized at the time.)

Third, the return to power of General de Gaulle in May 1958 assured that France would manufacture an atomic bomb and led to an acceleration of the French nuclear effort. De Gaulle's romanticization of the 'force de frappe' and his justifications for it, based as much upon 'independence' and 'military autonomy' as upon questioning the validity of the American nuclear guarantee, struck a receptive chord in some British hearts. Maintaining a nuclear capability separate from that of the United States also fitted in well with the growing concept of an economically and politically resurgent Europe.

Fourth, the unsatisfactory experience with the Blue Streak ballistic missile had a great impact in Britain. The Macmillan government relied heavily on Blue Streak as the basis for the future of the independent deterrent and research and development on the missile were depicted as the means for keeping Britain abreast of the latest advances in defence technology. Blue Streak's cancellation led to the widespread conclusion that Britain could not afford a significant nuclear force in the missile age and that a credible 'independent deterrent' policy was therefore beyond its grasp. This over-reaction in turn influenced the Labour party's decision to withdraw its support from the continuation of the nuclear force.

Fifth, the Eisenhower administration undertook a series of measures which relaxed previously tight restrictions upon nuclear sharing and thereby indirectly heightened European desires for a role in nuclear strategy. Tactical nuclear weapons were put in the arsenal of NATO ground forces in Germany, and some NATO countries were asked to accept American IRBMs on their soil. Arrangements were made in 1958 for the installation of sixty Thor missiles on British bases. The revisions of 1958 to the United States Atomic Energy Act which brought Britain into a full nuclear partnership with the United States, and which discriminated in her favour among other NATO allies, seemed to legitimize for officials of both nations her full nuclear role. The above five elements all contributed to Britain's increasing nuclear-mindedness.

Two central questions which dominated the great debate of 1957–64 can be distilled from the large mass of rhetoric which surrounded the issue. The first asked in what circumstances nuclear weapons would be employed in case of a military threat. This was a question of strategy, as much of NATO's nuclear strategy as of British security policy. The second concerned Britain's possession of its own nuclear weapons and asked whether the nation should continue its policy of maintaining an 'independent deterrent', or whether in the light of the growth of doubts concerning the military, economic, and technological feasibility and necessity of doing so, the effort should not be renounced. This was a separate question from that of the alliance's nuclear strategy, although in the public debate the two issues often became blurred and entangled with one another. Nevertheless, for analytical purposes, this is a useful and important distinction to make.

The concept of nuclear deterrence has a deceptive simplicity which encouraged public discussion. Being a 'war and peace' issue of the type that the British public had been quick to respond to since 1945, politicians were eager to articulate their views. This led to much shallow and emotional discussion lacking in concrete analysis. The nuclear debate became enmeshed with ideological disputes and personal rivalries, within the political parties and between the three parties. Because the nuclear force was believed to cut into the defence allocations for conventional forces it became a matter of inter-service conflict. Technological advances and weapons procurement decisions, alterations in the strategic doctrine of the United States, NATO alliance politics, and the ebbs and tides of East-West relations, all continuously interacted with the national debate in Britain causing shifts in the positions of the participants and generally confusing the debate.

1. The Question of Nuclear Strategy

Liddell Hart has observed that British public and parliamentary concern about the vulnerability of the British Isles to Soviet missile attack was surprisingly slow to develop.[1] The first real public impression of the menace of Soviet missiles was made at the time of Suez with Bulganin's rocket-rattling message to Eden. Not until the launching of Sputnik did the danger of Soviet nuclear attack become fully apparent. American atomic bombs had been located on United States Air Force bases in the United Kingdom since the Berlin Crisis of 1951, but it took a casual statement in November 1957 by General Powers, the Commander of SAC, regarding the state of readiness of SAC bombers to alert many Englishmen to their exposed position. This helps explain why the strategic nuclear doctrine given the following February in the 1958 Defence White Paper aroused such controversy. Though it merely restated in plain terms the established British and NATO policy, it was portrayed in the press and public discussion as a new departure of policy.

Duncan Sandys had chosen to give a somewhat stark account of the doctrine of massive retaliation. After noting that the Western powers relied primarily on the nuclear deterrent for their security, paragraph 12 of the 1958 Defence White Paper stated:

. . . it must be well understood that if Russia were to launch a major attack on them *even with conventional forces only* (italics mine) they would have to hit back with strategic nuclear weapons. In fact, the strategy of NATO is based on the frank recognition that a full-scale Soviet attack could not be repelled without resort to a massive nuclear bombardment of the sources of power in Russia.

The Government's statement then went on to claim that although Britain's nuclear power could not be compared in magnitude to that of the United States, nevertheless 'when fully equipped with megaton weapons the *British bomber force will in itself constitute a formidable deterrent.*'[2] (Italics mine.)

[1] B. H. Liddell Hart, *Deterrent or Defence*, pp. 51–2, 68, 217.
[2] *Report on Defence: Britain's Contribution to Peace and Security: 1958*, Cmnd. 363, p. 2.

MNP

The question to be asked is whether this constituted a viable defence policy. Critics of the Government—and they included the opposition party, some Tory backbenchers, much of the press, and other defence commentators—clearly thought not. With the growth of Russia's nuclear retaliatory capability in the mid-1950s (marked by the first Soviet thermonuclear explosion in 1953, the rapid production of long-range bombers, and Sputnik) a strategic first-strike by Britain or the United States looked increasingly less plausible. The White Paper's contention that Britain would attack Russia's 'sources of power' with nuclear weapons if the Soviets made a large-scale attack on Western Europe using conventional weapons only was not convincing. While the R.A.F. could perhaps destroy some Russian cities or some bomber bases on first-strike, Bomber Command did not possess a sufficiently powerful delivery capacity (and perhaps also a large enough stockpile of warheads) to overwhelm Soviet air defences so thoroughly as to eradicate Russia's retaliatory power. Not having the necessary counter-force strength, a British-initiated nuclear attack would invite a reprisal which would reduce to ruins the densely populated British Isles. Indeed the Government had admitted as much in the 1957 Defence White Paper when it noted that it must be 'frankly recognised' that:

There is at present no means of providing adequate protection for the people of this country against the consequences of an attack with nuclear weapons. Though, in the event of war, the fighter aircraft of the Royal Air Force would unquestionably be able to take a heavy toll of bombers, a proportion would inevitably get through. Even if it were only a dozen, they could with megaton bombs inflict widespread devastation.[1]

Therefore without a large-scale civil defence programme and a highly effective air defence the adopted nuclear strategy was not credible. Would a rational Prime Minister start a nuclear exchange if even a single Soviet aircraft carrying a thermonuclear bomb *might* get through? As a *Times* leader commented: 'A threat to commit suicide is not a rational defence policy.'[2]

Another question is whether British strategy was at variance with the accepted NATO strategy. Since his appointment as SACEUR in November 1956, General Lauris Norstad had been persuading the allies to develop the kind of military plans and forces that would relieve NATO of exclusive

---

[1] *Defence: Outline of Future Policy: 1957*, Cmnd. 124, pp. 2–3.

[2] 'What Kind of a Deterrent?' 25 February 1959. Press comment on the declaratory nuclear strategy was almost universally sharply critical. The *New Statesman* observed that 'British defence policy has ceased to be a merely military affair: it has become a problem in logic' in 'The Logic of Annihilation', 2 February 1958. See also 'Mystique of Our Deterrent' by 'Nucleus' (pseudonym for a recently retired senior naval officer), *Observer*, 7 December 1958.

dependence upon nuclear retaliation. The adopted five-year plan, MC-70, was designed to create a 'shield' of thirty divisions in Western Europe which would introduce a new measure of political and military flexibility. The role of the shield forces was to impose a 'pause' by non-nuclear means during which the aggressor would presumably weigh the costs of continuing his attack; conversely, the 'pause' permitted the defender to avoid a forced early choice between reliance on nuclear retaliation or passive acquiescence. Thus the then current SHAPE intentions no longer involved the early use of nuclear weapons against a conventional attack as was implied in much of the discussion on the British strategy.[1] On the other hand, if the 'major' or 'full-scale' Russian attack mentioned in paragraph 12 of the 1958 White Paper referred to an expedition of a magnitude sufficient to overwhelm or pierce through the allied forces, then the NATO countries were still pledged to a nuclear reprisal—despite the increase in Soviet nuclear offensive power since the strategy had first been adopted. Furthermore, the force goal of thirty divisions had not been met, nor had the 'official' NATO strategy been altered. Therefore, one must conclude that although the Sandys strategy seemed to be turning the clock back to 1954, it was in accordance with the alliance's unrevised nuclear doctrine, if not with the then current ideas of many of its adherents.[2]

The Labour party's spokesmen on defence in Parliament were quick to criticize a strategy which, in the words of John Strachey 'produces the end of the world at the first stage'.[3] In the debate on the 1958 Defence White Paper, Strachey suggested that paragraph 12 was a strategy of massive retaliation cruder in form than that of John Foster Dulles,[4] and predicted that its effect would be not to frighten the Russians but to turn some of the British people towards a 'nothing can be done' defeatism —a correct prophecy given the subsequent rise of the movement supporting unilateral disarmament. In the late 1950s Labour parliamentarians such as George Brown, Denis Healey, Fred Mulley, and John Strachey consistently took the Government to task for its 'unbelievable' nuclear

[1] See Robert E. Osgood, *NATO: The Entangling Alliance* (Chicago, University of Chicago Press, 1962), pp. 160–3.

[2] *The Times* found the strategy shocking not for its novelty, but its antiquity. 'Are we to assume that Mr. Sandys has learnt nothing since 1954?... If we are deterred from using thermo-nuclear weapons because Russia also possesses them now, then we ought not to base our defence plans on the pretence that we are not deterred.' 'Defence is Defence', 26 February 1958.

[3] 583 H.C. Deb. col. 656 (27 February 1958). The following year Strachey saw it as the 'perfect recipe for capitulation'. 600 H.C. Deb. col. 1411 (26 February 1959).

[4] The previous year George Brown citing Dulles' further retreat from 'massive retaliation' in a *Foreign Affairs* article observed that Sandys was now 'left standing alone' on the brink. 577 H.C. Deb. col. 320 (7 November 1957). See John Foster Dulles, 'Challenge and Response in United States Foreign Policy', *Foreign Affairs*, Vol. XXXVI, No. 1 (October 1957), pp. 25–43.

strategy (while at the same time the 'shadow' cabinet agreed with the Government, as we shall see later in this chapter, that Britain should retain its nuclear force).

One tactic used in order to try to show that the stated nuclear strategy was a 'bluff' was to attempt to force the Government to specify the circumstances under which it would resort to nuclear weapons. Following the widespread disparagement of his 1958 White Paper, Duncan Sandys conceded that limited or localized acts of aggression in Western Europe might be resisted using solely conventional arms. Prime Minister Macmillan defined the provocation required to unleash a strategic nuclear reprisal as 'the mobilization of large forces, say 200 divisions, or an all-out attack on Europe, or the bombing of London'.[1] But generally cabinet members resisted Labour's attempts to have them categorize the spectrum of responses to contingencies between a 'full-scale' Soviet conventional attack, which would be met by sizeable nuclear retaliation, and 'minor' incidents which would receive a non-nuclear response.[2] In the pre-McNamara era, before theories of controlled response became current, Conservative leaders were undoubtedly influenced by a genuine concern not to weaken the deterrent by casting doubt on the certainty of retaliation in response to any attack on Western Europe.

Britain's strategic doctrine, according to the critics, also failed to provide a method to deal with limited threats in the grey area between a border incident and all-out war. As the United States and the Soviet Union were seen as approaching a time of strategic nuclear stalemate, the most likely form of future conflict was thought to be limited war. The Sandys doctrine, according to the critique, failed to provide a 'middle game' strategy; indeed it had provided the rationale in 1957 for the reduction of Britain's conventional forces and her limited war capabilities. One of the principal criticisms of the priority given to the British nuclear force, as is discussed subsequently in this chapter, was that it weakened Britain's resources to wage medium-sized wars. Although Labour leaders favoured the retention of the nuclear force (until 1960), they wished to alter the order of priorities.[3] The major responsibility for providing the nuclear deterrent belonged in any case, they noted, to the United States.

[1] Macmillan added that he meant the bombing of London with conventional bombs. 583 H.C. Deb. col. 408–9 (26 February 1958). One wonders if 'mobilization' alone would in fact have led to the slightest consideration of a nuclear response.

[2] For example, Sandys himself spoke of 'an area in between about which I will not speculate and which I will not define'. 583 H.C. Deb. col. 410 (26 February 1958). See also *The Times* leader 'The Area in Between', 28 February 1958.

[3] For example, during the debate on the 1959 Defence White Paper, George Brown, then 'shadow' defence minister, castigated the Government for over-insuring at the nuclear level and under-insuring at the conventional and tactical atomic level. 600 H.C. Deb. col. 1165 (25 February 1959).

In view of the wide range of her commitments throughout the world, Britain's primary role should be to provide highly mobile conventional forces with modern equipment and the necessary air transport. As to the defence of Western Europe, critics suggested that less faith be put in the efficacy of the massive retaliation concept to inhibit Soviet aggression and that greater priority be given to increasing NATO 'shield' forces, thereby seeking to raise the size of limited threats that could be contained without recourse to atomic weapons.

Labour's 'shadow' cabinet could not, however, press its case for augmenting conventional capabilities too strongly, for the logic of the argument required the return of conscription—a step which most politicians equated with political suicide.

Along with its increased reliance on strategic nuclear weapons in order to avert the 'big war', the Government implied that tactical atomic weapons would help offset manpower deficiencies in 'limited' wars, particularly as a compensation for reductions in the size of the British Army of the Rhine. As in the United States, defence experts were confused and divided in their views as to whether battlefield atomic weapons could be used without provoking a central war. Not untypical was the case of John Strachey who supported in 1958–9 the dispersion of tactical atomic warheads in Europe but by 1962 had changed his mind.[1] The debate in Britain was strongly influenced by the writings of P. M. S. Blackett and B. H. Liddell Hart, both of whom doubted whether equipping NATO forces with tactical nuclear weapons brought benefits comparable to the added risks, were sceptical of the feasibility of maintaining a distinction between tactical and strategic weapons and of devising agreed upon 'rules of the game' for limited nuclear warfare, and recommended instead a non-nuclear defence of Europe.[2]

The British Army of the Rhine adopted an atomic strategy even before nuclear warheads were available for its implementation. By 1958 the defence planning and tactics of British units in Germany were conceived in nuclear terms, although American nuclear artillery was hundreds of miles away and the BAOR did not receive warheads of its own (subject to American custody) for Honest Johns and Corporals until 1960.[3]

---

[1] 600 H.C. Deb. col. 1407–11 (26 February 1959); 'Nuclear Chess', *Encounter*, Vol. XI, No. 2, August 1958, pp. 3–6; *On the Prevention of War* (London, Macmillan, 1962), p. 94.

[2] P. M. S. Blackett, 'Thoughts on British Defence Policy', *New Statesman*, 5 December 1959, pp. 783–90; B. H. Liddell Hart, *Deterrent or Defence*, pp. 59–61, 80, 139–43. Although over-optimistic in his conclusions as to the imminent 'last funeral rites upon the remains of the 1957 policy', an excellent summary of the interplay of British, American, and NATO theories on tactical atomic war, 1957–61, is given by the defence correspondent of *The Times* in 'Strategic Planners Think Again', 6 November 1961.

[3] Fred W. Mulley, *The Politics of Western Defence* (New York, Frederick A. Praeger, 1962), pp. 144–5.

Although Labour defence spokesmen advocated the dispersion of tactical atomic warheads in the late 1950s, they later criticized the Government for its over-dependence on nuclear weapons in the BAOR and were able to cite the warning of the Minister of Defence's own Scientific Adviser, Sir Solly Zuckerman, concerning the danger inherent in the employment of tactical nuclear weapons. Zuckerman, discussing the thorny problems of command and control of tactical nuclear weapons, feared that as they became part of a set-piece their use would simply become one part of a programme of predetermined strategic action which might set into operation the whole 'panoply' of strategic nuclear forces.[1]

By 1960 a wide spectrum of opinion could be found in Britain in opposition to the Government's declared nuclear strategy. It included a number of influential Tories, high-ranking officers of the Army and Navy (though not the Air Force), most of the national press, and the majority of defence commentators, in addition to the Labour party. This community of dissent was somewhat parallel to the opponents in the United States of the Eisenhower administration's 'New Look' defence policy. Critics on both sides of the Atlantic benefited from personal contacts with each other and from reading the rapidly mounting literature on nuclear strategy being written by the defence intellectuals of the Anglo-Saxon world.

There were, however, important differences between the two nations which derived from the differing historical and geographic situation of Britain as compared with America. Britain was the first middle-ranking power to have her own nuclear weapons and the first to debate their credibility and usefulness. The United Kingdom also was the first atomic power to find herself—by accident of geography—indefensible against a hostile and much larger nuclear power. British society, at least its attentive elites, was therefore forced to give attention at an early stage to the many-sided ramifications of basing her security policy on nuclear deterrence. It was no accident that unilateral disarmament was first seriously debated in Britain. Robert Osgood has suggested that even several years after Sputnik, Americans did not feel the immediate sense of physical vulnerability to nuclear devastation that aroused the British; he notes that in all the multitude of congressional investigations and hearings on defence policy there was no counterpart to the efforts of members of Parliament to force the Government to elaborate the circumstances under which it would use nuclear weapons.[2]

The years before the Nassau Conference of December 1962 were marked by a gradual diminution of the more extreme conceptions of nuclear

---

[1] 'Judgement and Control in Modern Warfare', *Foreign Affairs*, Vol. XL, No. 2, January 1962, pp. 197–202.
[2] *NATO: The Entangling Alliance*, p. 140.

deterrence of 1957–8.[1] Unlike the Defence White Papers of the previous two years, the 1959 document contained no statement of the deterrent doctrine. In 1960 the White Paper noted that the nuclear power of the West 'is only one component of the deterrent. Because of the need to meet local emergencies which could develop into a major conflict, conventionally armed forces are a necessary complement to nuclear armaments.'[2] The new Minister of Defence, Harold Watkinson, announced that contrary to what had been planned in 1957 the BAOR would not be reduced below seven brigades of 55,000 men. Watkinson affirmed that the R.A.F. Transport Command would receive more airlift capability while the fighter squadrons in Germany would be kept at present strength, and he generally tended to underplay dependency on nuclear weapons while stressing the flexibility and mobility of conventional forces.

Although the Government claimed continuity in its defence policy, the replacement of Sandys by Watkinson was interpreted as marking a switch of emphasis in the nuclear/conventional equation and was seen as a change in the direction of policy 'without losing face'[3] politically. In the debate on the 1961 Defence White Paper, Watkinson spoke of the 'necessity for deterrence over the whole spectrum of defence.'[4] The doctrinal paragraph of the 1962 statement stood in marked contrast to its stark predecessor of 1958:

We must continue to make it clear to potential aggressors, however, that we should strike back with all the means that we judge appropriate, conventional or nuclear. If we had nothing but nuclear forces, this would not be credible. A balance must be maintained, therefore, between conventional and nuclear strength. Neither element must be so small as to encourage an aggressor to seek a quick advantage, or to risk a provocative local incident escalating into a major war.[5]

We thus see that after the strong emphasis on nuclear weapons in the first years after Sputnik there developed an awareness of the limitations of nuclear deterrence as a provider of security against the whole range of possible threats.

It would appear that the Conservative government was responding to

[1] P. M. S. Blackett, for one, contended that the Defence White Papers of these years left Britain without a body of military doctrine on which realistic military planning and training could be based and therefore Britain 'cannot be said to have an intelligible defence policy'. See his 'Thoughts on British Defence Policy', *New Statesman*, 5 December 1959. Liddell Hart called for a workable deterrent that 'does not impale us on the horns of the dilemma: suicide or surrender', *Deterrent or Defence*, p. 45.

[2] *Report on Defence: 1960*, Cmnd. 952; *The Times*, commenting on the White Paper, found it far less rigid than those of the previous three years, 17 February 1960.

[3] In the words of a *Times* leader: 'New Thinking on Defence', 3 March 1960.

[4] 635 H.C. Deb. col. 1199 (21 February 1961).

[5] *Statement on Defence, 1962: The Next Five Years*, Cmnd. 1639, p. 5.

pressures from many sources. A majority of its backbenchers were concerned with Britain's ability to fulfil its overseas commitments and viewed the strategic doctrine with uneasiness since it implicitly supported expenditures for Britain's nuclear weaponry at the expense of conventional arms.[1] The same was true of the Army and Navy. The Foreign Office had viewed Sandys' unilateral defence planning as contributing to a growing estrangement from the continental European nations. The change of administration in the United States in 1961 brought with it a new emphasis at the non-nuclear end of the defence capabilities spectrum. Most important of all: the nuclear strategy issue faded into the background as, with the cancellation of Blue Streak in 1960 and Labour's subsequent change in policy, the spotlight shifted to the question of the purpose and continuation of Britain's own nuclear force.

2. The Question of Independent Possession— the Case for Retention

A. Strategic Justifications

The first rationale of a strategic nature given for the need for an independently owned and controlled British nuclear force was, as we have seen, that made in 1955 by the Churchill government: since in the crucial selection of enemy targets Britain might have a different order of priorities than the United States, it was essential that she have her own nuclear capabilities. Churchill's Minister of Defence at the time, Harold Macmillan, upon becoming Prime Minister put the 'independent nuclear deterrent' at the centre of his defence policy. But he had other reasons for doing so. Reliance on the British nuclear force for national security made possible the end of national service. In the Conservative party's programme for political recuperation following Suez, the abolishment of conscription was a major step towards avoiding defeat in the following general election. If this and the reduction of defence expenditure were for Macmillan the most important aspects of the 1957 White Paper, as many politicians in both parties believed, additional justifications of a strategic order for the nuclear force became readily available with the launching of Sputnik in October 1957.

The significance of Sputnik lay in the doubts that arose over the willingness of the United States to come to the aid of her European allies if it meant exposing American cities to nuclear retaliation. With the growth in

---

[1] Some of the leading Tory critics were former ministers who previously held defence portfolios in the Conservative government but were not inhibited from voicing their dissent in Commons debates. See Julian Critchley, 'Red Alert for Defence Policy?' The *Spectator*, 19 May 1961.

Soviet missile capabilities, as demonstrated by the rocket that thrust the Sputnik satellite into orbit, a widespread concern developed that the United States would be increasingly inhibited in using its nuclear retaliatory power for the defence of the European nations. If, for example, the Soviets at the outbreak of a war declared a 'limited' aim in Western Europe and further let it be known that the United States would be safe from nuclear attack if she did not intervene, could the Europeans be certain that the President would, while under tremendous domestic pressure, risk almost certain holocaust in order to honour the security guarantee? If nuclear weapons were used by the Soviet Union against Western Europe, the United States *might* feel compelled to retaliate in kind. Still more doubtful was whether the United States would initiate the use of nuclear weapons in response to a solely conventional assault upon Western Europe.

Another consequence of the advent of intercontinental missiles was thought to be the reduction of the strategic value of European territory for American security. The United States was no longer as reliant for her own defence upon European bases as when SAC bombers could reach the Russian heartland only from these bases. Eventually IRBM placements in Europe would also be unnecessary for American defence. The British came to feel that the American strategic stake in Europe was diminishing. If the American deterrent could not be depended upon to serve British interests in all circumstances, Britain, many persons reasoned, must place greater reliance on her own.[1]

The British alternated between two poles of fear: (1) The United States would *not* use nuclear weapons to defend interests vital to Britain unless its own safety and survival were threatened; (2) The United States *would* use nuclear weapons and destroy Britain in the process. The second fear was often associated with American involvements in the Far East (Korea, Vietnam) where it was thought that the 'local' use of nuclear weapons would escalate into a central war—hence, one of the reasons for wanting influence in Washington. But there were also intermittent fears that American actions in Europe would unintentionally push the Soviets over the brink. The first fear—that of abandonment by the United States—contributed to keeping Britain a nuclear power. In part because the American pledge to come to the aid of Europe was never fully convincing after Sputnik, successive British governments continued their own insurance in the form of the nuclear force. To be sure, American pronouncements did not always encourage them to keep the 'faith'.[2]

[1] Ironically, the immediate effect of Sputnik was to reinforce the American nuclear commitment in Europe with the placing of Thors in Britain and Jupiters in Italy and Turkey.

[2] Fred Mulley has suggested that the American guarantee 'really boils down to a question of confidence'. Op. cit., p. 81.

The years 1957–60 were marked by an increasing tendency on the part of American defence officials to discuss strategy in terms of passive deterrence and a second-strike capability.[1] Widely noted in Britain was the statement by Christian Herter on 21 April 1959 at the hearings on his nomination to be Secretary of State that he could not 'conceive any President involving us in an all-out nuclear war unless the facts showed clearly we are in danger of all-out devastation ourselves'.[2] Secretary of Defense McNamara's attempts to limit the nuclear end of the defence spectrum by enlarging the range of non-nuclear responses also stirred disquiet in Europe.

Few in Britain were inclined to claim seriously that the V-bombers provided a full-scale deterrent against the Soviet Union. An unfortunate if perhaps politically understandable tendency to discuss the strategic aims assigned to Britain's nuclear weapons without the necessary precision of terminology, led at times to vague or exaggerated claims and statements. Part of the obfuscation was created by the failure to make a distinction between a nuclear *'force'* and a nuclear *'deterrent'*. A 'force' is not a 'deterrent' until it is thought to be capable of deterring a hostile action by the threatened use of force. The deterrent value of the military force is therefore dependent upon the identity of the potential aggressor and the specific nature of his threat. *A* may be capable of deterring *B*, but not *C* or *D*. *A* may be capable (or thought to be) of deterring certain types of hostile actions by *B*, but not others. Most published British defence documents or oral statements by defence ministers failed to be sufficiently precise to permit useful distinctions regarding the claims made for the 'independent British deterrent'. Claims for the nuclear force were most often clothed in the habit of Britain's *'contribution'* to the Western deterrent. But the 1957 White Paper spoke of a wide measure of agreement that 'she must possess an appreciable element of nuclear deterrent power of her own' and in 1962 the defence statement claimed that the British contribution *'is by itself* [italics mine] enough to make a potential aggressor fear that our retaliation would inflict destruction beyond any level which he would be prepared to tolerate'.[3] In Commons debates and in public discussion British officials repeatedly spoke of the V-bombers or the Polaris flotilla as the British 'deterrent', failing to make the necessary distinction between a deterrent and a force.

[1] See Osgood, *NATO: The Entangling Alliance*, pp. 197–204.

[2] In fairness to Herter, it should be said that his statement would have been less alarming had it been given in its full context by the British press. See *Hearings on the Nomination of Christian A. Herter to be Secretary of State*, Committee on Foreign Relations, U.S. Senate, 86th Congress, 1st session, pp. 9–10.

[3] *Defence: Outline of Future Policy: 1957*, Cmnd. 124, p. 3; *Statement on Defence, 1962: The Next Five Years*, Cmnd. 1639, p. 6.

With respect to a threat from the Soviet Union, the strategic role for the British nuclear force presumably was to convince the Russians that a British retaliation could inflict 'unacceptable damage'—that is, sufficient damage to make a Soviet attack on the British Isles not worthwhile. Such a strategy was a counter-city strategy designed to maximize destruction so as to make the Soviets think twice about the price they would pay for starting an aggression. If a reasonable chance of a single thermonuclear bomb landing on a primary target such as Leningrad or Moscow was sufficient to make an attack on Britain seem less attractive, then a small British nuclear force might exercise a deterrent effect out of all proportion to its intrinsic power.

Thus the nuclear force could provide 'passive deterrence' to the extent that it succeeded in introducing the necessary doubts in the mind of the would-be aggressor against the British homeland. For a time proponents of the nuclear force spoke as if it were capable of providing 'active deterrence', that is, deterrence against aggression aimed at an allied country or an overseas colony.[1] Such claims were heard most often in the period after Suez when British officials, influenced by an acute sense of having been deserted by the United States, tended to ascribe to the nuclear force a compensating role in the protection of the remaining vital overseas interests, such as the Kuwait oil fields. But as the significance of the fast-growing Soviet missile power became recognized, the implausibility of 'active deterrence' became apparent. With a virtually unprotected civilian population,[2] no British government would seriously contemplate initiating the use of nuclear weapons against the Soviet Union in response to an attack upon an ally or as part of any peripheral situation. To do so would be suicidal unless the British force possessed the capacity to damage almost totally Soviet second-strike capabilities, a capacity even the most generous could not ascribe to Bomber Command.

Would the nuclear force provide 'active deterrence' of aggression by a non-nuclear power against Britain or one of her allies? Although Government statements were usually couched in terms of deterrence against a Soviet threat occasionally supporters of the British force referred to its possible use against a hostile power not possessing nuclear weapons.[3]

[1] To my knowledge the distinction between 'active' and 'passive' deterrence which subsequently gained currency in Britain was first made by the defence correspondent of *The Times*. He observed that although the nuclear force provided only 'passive' deterrence the Government spoke as if it possessed 'active' deterrence. See 'Britain and the Deterrent', *The Times*, 15 and 16 October 1958.

[2] For a discussion of the likely devastation caused by a nuclear attack on Britain and the supposed inadequacy of the Government's civil defence measures see Emanuel J. de Kadt, *British Defence Policy and Nuclear War* (London, Cass, 1964).

[3] 'Who can say that the way of checking the Castros, the Sukarnos, the Nassers and Perons of the future will not be the single nuclear missile accurately aimed at a vital military target

Such references were often made to sustain the belief that nuclear weapons provided a cheaper means of meeting British defence commitments. Certainly the nuclear force could have devastating effects upon nations not possessing an effective method of defence. But public attitudes in Britain concerning nuclear weapons are such that it is most unlikely that a government would use nuclear weapons against a non-nuclear state. There is no publicly available evidence to suggest that British military planners have ever seriously considered resorting to the practice of nuclear blackmail against a nation not possessing its own atomic weapons.

The strategic justifications given by successive Conservative Ministers of Defence simultaneously credited the nuclear force with providing independence for Britain while maintaining that it was a 'contribution' to the Western deterrent. Similarly, after the targeting plans of Bomber Command were co-ordinated with those of SAC, the Government claimed that the two nuclear forces were fully 'integrated' but insisted that the British retained full freedom of action in pursuing their own national security objectives. Such a double-edged approach was also evident in other claims made for the V-bombers. Since the weight Britain added to the deliverable American nuclear tonnage was relatively insignificant (approximately five per cent of America's), the primary contribution of Bomber Command to the Western deterrent was thought to be geographic. The V-bombers provided added dispersal and greater proximity to the Soviet Union, and complicated her own attack plans. They reduced the West's reaction time, in so far as manned aircraft were concerned. Duncan Sandys in the debate on the 1959 Defence White Paper cited the words of General Powers, Commander of SAC, that the V-bomber force was an essential element of the Western deterrent and that 'having regard to Britain's closer proximity we rely on her V-bombers to provide an important part of the first wave of the allied retaliatory force'.[1] But it could also be said that Britain's nuclear force sustained her declaratory nuclear strategy by providing the means for the early use of nuclear weapons. Though a first-strike against the Soviet Union by Britain alone would be clear suicide (and therefore did not provide a substitute for the American guarantee) such a threat would be meaningful to the Russians to the

after a period of warning?' *Sunday Telegraph*, 3 February 1963, quoted in Richard Gott, 'The Evolution of the Independent British Deterrent', *International Affairs*, Vol. XXXIX, No. 2, April 1963, p. 252.

[1] As quoted in 600 H.C. Deb. col. 1419 (26 February 1959); Sir John Slessor wrote in support of the nuclear force in 1962: 'It is entirely misleading merely to count numbers of first-line aircraft and deduce that the military value of Bomber Command is in direct ratio to its numerical strength compared to SAC, thus ignoring the important considerations of time and space, including the highly significant fact that Bomber Command is based several thousand miles nearer to its potential targets than is most of SAC.' *What Price Coexistence? A Policy for the Western Alliance* (London, Cassell, 1962), p. 109.

extent that it might automatically release or 'detonate' the American deterrent.

The claim that the real strategic function of the British nuclear force was to convince the Soviets that it might 'trigger' the use of SAC in a crisis in which the President would not assist Britain unless his hand were forced was based on the following type of scenario: following a hostile action or threat against Britain, Soviet radar screens pick up a missile coming towards it but are unable to distinguish whether it is a British or American attack. They are therefore forced to retaliate against the whole Western system—but the United States, assuming that the Soviets will act in this manner, immediately sets off its own large nuclear forces. A variation of this scenario would be as follows: the Soviets correctly identify the Union Jack painted on the British warhead and ask themselves if they can afford to accept the level of damage they are about to receive while leaving America's power untouched. If the British attack is certain to inflict 'unacceptable damage' to cities, industrial areas, or the Soviet Union's own retaliatory capability, the Soviets might reason that they should retaliate against the United States as well as the United Kingdom —but again, the American President fearing this line of Soviet reasoning might feel obliged to launch a pre-emptive blow against Russian territory. In both the main scenario and its variation the function of the British nuclear capability was to act as a catalyst which would 'trigger' the American nuclear deterrent. Some British officials and commentators thought that the possibility of such scenarios becoming reality (in the days before the 'hot line') would compel the Russians to be as cautious in provoking Britain as in provoking the United States.[1]

It is interesting but difficult to make a judgement on the reaction of the Soviet Union to the British nuclear force. The priorities in the procurement of nuclear delivery systems suggest that the Soviets were greatly concerned about Western Europe either as a source of potential aggression or as a hostage. The force of Soviet medium-range Badger bombers was built more quickly and in far greater numbers than the long-range Bears. In the same manner, the Soviets built a large IRBM force trained on Europe with greater urgency and in initially greater numbers than the ICBMs aimed at the United States. On the other hand, the Soviet literature

---

[1] British officials were understandably not eager to give public voice to the notion that their own nuclear force could make the United States extend its nuclear umbrella because America could not afford *not* to defend a country that had the power to involve it in a central war. Therefore this additional strategic justification for the nuclear force was never stated by the Government in an official manner, although it was discussed privately and in the press. See Denis Healey, *The Race Against The H-bomb*, Fabian Tract 322, March 1960, p. 7; Laurence W. Martin, 'Does Britain Need the Atom Bomb?' *Sunday Times*, 5 July 1959; Sir John Slessor, 'A New Decade for Defence', *The Listener*, Vol. LXIII, No. 1610, 4 February 1960, pp. 199–201; 'Britain's Bomb: Keep or Renounce', *The Economist*, 15 February 1964.

on nuclear war is comparatively bare of references to the British nuclear force. Little attention has been given to its strategic concepts, or to its targeting plans, and it has received even less commentary than the 'force de frappe'. What discussion there has been views the British force prin- cipally as an instrument of political conflict within the Western alliance, either to force adjustments to American strategy or as an element in the presumed struggle between Britain, France, and West Germany for European hegemony.[1]

B. *Political Justifications*

From its inception the rationale for an independent nuclear force given by British officials was as much political as strategic. As the task of main- taining a credible 'deterrent' became more difficult in the face of mounting strategic and economic counter-arguments, the justifications became increasingly political, emotional, and at times apologetic. To the Govern- ment and the Conservative party, the Royal Air Force, influential sections of British industry, and a public which opinion polls showed to be still quite chauvinistic, the nuclear force was a symbol of Britain's indepen- dence and status as a world power. Prime Minister Macmillan liked to speak of his belief that Britain was entering a 'second Elizabethan Age' in which, as in the earlier period before her imperial supremacy of the nineteenth century, Britain could play an influential international role without having all the resources of the greatest powers. Relying on the parallels of limited resources, the inability to establish herself as a great continental power in the sixteenth century and the loss of Empire in the twentieth, and the name of the Queen in each instance, he called upon the nation similarly to compensate for its smaller population and resources by a will to greatness. Nuclear weapons were seen as a way for a medium- sized but technically advanced nation to retain Great Power status.[2]

Possession of the nuclear force was thus thought to bestow prestige and influence. Alastair Buchan and Philip Windsor have referred to the 'psychological impulses' to exert a powerful influence upon the course of Western policy which they found in Britain (and France, but less so

---

[1] G. Anatolyev, 'Britain and European Security', *International Affairs* (Moscow), No. 2, February 1966, pp. 42–5; 'Nuclear Weapons and the West', symposium, *International Affairs* (Moscow), No. 9, September 1964, pp. 53–66; Thomas W. Wolfe, '*Soviet Commentary on the French "Force de Frappe"* ', RM 4359–ISA (Santa Monica, Calif., RAND Corp., January 1965). In June 1963 Krushchev told Harold Wilson and Patrick Gordon Walker, during their visit to Moscow, that the British manned bombers had no military significance since they had little prospect of getting through Soviet anti-aircraft defences, *The New York Times*, 11 June 1963.

[2] The intangible connection between Britain's thermonuclear bomb and the second Eliza- bethan age is discussed in Leon Epstein, 'Britain and the H-bomb, 1955–1958', *The Review of Politics*, Vol. XXI (August 1959), pp. 518–19.

in Italy).[1] Westminster politicians and Whitehall officials through their personal and official contacts with their American counterparts may well have realized that it was not to the nuclear force that Britain's influence in Washington could be attributed. Yet whatever real value the Americans put on her strategic nuclear 'contribution', the British government steadfastly insisted on the continuation of the 'independent deterrent' in order to enhance British influence. It was thought that the nuclear role helped Britain influence the evolution of American strategy, and thus the Western alliance's strategy, in a way which was not available to those NATO nations not possessing a nuclear arm. The willingness of the United States to give assistance on Blue Streak and make available Skybolt was interpreted as an expression of American confidence and respect. Not untypical was the statement of Minister of Defence Harold Watkinson in the debate on the 1961 White Paper that proposals to cast away the nuclear force were 'unrealistic' for to do so would merely weaken Britain's influence with the two Superpowers.[2] The Conservative party's political centre issued a pamphlet in 1959 written by Timothy Raison, a young, progressive Tory, which was a forceful defence of Britain's possession of the 'independent deterrent'. In a characteristic expression of Tory opinion Raison wrote:

We are still a major—though not a maximum—power with certain global responsibilities and sufficient strength both to strengthen and to influence the Western alliance. It is not being jingoistic to say that we often tend to underestimate our potential influence. . . . To some extent our contribution to the deterrent is a moral contribution. How would America react now if we renounced the deterrent? Would we not again hear the charge: 'Britain stinks of defeat'?[3]

As the disarmament negotiations in Geneva came to the fore at the turn of the decade the Government put forward an additional justification for the nuclear force. The 1961 Defence White Paper said that the nuclear contribution substantially increased British influence in negotiations for a nuclear test agreement and for disarmament.[4] Julian Amery, then Secretary of State for Air, told the Commons that he could say 'without hesitation' that the possession of the deterrent had been 'a strength to the Government' in international negotiations particularly over disarmament and other nuclear matters.[5]

[1] Alastair Buchan and Philip Windsor, *Arms and Stability in Europe: A British-French-German Enquiry* (London, Chatto and Windus, 1963), p. 184.

[2] 635 H.C. Deb. col. 1202 (27 February 1961).

[3] Timothy Raison, *The Missile Years*, Conservative Party Centre pamphlet No. 203, June 1959, pp. 11–12.

[4] *Report on Defence: 1961*, Cmnd. 1288, p. 5.

[5] 635 H.C. Deb. col. 1428 (28 February 1961).

But it was the idea that Britain might want to act independently of the United States that underlay the striving for 'influence'. Should a British government by an act of self-negation voluntarily make its national security more dependent on the United States than it need be? What guarantee was there that the American political system would always produce a President who placed a high priority on Britain's interests? What guarantee was there that a future United States Congress might not take a different view of nuclear co-operation with Britain, and restrict the supply of missile delivery systems? In a television interview, Macmillan connected the concepts of independence, influence, and Great Power status in justifying the nuclear force:

The independent contribution . . . gives us a better position in the world, it gives us a better position with respect to the United States. It puts us where we ought to be, in the position of a Great Power. The fact that we have it makes the United States pay a greater regard to our point of view, and that is of great importance.[1]

A nuclear force under British control provided a certain sense of assurance—even if strategic analysts could prove 'rationally' that this assurance did not have a valid foundation. Since Suez and Sputnik the Government had been haunted by a fear of American neutralism. The nuclear force was an expression of Britain's freedom of action—and of her sovereignty.

The Labour party supported the nuclear force until its official position changed in 1960, following the cancellation of Blue Streak. A growing body of dissent within Labour's adherents became increasingly vocal in the late 1950s, giving Duncan Sandys delight in watching the 'fission-fusion-fission' of honourable members opposite.[2] But the majority of the opposition within the rank and file came from unilateralists who starting in 1957 coalesced in the Committee for Nuclear Disarmament (C.N.D.), an organization which was essentially an extra-parliamentary movement and which did not have many members within the Commons. Among the Labour parliamentarians who did oppose the nuclear force, the non-pacifists such as Richard Crossman and George Wigg were in a distinct minority. In giving their reasons for retaining the nuclear force, Labour's front-bench spokesmen cited strategic and political justifications identical to those of the Government.

Given the views expressed by Labour leaders in 1960 to 1964 in opposition to the force, their statements of the previous years are of some interest. We have already noted Labour's support of the evolution of the

[1] *The Times*, 24 February 1958.   [2] 568 H.C. Deb. col. 1761 (16 April 1957).

concept of the independent deterrent during the Churchill and Eden governments following the Attlee government's manufacture of the British bomb. In 1958 Hugh Gaitskell approved of Britain's nuclear role because it brought 'influence and prestige and a measure of independence vis-à-vis the United States'.[1] The following year former Minister of Defence Emanuel Shinwell thought that Britain should not be dependent on the United States: 'We must stand on our own feet. After all we are a great nation and a great people and we still have great potentialities. We can afford to be independent.'[2] One of the most serious thinkers on defence problems in the party, John Strachey, was also one of the most vigorous supporters of the force. In a pamphlet issued by the party, Strachey rejected the new policy of the Liberal party that Britain should cease to manufacture its own nuclear weapons and rely on the American deterrent as a 'half way case', less logical and defensible than the pacifist case. According to Strachey, 'It would be really a nauseating piece of hypocrisy to protest that we were too holy to possess H-bombs ourselves, while at the same time saying under our breath that anyhow we didn't need them because the American H-bomb would always protect us.' He then went on:

To put the matter bluntly, surely we want a future British Labour government to be able in case of dire necessity to refuse to follow America in some policy of which we deeply disapproved and regarded as dangerous to peace . . . can we be sure that some future American government may not embark on some rash policy such as General MacArthur used to advocate in the Far East, for example, of which Labour utterly disapproves? In this situation we must retain the ability to take a different course, even though doing so might deeply alienate America and drive her towards isolationism. How can it possibly be maintained that a Labour Government's ability to do that would not have been greatly impaired if by depriving ourselves of defences, including nuclear weapons of our own, we had made ourselves wholly dependent on American protection?[3]

In evaluating such statements, one must bear in mind that Strachey and his colleagues were fighting a rearguard action against the unilateralists. They may therefore have been pushed into making cruder statements defending the Government's nuclear policy than they really desired. In other circumstances they may have preferred to develop a more sophisticated, complex, and non-unilateralist dissent.

As it was, the Labour leadership felt itself compelled to take a step

---

[1] 582 H.C. Deb. col. 1241 (19 February 1958).
[2] 600 H.C. Deb. col. 1335 (26 February 1959).
[3] John Strachey, *Scrap All the H Bombs* (London, Transport House, 1958), pp. 14–15, 18. By 1962 Strachey was arguing that Britain should not retain the nuclear force unless there was a world-wide proliferation of nuclear arms. See *On the Prevention of War*, p. 204.

towards advocating the renunciation of British nuclear weapons and did
so in its proposal for a 'Non-Nuclear Club'. Shortly after the National
Union of General Municipal Workers, normally one of the most docile
members of the Trades Union Congress, adopted a unilateralist position
and before the General Election of October 1959 the party made known
its proposal for preventing the proliferation of nuclear weapons in its
statement, *The Next Step*. Noting that Britain had a special responsibility
as the third nuclear power and that it was in a unique position to persuade
nations not yet in possession of nuclear weapons to desist from acquiring
them, Labour proposed that every nation with the exception of the United
States and the Soviet Union sign an agreement, preferably under the auspices of the United Nations, pledging itself not to test, manufacture, or
possess nuclear weapons. This agreement would be subject to full and
effective international controls. If such an agreement could be negotiated,
Britain would not only have to stop the manufacture of nuclear weapons
but would also have to give up those in her possession.[1]

Undoubtedly the 'Non-Nuclear Club' proposal was an attempt to avoid
the split in the party which ultimately came the following year, by side-
stepping the demands of the party's left wing for unilateral disarmament.[2]
But it also reflected a genuine concern among non-pacifist members of
the party regarding the dangers of proliferation, a concern less evident
in the Conservative party. The proposal also marked the first edging off
by the Labour front bench from its support of the British nuclear force.
Although the proposal came too late—on the eve of the first French atomic
test and after the Chinese had made known their nuclear plans—and was
not accepted by the Conservative government, it did offer terms under
which a Labour government would have the nation renounce nuclear
weapons. Despite the 'Non-Nuclear Club' proposal, defence and the British
bomb were ignored as political issues by the electorate in the 1959 General
Election, which the Tories won comfortably.[3]

By the spring of 1960 there was evidence of disaffection within the
Labour leadership with the independent nuclear force, although most of
its efforts and thoughts were turned towards holding back the tide of

[1] *Disarmament and Nuclear War: The Next Step*, Declaration by the Labour party and the
Trades Union Congress, Transport House, 24 June 1959.

[2] For discussion of the relationship between internal Labour politics and the Non-Nuclear
Club proposal, see 'A Non-Nuclear Club', *The Economist*, 27 June 1959; *Sunday Times*, 28 June
1959; 'Mr Gaitskell Does it Again', *Daily Telegraph*, 25 June 1959; P. M. S. Blackett approved
of the proposal, which he termed a plan for a 'Great Power Safety Catch Club', 'Thoughts
on British Defence Policy', *New Statesman*, 5 December 1959.

[3] David E. Butler and Richard Rose, *The British General Election of 1959* (London, Macmillan,
1960), pp. 50, 65, 72. Only the Liberal Party Manifesto said Britain should stop manufacturing
nuclear weapons. The defence correspondent of *The Times* saw 'no practical differences between
Conservative and Labour policy on the possession of the independent deterrent,' see 'Defence
and the Bomb', 24 September 1959.

unilateralism within the party which the 'Non-Nuclear Club' proposal had failed to appease. In that year's defence debate, Hugh Gaitskell weighed the advantages and the disadvantages of the 'independent deterrent' about equally, noting that this was a question which needed careful re-examination from time to time. He conceded that there was a powerful case against the British force on the basis of the costs of its future maintenance, the money it took away from conventional arms, and its contribution by example to the proliferation of nuclear weapons capabilities. Gaitskell nevertheless felt it was justifiable in order to avoid excessive dependence on the United States, in part because of doubts regarding America's willingness to engage in nuclear retaliation on Britain's behalf, given her own vulnerability, and in part in order to retain maximum influence in political discussions with the United States so that decisions were not forced on Britain against her will.[1]

In pursuing his course Gaitskell was certainly influenced by the knowledge that, according to the public opinion polls, the British people did not wish to see the nuclear effort summarily abandoned. The Gallup poll[2] asked the following question at intervals between April 1958 and April 1962:

'Would you approve or disapprove if Britain gave up her H-bombs even if other countries did not do so?'

Percentage	April 1958	Sept. 1958	March 1959	Sept. 1961	Dec. 1961	April 1962
Approve	25	30	30	21	31	22
Disapprove	61	57	50	62	55	64
Don't Know	14	13	20	17	14	14

Another set of more sophisticated answers suggested that there could be more support for renouncing the independent British force if it were to become part of a NATO nuclear capability (see table overleaf).

What is remarkable is the steadfastness of public support, if the polls be accurate, for the Conservative government's nuclear programme. The nation did not seek to escape from nuclear devastation by adopting a neutralist policy. Thus the Committee for Nuclear Disarmament, for all its vociferousness, did not command much support in the electorate. Labour's proposal for a non-nuclear club also received an unenthusiastic response, according to the polls. And when the Labour party did alter its policy in 1960 after the Blue Streak cancellation in favour of not

[1] 618 H.C. Deb. col. 1135–9, 1 March 1960).
[2] Data from the files of the British Institute of Public Opinion.

continuing the nuclear force beyond the life of the V-bombers, it failed
to carry along with it a noticeable portion of public opinion.

'What policy should Britain follow about nuclear weapons?'

Percentage	March 1960	June 1960	Oct. 1960	March 1961	June 1961	Aug. 1962
Give up nuclear weapons entirely	26	27	21	22	20	23
Pool all nuclear weapons with other countries and rely mainly on American production	19	34	32	29	30	25
Continue to make own nuclear weapons	31	28	37	41	35	37
Don't know	24	11	10	8	15	15

3. The Question of Independent Possession— the Case Against Retention

We now turn to the arguments against the retention of the British nuclear
force articulated by the doubters and dissenters, a heterogeneous group
which included much of the national press, academic analysts and other
private commentators, some Army and Navy officers, prominent backbenchers of both major parties, the Liberal party after 1957, and the
Labour party starting in 1960. The reasons for their opposition to the
Government's 'independent deterrent' policy included its lack of credibility, its costs, the simultaneous neglect of conventional capabilities
which some thought was a consequence of too great an emphasis on
nuclear arms, the unnecessary duplication of the American deterrent and
the ensuing conflict with American defence policy, doubt that the nuclear
force brought influence and prestige, and the incentive which Britain
was thought to be giving to the proliferation of nuclear weapons.

A. The Lack of Credibility

Deterrence of a large nuclear power by a smaller nuclear power is complicated because of the inherent asymmetry involved. It was virtually not
possible for a country with a nuclear force the size of Britain's to destroy
the whole of Russia's retaliatory power in a first-strike surprise attack,
or to defend itself successfully against the Soviet missiles and planes

which survived its attack. Therefore, the purpose of the British nuclear force was to threaten the destruction of some Soviet cities in retaliation against a Soviet first-strike or other aggression. The questionable credibility of such a strategic doctrine has been discussed in the first section of this chapter. Would a responsible and rational British government launch a strike against Moscow or Leningrad in retaliation for a massive conventional aggression in Western Europe, or in retaliation against a 'limited' nuclear attack on Britain—say, a strike on Southampton or an attack on R.A.F. bases in Britain? And would it do so knowing that the likely Soviet response would be fifteen thermonuclear bombs covering the British Isles? Probably not. As one commentator in the national debate remarked: 'There may be historical instances of nations committing suicide through lack of foresight or excessive trust or laziness or degeneration, but none springs to mind of national suicide as a result of a deliberate and considered judgement.'[1]

The most likely contingency for a Soviet nuclear attack on Britain would be a counter-force strike, with the purpose of neutralizing the V-bomber force at the opening stage of a large Soviet-American nuclear exchange. A British second-strike, counter-city nuclear force in order to be credible would have to meet the dual criteria of having the defensive capacity of withstanding an enemy counter-force strike and then having the offensive capability of piercing Soviet air defences to reach its targets. Critics of the V-bomber force as a nuclear *deterrent* doubted its ability to meet these two criteria.

Many believed that the British Isles were too vulnerable to act as a springboard for a nuclear deterrent, in part because their relative closeness to the Soviet Union reduced the warning time to a negligible amount. As long as the Soviet threat rested on manned bombers there was a reasonable chance that all the V-bombers would have time to get off the ground, however elaborate the Soviet attempt to achieve surprise attack. Once, however, that the Soviet threat came to rest principally on missiles, the vulnerability of the V-bombers, while on their ground bases, became acute. If a Soviet attack was preceded by a period of international tension, there would be time for the V-bombers to be widely dispersed to R.A.F. and civilian airfields in Britain and overseas. In case of a sudden surprise attack by Soviet intermediate range missiles launched from Western U.S.S.R., however, it was generally conceded that not more than four minutes' warning would be provided by the early warning system. Bomber Command was dependent upon information from the United States ballistic missile early warning system until the completion of the joint U.S.A.F.-R.A.F. station at Fylingdales in 1963.

[1] 'Mystique of Our Deterrent', by 'Nucleus', *Observer*, 7 December 1958.

The R.A.F. worked hard over the years to decrease the vulnerability of its nuclear bombers to on-site destruction. The most desirable antidote was to maintain a permanent airborne alert, but this was considered to be intolerably expensive. Furthermore, airborne alerts 'temporarily' put into effect at moments of less than extreme political crisis had the disadvantage of possibly becoming unduly provocative. One measure taken was the preparation of a pattern of dispersal, to be put into effect during a period of tension, of the V-bomber force (which at a maximum totalled 180 aircraft) to 100 British airfields plus a number overseas. In addition, V-bombers were stationed on Cyprus and some were reported to be stationed as far as Aden and Singapore. The dispersal pattern called for a maximum of four bombers on a runway, this being the number that could be airborne and at a safe distance within four minutes of warning time.[1] The bombers would stand on their runways ready to climb to safety on receiving radar warning of enemy missiles. Other measures included quick aircraft scramble techniques which were achieved with the use of powder cartridges to start all four engines simultaneously, together with a high level of training of the crews. In 1962 the Secretary of State for Air claimed that Bomber Command's state of readiness was such that its average reaction time from the time of receiving warning of oncoming missiles was two minutes.[2] Presumably in later years the R.A.F. was tied into the U.S.A.F. Midas orbital satellite early warning system. It remained, however, a matter of contention whether in fact the V-bombers could get off in time to escape destruction by a surprise Soviet missile attack.

Vulnerability at the take-off stage was one side of the problem; quite another was the ability of the V-bombers to get through Soviet air defences to their targets. A nuclear force must have the capability of inflicting 'unacceptable damage' on a potential aggressor in order to be a credible deterrent. It had been assumed that the attrition rate of the V-bombers due to sophisticated Soviet air defences would be high—a possible loss of 70–90 per cent of the attacking force was conceded. Because of the traditional emphasis placed in Soviet military doctrine on the defence, Soviet anti-aircraft defences were generally quite advanced and sophisticated. Supersonic fighter interceptors, surface-to-air anti-aircraft missiles, and an extensive radar system made possible several 'area defence' perimeters; and around key objectives 'point defence'

[1] Neville Brown pointed out that even this limited time span would not be sufficient if the Soviets produced and targeted enough missiles to bracket each airfield with a dispersed group of three or four airbursting missiles. In his estimation the only remedy for such a threat was a continuous airborne alert. See his 'Britain's Strategic Weapons: 1. Manned Bombers', *The World Today*, Vol. XX (July 1964), p. 296.

[2] 655 H.C. Deb. col. 908–11 (12 March 1962).

complexes were set up. The Government steadfastly maintained that, in the words of the 1961 Defence White Paper, 'The force has the capacity to penetrate to its assigned targets.'[1] Although critics doubted this assertion, they were unable to disprove it.[2] An independent action by Britain, not in conjunction with SAC, was all the more difficult since Soviet defences could be concentrated on a relatively small number of intruding aircraft.

In order to maximize the chances of delivering its bomb load, the R.A.F. made a number of modifications to the V-bombers. Chief among these was the Blue Steel 'stand off' bomb, a missile attached to the bomber which could be fired to the ground target from the stratosphere while the aircraft was 200 miles from the target. Work on Blue Steel Mark I began in 1955 but it did not become operational until 1962 when it was fitted on Mark II Victors and Vulcans. This second series of V-bombers had a shorter take-off time, longer range, and greater height capability than the first. Some experts believed, however, that Blue Steel was as vulnerable as its parent bomber because of its limited range and because of its inability to conduct sophisticated electronic warfare by taking spontaneous evasive action in response to unexpected threats. Awareness that these objections would hold good for a proposed Mark II Blue Steel missile influenced the decision in 1960 of Minister of Defence Watkinson not to proceed with it.[3] Another step taken to achieve penetration of heavily defended air space was the development of electronic countermeasures to blind or confuse Soviet radar. A variety of techniques, such as infra-red deception against heat-homing missiles and radar jamming devices were designed to reduce bomber attrition to an acceptable minimum. In 1964 the V-bombers were converted into a low flying role in order to limit their visibility on Soviet radar screens. This came about as a concession to the suspicion that the West was losing its superiority over the Soviet Union in the field of high altitude military electronics. Although antidotes to this tactic were available in the form of close-range ground-to-air missiles and long-range advanced interceptors patrolling high aloft, the R.A.F. claimed that the life of the V-bombers had been extended to 1972.[4]

It is interesting to note that the expected life span of the V-bombers was extended far beyond that originally forecast. When in 1957 it was

[1] *Report on Defence: 1961,* Cmnd. 1288, p. 6.

[2] The U-2 incident of 1960 was cited as evidence that the Soviet Union could probably shoot down a high-flying (50,000 feet) V-bomber.

[3] Neville Brown, *Nuclear War: The Impending Strategic Deadlock* (London, Praeger, 1964), p. 37.

[4] *The Times,* 5 February 1964. See also Brown, 'Britain's Strategic Weapons: 1. Manned Bombers', pp. 295–6; Divine, *The Broken Wing: A Study in the British Exercise of Air Power,* p. 251.

decided to cancel a supersonic manned bomber, the AVRO 730, this was done on the expectation that the manned bomber had no future. Britain's deterrent role was to be entrusted to the Blue Streak ballistic missile. Following the cancellation of Blue Streak in 1960 it was said that without the acquisition of the air-launched Skybolt ballistic missile to be placed on bombers, the V-bomber force would be obsolete by 1965. When the Nassau Conference replaced Skybolt with Polaris, government statements extended the life of the bombers still further. The announcement of the intended conversion of the V-bombers to a 'tree-top level' attack plane came in the midst of the extended election campaign of 1964 in which the independent nuclear deterrent was a major issue. At the time it was suspected that faced with a prospective gap in the 'deterrent' between the end of the effectiveness of the V-bombers and the introduction of British Polaris submarines, the Conservative government was engaging in a piece of politically motivated aeronautical salesmanship.[1]

It does appear, however, that the obsolescence of the V-bombers came about more slowly than had been first expected. Part of the credit must be given to Bomber Command's ingenuity and its determination to stay in the air. Equally significant, the Soviet Union in the mid-1960s did not modernize its anti-aircraft defences as rapidly as was expected by Western intelligence specialists. Perhaps because of the attention given to anti-missile defence systems, the Soviets did not develop advanced manned interceptors as quickly or in as large numbers as expected, nor did they widely deploy the best possible surface-to-air missiles. Furthermore, metal fatigue in the V-bombers set in more slowly than expected, although in early 1965 the Valiants had to be taken out of service because of this. By 1967 there were approximately 80 Mark II Vulcans and Victors in operation, over half of which carried Blue Steel missiles. The following year the Victor squadrons were disbanded and the remaining Vulcans did not lose their strategic nuclear role until 1969, after the third Polaris submarine came into service.

B. Bayonets versus Bombs

One of the principal objections to the strategic force was that the heavy expenditures on nuclear weapons and their delivery systems distorted

[1] 'If the V-bomber force is to provide an effective nuclear striking force against the Soviet Union in the 1970s as is now claimed, either the potential development of Russian aircraft defence has been grossly overestimated in the past, or something quite remarkable has happened to the V-bomber. In any case, one of the major assumptions of British defence policy appears to have been changed virtually overnight . . . suspicion will persist that the latest movement in the manned bomber game has more political than military significance.' *The Times* leader, 10 February 1964. See also, David Divine, 'The "New" V-bomber Fallacy . . . Could They Really Get Through?' *Sunday Times*, 9 February 1964; Divine, 'Shooting Down the V-bombers', *Sunday Times*, 16 February 1964.

the entire British defence programme. The deterioration of conventional war capabilities—the reduction in size of the armed forces and the failure to modernize equipment—was attributed to the increased reliance on nuclear deterrence. British security policy was entangled in a cycle caused by the interplay of manpower and technology. In the early 1950s the Churchill government, in the belief that the West should not compete with the Soviet bloc in military manpower, thought that compensation could be found in atomic arms. From this theorizing grew the doctrine of nuclear deterrence. The subsequent large investment in atomic explosives and their delivery system created pressures further to reduce spending on non-nuclear forces, as was determined in the Defence White Paper of 1957. But as the Soviet Union and the United States approached a period of mutual deterrence at the end of the decade, the most likely engagement for British forces was seen to be in limited wars. For these, it was argued, Britain was insufficiently prepared unless she increased her conventional capabilities.

The Government's dilemma was twofold. First, the cost of maintaining a credible nuclear force was growing at the same time that the cost of adequately equipping conventionally armed forces was also rising. When the V-bomber force was being planned and Blue Streak was first on the drawing boards no one foresaw that the bombers would be required to move from dispersed bases on a four minute alert. Nor was it foreseen that because of the unexpected accuracy of ballistic missiles, British missiles would be vulnerable unless they were 'hardened'. Similarly, the requirements of modern conventional warfare, in particular the need for rapid transportation and communication, necessitated new and expensive equipment. Though the costly technological character of modern conflict indicated that, barring effective arms control or disarmament, spending on defence ought to be measurably increased, the British government for internal political and economic reasons was unlikely to do so at a time when the nation was belatedly coming out of a long period of austerity. Thus one dilemma was how to increase certain items in the defence budget at the expense of others without ruining the whole existing pattern.

Second, the Macmillan government had committed itself to the end of national service, not taking into complete account the relevance of conventional forces in the approaching era of mutual deterrence in the Soviet-American nuclear balance. Limited war capabilities were seen as increasingly important not only in the NATO area but in Africa, where the transition to independence was unloosing a variety of destabilizing pressures in a number of states where the British had historical interests and commitments, as well as in the Far East, where Indonesia was to wage war against the British-supported Malaysian Federation. Even though semi-unexpected technological and political developments had eroded the Government's original justification for ending conscription, once the step had been taken it seemed politically unfeasible to undo it. Adequate conventional forces for limited war were becoming more crucial to British defence policy just as they were becoming more difficult to come by.

When in 1957 Sandys had announced the planned reduction of the military services by over 300,000 to a new manpower total of 375,000 by the end of 1962, the time when the last conscripted soldier was to be discharged, the size of the revised Army was set at 165,000. Doubts immediately set in as to whether a 165,000 man army was sufficient to give British defence planners the flexibility they needed.[1] These doubts were reinforced as it came to be believed that the 165,000 figure represented not a careful matching of forces with commitments but an actuarial estimate of the highest possible voluntary recruitment following the end of conscription. Under Anthony Head, Eden's Minister of Defence and Secretary of State for War from 1951 to 1956, a committee of experts chaired by General Sir Richard Hull had examined the Army's manpower requirements and recommended 200,000 as the minimum necessary. This had put Head in conflict with the Chancellor of the Exchequer, Harold Macmillan, who wanted further reductions for fiscal and economic reasons. The issue was resolved when Macmillan became Prime Minister and Head resigned, unwilling to reduce the Army beyond the advice of the Hull committee. Sandys, his successor, asked the Chiefs of Staff for their *military* appraisal of how they would deploy a hypothetical 165,000 and once this was given, declared it to be a *political* decision by the cabinet that such a deployment would be sufficient.[2] Thus the minimum Army which was deemed necessary at a time when the oncoming nuclear stalemate was enhancing rather than diminishing the importance of conventional forces was thought to be set by a hopeful estimate of what the services could recruit without resorting to conscription, rather than by the real need.

The Government claimed that the development of the British nuclear capability made possible the reduction in the armed forces. Accordingly British forces in Korea, Libya, and other overseas garrisons were reduced but the most significant cutback was in the British Army of the Rhine. Eden had publicly undertaken to maintain four divisions totalling 75,000 men on the continent at the time the Paris Agreements of 1954 were signed, in a step which was regarded as the price for obtaining French consent to German rearmament. The 1957 plan for the Army's deployment called for a reduction of the BAOR to 45,000 and a cut in half of

---

[1] See 'The Army We Need', *Observer*, 21 April 1957.

[2] For an unusually perceptive analysis of the formulation of defence policy under Duncan Sandys, with special attention to the bargaining process between the military services and the civilian executives, see Laurence Martin's 'The Market for Strategic Ideas in Britain: The "Sandys" Era', *American Political Science Review*, Vol. LXI, No. 1, January 1962, pp. 23–41.

the R.A.F.'s Second Tactical Air Force in Germany, although after strong protests from the United States and Germany the British agreed in 1958 to maintain the BAOR at approximately 55,000 men. To compensate for these reductions it was announced that tactical nuclear weapons were to be introduced into the BAOR and that the air force units in Germany were to be provided with atomic bombs.[1] The nuclearization of the BAOR, along with its reorganization into Brigade Groups, was said to make possible a reduction in its size without a diminution in its effectiveness.

In the following years a deep uneasiness grew about the feasibility of meeting the nation's worldwide commitments with an army of 165,000. There was also doubt about the sufficiency of 55,000 men as Britain's military representation on the continent, and concerning the adequacy of the equipment of the armed forces. A number of instances in which the armed forces were operationally involved—Jordan in 1958, Kuwait in 1961, and the Berlin crisis of August 1961—drew attention to shortages in manpower and arms. The Berlin crisis revealed that in order to reinforce the BAOR, which was in fact below the rock-bottom 55,000 level,[2] the Government was forced to seek legislation extending the duty of the remaining national service conscripts by six months and permitting the recall of those recently discharged. Much attention was given to recruitment statistics as it was questionable that the goal of 165,000 volunteers could be reached before the last conscript returned to civilian life.[3]

But even an Army of 165,000 was thought to be inadequate and too inflexible to provide for both a strong BAOR and the means to deal with 'brushfire' activities from Britain's overseas bases. Some alleged that Britain could not have met the Kuwait crisis and the Berlin crisis at the same time. In addition, much of the equipment of the armed forces was of World War II or Korean War vintage. The Navy was depleted in number of ships and especially deficient in anti-submarine warfare, the Air Force needed long-range transport aircraft to provide the necessary mobility for limited war, and the Rhine Army did not have modern equipment to match that of Soviet ground forces in Eastern Europe. Indeed, the end of 1962 was set as a goal for replacing the last of the World War II stock in the BAOR. A report of Brigadier Fernyhough, the Director of Munitions and Stores in the War Office, described the British Army as being, in relation to its

[1] *Defence: Outline of Future Policy, 1957*, Cmnd. 124.

[2] The BAOR force level always seemed to be below the 'minimum' of 55,000 by one to five thousand for 'temporary' reasons when visited by members of Parliament and defence correspondents. This led *The Economist* to comment that 'men still insist on going sick or on leave even when Mr. George Brown has arranged a visit'. In 'Ever Ready', 4 November 1961.

[3] This was a matter of considerable speculation and political debate for a number of years. The Air Force and the Navy were able to fill their quotas without great difficulty; the Army reached its goal five months before the deadline of January 1963 by using imaginative recruiting techniques and with indirect assistance from high unemployment pockets in Scotland.

small size and large commitments, 'one of the worst equipped in the world'.[1]

The dependence of BAOR strategy upon a conflict escalating into a nuclear war was particularly troublesome. The use of tactical nuclear weapons was repeatedly cited by the Government as compensating for shortages of manpower in British units in Germany. Those who were concerned with guaranteeing British independence of action could take alarm from the fact that the atomic warheads remained under American control. Other critics, less chauvinistically inclined, were concerned by the inability of the Rhine Army to defend itself even for a relatively short time without recourse to nuclear weapons. In the fall of 1961 Exercise Spearhead, the largest BAOR manœuvres since its inception, took place. Observers of the manœuvres noted that the BAOR was trained to use atomic weapons from the onset, despite Whitehall's public assurances about the BAOR's capability to limit itself initially to conventional weapons.[2]

With the Kennedy administration's promotion of a strategy for a conventional defence of Western Europe the debate over the size and strategy of the BAOR received renewed impetus. Many in Britain, especially commentators outside the Government, thought that British policy should be in accordance with the fresh thinking in the United States. The Macmillan government made an effort to carry its share with the limited reinforcement of the BAOR during the Berlin crisis of 1961. But in truth it was never persuaded, despite determined American salesmanship, of the practicality or desirability of a conventional response to a Soviet aggression. British planners noted that the concept of 'forcing a pause' first assumed that the Russians did not begin with nuclear weapons, an uncertain assumption in their view. They were slow to accept the American intelligence community's 'reappraisal' of the Communist bloc's armed manpower which lowered the number of effective enemy forces so as to make a conventional confrontation in Europe more 'equal'. Finally, they contended that the Russians would simply interpret their forced pause as a defeat and would quickly resort to nuclear weapons. This would leave NATO forces greatly disadvantaged since in a conventional war deployment they would be highly vulnerable to tactical nuclear attack.[3]

---

[1] Cited in 627 H.C. Deb. col. 598 (20 July 1960); for further discussion of shortages of manpower and material, see Richard Goold-Adams, 'Conventional Forces and British Defence Policy', *Political Quarterly*, Vol. XXXI, No. 1, January–March 1960, pp. 26–35.

[2] See *The Times*, 17 October 1961.

[3] See 'Arms and Men', *The Economist*, 28 October 1961. The 1962 Defence White Paper openly acknowledged that the Government did not believe that the defence of Europe 'could be decided by long drawn out fighting limited to conventional forces'. *Statement on Defence, 1962: The Next Five Years*, Cmnd. 1639.

Furthermore, the Conservative government thought that a strong build-up of conventional forces might be provocative and invite attack.

The Labour front bench took the position that the Government's allocation of expenditures between nuclear and conventional forces was not the right one, that Britain should make a greater contribution to the conventional armament of NATO by not 'starving' the BAOR, that the nuclear threshold should be raised, and that Britain should accept the concept of the 'pause' rather than being dependent on the early use of tactical weapons. But it failed to face up to the logic of its advice by calling for the reinstatement of national service. Instead, Labour leaders suggested that some of the anachronistic 'imperial garrisons' for a 'non-existent empire' be liquidated to be replaced by a mobile strategic reserve kept at a high state of readiness in Britain or Germany. They would give priority to British forces on the continent by a major reduction in overseas commitments in the Far East, Africa, and the Middle East. This did not satisfy two Labourites, Richard Crossman and George Wigg, who consistently argued that the ending of conscription was an irresponsible mistake and that in order to increase conventional forces and deflate Britain's reliance on nuclear weapons there should be a return to some form of conscription.[1] Their tangent of criticism was separate from that of the unilateralists who deplored British nuclear weapons still more ardently but were unwilling to have conscription reinstated.[2]

In a sense the predicament of the armed forces was more painful to the Government's own backbenchers than to the Labour opposition. There has always been a greater rapport between Conservatives and the professional officers of the military services because of their more common social and educational backgrounds and the elite nature of the regimental career. Furthermore, the Tories were by temperament closer to Britain's imperial role and her past tradition of colonial administration. So it was with grave disquiet that many Conservatives watched their own Government sharply reduce Britain's ability to act overseas. Starting in 1958 a number of prominent Tory backbenchers voiced their alarm over the thinness of Britain's armed forces and called for an increase in expenditures on conventional forces at the expense of the strategic nuclear force. Much notice was taken when Anthony Head, eighteen months after his departure from the Ministry of Defence, told the Commons that in his opinion national service should not be abandoned.[3] A trickle grew into a stream in succeeding years as influential Conservatives such as Sir

[1] See their joint article, 'Defence After Blue Streak', *New Statesman*, 14 May 1960; and Crossman's article 'Facing Realities', *Guardian*, 23 February 1963.
[2] See 'Unilateral Inconsistencies', *The Economist*, 19 June 1960.
[3] 592 H.C. Deb. col. 986–94 (28 July 1958).

Fitzroy MacLean (former Under-Secretary of War), Sir Alexander Spearman, Nigel Birch (by then a former Secretary of State for Air), Aubrey Jones (former Minister of Supply), and Viscount Lambton sought a higher priority for conventional forces. Most of the back-bench critics felt that Britain should return to some form of conscription rather than abandoning Commonwealth responsibilities by reducing or withdrawing overseas garrisons in such places as Singapore, Hong Kong, Aden, and Kenya, or by defaulting on NATO commitments.

Some also reasoned that Britain's influence in the Western alliance would be proportionate to her capacity to supply what the alliance really needed and wanted, namely manpower rather than 'independent' British nuclear weapons. The nation should not devote her limited resources to the nuclear force if this hampered her raising an adequate number of armed soldiers. At a private meeting of the Conservative Party Defence Committee in the fall of 1961, a group of M.P.s argued that rather than diminishing Britain's influence abroad, or imperilling her security by cutting the coat to fit the cloth, the cabinet should increase the size of the cloth by resorting to national service even if this were unpopular with the electorate.[1] A Bow Group study observed that it seemed 'incredible that the Government should have decided to end conscription'.[2] By the time of the debate on the 1962 Defence White Paper a majority of the influential Tory backbenchers who concerned themselves with defence affairs, according to one of them, were firmly of the view that even if voluntary recruitment filled the Government's existing quota, this quota would not be sufficient to meet commitments adequately, and that in order to increase the size of the services the Government should revert to conscription.[3]

Within the military services the Sandys doctrine of primary reliance on the nuclear force led to Whitehall battles of a ferocity unknown since the Second World War. For with the drastic 1957 reductions the point had been reached where one military service in putting forth a programme which met what it thought were its minimum requirements was forced to call implicitly for reductions in the other services. Although the Chiefs of Staff all paid lip service to the doctrine of independent deterrence, only the R.A.F. was relatively content, while the other two services struggled to maintain their forces and missions and opposed the diversion of funds from the re-equipping of conventional forces. The period of Sandys' tenure was marked by service rivalries and appeals to parliamen-

[1] According to the political correspondent of the Conservative-inclined *Daily Telegraph*, in 'Mr. Watkinson under Fire', 3 November 1961.

[2] *Stability and Survival: A Bow Group Discussion about Defence Policy,* February 1961, p. 30.

[3] Anthony Kershaw, 'The Services from Parliament', *Brassey's Annual* (London, Clowes, 1962), p. 254.

tarians and the public far beyond the more characteristic British pattern of a rigorous but closed internal debate.[1]

With the nuclear force's fixed—and growing—claim on the defence budget, each of the services was dissatisfied with some aspect of the Sandys policy and attempted to reverse it. But in many hard fought sessions with a Minister of Defence known for his tenacity and doggedness the Chiefs of Staff were unable to sway him from a concept of national security conceived more on the basis of politics and economics than military strategy. So the services resorted to circumferential tactics by making known their grievances to friendly members of Parliament, the press, and the defence-oriented industries. The Admiralty sponsored the 'Fairlead' Conference at Greenwich during which, in the face of prospective cuts in the number of ships, it made its case to influential industrialists and 'opinion-makers' for a 'balanced' fleet; upon its prompting, Commonwealth countries reminded Prime Minister Macmillan of the importance they attached to the Royal Navy for their own defence; and naval officers outlined for defence correspondents of the London press the particulars of the Soviet submarine threat, stressing the importance of anti-submarine capabilities.[2] The Navy's interest in a nuclear role was essentially limited to the aircraft carrier based Buccaneer bomber. It was slow in developing interest in the Polaris submarine, fearing that it would divert funds from the traditional fleet.

The Army, which was in the process of losing the most, shot the most sensational cannonball at the cabinet's policy. In a widely publicized lecture at the Royal United Service Institution on 4 November 1959, General Sir John Cowley, on active duty as the Comptroller of Munitions, took aim at the entire concept of a British independent deterrent. *The Times* subsequently commented: 'Here at last was someone saying openly . . . what two of the services have been privately thinking for the last three years.'[3] Cowley's talk came very shortly after the departure of Sandys and before the new Minister, Harold Watkinson, was firmly in control. It had been circulated at the War Office where a large number of senior officers were known to agree with Cowley's well-reasoned criticisms. But serving officers in Britain do not normally make speeches which

[1] Interservice conflict and bargaining exists in Britain as in the United States. Although equally intense, it is usually carried on with greater discretion and less publicity. In addition to Martin's, op. cit., successful scholarly analysis of defence politics during the Sandys administration, a more general discussion of the defence bargaining process may be found in William P. Snyder, *The Politics of British Defence Policy, 1945–1962* (Columbus, Ohio State University Press, 1962), pp. 151–80.

[2] From the safe haven of a NATO command, Admiral Sir John Eccles fired a broadside against massive retaliation and reopened the case for 'broken-backed' warfare. See 'Seadog off the Leash', *The Economist*, 5 October 1957.

[3] Leader, 12 November 1959. For the published text of the lecture see 'Future Trends in Warfare', *Journal of the Royal United Service Institution*, Vol. LV, No. 617, February 1960, pp. 4–16.

contradict government policy and, as an embarrassed Watkinson assured the Commons, such an incident was not to be repeated.[1] Although the Army deplored its weakened condition, it was not eager to have national service brought back. The constant training of new recruits and the quick rotation of personnel from overseas bases made necessary by conscription decreased its efficiency and detracted from its aspirations for a highly trained professional corps.[2]

Even the Royal Air Force, whose strategic nuclear mission was so wholeheartedly backed by the Government and which was least disturbed by the 1957 reductions, lobbied openly for the expansion of its extra-nuclear role. It sponsored the 'Prospect Conference' for 300 participants in May 1958 at which its shopping list for fighters, helicopters, transport aircraft, and a replacement for the V-bombers was unfolded with, it should be noted, remarkably little attention given to the ballistic missile.[3] But the R.A.F. also upheld the emphasis on the nuclear deterrent as the only feasible security policy. After Labour took the position that the nuclear force should not be continued beyond the V-bombers, the R.A.F.'s supporters stepped into high gear and at times spoke as if Labour's suggestion was almost downright unpatriotic.[4] The R.A.F. clearly had a vested interest in the deterrent policy.

Part of the reason for the rise in temperature of military affairs was that the increase in emphasis on nuclear deterrence was made possible and accompanied by a growth in the powers of the civilian political leadership. The nuclear age has given a new relevance to a nation's declaratory defence policy, in contrast to its military tactics. This is not only because of the possible instantaneousness of annihilation. The cost and complexity of modern weapons systems has forced a greater rationalization of defence expenditures. In post-war Britain the political establishment seized the initiative from the military services at the time of the defence reappraisal following Suez. Prime Minister Macmillan gave Sandys, upon his appointment, a far broader authority than that of his predecessors.[5] The strait-jacket into which the services were forced to fit because of the 1957 reductions was tailored by the Prime Minister and his colleagues, as was

---

[1] Cowley's speech was so unusual that it gave rise to jocular speculation about a 'general's plot' against the official defence policy. See Cyril Falls, 'The Minister and the Soldier', *Illustrated London News*, 21 November 1959; 'The Case of General Cowley', *The Economist*, 14 November 1959.

[2] An impressive analysis of the Army's tasks and resources at this time is to be found in the Report of the Army League Study Group, *The British Army in the Nuclear Age* (London, 1959), Richard Goold-Adams (rapporteur).

[3] See 'The Air Force Shows Its Shopping List', *The Economist*, 10 May 1958; John R. Taylor, 'The RAF—Today and Tomorrow', *Air Power*, Vol. 5 (July 1958), pp. 283–91.

[4] See, for example, the Commons speech of Sir Arthur Vere Harvey, 655 H.C. Deb. col. 153–63 (5 March 1962).

[5] See Macmillan's statement, 563 H.C. Deb. col. 396 (24 January 1957).

the increased reliance on nuclear weapons. In the process the Ministry of Defence ceased to be a clearing house for the individual service interests, but became a centre for control and integration; the Minister of Defence became less of a co-ordinator and more of a director. This did not occur overnight and even in the late 1960s the civilian revolution had not come to the point reached in McNamara's Pentagon. But as Michael Howard has written, if any single year must be chosen as marking a transition in the United Kingdom from a defence organization based on co-ordination to one based on control that year would be 1957.[1] The following year the amplified powers of the Minister of Defence were confirmed in a formal reorganization of the defence machinery.[2] To some extent the friction generated in Whitehall by the Sandys policy was an unfortunate consequence of the abrasiveness of the Minister's manner.[3] But the existence of nuclear weapons increased the necessity of the military to submit to political instruction, and this in turn made it easier for the cabinet to base its defence policy on the nuclear force.[4]

Michael Howard has also suggested that the primary emphasis on the nuclear force ran counter to well-established military tradition. After reviewing campaigns fought by the British Army in the nineteenth century, he observed that the 'need to be able to fight limited wars in the furtherance of national policy has always been taken for granted in British planning . . . and the organization of our armed forces has been unique in that their function has never been primarily to engage in a desperate battle with an adversary of our own strength, but rather to meet an emergency in any corner of the globe.'[5] Many observers thought that the priorities of the Government's defence policy ought to be the reverse of what they were. Instead of having what they thought to be an independent deterrent policy with some conventional forces tacked on to it, they wanted a larger conventional war capacity with some nuclear capabilities.

[1] 'Organisation for Defence in the United Kingdom and the United States, 1954–1958', *Brassey's Annual* (London, Clowes 1959), p. 74.

[2] *Central Organization for Defence: 1958*, Cmnd. 476. For comment see Michael Howard, 'Central Defence Organization in Great Britain, 1959', *Political Quarterly*, Vol. XXXI, pp. 66–70; a further important reorganization of the defence establishment was undertaken in 1963, strengthening still more the authority of the Minister of Defence. See *Central Organization for Defence: 1963*, Cmnd. 2097.

[3] Leonard Beaton, then defence correspondent of the *Guardian*, characterized Sandys as 'something of a one-man OKW making the bulk of the important decisions affecting the armed forces' in 'Men and/or Missiles', *Crossbow*, Summer 1958.

[4] For a retired officer's acknowledgement of the increased importance of the political leader in the evolution of defence policy see Air Vice-Marshal Kingston-McCloughry, op. cit., pp. 101, 254. See also, Major-General B. T. Wilson, 'The Modern Relationship of Statesmen and Military Leaders', *Brassey's Annual* (London, Clowes, 1958), pp. 14–21. Max Beloff has stressed the key role of the Prime Minister himself, *New Dimensions in Foreign Policy* (London, Allen & Unwin, 1961), p. 184–5.

[5] 'Strategy in the Nuclear Age', *Journal of the Royal United Service Institution*, Vol. CII (November 1957), p. 477.

ONP

The Government maintained that the nuclear/conventional balance of the armed forces was the right one and to support its claim cited the cost of the nuclear force. Successive Defence White Papers and statements in the Commons set the expenditure on the strategic bomber force, its nuclear bombs, and on the related research and development (including Blue Streak before its cancellation) at 10% of defence expenditures. Related expenses for warning and control systems, and fighter defence air bases, were put at another 5–10%. A total of 15–20% of the defence budget for the nuclear force was not thought to be excessive. Critics were somewhat sceptical of this accounting but were hampered by the paucity of statistical data made available with the Government's official reports. It was doubtful, however, that scrapping the nuclear force would produce an immediate saving of £300 million a year (approximately 15% of the defence budget) to be used for conventional arms. Many of the expenses related to the nuclear force, such as radar nets and fighter defences, would have to be continued. Furthermore, the professional personnel of R.A.F.'s Bomber Command could not be converted into infantry battalions. Thus the manpower and material resources of the nuclear force were only marginally transferable to increasing the Army's conventional forces.

By 1962 a wide spectrum of opinion had come to the conclusion that some form of selective service was necessary if Britain was to fulfil its commitments and not be over-dependent on its nuclear force of doubtful credibility.[1] Some based their contention on the improbability of recruiting quotas being filled by voluntary means; others believed that an army of 165,000, or even 180,000 as the Government said could be achieved by the mid-1960s, was too small. In order to retain British influence in NATO at a time when West Germany was planning an army of twelve divisions, in order to give SHAPE the greater flexibility below the nuclear threshold which General Norstad and President Kennedy wanted it to have, and in order to maintain the British military presence outside Europe, an Army of 250,000 to 300,000 was needed. In Parliament the call for conscription came from both back benches, from such strange bedfellows as George Wigg and Nigel Birch. Neither the Government nor the opposition shadow cabinet, however, was willing to support a measure which it was thought would be politically extremely unpopular.

C. The Cost of Delivery Technology

For a nation a desirable deterrent must be credible to the enemy at a cost which is considered 'manageable' at home. As Britain prepared to make

[1] See, for example, *The Times* leader, 27 October 1961; 'Defence in the Next Five Years', *The Economist*, 2 December 1961; 'First Target', *The Economist*, 25 August 1962; 'Defence by Cowardice', *New Statesman*, 3 November 1961.

the transition in its nuclear force from bombers to missiles, the expense of the delivery system appeared about to rise sharply. The nuclear deterrence policy which had originally appeared attractive because of its relative cheapness now seemed to be becoming increasingly expensive as electronics became more sophisticated and costly, and as missiles had to be made invulnerable in order for the deterrent to be credible. As the defence estimates of each succeeding year showed, the weapons and manpower concept outlined in the 1957 White Paper was not succeeding in holding down defence expenditures.[1] There was little inclination on the part of political leaders to decrease the percentage of the Government's revenue spent on social and economic services in order to increase defence spending. On the contrary, the proportion allocated to defence was already relatively high. In 1962, of the fifteen members of NATO, Britain was third highest in percentage of Gross National Product spent on defence, being exceeded only by the United States and Portugal. Thus the question was raised whether Britain could afford to allocate sufficient funds for a credible, second-strike, missile-based, nuclear force.

The cancellation of Blue Streak in April 1960 was an important juncture in the evolution of the nuclear force for it was widely interpreted to indicate that Britain could not afford to continue an 'independent deterrent' of its own. It signalled a reversal in the Labour party's position and led to a new dependence on the United States for technological assistance in maintaining the nuclear force. Blue Streak was an intermediate range ballistic missile started in 1955. Following the decision in 1957 not to continue development of a supersonic manned bomber, Blue Streak was selected as the second generation delivery system for the nuclear force and was given the highest priority. It was liquid-fuelled and designed to be launched from underground sites, with a range in excess of 2,000 miles. The Macmillan government had expressed unbounded confidence in its successful development, despite a rising tempo of scepticism among defence commentators in the press and the Labour party. The Government took the position that the future of the 'independent deterrent' rested on Blue Streak.[2] Furthermore, Blue Streak was cited as an example of Britain's ability to stay in the forefront of technological research and development. Not until after its cancellation did it become publicly known that its rocket engine and inertial guidance system were based on the American made Atlas and were being manufactured in Britain under licence from American companies.

[1] See Table 2.
[2] The decision to proceed to an advanced stage of development of Blue Streak was announced on the eve of the Prime Minister's trip to Moscow in February 1959. A Ministry of Defence press briefing encouraged reports such as: 'The secret new strength at Macmillan's elbow. . . . The news is proof that when the British Prime Minister talks on matters of defence, he will be speaking from great potential strength.' *Daily Express*, 9 February 1959.

Blue Streak was cancelled (as a military missile, for it was later to be continued for space research as Britain's part of the European Launcher Development Organization) for two reasons, but only after London had been assured of the availability of Skybolt. The unexpected Soviet and American advances in the accuracy of their ballistic missiles created considerable doubt about the ability of the missile to remain invulnerable even when placed in a silo. Concern about a pre-emptive Soviet strike was heightened by the cumbersome nature of the liquid fuel missile, which took ten to fifteen minutes of preparation prior to launching. The second reason for the cancellation was its rapidly mounting cost history. When it was started Blue Streak was intended to be above ground, but as the Soviet Union put missile placements near its Western borders forcing Britain to undertake pioneering research in underground 'hardening', the costs rose to an unforeseen level. At the time of its cancellation, £65 million had been spent on Blue Streak and it was estimated that it would have cost between £500 and £600 million to complete the project. Blue Streak was overtaken by technology, especially by solid fuel rockets which were less vulnerable and expensive—as, it should be noted, were its American and Soviet counterparts.

The moral of Blue Streak, as it was widely drawn at the time, was that Britain could not afford to remain an independent nuclear power. The cancellation of the missile on which the hopes and expectations for the future of the British deterrent had been placed had a great impact in Parliament, the press, and on the public. The conclusion drawn was that Britain had overreached herself. The experience of Britain seemed to suggest that in the age of missiles no nation other than a superpower could afford to create and maintain an independent deterrent of its own.[1] Yet in announcing its intention to replace Blue Streak with Skybolt the Government insisted that this action would maintain the 'independent contribution' to the Western deterrent. Minister of Defence Watkinson emphasized that nothing had changed but the mode of delivery of the British warhead. But critics noted that Britain had become dependent on the United States for the supply of the delivery system. Whether or not the claim of 'independence' was fictitious depended upon whether one used *control* or *manufacture* as the criterion.[2]

[1] See 'The End of Blue Streak', *The Times*, 14 April 1960; 'What for?' *Observer*, 1 May 1960; Norman Gibbs, 'The Way Ahead for the Western World's Deterrent', *Fifteen Nations*, No. 15, October–November 1960, p. 24; *The New York Times*, 15 April 1960, predicted that France, like Britain, would also find the costs of a strategic delivery system beyond its means.

[2] Contrast Watkinson and the *Guardian*. The Minister: 'If the weapon is developed and we purchase it without strings, fit it with our own warhead, and carry it in our own aircraft, then it is an independent deterrent.' 625 H.C. Deb. col. 397 (22 June 1960). The newspaper: 'One cannot call oneself independent if the wherewithal for independence is supplied by someone else. If Britain is to depend on the U.S. for supplies of modern nuclear weapons she will not

Although outwardly the Macmillan government insisted that the cancellation of Blue Streak brought no change in its independent deterrent policy, the episode could not help but occasion fresh thought. According to Nora Beloff, a number of Conservative ministers developed doubts as to whether continuing a nuclear force was essential to British defence. Other cabinet members continued to believe that nuclear sovereignty was a necessity for political reasons—but the contrary view was 'no longer taboo'.[1] In the Commons such former Conservative ministers as Nigel Birch, Aubrey Jones, and Anthony Head made criticisms of the nuclear force more substantive and eloquent than those of the Labour front bench. Jones, for example, argued that the nation was witnessing the 'visible collapse' of the aspiration for nuclear independence which was embodied in the 1957 Defence White Paper. With the passing of Blue Streak, the former Minister of Supply observed, Britain ceased to be able to develop and manufacture a 'deterrent' weapons system. He was disturbed, he said, because he was not certain that this truth had as yet been recognized by the Government.[2] Former Minister of Defence Anthony Head could find no reason, based either on national security or on the enhancement of political influence, which justified the continuation of the great nuclear effort. He counselled the Government to make certain that it could afford nuclear weapons delivery systems in the future and to know why it wanted them.[3]

Following the cancellation of Blue Streak, Whitehall gave new attention to how defence expenditures could be restrained from spiralling upwards. One way was to increase interdependence in research and development, both in NATO and within the Commonwealth. The Defence White Papers of 1961 and 1962 spoke somewhat wistfully on this subject. Minister of Defence Watkinson announced a new five-year forward planning R & D programme designed to provide a method for an earlier selection of projects for advanced development and better procedures for monitoring the costs.[4] The provision of facilities at Holy Loch for a depot ship and a floating dock for Polaris submarines of the United States Navy, in implicit exchange for the Skybolt missile, was seen as one form of the desirable interdependence.

In addition, thought had to be given to the expense of the delivery system which was to replace Skybolt. The most attractive aspect of Skybolt

be an independent nuclear power—and no amount of rhetoric will convince anyone outside the backbenches of the Conservative party that she is.' In 'Shared Streaks', *Guardian*, 20 April 1960.

[1] 'Cabinet Doubts on Own Deterrent', *Observer*, 6 March 1960.
[2] 635 H.C. Deb. col. 1247–52 (27 February 1961).
[3] 622 H.C. Deb. col. 253–9 (27 April 1960).
[4] 635 H.C. Deb. col. 1215–16 (27 February 1961).

was its relative cheapness. Not only was it to be sold to Britain without R & D charges, but the air to surface missile was to be added to the existing V-bombers. On the other hand, the lifespan of Skybolt could be relatively short because of the expected obsolescence of bombers as nuclear delivery systems against modern air defences. Because of the vulnerability of the V-bombers knowledgeable observers of the British defence establishment had long been advocating the acquisition of Polaris rather than Skybolt. The Royal Navy, however, did not want Polaris and the Royal Air Force did not want to lose Skybolt, upon which the continuation of manned bombers depended. Both services, for parochial interests, wished the 'nuclear deterrent' to remain R.A.F. property.

In 1961 a committee of the Conservative Bow Group studied Britain's defence policy and concluded that the Skybolt contract should be cancelled, to be replaced by six Polaris submarines, which hopefully could be purchased from the United States.[1] Polaris would permit the nuclear force to be moved out to sea, away from the highly vulnerable British Isles, thereby making for a more credible, second-strike deterrent. But the Macmillan government gave no indication of any interest in leap-frogging Skybolt for a more advanced weapons system. The reason for this attitude could be found in the domestic political commitment made to Skybolt after the end of Blue Streak. It was also the consequence of the apathy of the military services, and of the fact that the price of six Polaris submarines was estimated at double the cost of equipping the bombers with Skybolt. Therefore, as Britain decided to seek entry into the Common Market, and as doubts over the availability of Skybolt deepened, cabinet-level attention was first given in 1962, as we shall see in the next chapter, to the possibilities of future collaboration with France on ballistic missiles.

In retrospect the failure of the Royal Navy to make a strong case to the cabinet for acquiring Polaris rather than Skybolt before, and at the time of, the Blue Streak cancellation, was an irresponsible mistake. The Admiralty had been watching the development of Polaris closely since 1956 and recognized that it was an ideal strategic system for Britain because it was not subject to surprise attack (as was any weapon located on British soil), because it permitted a delay in retaliatory action (and, therefore, gave time for verification of the source of an enemy attack and consultation with the United States), and because it moved the nuclear force away from the homeland. But the Navy chiefs were not enthusiastic about Polaris, being worried about its costs and the accompanying drainage of skilled technicians. The 'senior service' was more interested in maintaining

---

[1] *Stability and Survival: A Bow Group Discussion About Defence Policy*, February 1961, p. 22. See also the remarks of Julian Critchley, a Bow Group member, in 632 H.C. Deb. col. 289–94 (13 December 1960).

the 'traditional' navy of surface ships which controlled the seas and was fighting for a new generation of aircraft carriers. It was unwilling to sacrifice a 'balanced' fleet on the altar of a seaborne nuclear force. The Board of Admiralty, therefore, put forth strong reservations to the entire 'independent deterrent' concept, rather than advising the cabinet that if it was the Government's *political* policy to maintain the nuclear force, Polaris was the most suitable weapons system for it. If the costs of the Polaris submarines were to be separated, so that either they were not part of the regular Navy budget or the budget was proportionately increased, there would have been less opposition to the Navy's taking over the deterrent mission. But given the past rigid pattern of defence allocations this was not considered likely to occur. Nevertheless, some senior Navy officers acknowledged that the choice of Skybolt in 1960 was perhaps only a 'postponement' of Polaris, and that the undersea missile might become the successor to Skybolt in the 1970s.

D. *Labour: The Politics of Principle*

For the Labour party the end of Blue Streak served as a potent catalyst which led the party into opposition to continuing the 'independent deterrent', thereby providing one of the principal issues between the two major parties until after the General Election of 1964. The forces which led to Labour's transition were a curious combination of technology, politics, and ideology and serve as an excellent example of the interaction of such in the formulation of national security policy attitudes. The Labour leadership was now able to argue that it could no longer support the 'British independent deterrent' because the costs of technology put it beyond Britain's resources. This was a convenient position, for it enabled the party's leaders to grant to their Left wing on the *practical* grounds of the inevitable trends of technology what they wanted as a matter of *principle*. It was also an attempt to end by compromise the civil war which was engulfing the party on the issue of unilateral disarmament.

The shift in the shadow cabinet's policy first became perceptible in the parliamentary debate on the Blue Streak cancellation. The announcement of the decision had been greeted in the Commons by a 'storm unequalled since the Suez debates'.[1] In the subsequent debate on Blue Streak's demise, George Brown asked that a Committee of Inquiry be established to determine why Sandys had persisted with the project so long against the weight of accumulating evidence that Blue Streak could not succeed as a weapon of deterrence, and described the costly cancellation as the 'biggest ministerial collapse of modern times'. Brown then

[1] *Daily Telegraph*, 14 April 1960.

adroitly withdrew Labour's past support of the 'independent deterrent' on the grounds that it was no longer certain that one was feasible in the future at a reasonable cost.[1] In the following weeks, Brown together with Denis Healey, Richard Crossman, and Morgan Phillips drafted a statement of a proposed new Labour defence policy, which after consultations with the Trades Union Congress and representatives of the Parliamentary Labour party was issued in July 1960 jointly by the National Executive Committee of the Labour party and the General Council of the Trades Union Congress. This took place under chaotic conditions as the labour unions were being swept by an avalanche of unilateral disarmament sentiment.

The new Labour policy said that in the future the provision of nuclear weapons in the Western alliance should be left exclusively to the United States, while Britain's contribution should be in conventional terms only. It did not specify what should happen to existing British nuclear weapons but noted that with the cancellation of Blue Streak it was clear that in a few years' time Britain would no longer possess a 'truly independent strategic deterrent'. The end of Blue Streak meant that the Sandys-Macmillan defence policy 'so proudly launched in 1957 is now in ruins'. If British strategy was to be based on military rather than prestige considerations 'we must accept the truth that a country of our size cannot remain in any real sense of the word an independent nuclear power.' The statement endorsed Britain's membership in NATO but deplored the alliance's dependence upon atomic arms and declared that the West should never be the first to use nuclear weapons. NATO ground forces should be effectively equipped for conventional defence; although tactical weapons might be deployed, they too should continue to be manufactured solely by the United States.[2]

Such a policy had long and persistently been advocated by Richard Crossman, and in the previous year partially by Denis Healey and George Wigg, but until now had been rejected as impractical by Gaitskell and the party's official defence spokesmen, George Brown and John Strachey. Since 1954 Crossman had shown great foresight in warning of the costs that would be incurred in continuing the nuclear effort and in the danger that Britain would encourage, by her example, the proliferation of nuclear weapons in Europe. He charged that the nuclear force was being built for reasons of prestige rather than security and criticized Strachey for thinking that Britain could have a nuclear deterrent, better conventional forces

[1] 622 H.C. Deb. col. 211–28 (27 April 1960). Emanuel Shinwell observed that although it was not originally intended the debate was turning out to be one of the most important in many years as Labour was on the threshold of a remarkable change in its defence policy. Ibid., col. 261.

[2] For the complete text see *Report of the Fifty-Ninth Annual Conference of the Labour Party* (London, Transport House, 1960), pp. 13–16.

and a smaller defence bill all at once. Gaitskell made several efforts to suppress Crossman's criticisms of official Labour policy and was driven to oust him from his position as spokesman on pensions in the shadow cabinet following his failure to vote for the opposition amendment in the 1960 defence debate. Subsequently Crossman and Wigg published several articles in the *New Statesman*, which served as a precursor for the 1960 statement, criticizing their front bench's defence policy.[1]

Labour's revised policy was also essentially the same as that which had been advocated by the Liberal party for several years. Soon after his elevation to the leadership, Jo Grimond began voicing doubts about the necessity of building up the nuclear force. As early as March 1957 the Liberal Parliamentary party issued a statement which declared that Britain 'should give up the separate manufacture of nuclear weapons and confine ourselves to contributions to the nuclear programme of the free world primarily through research.'[2] The Liberal Assembly of 1958 passed a resolution condemning the British government for 'providing the excuse for other countries to compete in the production of nuclear weapons'.[3] In the late 1950s Grimond was a perceptive critic in the Commons of the assumptions underlying the Government's nuclear policy.[4] Thus in 1960 the Labour leadership was only catching up with the Liberals, though it did not have the same success as the latter in warding off a unilateralist movement.[5]

The new Labour defence policy was rejected by the Labour Party Conference on 5 October 1960. To understand the reasons for this step, one must look at a number of prior developments within the party. The policy proposed to the conference at Scarborough had been a frank attempt to accommodate the pacifist wing of the party by formulating a programme which would gain the broadest possible measure of agreement.[6] The

[1] 'Left Holding the Deterrent', 12 March 1960; 'Defence After Blue Streak', 14 May 1960.

[2] Jorgen Scott Rasmussen, *The Liberal Party: A Study of Retrenchment and Revival* (London, Constable, 1965), p. 124. See also Grimond's exchange of letters with Erwin D. Canham, editor of the *Christian Science Monitor*, in 'Anglo-American Attitudes No. 3: Defence and Disarmament', *Observer*, 1 September 1957.

[3] *Liberal Assembly Resolutions Adopted at Torquay, 1958* (London, The Liberal Party Organization, 1958), p. 4.

[4] See, for example, 600 H.C. Deb. col. 1189–99 (25 February 1959). The Rasmussen study, op. cit., indicates that the initiative for the Liberal position came from Grimond personally. It should be noted that the Liberal party's small size and the remote chance of its coming to office made it easier to adopt a 'progressive' and perhaps less popular position.

[5] The Liberal form of unilateralism would have had the United Nations replacing NATO to provide collective security. At the 1960 Liberal Assembly at Eastbourne such an amendment, moved by Lieutenant Colonel Patrick Lort Phillips, was rejected 607 to 78. See his *Towards Sanity* (Carmarthen, Radical Publications, 1960). Professor Max Beloff stated the argument against Liberal unilateralism in the *Guardian*, 21 September 1960.

[6] See George Brown's acknowledgement of this, *Report of the Fifty-Ninth Annual Conference of the Labour Party*, p. 185; for examples of the attempt to sell it to the Left wing, see Denis

history of the growth of support in Britain for unilateral disarmament through the rise of the Campaign for Nuclear Disarmament has been told elsewhere and need not be re-examined here.[1] What distinguished those favouring the revised Labour policy of renunciation of British nuclear weapons from the unilateralists was that the latter also held that Britain should withdraw from any alliance that relied on the possession or use of nuclear arms, that is, from NATO.

Most unilateralists came to this view through a great fear of nuclear war, a rejection of the concept of nuclear deterrence, and a sense of moral guilt about the existence of nuclear weapons. They were inheritors of a radical tradition of dissent from government policy combined with a penchant for pacifism. Their beliefs were characterized by neutralism mixed with anti-Americanism. Yet, curiously, they were also motivated by national pride and a desire for moral influence, for they yearned for Britain, by her act of renunciation, to set an example for the world. The Campaign for Nuclear Disarmament was organized in the spring of 1958 following the Government's own admission that Britain was defenceless against a nuclear attack, and as alarm was spreading that the installation of the Thor missiles in eastern England would provoke or tempt a Soviet attack. It probably reached its zenith of popular support with the 'Ban the Bomb' march from the Aldermaston Research Establishment to Trafalgar Square on Easter Sunday, 1960. This date was roughly coincidental, it should be noted, with the cancellation of Blue Streak and Labour's proposed change of policy.

There was another dimension, however, which helps explain the revolt against the party's leadership on defence. This was a struggle for the very control of the Labour party. The genuine protest of the pacifists was used

Healey, 'This Plan Can Make Britain Safe and Speed Disarmament', *News Chronicle*, 27 June 1960, and Richard Crossman, 'This is No Compromise—It is a Sober, Workmanlike Policy', *News Chronicle*, 28 June 1960.

[1] The best and most extensive study of the CND is Christopher Driver's *The Disarmers: A Study in Protest* (London, Hodder & Stoughton, 1964). The diverse composition of unilateralist support is discussed in: Hedley Bull, 'The Many Sides of British Unilateralism', *Reporter*, 16 March 1961, pp. 35–7; David Marquand, 'England's Labour Party and its Discontents', *Commentary*, Vol. XXX, December 1960, pp. 489–96; Drew Middleton, 'The Deeper Meaning of British Neutralism', *The New York Times Magazine*, 11 December 1960; Harvey A. DeWeerd, *The Labour Party and Unilateralism*, RM-2914-PR (Santa Monica, Calif., The RAND Corporation, February 1962). Back-bench attitudes in the Labour party towards nuclear weapons and pacifism are analytically reviewed in S. E. Finer, H. B. Berrington, and D. J. Bartholomew, *Backbench Opinion in the House of Commons, 1955–1959* (London, Pergamon Press, 1961), pp. 23–8, 33–136. The principal literary advocate of nuclear disarmament was Bertrand Russell: see his *Common Sense and Nuclear Warfare* (London, Allen & Unwin, 1959), *Has Man a Future?* (London, Allen & Unwin, 1961), and *Unarmed Victory* (London, Penguin, 1963). An original work is that of a distinguished retired Naval officer who advocated a strategy of 'non-violent resistance' and unilateral disarmament not on moral or emotional grounds but on the military case of 'better Red than dead', Sir Stephen King-Hall, *Defence in the Nuclear Age* (London, Gollancz, 1958); see also his *Power Politics in the Nuclear Age* (London, Gollancz, 1962).

as a vehicle by others whose principal object it was to use the defence controversy as a means of ousting Gaitskell from the leadership.[1] After Labour had suffered its third successive General Election defeat in 1959 the tensions between the Left and Right wings of the party intensified. The fundamentalists on the Left thought that the party had not advanced a sufficiently socialist programme whereas the pragmatic party leaders on the Right viewed the old-fashioned socialist dogma as an electoral disadvantage. The intra-party dispute initially centred on Gaitskell's attempt to modify the anachronistic Clause IV of the party's constitution, which since 1918 had committed Labour to common ownership of means of production, distribution, and exchange. Gaitskell, after encountering considerable opposition, was forced to retreat on Clause IV as the Left wing mounted an offensive designed to commit the party to unilateral nuclear disarmament, a far more serious matter from the viewpoint of a 'responsible' leadership. In the summer of 1960 several unions passed unilateralist resolutions and at the Trades Union Congress in September the revolt of Frank Cousins, head of the Transport and General Workers Union, was confirmed as he introduced and had accepted a resolution demanding unilateral disarmament. The die was cast. Cousins, who had been personally feuding with Gaitskell for some time, introduced the resolution passed at the 1960 Annual Labour Party Conference which, *inter alia*, called for 'a complete rejection of any defence policy based on the threat of the use of strategic nuclear weapons'.[2]

The challenge to Gaitskell was direct but equivocal; it had never been resolved whether final authority on Labour policy rested with the Annual Conference, as the Left preferred, or with the Parliamentary Labour party, two-thirds of whom were not unilateralists.[3] The man who sought to wrest the leadership from Gaitskell by standing against him in a caucus of the Labour members of Parliament the following month was Harold Wilson. Though not a unilateralist himself, Wilson tried to make himself acceptable to the Left and Right wings in his first bid for the leadership by arguing that the controversies over unilateralism and conference authority, on which the Party Conference and the Parliamentarians were at opposite poles, were not ones of 'principle'. He claimed that the differences could be resolved through compromise by a less recalcitrant party

---

[1] See Shinwell, *The Labour Story*, p. 207.

[2] *Report of the Fifty-Ninth Annual Conference of the Labour Party*, p. 178. Other clauses in the resolution called for a permanent stop to the manufacture and testing of nuclear weapons, a termination of aircraft carrying nuclear weapons operating from bases in the United Kingdom, and advocated continued opposition to missile bases in Britain.

[3] For a relevant discussion of the question of Parliamentary party freedom from control by a mass membership organization, see Leon D. Epstein, 'Who Makes Party Policy: British Labour, 1960–61', *Midwest Journal of Political Science*, Vol. VI, No. 2, May 1962, pp. 165–82.

leader for the sake of unity against the Tories. Wilson was accepted by the unilateralists as a means of dethroning Gaitskell, but he was defeated 166 to 81.

The unilateralist resolutions passed at Scarborough were intentionally ambiguous with respect to NATO. They did not specifically say that Britain should leave the military alliance, but they implied as much, so long as NATO relied on the use of any nuclear weapons. Knowing that the vote would be going against the National Executive Committee's defence statement because of predetermined bloc voting by the union representatives, Gaitskell set out to educate the party to the fact that the logic of unilateralism led to neutralism, and to the rejection of NATO and the alliance with the United States. He also reserved the right of the Parliamentary party not to follow a conference decision. In his famous speech to the Scarborough conference, which Robert McKenzie has called 'one of the boldest and most forthright in the whole history of British party leadership',[1] Gaitskell served notice that he and his parliamentary supporters would 'fight and fight and fight again to save the Party we love. We will fight and fight and fight again to bring back sanity and honesty and dignity. . . .'[2]

And so they did. Following the defeat of Wilson, an organization called the Campaign for Democratic Socialism was formed within the party to challenge the unilateralists at the grass root level. 'Cell' groups were organized at which the 'multilateralists' stated their case: renunciation of British nuclear weapons but continued participation in NATO; Western disarmament but only following internationally agreed upon measures. Gaitskell spent an arduous year recapturing control of the party and educating it on defence—with success. According to one study, one in three of the unilateralists switched their position to multilateralism between 1960 and 1961. The authors concluded also that despite the union bloc votes at the 1960 Conference, a majority of the party at the constituency level supported the defence policy of the National Executive Committee even then.[3]

At the 1961 Conference at Blackpool the party reversed itself on unilateralism. It approved a new defence statement—'Policy for Peace'— which reproduced in essence the position worked out after the cancellation

[1] *British Political Parties: The Distribution of Power Within the Conservative and Labour Parties,* 2nd rev. ed. (London, Mercury Books, 1963), p. 615.

[2] *Report of the Fifty-Ninth Annual Conference of the Labour Party,* p. 201.

[3] See Keith Hindell and Philip Williams, 'Scarborough and Blackpool', *Political Quarterly,* Vol. III, No. 3, July–September 1962, pp. 306–20. See also Alastair Buchan,' The Odds Against Gaitskell', *Reporter,* 22 December 1960, pp. 30–3; 'Gaitskell's Road Back', *Observer,* 8 October 1961. The case against unilateralism was cogently made by John Strachey in his *The Pursuit of Peace* (London, Fabian Tract No. 329, December 1960).

of Blue Streak. As to the nuclear force, it said that 'Britain should cease the attempt to remain an independent nuclear power, since this neither strengthened the alliance nor is it now a sensible use of our limited resources.'[1] The Left wing did pass two resolutions which the parliamentary leadership viewed with disfavour. The first condemned the establishment of an American Polaris submarine base at Holy Loch and the second objected to the training of German troops on British soil. Gaitskell, though arguing against the resolutions, decided not to make them an issue of principle, preferring to regard them as 'consolation prizes' for the losers of the principal contest.

E. Influence and Duplication

Another tangent of opposition to the nuclear force could be found among those who were sceptical of the claim that the possession of nuclear weapons enhanced the nation's influence. As the military credibility of the V-bombers declined, the Government increasingly based its justifications for the nuclear force on a political rationale, rather than on strategic analysis. Thus the argument that the nuclear effort did not create greater influence than Britain would have had without it became an integral part of the public debate.

It was the claim of influence on United States policy that was especially controversial, because of the Government's tendency to see in the nuclear force both the means for retaining *in*dependence and a mechanism for obtaining *inter*dependence. Critics of the Government thought that it held too high an estimate of the influence which nuclear weapons automatically confirm. They found no evidence in the record that the Pentagon or the State Department paid greater attention to the British point of view with respect to Suez, or to events in the Far East in the 1950s— to cite two examples where London and Washington policies were at odds—because of the V-bombers.[2] Jo Grimond declared in 1959 that, as far as he could see, the nuclear force had no utility as an instrument of persuasion on the United States.[3] Many would grant that the separate development of atomic weapons after World War II had reopened the doors of atomic co-operation, but this aim, it was thought, had been

[1] *Report of the Sixtieth Annual Conference of the Labour Party* (London, Transport House, 1961), p. 8.

[2] 'Ironically enough, Britain had a much more decisive influence on American policy in those crises of the Cold War which arose before she was an operational nuclear power, the Berlin blockade, Korea, and Indochina, than those which occurred after she had become one, Quemoy, Laos, and Cuba. By a double irony, the Suez crisis occurred at almost exactly the moment when she became an operational nuclear power'. Alastair Buchan, 'Europe and the Atlantic Alliance: Two Strategies or One?', *Journal of Common Market Studies*, Vol. I, No. 3, Spring 1963, p. 229.

[3] 600 H.C. Deb. col. 1195 (25 February 1959).

fully achieved with the 1958 American atomic energy legislation. Following Labour's change of policy in 1960, its leaders argued that the United States would not be unhappy if Britain gave up trying to maintain the nuclear force. Upon returning from Washington in 1962 Harold Wilson insisted that 'there is not one person in authority there who thinks that our nuclear deterrent adds one iota to the strength and credibility of the Western deterrent.'[1]

In the United States the arrival of the Kennedy administration, which sought to discourage independent nuclear deterrents, centralize nuclear control in Washington, and increase the conventional contribution of the allies, rendered still less tenable the claim that the British nuclear force brought influence. One did not hear as often the kind of comment made by Minister of Defence Watkinson about his discussions with Secretary of Defense Gates and other Eisenhower administration officials:

. . . they have made it plain to me that for reasons of geography, for reasons of the strength of our alliance, and for other reasons of a more technical and secret character, they very much welcome this essential contribution to the present strategic forces of the West.[2]

Certainly the level of concern about the dangers of nuclear proliferation had been less in the Eisenhower presidency than under Kennedy. When Eisenhower promised Skybolt to Macmillan at Camp David in 1960, or when he asked the Congress to amend the atomic energy law in 1958, he does not appear to have been greatly concerned about the impact such actions would have upon the French or other nations in terms of the inducements to acquire atomic weapons for their own political purposes, or to develop their own 'special relationships'.[3]

On the other hand the Kennedy administration was less disturbed by the British nuclear force than by the 'force de frappe'. General de Gaulle was using his bomb to harass the Americans in a quite un-British manner. Bomber Command, unlike the fledgling French force, eventually had its target plans closely integrated with those of SAC and there was no worry about the political stability of the British state après Macmillan. Nevertheless, when McNamara, at the NATO ministerial meeting in Athens in the spring of 1962 and at Ann Arbor in June, spoke of limited nuclear capabilities operating independently as being 'dangerous, expensive, prone to

[1] 655 H.C. Deb. col. 228–9 (6 March 1962).

[2] 635 H.C. Deb. col. 1505 (28 February 1961).

[3] Robert Bowie has questioned whether in the 1950s it was wise for the United States to bolster the 'special relationship' with Britain and so encourage an outdated image of Britain's influence and options. See his *Shaping the Future: Foreign Policy in an Age of Transition* (New York, Columbia University Press, 1964), p. 50. See also, William B. Bader, *The United States and the Spread of Nuclear Weapons* (New York, Pegasus, 1968), *passim*.

obsolescence and lacking in credibility as a deterrent', the meaning was clear. The London reaction was predictably cool in Whitehall and fervent among the Government's critics. Labour and Liberal leaders and much of the press aligned themselves with McNamara; British defence officials insisted that the U.S. Secretary of Defense must have been referring solely to the French since the British force was fully 'co-ordinated' with that of the United States. A week later McNamara said he had not been referring to the British, but this disclaimer did not dispel the impression that his University of Michigan graduation speech was meant to be heard in London as well as in Paris.[1]

In the words of a former Conservative Minister, the nuclear force was a 'decaying asset'. Aubrey Jones told the Commons that in his opinion the British force was becoming a source of embarrassment and a discomfort to the United States, as well as a source of estrangement between the two countries.[2] As the Kennedy administration sought ways to inhibit incentives for atomic arms in Germany and defuse the desire for nuclear proliferation elsewhere, the 'special nuclear relationship' got in the way. Many in Britain felt that America would not regret the United Kingdom's retirement from the nuclear business. What Washington wanted, they argued, was not additional nuclear weapons, which it did not need, but more conventional troops, flexible sea and airborne forces, and economic assistance to the underdeveloped world. As the defence correspondent of *The Times*, Alun Gwynne Jones (later Lord Chalfont) reported on the basis of conversations with American officials:

The very sincere regard which many Americans feel for Britain is largely instinctive and emotional. The only special feeling that exists as a direct result of Britain's own military policies is one of exasperation. . . . Much official opinion, not only in the Pentagon but in the State Department and the White House as well, finds Britain's nuclear pretensions ridiculous and its position as the only major NATO power without some form of compulsory military service incomprehensible. It is arguable that British planners should take a little more seriously what is done and said in the United States. For America powerful allies are desirable, for Britain they are indispensable.[3]

Those who denied the influence of British nuclear weapons often saw them as an unnecessary duplication of the American defence programme. They would have preferred the guiding principle of British defence policy to be that Britain complement, rather than supplement, United States weapons. Since they tended to have a high esteem for the reliability of the American nuclear guarantee, they advocated that Britain's contribution to

[1] *The Times*, 19, 20, 23 June 1962; *Observer*, 17, 24 June 1962.
[2] 655 H.C. Deb. col. 75 (5 March 1962).
[3] 'Realistic Tactics for Britain', *The Times*, 2 August 1963.

Western defence be solely conventional, on the assumption that the United States would automatically come to the defence of Britain with nuclear weapons should it prove necessary. No one doubted that the United States alone possessed nuclear bombs in sufficient strength to inflict 'assured destruction'. Thus they were scornful of the Government's pride in Britain's 'contribution to the Western deterrent' since they felt that it was being made simply for Britain's own political purposes. Furthermore, they noted that the United States had continued its own nuclear programme in a self-sustained and self-sufficient manner; there had been no known comparative reduction in the production of American armaments because of the V-bombers, or because of the R & D work on Blue Streak. The fact that both the United States and the Soviet Union spent more on defence research and development alone than the British defence budget in its entirety was seen as evidence of the need for greater specialization in armaments and defence functions. Britain's willingness to give up the nuclear force would help fulfil the intended logic of the NATO alliance.

What was the true source of British influence in international politics? Critics of the nuclear force thought that whether Britain's advice was sought or needed depended on a number of factors of which nuclear power was one of the least relevant. It depended on the soundness of the advice, and the personality and skill of the Prime Minister and his colleagues, and their perceptions of world affairs. It depended upon the closeness of the ties with the United States and the ability of British statesmen to continue to cultivate this long, historical relationship. It depended on Britain's non-nuclear contribution to European defence and her relationships with the continent. It depended on the handling of her worldwide peacekeeping role, the process of decolonization, and the ties with the Commonwealth. It depended on the strength of sterling and the resilience of the economy. As the *Guardian* editorialized: 'Not bombs but brains, and not a threat to separate but a commitment to unify, determine whether one's voice has a chance of being heard in Washington.'[1]

The 'independent nuclear deterrent' was thus seen as a prestige symbol to help protect Britain's status as a Great Power. Having long been a world power with strong military forces including a great strategic fleet, Britain was reluctant to relinquish that role. The nuclear force was viewed as an attempt to keep up with the Russo-American Joneses. As late as 1960, former Minister of Defence Anthony Head found it necessary to say in the Commons: 'It is extremely dangerous to think and to behave like something you no longer are. . . . We shall never be one of the two Great Powers. We have not realized—I do not believe that the British public

[1] 'Sharing', 28 April 1960.

has realized—our true position in world affairs today.'[1] The attempt to maintain a credible deterrent was seen as symptomatic of the wishful thinking of a declining nation.

F. Contribution to Nuclear Proliferation

Britain has had a special position in the history of the spread of nuclear weapons. As the third power to test an atomic bomb, she was the first country other than the Superpowers to acquire a nuclear capability. Because of this unique situation it was felt by many that Britain could have a major influence on the decisions of other states regarding the manufacture of nuclear weapons. By the example which she set Britain could measurably affect the dispersion of nuclear capabilities. (Had she made the choice not to acquire nuclear arms, Britain, as potential atomic power number three, might have created conditions discouraging number four.) Furthermore, the United Kingdom was the first country to run into difficulties in maintaining a credible deterrent and was the first to debate in earnest the merits of giving up nuclear weapons that had already been acquired. Thus some contended that by voluntarily renouncing her nuclear weapons Britain might slow their spread; or that by agreeing to contribute her weapons to NATO or a European nuclear force she might lay the groundwork for a viable system of nuclear sharing.

It is probably fair to say that the British were among the first to take seriously the danger inherent in the world-wide proliferation of nuclear weapons. The Baruch Plan of 1946 was designed to deal with the problem but in a somewhat utopian manner. Following the failure to have it accepted, the American government's policy seemed to be directed more towards restricting the dissemination of American nuclear secrets than in the more positive aim of channelling the atomic inspirations of other nations, or in constructing an effective system of international control. In the 1950s American defence policy indirectly encouraged the dissemination of nuclear weapons in Europe by the installation of IRBMs in Europe under 'dual key' arrangements, the promotion of the use of tactical nuclear weapons for defence of the continent, the emphasis upon 'massive retaliation', and the general importance given to nuclear weapons. The British as a society were conscious of their position as the first 'Nth power' and seemed to be more aware of the dangers of 'secondary' nuclear arms races. As a government, however, Britain failed to set the sort of example which might have discouraged the dispersion of nuclear capabilities.

Those who were most concerned about the dangers of nuclear

[1] 622 H.C. Deb. col. 259 (27 April 1960).

proliferation, apart from the pacifists who rejected military arms on principle, tended to come from the centre-left of the British political spectrum. P. M. S. Blackett believed that the 'single most important reason' why Britain's defence policy was of 'international significance' was her 'key situation in relation to the spread of nuclear weapons to other countries' and her ability to have a 'decisive influence, for good or ill, on the vital task of attempting to check their spread'.[1] Though his estimate of Britain's influence may have been more modest, Denis Healey saw the spread of nuclear weapons as the 'most urgent problem facing mankind'.[2] Kenneth Younger, Director-General of the Royal Institute of International Affairs and a Minister of State for Foreign Affairs in the second Attlee government, argued that Britain had a 'special responsibility because it is undeniable that our example in being the third power to make these weapons has played some part in the desire of other countries to do the same'.[3] In 1958 Richard Crossman asked, 'How can we possibly prevent the Germans, the French, and every other nation in the alliance saying—"What the British demand for themselves we demand for ourselves?" The right to distrust the Americans', Crossman observed, 'cannot remain a British monopoly.'[4]

Labour's proposal of 1959 for a 'Non-Nuclear Club', discussed earlier, which all countries would join except the two Superpowers, and which Britain would join through an act of renunciation, was an attempt to deal with the proliferation phenomenon. But it came late in time and even then was still an aberration from Labour's continuing support of the British nuclear force. When Labour did alter its policy in 1960–1, non-proliferation was cited as one of the several reasons for the new policy. Within the confines of the Left wing of the Labour party, the concern over the spread of nuclear weapons was often equated with the 'German problem', for it was the acquisition of nuclear armaments by the West German military forces that was most dreaded. Following Labour's reversal of policy, its leaders insisted that Britain must look at her policies in the light of their impact on the intentions of other governments. Labour and the Liberals argued that the Conservative government's stated policy of continuing an 'independent deterrent' would encourage the proliferation of nuclear weapons in Western Europe, and eventually in Asia and the Middle East. Denis Healey pointed out that for Britain to continue

---

[1] 'Thoughts on British Defence Policy', *New Statesman*, 5 December 1959.
[2] *The Race Against the H Bomb*, Fabian Tract No. 322, London, 1960, p. 1.
[3] *Britain's Role in a Changing World*, Fabian Tract No. 327, London, 1960, p. 15.
[4] 583 H.C. Deb. col. 634 (27 February 1958). Crossman urged the British government to propose to NATO a ten-year pact under which the United Kingdom would renounce nuclear weapons on the condition that all NATO members but the United States do likewise. See his 'The Nuclear Obsession', *Encounter*, July 1958, Vol. XI, No. 1, pp. 3–10.

the nuclear force would require American assistance, which would set a dangerous precedent. If Britain compelled the United States to offer technological assistance, this would create a tremendous incentive for America's other allies to produce their own warheads and thereupon lay a claim in Washington for assistance with delivery systems.[1]

The unhappy irony of the rise of concern in Britain regarding proliferation is that it came too late. The cancellation of Blue Streak, which led to Labour's new defence policy, occurred the month after the first French atomic explosion in the Sahara. The advent of France as a nuclear power guaranteed that no British government would cast away its nuclear weapons except as part of some type of international arms control agreement. A British government by voluntarily giving up nuclear weapons in the early or mid-1950s might have induced the French not to develop their own atomic arms, for there is considerable evidence to suggest that the British lead encouraged the French to follow. The significance of this lies in that the French, in turn, may have kindled nuclear desires in Germany and elsewhere in Europe. The spectre of nuclear proliferation in Europe may have brought to the attention of countries in Asia, Africa, and the Middle East the national security and prestige merits of possessing a nuclear capability. Such a line of reasoning is candidly subjective and therefore impossible to substantiate. It does seem certain, however, that the British example had an unsettling effect on the rest of Europe.

Was it not true that most of the strategic and political arguments used by the British government to justify the creation and continuation of its 'independent nuclear deterrent' could have an equal validity when applied by other governments to their own national interests?

The French case serves as the most obvious and relevant example of the impact of Britain's nuclear policies. The 1955 Defence White Paper, announcing the decision to manufacture a hydrogen bomb and confirming the intention to develop a nuclear force, stimulated French political leaders to reconsider the orientation of French national security policy. 'In the view of many Frenchmen', according to Lawrence Scheinman, 'France's interests were as extensive as those of Great Britain. If Great Britain felt that her security obligations required that she possess a nuclear weapons arsenal, then France should recognize the same need and take steps to assure herself a nuclear force.'[2] French military leaders in the mid-1950s pointed to Britain to help them justify their claim that atomic weapons were not the peculiar province of the Superpowers.

---

[1] 635 H.C. Deb. col. 1218–22 (27 February 1961).
[2] Lawrence Scheinman, *Atomic Energy Policy in France under the Fourth Republic* (Princeton, Princeton University Press, 1965), p. 119. French military thinking was also influenced by the 1957 White Paper, ibid., p. 188.

A recent study of French nuclear policy concluded that the French watched British nuclear developments closely and that each major step in Britain could be matched by corresponding later developments in France. The first British atomic tests, for example, stirred interest in a weapons programme within some French military circles. The justifications of a strategic nature given for the British independent deterrent found their echo in the writings of a small military pressure group which appeared in the *Revue de Défense Nationale*.[1]

If the British nuclear force spurred the French, America's discrimination in favour of Britain further increased the incentive for the French to follow suit. The 1958 revisions of the United States atomic energy legislation (which by coincidence of timing came almost simultaneously with General de Gaulle's return to power), permitting privileged access to countries that had already made 'substantial progress' in the nuclear field, could only encourage the conviction in Paris that access to American nuclear secrets depended upon possession of a French bomb. The French felt a sense of injustice in being 'beaucoup moins favorisée' than Britain[2] and found the American attitude to be that the transfer of nuclear secrets became more dangerous when crossing the Channel than when they crossed the Atlantic. For a time the objective of French policy was to achieve the status of an atomic ally of the United States so as to receive advanced nuclear weapons information without the great costs of further research and development.[3] Equal treatment of Britain and France by the United States would pave the way for de Gaulle's desired triumvirate within the alliance.[4]

The debate in Britain on the retention of the nuclear force did not pass unnoticed in Paris.[5] The British nuclear force was frequently evoked in the important debate in the Assemblée Nationale preceding the vote in 1960 on the 'loi-programme militaire' authorizing funds until 1965 for the French nuclear force. De Gaulle's parliamentary spokesmen used the British example as a precedent to justify their own policy, and as proof that a national force would not necessarily damage the Atlantic alliance and could be achieved within the economic resources of a middle level

---

[1] Wolf Mendl, *Deterrence and Persuasion: French Nuclear Armament in the Context of National Policy* (London, Faber & Faber, 1970), pp. 40–8.

[2] Goldschmidt, *L'Aventure atomique*, p. 203.

[3] Ibid., p. 253. See also Edgar S. Furniss, Jr., *De Gaulle and the French Army* (New York, The Twentieth Century Fund, 1964), p. 207; Wolf Mendl, 'The Background of French Nuclear Policy', *International Affairs*, Vol. XLI, No. 1, January 1965, pp. 22–36.

[4] For an excellent appraisal of de Gaulle's use of the 'force de frappe' as an international political instrument, see the forthcoming Wilfrid L. Kohl, *French Nuclear Diplomacy* (Princeton, Princeton University Press).

[5] See, for example, Maurice Megret, 'L'Angleterre et le "Deterrent National",' *Revue de Défense Nationale*, March 1961, pp. 423–36.

power.[1] At the first Conservative party conference following the Blue Streak cancellation, Minister of Defence Watkinson told his fellow Tories that the Conservative government had no intention of abandoning Britain's role as the third nuclear power because 'We would be sheltering behind the Americans and our voice in NATO and elsewhere in the world would be of no significance.' Twenty-four hours later French Foreign Minister Couve de Murville quoted the Watkinson speech extensively in defending the 'force de frappe' before the Foreign Affairs Committee of the Assemblée Nationale. By early 1962, when the continuation of the British nuclear force was highly contentious, Le Monde was asking whether some of the questions being asked in the House of Commons in that year's defence debate concerning the costs, credibility, and justification for the force did not also apply to France.[2] Nevertheless, as The Economist commented, Whitehall could 'partly thank itself that the British chickens of insularity and independence in deterrents were being brought home to roost by General de Gaulle'.[3]

If Britain were to renounce her nuclear weapons unilaterally, who would follow suit? This question came to be asked as France became recognized as a nuclear power. It was the standard Tory reply to Labour's policy of renunciation. Conservative government leaders said they could 'understand' the reasons for France's development of her own nuclear capability.[4] They argued that 'the General' would continue his nuclear programme no matter what Britain did. In truth, it would have been difficult for the British government actively to discourage the acquisition of nuclear weapons by others when it itself spoke forcefully of the need for maintaining an 'independent nuclear deterrent'. Thus Macmillan could only register 'surprise' upon being told by President Kennedy in a private letter in February 1962 that a British effort to continue the nuclear force through the sixties 'might both confirm de Gaulle in his own course and hasten the day when the Germans would demand nuclear weapons for themselves'.[5]

The view of French strategic theorist General Pierre Gallois that the peace of the world was more likely to be endangered by there being too few nuclear powers rather than too many was never very popular in Britain, although it did have an occasional adherent.[6] As the danger of nuclear proliferation was recognized—belatedly in terms of Britain's

[1] République Française Journal Officiel, 25 October 1960, passim

[2] 'La Défense de l'Angleterre', Le Monde, 8 March 1962.

[3] 'Autumn Manœuvres', 22 October 1960.

[4] For a typical statement, see Prime Minister Macmillan's, 661 H.C. Deb. col. 958 (26 June 1962).

[5] Arthur M. Schlesinger, Jr., A Thousand Days: John F. Kennedy in the White House (Boston, Houghton Mifflin, 1965), p. 849.

[6] See, for example, Vice Admiral J. Hughes Hallet, 'Thoughts on the New British Defence Policy', Brassey's Annual (London, Clowes, 1957), pp. 268–9.

perhaps being capable of holding back a chain of nuclear dominoes—
two sets of priorities emerged. Some thought that a unilateralist act, such
as a jettisoning of the British warheads into the North Sea, might turn
the course of nuclear dispersion. Such a view was flattering to British
visions of moral leadership but became increasingly less plausible with
the passage of time. Others thought Britain should concentrate her efforts
on securing a European arms control or disarmament agreement under
which a voluntary British renunciation would be used as a *quid pro quo*
for the agreement of other countries not to develop their own nuclear
arms. In such a case, the British nuclear force could be a trump card of
great value which should not be needlessly thrown away beforehand.

9 | Skybolt, Nassau, the MLF, and the 1964 General Election

In the year before the Nassau Conference of December 1962, the future of the nuclear force appeared to be very much open to question. The conditions for giving up the 'independent' endeavour, or merging it into a bilateral or multinational venture, seemed to be emerging. Then the pattern of events which was settling in was suddenly ruptured. The Skybolt crisis precipitated an awkward weapons system decision at Nassau which was to have long-term consequences. Nassau brought to the fore the problem of nuclear sharing and control within the alliance, and unleashed the acrimonious debate over the American proposal for a multilateral nuclear force; it laid bare the opposing visions of Charles de Gaulle and John F. Kennedy for the future of the Atlantic relationship; and it brought to a climax the debate in Britain over its 'independent nuclear deterrent'.

1. The Range of Choice before Nassau

A large variety of proposals as to what Britain should do with its nuclear force were put forth in the period before the Nassau Conference. Especially after the cancellation of Blue Streak, much informed opinion felt that Britain should no longer seek to remain an independent nuclear power. This view could be found in varying gradations in all three political parties and had particularly strong support in the press, notably in the *Observer, Guardian, The Times,* and *The Economist.*[1] The following attempts to cover the panorama of proposals which were tabled but, because of the shifts of opinions and ideas, does not attempt a firm classification as to the supporters of each point of view.

One strand of thought was that there should be a firm decision that there would be no weapons system developed to follow the V-bombers once they became obsolete. In this manner Britain might gracefully bow out of the strategic nuclear weapons field. The existing V-bombers should not be scrapped, but they should not be replaced either, and to accelerate the process of denuclearization they might be given a purely conventional role of interdiction in NATO strategy. This was in essence the policy of the Labour party. In the Commons, George Brown speaking for his party insisted that the demise of Blue Streak represented not only

[1] Cf., 'Dropping the Bomb: When and How Britain Might Usefully Give Up Its Nuclear Arms', *The Economist,* 17 March 1962.

the termination of a weapons project, but the end of an entire concept of defence, that is, the era of the 'independent British deterrent'. With Skybolt the Government was grasping at straws, for clearly Britain had now become dependent on the United States for its delivery system.[1] Thus Labour charged that the Government's claim that Skybolt preserved the 'independent deterrent' was a pretence. The escalating costs of technology made it no longer possible for Britain alone to develop and manufacture a weapons system which would constitute a credible deterrent. The failure of Blue Streak, said Harold Wilson, was the 'moment of truth' for the British deterrent.[2]

Labour also cast doubts as to whether Bomber Command would ever get Skybolt, pointing out that it was a highly sophisticated, yet unproven, weapons system which was therefore a calculated risk. Plans for the British 'dependent' deterrent, Labour insisted, were therefore pinned on a missile which was still in the research and development stage and which had not yet been 'bought' by the Pentagon.

The idea that Britain should 'drop the bomb'—in the constructive sense of the phrase—by leaving to the United States the future provision of all nuclear and delivery systems had widespread appeal. But it neglected the fact that the nuclear innocence of Britain and France had been lost beyond all recall. The two 'independent deterrents' which had been sired out of the wedlock of the NATO alliance could only be legitimized by becoming part of a larger grouping. Thus proposals for a European or NATO nuclear force were made as a device to absorb and legitimize the nuclear offspring.

The British nuclear force could form the principal component of a 'European nuclear deterrent' sponsored by the European Community or a new European Defence Authority. Before the 1963 veto of Britain's application for admission into the Common Market, this seemed to conform with the emerging long term economic and political pattern of the alliance. It could buttress the European pillar in the 'twin pillar' concept of Atlantic partnership. Britain could make the most important contribution to an incipient European force by way of her advanced nuclear weapons programme and her large aircraft industry. Acceptance by the continentals of Britain's nuclear arms as the centrepiece of a new European military organization would strengthen the sense of common identity between the United Kingdom and her cross-Channel allies. It would also lead to broadened collaboration in advanced technology. Some of the British supporters of a European nuclear deterrent privately hoped that

[1] 635 H.C. Deb. col. 1493–6 (28 February 1961).

[2] 655 H.C. Deb. col. 230 (6 March 1962). This position, one should note, failed to make the necessary distinction between independent *control* and independent *manufacture* of nuclear systems.

it would make it less likely that France would press ahead with her 'force de frappe' and viewed it as a way to harness West Germany's military strength and ambitions. The Conservative government occasionally hinted that, if Britain did become a member of the E.E.C., it would give sympathetic consideration to a European system of nuclear deterrence as the community acquired a political framework. Edward Heath, then the chief British negotiator at Brussels, told the Ministerial Council of the Western European Union on 10 April 1962 that 'We quite accept that the European political union, if it is to be effective, will have a common concern for defence problems and that a European point of view on defence will emerge.'[1] A first step towards a European deterrent could take the form of an Anglo-French nuclear collaboration arrangement.

For Britain, participation in a European nuclear force would have meant sacrificing the intimate military relationship with the United States. Despite an occasional word of support for the concept of a European deterrent from individual American officials representing a government which was not of one mind on the subject, it was not likely that Washington would maintain in the 1960s the special nuclear relationship with a British government that joined its atomic arms with the French in a European strategic force. It was here that the 'twin pillar' concept collapsed, for the American insistence on centralized nuclear command and control in the alliance made it impossible to support a European nuclear force that was not integrated with its own in such a manner that the ultimate power of veto remained in American hands. Under such conditions, however, much of the European rationale for a deterrence capability of its own was dissipated.

In addition, a European deterrent would raise a myriad of awkward, but crucial, questions. Would the Germans, Italians, and other Europeans accept an Anglo-French force operating 'on behalf of Europe', or would they insist on a greater participation of their own? Does the control of the trigger not require a genuine European political federation, if not a concentration of responsibility in a 'President of Europe'? Might not the Soviet Union become so alarmed by the prospect of a second major nuclear force in the West that it would be driven to take pre-emptive action before it was created? And finally, would a European deterrent not lead to a weakening of the American commitment in Europe, a growth of European neutrality, and to a decrease in confidence between the two halves of the alliance?[2]

[1] Quoted in *The Control of Western Strategy*, Adelphi Papers No. 3 (London, The Institute for Strategic Studies, April 1963), p. 7.

[2] For examples of support for British participation in a European deterrent see Roy Jenkins, 'Europe After Blue Streak', *Spectator*, 6 May 1960, and Richard Goold-Adams' letter to *The Times*, 6 February 1962. Excellent critical appraisals pointing out the disadvantages noted above

One possible framework for a European nuclear force existed in the Western European Union, which already brought together Britain and the Six. In his capacity as rapporteur of the W.E.U.'s Defence Committee, Fred Mulley, a Labour member of Parliament, proposed in late 1959 that the W.E.U. organize a nuclear force with a joint power of decision on the use of strategic weapons. Mulley suggested that Britain could take the lead by placing some, if not all, of her V-bombers and nuclear warheads under W.E.U. control. His plan, however, failed to win the approval of the Labour leadership because it was thought that it might lead to the dispersion of nuclear capabilities.[1]

Another formula for enfolding the British nuclear force within an international framework was the proposal for a NATO deterrent, which received its first full public exposition from the pen of Alastair Buchan.[2] A NATO nuclear force would differ from a European nuclear force, or one based on the W.E.U., in that it would preserve the interlocking military relationship with the United States. Buchan rejected the notion that all nuclear weapons in NATO be left in American hands as this would create a division of outlook and responsibility within the alliance. He recommended the reorganization and strengthening of the military command structure of NATO, including the creation under the Standing Group of the position of the Supreme Allied Commander Deterrent (SACDET), an office to be held preferably by a European. To SACDET would be assigned all strategic nuclear weapons, including American bombers and missiles such as Thors and Jupiters, which were based in Europe. In this manner Britain would at first commit her V-bombers to the operational control of a NATO commander. By taking such a step she would receive the bonus of diminishing the vulnerability of the V-bombers, since in an impending crisis they could be dispersed to airfields throughout NATO countries in Europe. In the following stage Britain would contribute to the development of a NATO missile force which would have a second-strike capability to act as a counterweight to the Soviet IRBMs in Western U.S.S.R. The rationalization of the British and French nuclear forces into a NATO nuclear force would enhance their credibility, strengthen the Western deterrent, reduce the economic burden of the national

---

are to be found in Buchan and Windsor, *Arms and Stability in Europe: A British-French-German Enquiry*, pp. 201–12 and Buchan's 'Partners and Allies', *Foreign Affairs*, Vol. XLI, No. 4, July 1963.

[1] For the details of his proposal, see Mulley, op. cit., pp. 86–91.

[2] *NATO in the 1960's*, first edition (New York, Praeger, 1960), pp. 70–81. For his British audience during the post-Blue Streak debate Buchan wrote 'Britain, NATO and the Bomb' and 'Future of British Deterrent: A NATO Retaliatory Force?' *Guardian*, 31 May and 1 June 1960; for the Americans, 'Should NATO Become a Nuclear Power?' *Reporter*, Vol. XXII, 14 April 1960, pp. 21–3.

nuclear weapons, and hopefully, would diminish the likelihood of further nuclear forces in Europe.

Although the concepts of a European, W.E.U., or NATO nuclear force were designed in part to moderate and confine proliferation, it could also be held that they would involve the diffusion of nuclear capabilities, at least in appearance if not in reality. There was concern, particularly on the Left side of informed opinion, that the Germans would thus be closer to having access to nuclear weapons. A more widespread objection to an internationally integrated nuclear force was that it would enormously complicate disarmament negotiations between the Soviet Union and the Western powers. The Soviets could claim that the new nuclear force represented an expansion in the distribution of nuclear weapons in Europe, and they too could be expected to be especially concerned about Germany. There were therefore grounds for caution before establishing a collective nuclear power, even if it might provide a convenient basket into which to place the British and French nuclear capabilities.

The Macmillan government did not openly accept any of the proposals for a European, W.E.U., or NATO nuclear force, in part because it was enmeshed in its own incompatible objectives. In the period before the Nassau Conference and the 1963 Common Market veto there were two major strands in Britain's foreign policy. One strand concerned her future *economic* partners—Britain was intent on joining the Common Market. The other strand concerned her future *military* partners—in replacing Blue Streak with Skybolt Britain seemed to have opted for a closer strategic weapons partnership with the United States. Yet while having accepted dependence on the United States for the missiles themselves, the Government insisted that it was maintaining the 'independence' of its nuclear force. At the same time, a few members of the Macmillan government favoured opening a nuclear relationship with the French, which might in time lead to a European nuclear force. These contradictory objectives gave British policy a markedly schizophrenic quality.

In retrospect, it is unfortunate that Macmillan failed to educate the Conservative party and the public on the diminishing feasibility of a truly 'independent deterrent'. Some of his colleagues urged him to do so, in the same manner that he was then taking the lead in fostering the acceptance in the nation of British entry into the Common Market. What the two issues had in common is that they both involved recognition by the public that Britain was no longer an independent world power. Acceptance of Britain's presumed new 'economic' role may have seemed easier, for at first sight it did not seem to involve a major loss of sovereignty. Britain's 'nuclear independence', on the other hand, had through the Government's own rhetoric become associated with her military autonomy and sovereignty. This symbolism had gained currency with the public and was especially popular among Tory backbenchers and many supporters of the Conservative party, as the Prime Minister knew well. By his failure to educate, Macmillan locked himself into a political position which was to shape his attitude at the Nassau Conference.

In the summer of 1962 certain members of the Macmillan cabinet turned their attention to the possibility of collaboration with France on ballistic missiles and perhaps warheads. This was at a time when the negotiations for entry into the Common Market were reaching an intensive stage and the prospects for Skybolt were increasingly gloomy. Peter Thorney-croft, the new Minister of Defence, was a good 'European' who was attracted by the opportunity of integrating Britain's armaments industry and her defence policy with the continentals. In 1958 he had resigned as Chancellor of the Exchequer in protest against the money allocated to defence at the expense of the welfare services and the economic solvency of the country. On that occasion he had warned of the costs of the attempt to remain an independent nuclear power.[1] Now he viewed collaboration with Europe, and in particular France, as a good way to reduce research and development expenditures. Furthermore, he shared with Julian Amery, the new Minister of Aviation, a belief in the desirability of decreas-ing Britain's dependence on the United States—a vision not unlike that of General de Gaulle's.

It is generally believed that Thorneycroft and Amery during several official and private visits to Paris indicated to their French counterparts that they would personally favour a future 'entente nucléaire'.[2] At the time de Gaulle was under pressure from some of his military and scientific advisers and from within his cabinet to get assistance for the costly 'force de frappe'. One most desirable form of assistance would have been the supplying of enriched uranium, thus avoiding some of the very expensive investment in the isotope separation plant at Pierrelatte. Britain had a surplus of fissile materials and had even reduced the output of her nuclear installations, in part because enriched uranium could be obtained more cheaply from the United States. Co-operation would also be valuable as a way to limit the strains on French resources which could be expected in developing the means of delivery to follow the Mirage IV, be it a solid fuel rocket, a nuclear submarine, or both. A precedent for an Anglo-French arrangement existed in the joint development of the Concorde civil aircraft.

[1] 580 H.C. Deb. col. 1294–6 (23 January 1958).
[2] See Nora Beloff, *The General Says No: Britain's Exclusion from Europe* (London, Penguin Books, 1963), p. 150.

Macmillan was well aware of the logic of a nuclear partnership with France, especially one starting after Britain's prospective admission into the Common Market. But he placed a greater value than his Minister of Defence on the Anglo-American relationship. The Kennedy administration in the spring of 1962 had reaffirmed its policy of restricting nuclear aid to France, and therefore it was not sympathetic to Anglo-French nuclear collaboration. To assist France without American consent would have been incompatible with United States-United Kingdom nuclear agreements and the whole history of the 'special nuclear relationship' with the United States. When Macmillan met de Gaulle at Chateau des Champs in June 1962 the subject of nuclear co-operation was not discussed. The French President preferred not to be seen making a specific request for Britain's nuclear help, although he was left with the impression that in time Britain would be willing to move in this direction. For his part, the Prime Minister thought that the right time formally to ask Washington to revise the 1958 United States-United Kingdom nuclear arrangements so as to assist France would be after Britain was admitted into Europe.[1] He evidently did not consider the nuclear force to be the entry ticket to the Common Market.

After the British had heard that Skybolt would be cancelled, and only three days before the Nassau Conference, Macmillan met de Gaulle again at Rambouillet. Although the Quai d'Orsay and Foreign Office versions of what took place were never reconciled, it appears most probable that Macmillan made no effort to reach a bilateral nuclear arrangement. This time de Gaulle did broach the subject but only to receive a non-committal reply.[2] Macmillan told de Gaulle that he was determined to maintain the British nuclear force, possibly on the basis of Polaris. The French President would presumably sympathize since he cherished his own independent deterrent.

Perhaps if Macmillan had taken a more enthusiastic and constructive lead in proposing a nuclear partnership with France, and had spelled out the specific details of what a joint venture might look like, all as part of Britain's becoming 'European', de Gaulle would not have been able to resist. And it is difficult to conceive of a significant Anglo-French nuclear arrangement with Britain remaining out of Europe. (More difficult than to imagine the United Kingdom in the E.E.C. without an Anglo-French nuclear accord.) If a nuclear accord with France and the subscription of the British nuclear force to a European deterrent was the implicit price

[1] Ibid., p. 151.

[2] Ibid., pp. 157–8; André Fontaine, 'What Is French Policy?' *Foreign Affairs*, Vol. XLV, No. 1, October 1966, p. 74; Robert Kleiman, *Atlantic Crisis: American Diplomacy Confronts a Resurgent Europe* (New York, Norton, 1964), pp. 49–50.

for admission into the Common Market, Macmillan either did not recognize this or gambled that he could finesse the entrance without shedding the Anglo-American relationship. In any case it is clear that in his personal system of preferences, as well as in Foreign Secretary Alec Douglas-Home's, greater priority was given to maintaining the political and strategic relationship with the United States at Nassau than to entering into a new military relationship with France and Europe at Rambouillet.

As to the 'Gaullists' in the British cabinet, the weeks before Nassau were marked by the dropping of hints from them that London was now more interested in a European nuclear force under solely European control. On 4 December Thorneycroft in a speech in Paris before the Western European Union Assembly spoke of Europe as a potential world power which must be equipped with commensurate military capability. In closed sessions he reportedly discussed how the weapons for a European nuclear force might be procured.[1] This may have been designed to ease Britain's passage into Europe. But it could also serve to exert pressure on the Americans by making them more aware of the risk of leaving Britain without Skybolt or a suitable replacement. So long as it was not prepared to countenance the emergence of a separate European deterrent based on Anglo-French co-operation, Washington could not afford to deal in a cavalier manner with the British 'independent deterrent'.

2. The Skybolt Crisis

The decision to end research and development on the Skybolt missile led to a veritable political eruption in London, a wave of anti-Americanism in the British public, and at the official level the greatest crisis between the two countries since the Suez affair. Since this response to the American action in turn helps account for a great deal of what happened at the Nassau Conference it is of significance here. To assist in understanding the British reaction to the Skybolt cancellation one must take into account several events in the autumn of 1962 which cumulatively led to a rapid transformation in the atmosphere of Anglo-American relations.

The Cuban missile crisis in October 1962 greatly strengthened a latent sense of irritation with Britain's dependency upon the United States. Britain was informed but not consulted as her principal ally took rapid decisions involving the serious risk of nuclear war while acting essentially alone. With whatever admiration the British may later have viewed President Kennedy's decisive but restrained handling of the world's first

[1] See Geoffrey Warner, 'The Nassau Agreement and NATO', *The World Today* (February 1963), pp. 63–4.

'nuclear confrontation', as some have referred to it, the lack of consultation seemed to reveal the weakness of the 'special relationship' and the small amount of political influence attached to Britain's role as a nuclear power. 'The British government', one London journalist wrote, 'could hardly have had its dependent status more brutally spelled out to it than it has been this week.'[1] The initial reaction of the British public and press, regardless of political persuasion, was one of doubt and scepticism regarding Washington's actions and fear that Britain was being drawn by an irresponsible America into her war.[2] In order to counter this sentiment, Ambassador David Ormsby Gore persuaded the President to release some of the aerial photographs of the missile placements in Cuba. The British government thereupon loyally supported the United States in the Security Council. Even Macmillan, however, had to be reassured by Kennedy that his policy was not a response to anti-Castroism at home, but was guided by his appraisal of a serious Soviet threat to the West.[3] There was a tendency in Whitehall to see the American naval quarantine of Cuba as needlessly aggressive and to wish for Britain's dissociation from America's actions. The events of Cuba, like Suez, provoked new demands for independence from the United States.[4]

An additional irritant came in the form of a speech by Dean Acheson at West Point on 5 December 1962 in which he commented that 'Great Britain has lost an empire and has not yet found a new role'. The former Secretary of State's observation, which was only a minor theme in a wide-ranging talk on the Atlantic alliance, was trite but true. Nevertheless, it struck a sensitive nerve in the British body politic and inflamed political passions out of all proportion to the importance of the speech. The front pages of the London press joined together in jingoistic protest, some in Whitehall suspected that the speech was politically inspired, and Macmillan felt compelled through the device of a letter to the Institute of Directors to give a sharp rebuke. By then news of the imminent Skybolt cancellation had reached the public and the atmosphere between London and Washington had become electric.[5]

[1] Anthony Howard, 'Caution in Westminster', New Statesman, 26 October 1962.

[2] For a detailed analysis of the British press during the 'week of Cuba' supporting this conclusion see Encounter, Vol. XX, No. 1, January 1963, pp. 84–95.

[3] Schlesinger, Jr., op. cit., pp. 815–16.

[4] John Mander later wrote: 'If any one day saw the death of Britain's "special relationship" with America it was Tuesday, 23 October 1962. . . . Who can doubt that the Skybolt affair, Nassau and Mr. Acheson's speech were influenced by it? . . . I believe that there are features of the Cuban crisis that argue against too close a dependence on American power. There are, I believe, good arguments why Britain (or Britain-and-Europe) should maintain an independent deterrent.' Great Britain or Little England? (London, Penguin Books, 1963), p. 21.

[5] The Acheson speech, said The Economist, 29 December 1962, 'sparked off what has always been the most disturbing feature of postwar Conservatism's inferiority complex: namely, the feeling that when in travail, it is an appropriate reflex to turn anti-American.'

The Conservative Party in late 1962 was in deep political trouble and Macmillan's position as leader of the party was becoming increasingly questioned. Dissensions over the rebuffs at Brussels, rising unemployment and a stagnating economy, dissatisfactions over the cabinet's African policies, and a series of disastrous losses in by-elections put the Tory government in its worst shape since it had taken office eleven years earlier. There was much speculation of a General Election being forced on the Conservatives and of a subsequent Labour victory. The Gallup Poll in mid-1962 reported that only 36 per cent of the electorate expressed approval of Macmillan's performance as Prime Minister. Support for a Prime Minister had sunk to so low a level only once before, in 1940 during the final days of the Chamberlain government.[1] The Skybolt cancellation —which the public, not being privy to the many prior warnings, saw as an abrupt and rude treatment of Britain by the United States—served as a catalyst. The 'independent deterrent' became ever more a symbol of Britain's greatness which Conservative supporters and backbenchers refused to do without. And as Macmillan flew to Nassau his personal position in the party was very much at stake.

As we have seen, the scrapping of Skybolt came at a particularly bad moment: following the Cuban missile crisis, the Acheson speech, and at a time when the governing party in Britain was in grave domestic political difficulties. In addition, it came about shortly before the negotiation for admission into the Common Market was expected to reach a conclusive stage. Since the details of the Skybolt crisis have been written about fairly extensively elsewhere, they will be reviewed only briefly here. The reader should note, however, that most of the analysis thus far has focused on questions regarding the failure in communications between the two Governments and bureaucratic politics within the Governments, rather than on the significance of the cancellation of Skybolt in the context of the long history of the British nuclear force.[2]

After it was finally recognized by the British cabinet that Blue Streak could not be continued, Prime Minister Macmillan obtained a promise from President Eisenhower at Camp David in March 1960 that the British

[1] McKenzie, op. cit., p. 594a.

[2] The most complete and accurate published account is the post-mortem written a year later by the respected Washington correspondent of the *Sunday Times*, Henry Brandon, 'Skybolt: The Full Inside Story of How a Missile Nearly Split the West', 8 December 1963. See also: Schlesinger, Jr., op. cit., pp. 856–62; Ward S. Just, 'The Scrapping of Skybolt', *Reporter*, Vol. XXVIII, 11 April 1963, pp. 19–21.

President Kennedy was so perplexed by the miscalculations of the two Governments that he asked Professor Richard E. Neustadt to make a confidential study. Neustadt looked at the internal political decision-making processes on Skybolt within Whitehall and Washington as well as the transatlantic communications network. His study was read by the President the week of his assassination and subsequently provided the basis for one of the two case studies in his suggestive *Alliance Politics* (New York, Columbia University Press, 1970).

would be sold the Skybolt missile when it reached the production stage. On the same occasion the British undertook to make available in Scotland facilities for a base for the new nuclear-powered Polaris submarines of the United States Navy. Although the subsequent formal agreements dealing with Skybolt and Holy Loch made no mention of the link between the two, there is no doubt that the British felt that the United States was under a moral obligation to provide a strategic missile in one form or another in exchange for Holy Loch. Since at the time Skybolt was little more than a drawing board concept, the agreement contained a termination clause that either party could end its interest in the project at any time, but neither would do so without prior consultations.

In all probability the British could have obtained Polaris rather than Skybolt at Camp David if they had so wished. Indeed, the United States Navy attempted to 'sell' Polaris to the British contingent at Camp David through President Eisenhower's naval aide. For a number of reasons discussed in Chapter 8, and chiefly related to inter-service rivalries, costs, and strategic concepts, both the Royal Navy and the Royal Air Force preferred Skybolt to Polaris. Moreover, American defence officials had indicated that any arrangement on Polaris should be part of a wider NATO missile undertaking, such as General Norstad was seeking. Watkinson therefore advised Macmillan that since an American offer of Polaris would be tied to NATO, only Skybolt would keep Britain's nuclear force fully independent.

How different might the course of events in the Atlantic alliance have run if the British had opted for Polaris in 1960! There would have been no Skybolt crisis to jeopardize Anglo-American relations, no confrontation over nuclear weapons at Nassau, de Gaulle would not have been affronted with a new manifestation of the 'special relationship' at a delicate stage in the negotiation of Britain's entry into the Common Market, and the entire approach to nuclear sharing based on multilateralism would certainly have evolved in another manner.

In the twenty months between the Camp David meeting and the fall of the curtain on Skybolt its progress was carefully watched by British officials. An R.A.F. group captain at the Pentagon, assisted by various technicians, had the sole task of following the tantalizing progress of the missile. The record is studded with meetings at which American officials at the policy-making level warned the British by expressing their doubts that Skybolt would ever go beyond the research and development stage. Following the Nassau meeting the chairman of the British military defence staff in Washington from 1959 to the autumn of 1962 took the most unusual step of denying in a letter to the *Daily Telegraph* that Britain had been 'let down' by the United States. 'We have been warned constantly from the

Q NP

beginning that the continuation of the project was not 100 per cent certain and that the Americans would have to scrap it if it did not meet their requirements over date or cost. In fact I cannot recall any conversation between senior American and British people when Skybolt was discussed and this straightforward warning was not given.'[1]

Even before the arrival of Robert McNamara at the Pentagon, Secretary of Defense Thomas Gates had warned London that the Skybolt missile might be abandoned. In late 1960 he had sent a message to Minister of Defence Harold Watkinson through the latter's Chief Scientific Adviser, Sir Solly Zuckerman, advising of the risk in making a political issue of Skybolt. Throughout 1961 and 1962 Whitehall had been well informed of the mounting odds favouring the project's cancellation, yet the Government failed to modify its declaratory policy to suit a most probable contingency. Watkinson stated in the Commons that Skybolt would continue the British deterrent throughout the 1960s and that, as long as Britain owned the warhead and the delivery vehicle, the weapon system maintained Britain's 'independence'.[2] Recurrent reports in the press, or reaching the ears of Labour politicians, that the Skybolt project was in terms of cost-effectiveness becoming an increasingly poor investment in comparison to Minuteman and Polaris and therefore might be cancelled were repeatedly scoffed at. The Secretary of State for Air, Julian Amery, following a visit in early 1962 to Douglas Aircraft in California, told the House that he returned home convinced that Skybolt would come into service on time.[3] He did not speak of a luncheon at the White House where, according to a reliable account, he became so upset he nearly fell off his chair upon hearing from President Kennedy that the Skybolt missile might not work out.[4]

Why then were the British so 'shocked' and 'surprised' when the cancellation did come? One reason is the high estimate which Whitehall officials gave to the power of the United States Air Force, the Joint Chiefs of Staff who had recommended continuation of the project, and the ndustrial interest, chiefly the Douglas Aircraft Corporation, to force the Secretary of Defense to accept Skybolt for the American strategic arsenal. These same. nterests encouraged the British to bring pressure upon the Pentagon leadership, and on at least one occasion it was such pressure which kept funds for Skybolt from being sharply curtailed. Britain's participation in Skybolt, one observer believes, assured the survival of the programme for an additional six months.

[1] Reprinted in *Survival*, Vol. V, No. 3, March–April 1963, p. 51.
[2] 635 H.C. Deb. col. 1207 (27 February 1961); 655 H.C. Deb. col. 330 (6 March 1962).
[3] 655 H.C. Deb. col. 914 (12 March 1962).
[4] Henry Brandon, 'Skybolt: The Full Inside Story of How a Missile Nearly Split the West', *Sunday Times*, 8 December 1963.

London, however, underestimated the managerial revolution which McNamara had brought to the Pentagon, and his ability to use cost-effectiveness analysis to discriminate between weapons systems. On the basis of cost, vulnerability, and effectiveness Skybolt more and more compared unfavourably with Polaris and Minuteman. In explaining his reasons (after the Nassau Conference) for cancelling Skybolt, Secretary of Defense McNamara said that it promised to combine the disadvantages of the bomber with those of the missile. It would have had the bomber's disadvantage of being 'soft', 'concentrated', relatively vulnerable on the ground, and slow to target; but it would not have had the bomber's advantageous payload and accuracy, or the advantages usually associated with a manned system. Furthermore, the Skybolt-bomber system would have had the lower payload and poorer accuracy of a missile, without the relative invulnerability and short time to target of a Minuteman or Polaris.[1] An additional consideration was that the Skybolt-bomber system was a far less satisfactory instrument for the strategy of controlled response.

Certainly, also, there was an element of wishful thinking in London at the cabinet level. Every straw of evidence that the missile would be continued was seized upon by the Ministers of Defence and Aviation. The Skybolt story is a superb case of a Government 'hearing what it wants to hear' and hoping that all will go well in the end. Thus as Skybolt became a political issue, the advice of the technical experts carried less and less weight. For in the final analysis the Conservative leaders expected that *political* considerations could pull the chestnut out of the fire. This was a facile assumption to make for politicians who had entered into the habit of basing some of their principal defence decisions on domestic political factors. One must bear in mind that the reason Skybolt was of such importance to the cabinet was the accusation of the critics that the 'independent deterrent' could not be maintained.

United States officials looked upon the Skybolt cancellation as essentially a technical rather than a political matter. When President Kennedy gave McNamara authority to settle the issue with the British, and Dean Rusk and the State Department's seventh floor failed to show a strong interest in this 'weapons system' matter, there was little understanding that a major political crisis was on the horizon. It may be that in the euphoria following the Cuban missile crisis the President's usually sensitive political antenna was slightly dulled. As Sorensen was to write of the initial handling

---

[1] *Hearings on Military Posture*, Committee on Armed Services, House of Representatives, 88th Congress, First session (Washington, GPO, 1963), p. 312. See also Alain C. Enthoven and K. Wayne Smith, *How Much is Enough? Shaping the Defense Program, 1961–1969* (New York, Harper & Row, 1971), pp. 251–62.

of Skybolt, 'After Cuba it seemed a small problem. All problems did.'[1] Later Kennedy was to ask why he had not been warned of the coming storm.

The high point of the cancellation drama came when McNamara met Thorneycroft in London on 11 December and in effect presented him with a *fait accompli*, while indicating a willingness to work out a suitable alternative to Skybolt. At that time McNamara was not fully cognizant of the symbolic importance of the 'independent deterrent' to the Macmillan government, and the degree to which that symbolism had come to depend upon Skybolt. Thus after McNamara had finished a characteristically comprehensive analysis of the budgeting and technical factors which had influenced his decision to cancel Skybolt he was surprised by Thorneycroft's insistence on discussing the matter primarily upon the basis of the grave political implications involved. In 'one of the bluntest talks ever within the Anglo-American alliance' Thorneycroft, after reminding McNamara of the relationship between Holy Loch and Skybolt, demanded to know if the United States wanted to deprive Britain of its 'independent deterrent role'. If such was not the case, was the United States willing to do everything possible to assist Britain in maintaining its independent role and to say so publicly?[2]

This question indicated the extent to which the Skybolt episode had become a British domestic political crisis as much as an Anglo-American dispute. McNamara's speech at Ann Arbor condemning independent nuclear forces, the entire direction of the controlled response strategy as articulated by numerous American officials, the attempt to revise NATO strategy by raising the nuclear threshold, the Acheson speech, and now the culminating Skybolt cancellation—all were interpreted by much of the public and press as signifying that Washington's policy was to take Britain out of the nuclear business.

There was a strong suspicion that Skybolt's extinction was a thinly disguised attempt to force Britain out of the nuclear club, thereby further polarizing nuclear matters between Washington and Moscow.[3] This was not an unreasonable assumption given the underlying rationale of the new American defence policy. Under such circumstances the Kennedy administration, which was highly admired in Britain, would seem to be supporting Labour's call for renunciation of the nuclear force. But such in fact was not the case. Whatever their private views on the British deterrent may have been, neither the President nor his Secretaries of State or Defense intended to use the Skybolt cancellation as the knife to kill the British

---

[1] Theodore C. Sorensen, *Kennedy* (New York, Harper & Row, 1965), p. 564–5.

[2] Brandon, *Sunday Times*, 8 December 1963.

[3] See, for example, *The Times*, 14 December 1962; *Daily Telegraph*, 18 December 1962.

nuclear force. After the decision to cancel Skybolt had been made, some planning level officials concerned with European affairs in the State Department saw an opportunity to use the situation to force Britain into a multilateral agreement. But at the cabinet level there was an inclination to make a special exception for the British to the arms control analysis opposed to national nuclear forces.[1] Thus when McNamara met Thorneycroft before the Nassau Conference there was already some hedged discussion about the possible replacement of Skybolt with Polaris.

Britain's experience over Skybolt illuminated the nature of the dependency which she had entered into after the cancellation of Blue Streak by deciding to purchase the American missile rather than developing a new British weapon. With Skybolt Britain had tied herself into the American order of priorities and thereby was forced to gamble on the risk of disappointment. The Macmillan government found itself politically embarrassed because in its past declarations it had refused to acknowledge that its nuclear deterrent policy had been at least partially placed in trust with the Pentagon leadership. It might have been wiser to draw attention to the fact that a certain loss of sovereignty is unavoidable if nations in alliance are to become interdependent.

3. The Confrontation at Nassau

Nassau was a great turning point in the history of the British nuclear force.[2] Before the conference a mix of events and ideas seemed to be forcing out the 'independent deterrent'; after the conference the continuation of an independent capability was assured for perhaps another twenty years. Nassau also raised to the top of the alliance agenda the question of devising multinational or multilateral formulae for nuclear control. It marked a partial reversal of the then orthodox American policy on nuclear sharing. Its long-range impact on the integration of Europe and the cohesion of the Atlantic alliance is more difficult to measure, but certainly cannot be denied.

Nassau was also one of the great confrontations in the history of

[1] Interviews.

[2] In this section I am more descriptive than in other parts of the study because although many analyses have been written of the inconsistencies of the Nassau Agreement, far less has been published on how these inconsistencies came about. What actually happened at Nassau can only be understood in the context of the overpowering British concern for the independent deterrent. Much of my information comes from extensive interviews with a number of the principals who attended the Nassau Conference. In addition, I have carefully culled from the British and American press of the time and from the most informative writings thus far available: Brandon, *Sunday Times*, 8 December 1963; Kleiman, op. cit., pp. 47–61; Schlesinger, op. cit., pp. 862–6; Sorensen, op. cit., pp. 566–71; George W. Ball, *The Discipline of Power* (Boston, Atlantic-Little, Brown, 1968), pp. 102–7.

Anglo-American relations and a crucial test of the 'special relationship'. The discussions were to have centred on Cuba and the East-West relations in the aftermath of the missile crisis, the Congo, joint efforts to help India improve her defences against China, and a nuclear test ban agreement. Skybolt was not on the agenda when the meeting was arranged. But for the British the preservation of the 'independent deterrent' was to be the single, overriding consideration. 18 December was a warm and clear day, Nassau as attractive as on a tourist postcard, but the British delegation arrived in a mood of nagging exasperation and bitter indignation. The uncertainty as to how the conference would end was far greater than usual since there had been no consultations or exchange of papers at the diplomatic level. Henry Brandon of the *Sunday Times* found in the British contingent a 'resentment and suspicion of American intentions such as I have never experienced in all the Anglo-American conferences I have covered over the past twenty years'.[1] The Skybolt episode had fostered the growth of a victimization complex in Whitehall leaving British officials uncommonly irritated. Macmillan himself was in a terrible mood, as he had every reason to be: two days earlier he had been told by de Gaulle at Rambouillet that the time for British entry into the Common Market had not arrived. Now the continuation of the 'independent deterrent' to which his Government was deeply committed was in serious jeopardy, the Conservative party was in a rebellious state, and his own position as leader was at stake.

On the flight to Nassau President Kennedy took with him his trusted friend, David Ormsby Gore, the British Ambassador. Ormsby Gore told Kennedy that for the European nations to see Britain let down would be cited by them as proof that the United States could not be trusted. Earlier he had warned the President that to drop Skybolt abruptly would be 'political dynamite' in London. Now he feared that a storm of anti-Americanism would sweep Britain if a suitable arrangement on a weapons system was not made. The two then worked out a proposal whereby the research and development of Skybolt would continue as a joint enterprise with each country paying half of the future cost. Britain would place a production order to meet her requirements, even if the United States did not make a purchase. This was a generous offer since the United States no longer felt a need for the missile. Had it been made earlier the British might well have either accepted it or by their own decision reached the conclusion that Skybolt was becoming too expensive, thereby averting the crisis atmosphere which Skybolt's cancellation brought about.

But Skybolt was no longer acceptable to the British. Ormsby Gore had not known that only hours prior to Macmillan's departure for Nassau the

[1] Brandon, *Sunday Times*, 8 December 1963.

cabinet had decided to attempt to obtain Polaris. Deep in their hearts the R.A.F. and the Royal Navy had come to admit that Polaris was a far preferable weapons system, even if they did not want it for parochial service interests. For Macmillan the deathblow to Skybolt had come in the deprecatory statements which Kennedy and McNamara had recently made of Skybolt before the press. They had 'compromised the reputation of the lady' in public. Skybolt had been discredited by the Americans. It could no longer be presented as a credible maintainer of the 'independent deterrent' to the British public. In rejecting the Nassau offer of continued development of Skybolt on a 50-50 basis, Macmillan cited the uncertainties regarding the date of completion and the final costs of the project. As a possible alternative the President suggested the air-to-ground Hound Dog missile, which could be adapted to the V-bombers. But the less advanced Hound Dog would have been a humiliating exchange for Skybolt, even if some technical difficulties could be overcome. Another suggestion, for a joint study of alternative weapons systems which might be made available, thereby providing the added advantage of a delay until the outcome of the then critical Common Market negotiations was clearer, was also unacceptable. It became evident to the President that only Polaris would satisfy the British.

President Kennedy had a historian-philosopher side to his personality, and Macmillan knew how to appeal to it. In an eloquent, emotional discourse memorable to those present, Macmillan spoke of the better days in the Anglo-American relationship. He opened with some of his nostalgic memories of working with Americans when Britain was more of a world power. Macmillan then retraced the long history of Anglo-American relations in atomic energy. He reminded the President of the initial work of the British scientists on 'Tube Alloys' without which, he said, the bomb would not have been developed; of the collaborative effort in the Manhattan Project; of the way Britain had been unfairly let down after the war by the McMahon Act; of the long road between 1946 and 1958 during which Britain was forced by America to 'pull its way alone'; of his personal role in re-establishing co-operation on atomic energy in 1958 and his efforts to restore the close Anglo-American ties after the Suez rupture.[1] At Camp David a broad and honourable understanding had been reached which included the stationing of United States Polaris submarines in Scotland. In asking for Polaris now he was only requesting what had already been offered to him in 1960 at Camp David, when his service chiefs had advised him, right or wrong, to choose Skybolt.

[1] This historical interpretation was believed by Macmillan and accepted by his listeners, even if contemporary scholarship might put the early collaboration during World War II in a somewhat different light. See Chapters 1–3.

Macmillan warned of the dire political consequences for Anglo-American relations if the United States was seen by the British public to be depriving the United Kingdom of her nuclear role. The preservation of the 'independent deterrent', he stressed, was essential for Britain's self-respect. He described himself as being like a ship that looked buoyant but was apt to sink. Did the President want to live with the consequences of sinking him? The collapse of his cabinet on this issue could bring into the Conservative leadership someone who would exploit anti-Americanism in order to keep the Tories in power. President Kennedy had been prepared for an argument that the Conservative government could fall on the issue, an unattractive eventuality for him. He had been well disposed to Labour until the previous September when Gaitskell, in his speech before the Labour party's annual conference, came out in opposition to entry into the Common Market. But rather than making such an argument, the Prime Minister was presenting him with the likelihood of a General Election being fought on a 'perfidious America' theme by the Tories, an even more unappealing prospect. The President was very sensitive to the bi-partisan nature of the support within the United States for the 'special relationship' with Britain.

Kennedy had no intention of letting Macmillan leave Nassau empty-handed and was determined to work out a mutually satisfactory solution. He accepted the British contention that the United States was under a moral obligation to provide a missile because of the understanding reached at Camp David. Therefore he was offering to continue Skybolt or to replace it with Hound Dog. Polaris would have to be dealt with somewhat differently. He was willing to give the submarine-launched missile to the British if it were 'irrevocably' committed to some type of a NATO nuclear force arrangement. Polaris could not be provided on unconditional, bilateral terms.

The President was now setting out on relatively uncharted waters. There had been surprisingly little staff work done in Washington in preparation for the Nassau Conference on a possible offer of Polaris to the British. There was no agreed United States position which had State, Defence, and White House concurrence on a NATO 'multilateral' force, or on a Polaris offer to Britain, and the 'specialists' were not present at Nassau to identify the hidden rocks. In the Bureau of European Affairs of the State Department there were a number of officials who saw in the Skybolt cancellation an unexpected opportunity to facilitate their conception of the 'Grand Design' by bringing an end to the 'special relationship'. The 'Europeanists' contended that the British should be denied Polaris as a straightforward replacement for Skybolt so as to 'lower' them to an equal level with Germany and France. Those who were supporting a multilateral force argued that any offer of Polaris should only be made within the context of such an arrangement, thus forcing Britain to join. Those who were primarily concerned with the Common Market believed that the ending of the preferential treatment for Britain on atomic energy, which was so resented in France, would be a step towards the successful outcome of the Brussels negotiations. The top State Department official at Nassau, George Ball, urged President Kennedy not to make an offer of Polaris outside the framework of a NATO multilateral force, as this would be regarded by the continentals as fresh evidence of discrimination benefiting the United Kingdom.

Macmillan, however, insisted that the claim to an independent nuclear capability should not be blurred. To return to London without the 'independent deterrent' would be fatal. He cited an angry cable he had received from the Chairman of the Conservative Defence Committee and signed by 137 backbenchers of his own party. 'From the Nassau Conference room', wrote *The Economist*, 'the Prime Minister could still hear 3,000 miles away the loud baying of the Tory troops for their independent nuclear deterrent.'[1] He knew better than anyone that within the Conservative party an emotion-laden, anti-American issue which affected Britain's historic status was the one type of revolt that a leader had to take seriously. Macmillan told Kennedy that he saw no reason why Polaris should be offered on an altogether different basis from Skybolt. To him the only difference was that one was fired from the air, the other from the sea. It was his impression at Rambouillet that General de Gaulle would not be upset by a straight switch of one for the other.

If there must be a parting, Macmillan went on, let it be done with honour and dignity. Britain would not break her past agreements— the Holy Loch depot could remain for American Polaris submarines, the Fylingdales station for early warning radar system would continue to operate, R.A.F. bases would be provided for American aircraft—all commitments, the Prime Minister noted, that brought added risks to the British Isles. Britain would want no more nuclear information from the United States—but—it would be understood that what information she had already received would not keep her under obligation from branching off on her own. Britain would be at liberty to co-operate elsewhere on nuclear matters. The obvious implication was collaboration with France.

Kennedy was unwilling to accept a rupture in Anglo-American relations on a weapons system issue, or, more specifically, on the 'irrevocability' of the commitment of Britain's nuclear force to an embryonic NATO venture. He accordingly steered his delegation to a compromise formula which would not contradict American aspirations for multilateralism,

[1] 'Tories in Arms', 22 December 1962.

yet would make it possible for Macmillan to claim that he had preserved Britain's independent deterrent. In a few hours, and without the aid of adequate staffs, the two delegations set out to resolve a complex of problems involving nuclear sharing and military integration which had baffled the American government and the Atlantic alliance for several years. The result was a document of extraordinary ambiguity which was later read with differing interpretations in Washington and London. The American bureaucracy spent weeks debating the nature of the commitments which had been made.

The Nassau 'Statement on Nuclear Defence Systems'[1] provided that the United States would make available to Britain on a 'continuing basis' Polaris missiles. Britain was to construct the submarines in which the missiles were to be placed and provide the nuclear warheads. From this point on the accord became imprecise, in part because the hasty drafting of the document precluded firmer agreement, but also because the participants got their terminology muddled. Paragraph Six provided for the assignment of allocations from Bomber Command, United States strategic forces, and tactical nuclear forces in Europe to a 'NATO nuclear force targeted in accordance with NATO plans'. Paragraph Eight committed the planned British Polaris submarines to assignment in the same manner as the forces described in Paragraph Six. This was the *multinational* approach. But Paragraph Eight went on to say that the British Polaris force would be made available for inclusion in a NATO *multilateral* nuclear force. In Paragraph Seven it was agreed that the purpose of the provision of the Polaris submarines 'must be the development of a *multilateral* NATO nuclear force in the closest consultations with other NATO allies'.

The British were under the impression that the future NATO force was to be organized on the basis of existing forces plus the projected Polaris submarines, and that the 'multilateral' commitment of Paragraph Eight referred to a force based on national contingents. In subsequent weeks, however, the Department of State indicated that its concept of the multilateral force was a new, jointly financed, mix-manned fleet. Americans supporting this proposal initially thought that the British at Nassau had agreed to participate, but in fact the question had not been settled there. On the contrary, the British were led to think at the time that the multilateral nuclear force (MLF) was only a distant aspiration and a secondary American objective.

To what extent did the assignment of the British Polaris submarines to a NATO force restrict London's ability to use them for national purposes? Paragraph Eight of the Nassau Agreement stipulated that the Polaris

[1] Text in Appendix B.

submarines would be used 'for the purposes of international defence of the Western Alliance in all circumstances', except 'where her Majesty's Government may decide that supreme national interests are at stake'. (Italics mine.) But could one imagine Britain considering the use of nuclear weapons in circumstances other than those involving the supreme national interest? And what was meant by the 'international defence' of the Western alliance? It could be argued that the Polaris force could only be used within a NATO context, not for example for the unilateral defence of Kuwait or Singapore. Successive statements by the Prime Minister in 1963, however, winnowed down any restrictive aspects of the commitment to NATO. In practice Britain was less inhibited in its independence than might appear to be the case. Clearly Britain would retain complete national control of her Polaris submarines, the *sine qua non* of Macmillan at Nassau. [1]

The conference in the Bahamas demonstrated how insensitive to the alliance as a whole the two nations could be when they met. Britain and the United States developed an important nuclear plan for NATO without consulting their allies, or even the alliance's other nuclear power, France. It was therefore understandable that the reaction to the Nassau Conference throughout Western Europe was one of cool suspicion. The failure of Britain to consult with the Common Market nations before concluding a compact of such long-term significance may have been a particularly serious mistake. At Nassau the British acted as if their future was tied to the United States rather than Europe. The French were later to make much of the fact that Britain negotiated for sixteen months with the Common Market, but reached a major defence agreement with the United States in forty-eight hours.

The manner in which the Nassau Agreement was concluded may have been more offensive to General de Gaulle than its content. The communiqué was transmitted to de Gaulle through diplomatic channels only after it was published in the press. This was a strange way to treat a man whose distrust of 'les Anglo-Saxons' was legendary. The Americans at Nassau proposed that the United States-United Kingdom Polaris arrangement

[1] This was recognized by President Kennedy in a press conference at Palm Beach shortly after Nassau. In answer to a question whether the 'escape clause' was only symbolic, Kennedy, in a reply which was widely quoted in the British press and which was subsequently cited by Conservative statesmen as proof of his 'understanding' of the need for a British independent deterrent, said: 'It was not merely symbolic. It was a recognition I think probably of the interests of any nation if they are going to put that much effort into it. Every nation is conscious that there may be a moment when it is isolated and when its national interests are involved. The British have had several such experiences. They had them certainly at the beginning of the Second World War. So I think that the concept of their having to be alone is a rather strong one for the British.' *Sunday Times,* 6 January 1963.

be discussed with de Gaulle before the accord was publicly concluded. But Macmillan insisted that the agreement had to be announced before he returned to London. Domestic politics must have dictated his priorities. He gave little indication of sharing Kennedy's concern regarding the effect of presenting de Gaulle with a *fait accompli*, arguing that the General would have no objections to the Polaris deal given his sympathetic understanding of the relevance of nuclear weapons to national sovereignty. Here again one suspects that Macmillan was preoccupied with his primary objective, the survival of the British nuclear force.

It was in fact the Americans who took the initiative in proposing that an offer of Polaris missiles also be made to France.[1] There had always been a minority within the Kennedy administration who favoured nuclear assistance to Paris as the price of a more co-operative French attitude. At Nassau when the British in return for Polaris missiles appeared to agree to commit their nuclear force to a NATO nuclear arrangement, it became possible for the first time to offer France equal treatment without accepting the concept of a totally independent French nuclear force. The President was told by some of his advisers that to give Polaris to the British and not to offer it to the French could be disastrous. Thus the cancellation of Skybolt was seen by some Americans as creating a new opportunity to accept a measure of the tripartism within the alliance that de Gaulle desired, thereby opening a bridge for the French to return to full co-operation within NATO. Shortly after Nassau a Gaullist spokesman pointed out that France possessed neither the submarines nor the warheads required for the Polaris missiles; but in the extended discussions that Ambassador Bohlen was instructed to suggest to de Gaulle, the possibility of collaboration on the entire Polaris submarine system was not excluded.

The British experience with Skybolt gave de Gaulle fresh evidence of the dangers that accompany leaving the manufacture of a critical component of an independent nuclear force to another nation. Even if his first preference remained that the 'force de frappe' be completely 'fabriqué en France', the delay before giving his negative response to the Polaris offer, and the impression of some persons who spoke to him at the time, suggest that he was strongly tempted by the offer. The pressures upon de Gaulle to find a way to avoid the rising costs of his nuclear force were substantial. The Nassau Agreement's *multinational* clauses opened the way for a co-ordinated, yet independent, French nuclear role. Unfortunately, immediately after Nassau the proponents of the MLF, contending that the

---

[1] The correspondent of *The Times* at Nassau saw the extension of the offer to Paris as signalling the probable end of the United Kingdom-United States 'special relationship', 22 December 1962.

conference had given a dangerous sense of exclusion to Germany, re-newed their efforts for a *multilateral* force. Under Secretary of State George Ball went to Bonn to see Adenauer, stopping on his way to discuss Nassau with Couve de Murville, the French Foreign Minister. Ball reportedly stressed the integrationist side of Nassau, suggesting that any Polaris missiles given to France would have to become part of a *multi-lateral* arrangement. This may have been what tipped the scales against the acceptance of the Polaris offer, the General sensing that Nassau was a roundabout way of bringing the 'force de frappe' under American or NATO management. But de Gaulle must also have realized that he could not enter into a closer nuclear relationship with the United States while simultaneously closing the door on Britain at Brussels.

The existence of a causal link between Nassau and the Common Market veto has been the subject of much debate and therefore need not be discussed extensively here. In all probability de Gaulle had determined his general course of action long before the Bahamas meeting. Nassau served as a splendid justification—for how could Britain enter an inte-grated Europe in 1963 while leaving her nuclear force outside until 1980? Nevertheless, the timing of Nassau was most unfortunate. It was an unnecessary mistake to cancel Skybolt at the critical juncture in Britain's negotiations with the European Community, thus laying the stage for a public reaffirmation of the special Anglo-American military relationship and consequently strengthening de Gaulle's hand in resisting British entry into Europe. The Skybolt timetable was prescribed by the American budgetary cycle and a special budget trimming exercise then under way because of the Kennedy administration's resolve not to exceed the peak budget deficit of the Eisenhower years. If the White House had agreed to a delay of a few months while orderly negotiations were carried out with the British for replacing Skybolt, it might have been possible to avoid budgetary considerations undermining foreign policy goals.

Similarly, there would have been merit in Macmillan's acceptance of the proposal made by Kennedy at Nassau that a decision on Polaris be post-poned by setting up a study group, until the Common Market negotiations had progressed further. Macmillan assured Kennedy that the Polaris agreement would not get in the way; the only remaining stumbling block at Brussels, he said, was agriculture. Whether Macmillan's optimistic attitude at Nassau on the Common Market question and his playing down of its relationship to the Polaris deal could be justified by what he had been told by de Gaulle a few days earlier at Rambouillet remains for history to judge. It has been said that the 'Non' was written on the wall when they met at the Chateau. De Gaulle was probably convinced before Rambouillet or Nassau that Britain did not fit into his conception of Europe. It is possible, though not probable, that Britain could have obtained admission into the Common Market if she had entered into nuclear collaboration with France and countenanced the emergence of a European nuclear force. Yet even this would have been distasteful to de Gaulle since it would have allowed the British to share his hitherto sole nuclear role in the European Community. Nevertheless, Britain demonstrated at Nassau that she did not believe that her fate was tied inseparably to that of Europe. Nassau and Brussels represented two different conceptions of Britain's future role and associations. Macmillan chose firmly a transatlantic connection while the Common Market question was still unsettled.

For American nuclear strategy Nassau was a deviation from—if not a reversal of—both the doctrine of limiting independent nuclear forces and the doctrine of controlled response. These canons had been prescribed by Secretary McNamara as recently as the week before the Bahamas meeting at the annual NATO Ministerial Conference in Paris. The offer of Polaris missiles to France was even more of a modification of past American policy than the offer to Britain. But the McNamara critique of independent nuclear forces, which he made in his famous Ann Arbor speech of June 1962 and which was thought to be directed primarily at the French nuclear force, could be applied with equal logic to the United Kingdom.

As Henry Kissinger has perceptively written, 'The Nassau Agreement attempted a *tour de force*. It tried to reconcile integration with independence, the American belief in the need for an indivisible nuclear strategy with the British desire for autonomy.'[1] Kennedy had hoped that the *multilateral* provisions of the accord, which were thought of as preventing the independent use of nuclear weapons, would complement its *multinational* provisions and the 'escape clause' for matters of 'supreme national interest'. The contradiction in these two approaches, however, was never reconciled so that in practice they tended to cancel each other out. The Americans left Nassau thinking that they had a further British commitment to multi-lateralization than the passage of time proved to be the case. The President was said to have been unhappy about the accord reached at Nassau not long thereafter. He felt that he might have been able to draw up a more watertight agreement on the commitment of the Polaris submarines to a NATO nuclear force (possibly subject to American veto) if the conference had been better prepared for in Washington and conducted in less of a crisis atmosphere at Nassau.

To understand further the President's Polaris decision one must look at his political environment at the time. Kennedy at Nassau was a captive of the previous administration's policy of 'interdependence', of assisting

[1] *The Troubled Partnership* (New York, McGraw-Hill, 1965), p. 83.

Britain on atomic energy and missiles. His sense of honour would not allow him to repudiate the obligation to provide a missile inherent in the Skybolt-Holy Loch understanding, even though the obligation remained unwritten. Neither did he wish to be seen publicly as forcing the British out of their nuclear role. An editorial in the *Washington Post* shortly before Nassau served as a reminder that a break with Britain would not be popular at home. The President was mindful of the undesirability of a sweep of anti-Americanism in Britain. Quite apart from the 'backlash' which this might create towards his administration within the country, the United States had solid foreign policy reasons for maintaining the best possible relations with Britain. As the nation's closest ally, the United Kingdom, with its worldwide military and diplomatic experience, remained the country with which Washington could best exchange views and discuss world problems. The United States and Britain did not always agree, but following misunderstandings their relationship had been characterized by what Richard E. Neustadt has termed a 'propensity to repair'. For reasons of history, culture, mutual faith in democratic government, and common purposes, the United States has always looked at Britain through a special prism.

Reference must also be made to a few of the personal relationships involved at Nassau, for they too contribute to the stuff of history. Macmillan was the Western leader whom Kennedy liked best and saw most often—four times in 1961 and seven times in his presidency. According to Theodore Sorensen 'a fondness developed between them which went beyond the necessities of alliance.' Told after Nassau that he had been 'soft' on Macmillan, the President is said to have replied, 'If you were in that kind of trouble, you would want a friend.'[1] Another unusual relationship was that of David Ormsby Gore with the President. The British Ambassador, who was related to both Macmillan and Kennedy by marriage, had been a personal friend of the President since 1938 and was usually well acquainted with the Prime Minister's frame of mind. The President often confided in him as he would a member of his own cabinet.[2] At Nassau the two talked together in between the formal sessions of the conference. Kennedy was anxious to help Macmillan in a domestic political crisis which he knew had its roots partly in United States actions. More than some in his entourage, he was sensitive to the political importance of the 'independent deterrent' to the Macmillan government. This is not to say that the Nassau Conference was all sweetness and light—on the

---

[1] Sorensen, op. cit., pp. 558–9, 576; see also Schlesinger, op. cit., p. 376; Anthony Sampson, *Macmillan: A Study in Ambiguity* (London, Allen Lane the Penguin Press, 1967), pp. 225–6.

[2] See Henry Brandon, 'Envoy Extraordinary', *Sunday Times*, 28 March 1965; Sorensen, op. cit., p. 559; Schlesinger, op. cit., pp. 423–4.

contrary. With Macmillan's survival at home at stake, Kennedy found a testier and more stubborn man than he previously had known. There was much hard bargaining; following the confrontation word passed among the Whitehall *cognoscenti* that Macmillan had persuaded Kennedy to overrule his advisers and had obtained Polaris through a combination of threat and charm. Neither leader, however, wanted to destroy the basic condition of trust between the two countries.

Nassau was a great achievement for Harold Macmillan and represents one of his finest hours—assuming, of course, acceptance of his perception of the British national interest. On returning to London he was able to declare that he had preserved the 'independent nuclear deterrent'. In Polaris he had obtained the best second-strike weapons system then existent. It was far more suitable to the vulnerable British Isles than either Skybolt or Minuteman. Unlike Skybolt it was then a proven and successful weapon, and the Soviet Union was far from developing a sufficient hunter-killer submarine capability to cut short its invulnerability. Polaris was also a better option for Britain than Skybolt because the latter was tied to the obsolescence of the V-bombers. Skybolt had been intended for the five-year gap between 1965, when the existing Blue Steel Stand-off bomb became obsolete, and 1970 when the V-bombers might no longer be credible; Polaris, on the other hand, would probably remain viable until the 1980s.

Moreover, the British obtained Polaris on extraordinarily favourable and inexpensive terms. This is a vignette of its own. In the hurried confusion of the Nassau meeting the matter of development costs had been overlooked. The British thereupon assumed that they would not contribute to the research and development costs but only pay for the missiles they purchased. They were surprised to discover later that the Pentagon expected them to share in the R & D expenses. On a *pro rata* basis, Britain's five planned submarines to America's forty-one, the United Kingdom would have paid 12 per cent. But in a mix-up President Kennedy made a cheaper deal with Ambassador Ormsby Gore than Secretary McNamara had wanted. Britain was only to pay a surcharge of 5 per cent on the final production price of the A-3 missile as a contribution to the massive research and development expenses.[1]

The early reaction to the Nassau Agreement in Britain was quite different from what Macmillan had expected. Labour and the portion of the press which had been critical of the independent deterrent policy continued to be so, as we shall see, with renewed vigour. What was surprising was the response of the chauvinistic element in the Tory Party which had been on the Prime Minister's mind at Nassau. They feared that the

[1] *Polaris Sales Agreement,* Cmnd. 1995.

'independent deterrent' had been 'sold out' in the commitment to a NATO nuclear force. Sir Arthur Vere Harvey, Chairman of the Conservative Defence Committee, was critical of the Nassau Agreement: 'I want Britain to have her own deterrent, not to share one where everyone has a key in the cupboard and America has the master key.'[1] The anxiety was so great that on New Year's Day Harvey and a delegation of leading members of his committee had an unusual meeting with Minister of Defence Thorneycroft in which they sought assurances that the Polaris missiles would not be fitted with radio 'locks' inhibiting their use without the sanction of the President, and that Britain would have an 'absolute right' to use Polaris independently if the Government thought that supreme national interests were at stake. In addition, they urged that Britain quickly develop a stand-off nuclear bomb of greater range than the existent Blue Steel to fill the expected 'deterrent gap' between the end of Blue Steel's credibility and the availability of Polaris submarines, so that at no time would Britain be left without an 'independent deterrent'.[2]

In the following months as the General Election approached the Conservative government made it abundantly clear that Britain's nuclear role had been preserved. Nassau, in retrospect, was the great turning point. If any occasion following the years of domestic debate would have been the logical time to make the decision to allow the nuclear capability to taper off, this would have been it. In deciding that the first generation of the nuclear force—the V-bombers—would be replaced by a definitely available second generation—Polaris submarines—the guarantee was made that the British nuclear force would continue in one form or another for many years to come.

4. Britain and the Multilateral Nuclear Force

The American proposal for a multilateral nuclear force (MLF) bedevilled the politics of defence in the Western alliance for the two years following Nassau. It is beyond the scope of this study to discuss it in detail. The British reaction to the MLF is of concern here, however, because unlike the other interested NATO powers the British response was closely tied up with the question of how their national nuclear force should be related to a NATO nuclear force. Some of the British counter-proposals—the 'Thorneycroft proposals' of 1963-4 and the Labour government's plan for an 'Atlantic Nuclear Force'—were drawn up with the future of the British nuclear force very much in mind. In addition, the placing of the

---

[1] *Observer*, 23 December 1962.

[2] *The Times*, 2 January 1963; 'Stop Clutching at Straws', *The Economist*, 5 January 1963; the *New Statesman*, 4 January 1963, commented that Harvey was becoming as near as a Briton could to being the counterpart of Senator Stuart Symington!

MLF project in the centre stage of alliance diplomacy was directly related to the Nassau Conference and its consequences.[1]

The idea of a multilateral NATO nuclear force grew out of some studies made at SHAPE in the late 1950s with a view to countering an estimated 750 medium-range ballistic missiles which the Soviet Union was deploying in Western Russia and which were considered sufficient to cover every important city and military target in Western Europe. The original proposal of General Lauris Norstad (SACEUR) for mobile land-based Polaris missiles in Europe under a double veto system did not commend itself to the American government; but a subsequent proposal drawn up by a study group headed by Professor Robert R. Bowie for a force of Polaris missile submarines to be jointly owned and operated under the control of SACEUR, and to be manned by crews of mixed nationality, was presented by outgoing Secretary of State Christian Herter to the NATO Council in December 1960. The Kennedy administration after studying the proposal let it drop, however, preferring to focus its energies on the centralization of control of nuclear weapons and on persuading the allies to meet their goals in conventional forces rather than on the creation of a new nuclear force within NATO. During the following year the lack of attention given to the MLF suggested that it was not considered very urgent, but in the second half of 1962 certain officials in the Department of State, who were concerned with giving Europe a worthy strategic role while preventing the proliferation of national nuclear forces in Europe (i.e., Germany), gave renewed attention to a multilateral nuclear force. At this time American officials acknowledged that such a force was not a military necessity and suggested that if the European nations desired it— which their lukewarm response did not appear to so indicate—it was up to them to formulate concrete proposals.

Whereas before the Nassau Conference the MLF was berthed at the planning level of the State Department, in the six weeks following the Bahamas meeting it was launched as a major diplomatic venture. The posture of American willingness to respond to European desires was in time dropped and replaced by Washington's insistence that the MLF be underwritten by the allies. What accounted for the sudden shift in American policy, which appeared to many Europeans as having been taken with undue and unthinking haste? First, President Kennedy's wish to furnish a replacement for Skybolt, but his reluctance to make a direct exchange with

---

[1] A complete study of the MLF episode remains to be published. The best available is Alastair Buchan's *The Multilateral Force: An Historical Perspective* (Adelphi Papers No. 13, London, The Institute for Strategic Studies, October 1964). Another reasoned analysis may be found in Kissinger, *The Troubled Partnership*, Chapter V. For an analytical statement on behalf of the MLF see Robert E. Osgood, *The Case for the MLF* (Washington, Washington Center for Foreign Policy Research, 1964).

Polaris without a British commitment to a broader NATO nuclear force, provided the opportunity to inject the multilateral force concept into the Nassau Agreement, albeit in a confused and imprecise manner. Second, when President de Gaulle in his press conference of 14 January 1963 announced his veto of the British entry into the Common Market he in effect declared war on the American concept of an Atlantic partnership. Washington officials, in retrospect somewhat naïvely, seized upon the MLF as an alternative route to the Grand Design. Third, the signing of the Franco-German Treaty of Collaboration on 23 January raised fears that the collaboration might be extended to the nuclear field. The MLF was promoted as a way to funnel the Federal Republic's supposed nuclear appetite, and to court her away from France by forging new German-American links.

The proposal for a multilateral force called for a fleet of twenty-five surface vessels (originally nuclear submarines), each armed with eight A-3 Polaris missiles possessing a range of 2,500 miles. The MLF was to be financed by the participating countries at a cost of five billion dollars, spread out over ten years, but no nation was to contribute more than 40 per cent of the total. The crews were to be 'mixed-manned' with each ship having at least three nationalities. The ostensible purpose of mixed-manning was to produce a partnership in nuclear management, deployment, and targeting; but of greater import was the fact that the national contributions were to be so scrambled that withdrawal by a country from the MLF would not leave it with a complete nuclear weapons system. The control system was not decided upon—it being the most thorny and crucial aspect—and although the proposal as originally presented required unanimity in voting, it later appeared likely that there would be an executive committee with a voting system providing initially at least a minimum of a veto for the United States.

The reaction in Britain to the MLF ranged from unenthusiastic to hostile throughout the military establishment and in the two principal political parties.[1] It must be recalled that Britain was the only country in Europe with sufficient experience in the handling of nuclear weapons to be able to make a valid critical assessment of the planning and assumptions made by the United States in the detailed presentation of the MLF proposal. Moreover, as Sir John Slessor has written of new military concepts at another time, 'New ideas seldom have a very strong appeal to Englishmen; it is one of our strengths that we look at them critically and like to measure their validity by empirical tests.'[2]

The MLF was strongly objected to in the Ministry of Defence, where it

[1] The author was dealing with the MLF while on the staff of the American Embassy in London at the time.

[2] 'Air Power and the Future of War', *Journal of the Royal United Service Institution*, Vol. XCIX, No. 595, August 1954, p. 344.

was regarded as militarily unnecessary and of doubtful practicality. The service chiefs argued that it was superfluous in that it merely added more nuclear weapons to the already abundant nuclear arsenal of the West. Furthermore, the surface ships would be too easily detectable and vulnerable, subject to 'incidents' such as collisions, demands to change course, et cetera, and might prove to be a highly provocative irritant to the Soviet Union. 'Mixed-manning' was derided by the Navy as a sailor's nightmare, unworkable on board ships. But underlying the Navy's objections was the matter of costs. The 'senior service', mindful of the relatively fixed share of each of the services in the defence budget and of the unlikelihood of a proportional increase in the entire defence budget, should the MLF come into being, feared that what was spent on the MLF would be taken out of funds for its traditional activities. The British contribution to the MLF was expected to be approximately 10% of the total costs, about £150m. spread out over ten years. For this the Navy could get two new aircraft carriers, or three more Polaris submarines. Having just received Polaris submarines at Nassau, the Navy feared that the MLF would become a further drain on scarce skilled manpower and would send it into financial shipwreck. Moreover, the demand created by the MLF for skilled specialists might force a delay in the British Polaris programme. Similarly the R.A.F., fighting for a new nuclear tactical strike reconnaissance aircraft, and the Army, pinched by the increasing costs of conventional equipment, were alarmed that the MLF would divert funds from the more needed traditional expenditures. The MLF failed to win the backing of either the Chief of the Defence Staff, Lord Mountbatten, the Chief Scientific Adviser, Sir Solly Zuckerman, or Minister of Defence Thorneycroft, all of whom thought it was military nonsense contrived for political reasons.

The Foreign Office accepted the Ministry of Defence's view that the MLF was of dubious military value and initially added some political demurrers of its own. If the principal of unanimity prevailed in the control structure, or even if only the United States retained a veto (which the British considered essential) the diplomats doubted if this would satisfy for long a Germany really interested in achieving influence over the use of nuclear weapons. If the Americans eventually withdrew from the MLF under a prospective 'European clause'—as American officials had hinted might eventually happen following satisfactory progress towards European unity—there might come about a more general disengagement of the United States from the defence of Europe. The Foreign Office was also concerned that the MLF would adversely affect relations with the Soviet Union, would render more difficult the achievement of a non-proliferation treaty, and would become a divisive force within the alliance, especially as long as France refused to participate.

But as State Department officials brought unusually heavy pressure on the British to join and let it be known that they would proceed without Britain if necessary, the Foreign Office came around to the view that if the MLF was to come into being Britain simply could not afford to remain outside. The potentially deleterious effect on Anglo-American relations was obvious. In addition, abstention from the force would further isolate Britain from Europe following only shortly after the Common Market exclusion. Nor was the prospect of a nuclear force consisting of Germany and the United States with several of the smaller European countries very attractive. Foreign Office officials tended to believe that by pushing the proposal so hard the United States had to some extent created a German appetite for nuclear weapons, but whatever its origins they came to agree that pressures for greater participation in nuclear strategy were building up in Germany. Joining the MLF, which seemed to have strong German support, might be the most acceptable way of satisfying the Germans and heading off a Franco-German nuclear arrangement. The change of opinion within the Foreign Office and the American call for participation in discussions on the MLF led to an unusually visible Whitehall dispute between the Foreign Office and the Defence Ministry in the fall of 1963, which was resolved when Prime Minister Macmillan announced that Britain would join the technical examination of the feasibility of the plan but without commitments as to participation.[1]

While agreeing to discussions on the MLF the British formulated proposals of their own which they wanted Washington to consider. The British would have preferred to start from the basis of Paragraph Six of the Nassau Agreement, which provided for a nuclear force consisting of national contingents of existing forces—the *multinational* approach. Such contributions, though part of an international command, would not be mixed-manned and would be subject to the right of recall in the event of a national emergency. Accordingly, a start in this direction was made in February 1963 when the whole of the V-bomber force was assigned to an 'inter-allied' NATO force along with three United States Polaris submarines. At the Ottawa meeting of NATO Ministers in May 1963 arrangements were made for a broader participation by officers of NATO countries in nuclear planning at SHAPE and in the co-ordination of operational targeting and planning at the headquarters of the Strategic

---

[1] See 'Pressures on Britain to Join', *Guardian*, 28 September 1963; 'Whitehall Split Over NATO Nuclear Force', *Observer*, 15 September 1963; Defence Correspondent, *The Times*, 25 June 1963, 8 July 1964; Vice-Admiral Sir Peter Gretton, 'NATO and the Mixed-Manned Force—A British View', *The Nuclear Deterrent in the Context of Anglo-American Relations*, Report of a conference held under the auspices of the Ditchley Foundation, 27–30 September 1963, pp. 23–5. In the House of Lords mixed-manning was damned by Lord Montgomery of Alamein as 'utter and complete poppycock!'

Air Command in Omaha. Although this gave the European countries for the first time (except Britain) some knowledge and influence in the selection of targets for strategic nuclear attack, the 'assignment' of the V-bombers was essentially a symbolic act. It did not restrict their independent use by Britain, nor did it diminish the national control of the V-bomber force. This was made clear when, as the British election came into sight, the Conservative government laid great stress on the capacity for independent action of the British nuclear force.

Prospects for the multinational approach were limited, however, by France's unwillingness to strengthen NATO and to integrate the alliance further by giving the non-nuclear members a significant share in nuclear planning. Furthermore, in the months following the post-Nassau presentation of the MLF the feeling grew that Germany—which tended to see the MLF as its own version of the British and French nuclear forces—would not be satisfied with the *multinational* approach and would seek more direct participation through a *multilateral* formula. This in turn necessitated a measure of mixed-manning.

Under growing American pressure to accept the MLF, the British drew up detailed plans for an alternative scheme which would achieve the same political result of giving the Germans a sense of participation, but at far less cost and without requiring the purchase of weapons not already planned on. The 'Thorneycroft proposals' were initially presented to the NATO ministerial meeting in Paris in December 1963 and were tabled in detailed form before the working group examining the MLF in July 1964. They called for the application of the multilateral concept to aircraft and missiles which had an interdiction role in European defence. There was to be mixed-manning, joint finance, and control under SACEUR of the British Canberras then operating with NATO forces, the F-104 Starfighters of the American and West German Air Forces, the Pershing 400 mile surface-to-surface missile then in service with American and German forces in Europe, the projected British tactical strike aircraft (TSR-2), the planned American F-111, and the V-bombers which would be redirected from strategic targets in Russia to NATO interdiction targets mainly in Eastern Europe. This proposed massive multilateralization would involve manning by mixed nationalities of units and squadrons, but not within individual aircraft.[1]

The 'Thorneycroft proposals', unlike the MLF, called for the multilateralization of weapons systems already in existence or scheduled to come into service. The British Polaris submarine force was, however, significantly omitted. Thus there was to be no sharing of the 'independent deterrent'. The advantage of the proposals from the British point of view

[1] *The Times*, 26 June and 3 July 1964.

was not only that they avoided a diversionary drain of financial and manpower resources for the establishment of a new surface fleet. Britain would also have a proportionately larger role in such a force than in the MLF, to which it was likely to make no more than a 10% contribution. The R.A.F. welcomed the plan as a way to ensure that the Ministry of Defence bought its controversial TSR-2. An additional advantage was that a force consisting essentially of European-based weapons of interdiction would be more closely geared to European interests in the early stages of a nuclear crisis than a seaborne force whose strategic purpose remained somewhat undefined.

Although the 'Thorneycroft proposals' were the result of considerable planning in the Ministry of Defence they were initially discounted in Washington as an attempt to impede the MLF. Their presentation was followed by comments from annoyed American officials that the United States and Germany would establish the MLF, if not with Britain, then without her. In the proposals the British did nevertheless commit themselves to the feasibility of mixed-manning. Washington subsequently agreed that the proposals should be seriously considered, though as a complement, rather than as an alternative, to the MLF. Not to be ruled out, however, was the possibility of a compromise package which would include the tactical aircraft and missiles in the British plan plus a smaller number of Polaris-equipped surface vessels.

Throughout most of 1964 the hard choices on the MLF were held in abeyance since no decision of consequence could be reached until the General Election was over. The Conservative government sent thirty Royal Navy officers and seamen to take part in the mixed-manning experiment on the United States destroyer *Admiral Claude V. Ricketts*, and actively participated in the MLF working group discussions. This was done without a commitment to join the MLF if the Thorneycroft proposals proved to be unacceptable to the United States as an alternative. The new Prime Minister, Sir Alec Douglas-Home, seemed sensitive to the danger that an announced intention to join the MLF would appear as a weakening of the nuclear independence to which he gave great weight in his pre-election platform. But there were also indications that following the election a new Conservative government, if pressed by Washington, would overrule the admirals and other Whitehall sceptics and agree to participate in the formation of the MLF.

The Labour party was even more strongly opposed to the MLF than the Tories or the defence establishment.[1] The objections of Labour

---

[1] The Liberals, however, gave the MLF their backing, see *Liberal Assembly Resolutions Adopted at London, 1964* (London, Liberal Party Organization, 1964), p. 3. See also the campaign leaflet, 'Defence—the Liberal Answer'.

spokesmen were not essentially derived from military considerations, although they agreed that there was no military need for the MLF and that it would involve unnecessary new expenditures. Rather, the Labour leaders feared that the MLF would encourage the spread of nuclear weapons by whetting appetites which might not previously have existed. Distaste for Germany and of any German nuclear role was at the heart of Labour's opposition to the MLF. The American plan, it was thought, would not placate German nuclear ambitions but might nourish and encourage them. Thus, Labour's objections were predominantly of a political order and included the fear that the MLF would be an intolerable provocation to the Soviets. It was thought that the MLF would weaken NATO by the creation of a second nuclear organization, and the talk of a possible 'European clause' was seen as a dangerous indulgence of the continentals.[1]

The alternative favoured by Labour was consistent with its policy of bringing to an end the British nuclear force. Labour wanted to gain a measure of influence and control over what really mattered—the 'independent' American deterrent. Only by having a greater share in the formulation of American policy and strategy would the European half of the Western alliance acquire what it wanted. The President would retain the right to press the nuclear trigger, but the allies would be involved in intimate consultations concerning the organization of the American nuclear forces and the strategy according to which they would be put to use. In return the allies would undertake to build up their conventional forces.[2] As the election approached and there was no sign that the United States was about to accommodate to Labour's views, the party's defence spokesmen, faced with the prospect of a quick decision on the MLF should they gain office, inserted loopholes and saving phrases into their statements of opposition to the MLF. Accordingly if it did not prove feasible to gain Washington's agreement to Labour's preferred solution of a more effective voice for the allies in the control of the American deterrent, some form of a multilateral force might, it was hinted, be found palatable. After the election, as we shall see, the Labour government drew up its own proposals for an 'Atlantic Nuclear Force'.

If ever there was an excellent example to disprove the Gaullist notion that Britain and America plan their nuclear affairs through a process of congenial and easy harmonization, not to mention a cabal, it was the MLF. For two years American officials arm-twisted the British and pressured

[1] In an unusual step, Labour's objections to the MLF were presented in a written memorandum to Foreign Secretary Douglas-Home by Patrick Gordon Walker, the 'shadow' Foreign Minister.

[2] See statements of Denis Healey, 673 H.C. Deb. col. 59–61 (4 March 1963) and Patrick Gordon Walker, 684 H.C. Deb. col. 495–6 (15 November 1963).

them to accept the MLF, eventually threatening to proceed on the project without Britain, if necessary. Although the central problem of finding a formula for the political control was sidestepped, Washington let it be known that British participation was expected. In part the American insistence could be attributed to the messianic zeal of a coterie of MLF enthusiasts in the State Department who refused to believe that the British would not in the last analysis march to the American tune. President Kennedy, who saw the MLF as an exploratory idea and who grew increasingly sceptical about it, was taken aback to learn from Sir Alec Douglas-Home about the pressures emanating from his own bureaucracy.[1] But following the assassination the MLF was presented to President Johnson in such a manner as to elicit a strong commitment to forcing quicker action on the plan than President Kennedy had ever intended.

As Alastair Buchan has noted, the American pressure on Britain also stemmed from Washington's practice of giving the demands of German internal politics priority over Britain.[2] December 1964 was set as a 'deadline' for concluding an agreement on the MLF on the rationale that if it was not ratified by the Bundestag before the 1965 German elections it might become prey to a political dispute in Germany. This overlooked the fact that a Labour government coming into office for the first time in thirteen years would have only two months to decide on the MLF and also have its own proposals considered. Underlying the American attitude was a tendency to pay too much attention to the nuclear neuroses of Germany and not enough to those of Britain, or in effect, to take the British for granted. Thus despite the repeated criticisms of the MLF by the Labour leaders while in opposition, a new Labour government was expected not to refuse to participate in a project which had advanced as far as it had.[3]

5. The General Election of 1964: The Tories and the Bomb

The principal foreign and defence policy issue in the General Election of 1964 which brought the Labour party into power was the retention of

[1] Schlesinger, op. cit., p. 875; see also Sorensen, op. cit., p. 569.

[2] Buchan, *The Multilateral Force: An Historical Perspective*, p. 10.

[3] In June 1964 Richard Neustadt spent some time in London assessing the attitudes of the Labour Party shadow cabinet and higher ranking Whitehall officials on the MLF. One of his aims was to help avoid 'another Skybolt', another situation where 'differences of interest are compounded by each side's misreading of the pressures and procedures on the other side.' Neustadt wrote a memorandum intended only for McGeorge Bundy and a few others. Included were recommendations on how to overcome Labour objections to the MLF, and how a new Labour government should be dealt with. Four years later it found its way into the press, billed as an example of the 'inside-dopester style'. For its complete contents see the *New York Review of Books*, Vol. XI, No. 10, 5 December 1968, pp. 37–46; or the *New Left Review*, September–October 1968, pp. 11–21.

Britain's 'independent nuclear deterrent'. During the twenty-one months between the Nassau Conference and the October election—a period which coincided with the longest 'unofficial' election campaign in fifty years—the issue was surrounded with a fog of confusion, distortion, and over-simplification. As the British bomb became the volley ball of the political arena both parties believed that it was in their electoral interest to accentuate the differences between them so that they became, in fact, grossly exaggerated. Wrongly, the Conservatives became the party of perpetual nuclear independence, and Labour the party which was going to drop the nuclear arms immediately into the Lake of Geneva. Both sides had an interest in creating the maximum obfuscation on the subject. The Tories wished to conceal their uneasy condition of dependence upon the United States for the nuclear force. Labour wished to cover the fissures which threatened to crack open the defence policy compromise reached in 1961.

Although the Labour party had withdrawn its support of the nuclear force and was critical of the Nassau Agreement, it was the Conservatives who decided to make the bomb a major electoral issue. In the speech in which he announced his intention to lead the Conservative party in the next election, Macmillan let it be known that he meant to fight the election on the retention of the 'independent deterrent'.[1] His successor, Sir Alec Douglas-Home, in his first address to the Commons after becoming Prime Minister, said in a jingoistic vein that he intended to put the question of the independent deterrent before the British electorate.[2] According to a Conservative M.P., knowledgeable on defence matters, 'the decision was quite deliberately taken and not without opposition from those who felt that such an appeal would lose votes at the "centre" but to no avail. The appeal was to "patriotism" and to the traditional Tory voter.'[3]

There were a number of considerations which moved the Conservatives to put the issue in the forefront. First, there was the hope of smoking out the divisions in the Labour party on defence by making a calculated attempt to exploit them. But although Labour was still not united on nuclear matters the chances of splitting the party anew and re-opening its civil war of 1960–1 were minimal. The unilateralists were not as effective as before and the excellent prospect for success in the coming election was likely to keep the party together. Second, the charge that a Labour government would 'hand over' Britain's defences to another country

[1] 'Macmillan was defending Britain's nuclear independence to the Conservatives of Bromley in words which de Gaulle might have used to justify his force de frappe', from 'Flying the Nuclear Flag', *Observer*, 14 April 1963.

[2] 684 H.C. Deb. col. 49–51 (12 November 1963).

[3] Julian Critchley 'Ending the Myth of Nuclear Independence', *Crossbow*, Vol. VIII, No. 31, April–June 1965, p. 29.

appealed to a sense of outraged patriotism. The Tories saw the 'independent deterrent' as a symbol of military power and national sovereignty which would catch the imagination of the voters—for nationalism is still the strongest of political emotions. It was, moreover, important to the Government that the electorate should forget the humiliation over Britain's exclusion from the Common Market.

Third, the Conservative position had a tactical advantage in that in electioneering terms it could be stated more simply than the Labour case for not continuing to maintain the nuclear force under certain semi-defined circumstances. In past practice in Britain (and as it turned out in 1964) defence and foreign policy issues did not have much influence on the way the electorate voted. But the very simplicity of the notion that Britain's greatness and independence rested upon the retention of the nuclear arms which the opposition wanted to throw away was expected to have some vote-getting appeal. Some of the political strategists in the Conservative Central Office had their doubts as to how many votes were in the issue, but they were mindful of the opinion polls which indicated strong public support for the nuclear force. Fourth, Sir Alec Douglas-Home adopted the 'bomb' as 'his' issue. A weak speaker who had made the mistake of admitting publicly that he did not understand economics, the new Prime Minister was more comfortable discussing his accustomed field of international affairs than domestic, social, and economic programmes. The nuclear force was emphasized by Sir Alec not because it was the issue which would draw the most votes, but because it was the issue on which he spoke most effectively with the most authority and conviction. Furthermore, the Prime Minister appeared genuinely to believe that saving the British deterrent was a matter of great importance and that it was his duty to make the public aware of its significance.[1]

In most of his public statements on the nuclear deterrent, Douglas-Home laid great stress on its function as a 'ticket of admission' to discussions on the major issues of war and peace. In particular, the possession of nuclear weapons was sought to bestow upon British representatives an added influence at disarmament conferences. Thus to abandon them would mean that Britain would no longer have, according to Douglas-Home, a 'place at the peace table as of right'.[2] It was said that without her nuclear role Britain would not have been present at the three-nation negotiations at Moscow which led to the signing of the partial Test Ban Treaty, and the implication was drawn that save for Britain's participation

---

[1] See David E. Butler and Anthony King, *The British General Election of 1964* (London, Macmillan, 1965), pp. 93, 128–9, 148. The authors quote (p. 93) one of Sir Alec's 'senior colleagues' as having said: 'Every P.M. has one issue he cares more about than anything else. Alec's is the bomb. He'd even be prepared to lose any election on it.'

[2] 684 H.C. Deb. col. 49 (12 November 1963).

there would have been no treaty.[1] The latter was a somewhat spurious contention, for the conditions which made possible the signing of the treaty, after several years of discussion, were mainly attributable to the detente between the Soviet Union and the United States that followed the Cuban missile crisis. It is true, on the other hand, that Britain maintained pressure over a number of years on the two Superpowers to come to an agreement, and that at a critical juncture the momentum of the negotiations was sustained by British seismological research which narrowed the divergent positions of the Soviet Union and the United States on the number of 'on site' control posts needed to monitor underground tests. Sir Michael Wright, the British representative to the Nuclear Test Ban Conference, believed that had it not been for British interventions the talks would have broken down in 1959–60, the Western attitude would not have been as 'constructive' as it was, and the initiative in the spring of 1963 which ultimately led to the agreement would not have been taken.[2] Whether the persuasive influence of Britain's advice was dependent upon her independent ownership of nuclear weapons remains, however, an open question.

The Conservative position was based on a goodly amount of nuclear chauvinism which was designed to solicit the 'patriotic' vote. Douglas-Home justified Britain's continued nuclear role in part by the contribution the nation could make to world peace. He was fond of talking of Britain's still valuable knowledge and experience in international matters and her 'unfanatical approach' to the problems of the world. 'We have decided', he stated on one occasion, 'that Britain must be equipped to be present in the councils of war and peace—and to be there by right. And this means nuclear power.'[3] Conservative politicians derided the Labour party for wanting to reduce Britain to the rank of a second-class power. They also implied that a Labour government would diminish Britain's status to below that of France without helping to arrest the spread of nuclear weapons in the process, for they dismissed the argument that Britain's unilateral renunciation would have much influence either on France and China, or on potential nuclear powers.[4]

[1] Following the election Douglas-Home made this claim explicit: 'I was in the negotiations all through on the Nuclear Test Ban Treaty. I have no doubt whatever that we would never have got that Treaty unless the United Kingdom had been in a position to intervene from knowledge and had a status which could not be denied. We would not have got it if it had not been that we were a nuclear power.' 704 H.C. Deb. col. 588 (17 December 1964).

[2] See his letter to *The Times*, 14 September 1963, written in rebuttal to that newspaper's leader of 11 September criticizing the 'comfortable fiction that the nuclear force gives Britain a decisive voice in the disarmament and defence policies of the West'; see also Sir Michael Wright, *Disarm and Verify* (London, Chatto & Windus, 1964), pp. 133–41.

[3] *The Times*, 22 May 1963.

[4] One anguished Tory backbencher declared: 'If the French bring about such an achievement (second-strike nuclear force) and we have not got a deterrent, where will Britain be? I

The principal justification for the maintenance of the nuclear force remained, however, the necessity of preserving Britain's freedom of action should her interests diverge from those of the United States or NATO. In citing his reasons for continuing the 'British deterrent' at Nassau, Macmillan told the Commons:

... and this perhaps is the most vital argument of all, there may be conditions, there must be areas, in which the interests of some countries may seem to them more vital than they seem to others. It is right and salutary that a British government, whatever may be the particular conditions of a particular dispute, should be in a position to make their own decision without fear of nuclear blackmail. ... I would hope that Britain will be able, for as long as possible, to maintain her position free from threat, and should be able, should the necessity arise, to make her independent decisions on issues vital to her life.[1]

This argument was based on the conviction that Britain could ultimately be defended against an enemy threat only by the possession of a national nuclear force. Thus the Defence White Paper of 1964 said:

To suggest that the independent deterrent might be abandoned in the interests of non-dissemination overlooks the fact that if there were no power in Europe capable of inflicting unacceptable damage on a potential enemy he might be tempted—if not now then perhaps at some time in the future—to attack in the mistaken belief that the United States would not act unless America herself were attacked. The V-bombers by themselves are, and the Polaris submarines will be, capable of inflicting greater damage than any potential aggressor would consider acceptable.[2]

The British government's doctrine of nuclear independence in 1963–4 had a remarkable similarity to the views expressed by General de Gaulle to justify the 'force de frappe'. Right-wing Tory politicians in the less guarded atmosphere of the election platform expressed doubts about reliance upon the American nuclear guarantee and stressed the need for national atomic arms in phrases which sounded like undiluted Gaullism. This was especially so following the death of President Kennedy, which served as a sharp reminder of the unpredictability of the future, the 'un-Britishness' of some Americans who achieve high office, and the consequent risk of becoming dependent now upon an unknown future President who might be isolationist or have little understanding of, or sympathy for, the 'special relationship'. The journal of l'Institut Français d'Études Stratégiques, in an article in the summer of 1964 reviewing alliance developments, noted that in contrast to the 'integrationist'

have seen Britain pushed around enough on other things. If we are allowed to be pushed around by General de Gaulle, that is just about the end.' 670 H.C. Deb. col. 1072 (30 January 1963).

[1] 670 H.C. Deb. col. 962 (30 January 1963).

[2] *Statement on Defence: 1964*, Cmnd. 2270, p. 6.

position taken at Nassau, the Conservative government's policy was approaching that of France and that the 1964 Defence White Paper put forth a nuclear policy very similar to that of Paris.[1]

A favourite Conservative theme before the election was that a Labour government would 'abandon' the deterrent, would leave the United Kingdom 'defenceless' and would 'hand over' the determination of the nation's future to the United States. There was a tendency to orate as if Britain was as independent as she once was in the nineteenth century. There was also a tendency to make apocalyptic remarks, such as Thorneycroft's charge that to give up nuclear weapons 'would not be an abdication of defence but of our role in the world'.[2] In his final television appeal before the election Sir Alec, after discussing domestic matters, moved to the issue of the British bomb:

As Foreign Secretary and now as Prime Minister I know that the world is still a dangerous place. It is just at this moment, when France and China are becoming nuclear powers, that the Socialists would propose to discard all control by a British government over Britain's nuclear arms. . . . I must be sure that each of you recognizes the consequences of such a Socialist decision. It would mean that we should surrender all our authority in world affairs and hand over the decision about the life and future of Britain to another country. This I am quite sure you cannot allow.[3]

And the eighty-eight-year-old Winston Churchill in one of his last public statements warned that, unlike times past, there would be no second chance if Britain again committed the folly of throwing away her arms.[4]

But within the Conservative party there were many members, including some cabinet ministers, who were by no means certain that Britain really had a credible 'independent deterrent', as the Government claimed, or that if it had one it could, or should, be maintained in the future. Such Conservatives were uneasy with the Prime Minister's contention that Britain needed her atomic arms to avoid 'nuclear blackmail', and would have preferred the Government's declaratory policy to have been based less upon an assumption of mistrust of the United States. They doubted that Britain would ever use her nuclear force without American consent; and they could not understand how Britain could ask the United States to make available her missile technology while simultan-

---

[1] Thorneycroft is quoted as declaring that Britain is 'in a large measure' in accord with the French thesis. Michael Eyraud, 'La Controverse nucléaire au sein de l'alliance atlantique', *Stratégie*, No. 1, Été 1964, p. 118.

[2] 690 H.C. Deb. col. 460 (26 February 1964).

[3] Butler and King, *The British General Election of 1964*, p. 126.

[4] In a well-publicized message to the Primrose League, Churchill wrote: 'Sometimes in the past we have committed the folly of throwing away our arms. Under the mercy of providence and at great cost and sacrifice we have been able to re-create them when the need arose. But if we abandon our nuclear deterrent there will be no such second chance. To abandon it now would be to abandon it forever.' *The Times*, 4 May 1963.

eously threatening to use the very same missiles 'independently'.[1] The moderate elements in the Tory party held a view akin to that of the First Lord of the Admiralty, Earl Jellicoe, who in the more reflective atmosphere of the House of Lords conceded that it would not necessarily be right for Britain to retain the option of an independent deterrent for all time since 'there might come a time when the organic structure of the Western Alliance was sufficiently strong for us to be able with entire confidence to place our nuclear armoury irrevocably in a common pool.'[2] It was a mark of the depth of Sir Alec's commitment to nuclear 'independence' that this eminently reasoned and balanced statement by a public official—which *The Economist* saw as a 'fragment of common sense riding on the electoral tide'[3]—was a source of embarrassment to the Conservative government and the Tory central office. The murmurs of dissent within the more enlightened of the Conservative ranks were muted by the need for maintaining the appearance of electoral unity and in the Commons by the very incisiveness of the opposition's attacks, which tended to have the effect of rallying the Government's back bench.

According to opinion polls, the public favoured the retention of the nuclear force and agreed with much of the Conservative rationale for it. In spite of years of national debate and the changed circumstances since the mid-1950s, public support for Britain's nuclear role remained constant ever since its early development. A week before the 1964 General Election 55 per cent thought that it was 'very important' that Britain keep the 'independent nuclear deterrent' ('fairly important'—17%, 'don't know'—4%). Asked if they believed that if Britain gave up nuclear weapons other countries such as France would agree to do without them as well, 63 per cent in July 1963 thought they 'would not agree' ('would agree'—18%, 'don't know'—19%). Yet as the chart below indicates, in February 1963 the British public did not view a German or even French nuclear force with the same equanimity as its own:

Question: 'Would you favour or oppose West Germany having its own nuclear force? How about France? How about Great Britain?

Answer:	*West Germany*	*France*	*Great Britain*
'Favour'	15%	23%	54%
'Oppose'	72%	57%	31%
'Don't Know'	14%	20%	14%

[1] See Aubrey Jones, 'Does Nuclear Independence Make Sense?', *Observer*, 26 May 1963; Peregrine Worsthorne, 'Trust America More', *Sunday Telegraph*, 6 January 1963; 'Who Stands Where on the Deterrent?', *Financial Times*, 5 July 1963; and Aubrey Jones in 690 H.C. Deb. col. 484–93 (26 February 1964).
[2] 256 H.L. Deb. col. 720 (17 March 1964).
[3] 'The Jellicoe Touch', 21 March 1964.

When in the summer of 1962 there was discussion of an Anglo-French accord on nuclear collaboration, 50% thought Britain 'should not share' her nuclear secrets with France ('yes, share'—28%, 'don't know'—22%).

The polls confirm that the British attitude towards the 'independent deterrent' was related to the nation's conception of itself as a world power and the desire to be able to 'face up' to the United States. Asked in September 1964 if Britain should try to be a 'leading world power' or if it should play a role similar to that of Sweden or Switzerland, 52% wanted Britain to work to 'remain a world power' ('more like Sweden or Switzerland'—27%, 'don't know'—21%). Yet in January 1964 to the question: 'Do you think that Britain is treated as an equal partner by the United States in affairs that concern them both, or don't you think so?', 59% thought that Britain was 'not being treated as an equal partner by the United States' ('equal partner'—21%, 'don't know'—20%).[1]

Given this sentiment of the nation as a whole, it is not surprising that in the aftermath of the ambiguous agreement reached at the Nassau Conference the Macmillan government put great effort into presenting the Polaris submarines as simply the next stage in the continued development of the 'independent British deterrent'. Since in addition to the Polaris missiles themselves, key components of the communications, navigation, and guidance systems of the submarines were to be provided by the United States, the question of whether the freedom of action of the Polaris submarines would be limited received much attention in Parliament. The Government stressed that the Polaris submarines would be entirely under British control, that the submarines were to be built in the United Kingdom, and that the missiles would become British property after they were bought. It went so far as to deny the existence of a secret protocol, which some Labour M.P.s suggested might have been signed at Nassau, requiring electronic locks which would be under American control in the Polaris warheads. Fears that the United States would 'do another Skybolt' by unilaterally terminating the Nassau arrangement were partially dispelled by the publication of the Polaris Sales Agreement in April 1963, and by a public statement of Secretary of State Rusk that even if the NATO nuclear force referred to in both the Nassau and the Sales Agreements was not created the Polaris missiles would still be supplied to Britain.

In the weeks after the Nassau meeting there was some talk of a 'deterrent gap' in the period between the obsolescence of the V-bombers without Skybolt and the operational availability of the Polaris submarines. Some Conservatives contended that the Government should embark on

[1] Data from the files of the British Institute of Public Opinion.

a crash programme to produce a new Blue Steel of extended range to fill the gap and to be a form of insurance against a change in American policy which could deprive Britain of the Polaris missiles. This the Ministry of Defence rejected as too costly, but the 1963 Defence White Paper announced that special measures were being taken to lengthen the operational life of the V-bombers. In addition, a new 'bonus' strategic nuclear role was given to the Tactical Strike and Reconnaissance Aircraft (TSR-2) which was due to enter into service with the R.A.F. in 1967.[1] The TSR-2 had been intended as a low-flying aircraft to replace the Canberra; knowledgeable critics doubted that its tactical specifications made it suitable for the new long-range strategic mission which the Government now claimed for it with considerable fanfare. They were probably right, as demonstrated by the costly cancellation of the TSR-2 in 1965.[2] All this was motivated in part by the Macmillan government's desire to assure the country that it had guaranteed the independence of the British nuclear force for an indefinite time ahead.

The Conservative government's policy was tantamount to a rejection of two of the principal tenets of the new American defence doctrine, despite the Nassau Agreement and President Kennedy's acceptance of the British need for an 'escape clause'. In the first place, many British officials were never really in accord with 'flexible response' and with Secretary of Defense McNamara's objective of a conventional build-up in Europe to the point that a Soviet conventional attack could be resisted by non-nuclear means. Pentagon planners in 1963 made a new estimate of Soviet conventional force capabilities based upon calculations of the number of administrative troops used to support front-line deployments. The purpose of this reappraisal seemed to be to demonstrate that by a relatively small strengthening of conventional forces the range of non-nuclear options for the defence of Western Europe could be increased, and that tactical nuclear weapons could be relegated to a reserve role. British military intelligence officers were sceptical of the Pentagon's contention that Soviet conventional capabilities had been consistently miscalculated and that at full strength there was only the equivalent of 60 combat-ready Russian divisions rather than the 175 that had hitherto usually been

---

[1] *Statement on Defence: 1963*, Cmnd. 1936, p. 67.

[2] The TSR-2 was cancelled because it was over-ambitious and therefore too expensive. It is quite possible that the TSR-2 would have been cancelled earlier, before the 1964 General Election, if the Conservative government had not linked it with the maintenance of the independent deterrent after the cancellation of Skybolt. For an excellent and unusually thorough analysis, see Dr. Geoffrey Williams, Frank Gregory, and John Simpson, *Crisis in Procurement: A Case Study of the TSR-2* (London, Royal United Service Institution, 1969).

SNP

estimated. They therefore continued to feel that a large-scale Soviet incursion in Western Europe could not be resisted without the early use of nuclear weapons. Moreover, in order to increase the BAOR the British would either have had to withdraw forces from the Far and Middle East or reintroduce conscription, neither of which were attractive alternatives.

The basic British objection was, however, far more fundamental. They were convinced that the result of strengthening conventional capabilities would be to degrade the credibility of the nuclear deterrent—Britain's as well as that of the United States. The very weakness of NATO's conventional forces gave plausibility to the assumption that strategic nuclear weapons would be used for Europe's defence. To plan for a prolonged conventional war would, in the British view, remove this assumption and therefore make a Soviet attack more likely. The McNamara strategy of 'flexible response' was perhaps in accord with American national security interests, and was tailored to the desire of the United States to limit a war in Europe to a conventional battle. But this was far less attractive to the Europeans, who remembering the havoc and destruction of two world wars, wished to avoid another large-scale conflict on European soil. For the United States 'flexible response' increased the range of defence options by permitting a carefully graduated involvement in a war. But for the Europeans 'flexible response' reduced their options in the sense that it cast doubts on the availability for their defence of the American strategic nuclear force. Moreover, British strategic analysis in its continued adherence to 'massive retaliation' was more in agreement with the views held in Germany and most other continental nations than the policy of Washington.[1]

British nuclear policy also implicitly rejected the American doctrine of limiting independent nuclear forces. In the previous chapter it has been noted that although the United States was not enthusiastic about the British nuclear force, it was far more disturbed about the development of the French nuclear force, its use as a political weapon by de Gaulle, and the lesson which would be drawn in Germany from the separatism of Britain and France. Nevertheless, even taking into account the much heralded co-ordination of the nuclear target planning of Bomber Command and SAC, it could not be denied that McNamara's strictures against independent but limited nuclear forces as being 'dangerous, expensive,

---

[1] See the interview of Thorneycroft by the Defence Correspondent of *The Times*, 9 September 1963. See also Hedley Bull's excellent criticism of the political premises of the American defence doctrine in *Strategy and Atlantic Alliance: A Critique of United States Doctrine*, Policy Memorandum No. 29 (Princeton University, Center of International Studies, 15 September 1964), pp. 25–33. The Pentagon 'case' for a conventional build-up is given in Timothy W. Stanley, *NATO in Transition* (New York, Praeger, 1965), Ch. V.

prone to obsolescence and lacking in credibility' applied with equal logic to Britain. The creation of divergent policies was, however, caused by a shift in Washington's nuclear strategy rather than London's for, as was sometimes overlooked by the policy makers of the Kennedy administration, throughout most of the 1950s the United States had in fact aided and encouraged the growth of the British nuclear force.

The quest for centralized nuclear control and a monopoly in the ultimate decision-making power may well have been in America's presumed interest, but the questionable assumption was usually made that this was also in the interest of Britain and the other allies. Some American planners feared that independent nuclear forces might involve the United States in a nuclear war against its will, or make more complex, and therefore less controllable, the conduct of a war once it had begun. Accordingly they sought the prevention of additional national nuclear forces within NATO and, if possible, the eventual dissolution of existing ones, or their supersedence into a broader framework. American officials—too often with a certain arrogance—sought to persuade the British to climb down the nuclear ladder. They contended that if Britain renounced her nuclear weapons the Germans would no longer feel inferior because of their lack of them. Some even thought that a British and German renunciation, coupled with the recognition in Paris of the high costs of second generation delivery systems and thermonuclear bombs, might convince France to discontinue its own military nuclear programme.

But this presupposed an indivisibility of interests within the alliance which was not in accordance with the true situation. In Britain, as in other European NATO countries, an element of uncertainty was believed to be essential to the success of nuclear deterrence. Complications in the calculus of deterrence caused by the existence of more than one centre of nuclear control in the Western alliance were thought to add to the credibility of the Western deterrent by extending the range of contingencies with which the Soviets would have to contend. Furthermore, British political and military objectives in a nuclear war might not be the same as the objectives of the United States. The existence of a separate nuclear force would help ensure that British interests were properly taken into account. For these and the other reasons for maintaining the nuclear force already discussed, the American appeal to limit such forces fell on unreceptive ears—at least as far as the Conservative government was concerned with respect to British nuclear arms.

The differences in strategic doctrine between Whitehall and Washington contributed to the national debate in Britain on the 'independent deterrent'. The political impact of the American views went beyond the strategic arguments in which they were couched. For as Henry Kissinger has written, 'To ask a government to confess to the bankruptcy of a policy which it has pursued at heavy expense for over a decade is to undermine its domestic position and to evoke reactions of hostility.'[1] The Conservative government's justifications for the nuclear force consequently became more elaborate, emotional, and dependent upon conflicting interests with the United States. Conversely, the Labour party, sensing an invaluable electoral ally in President Kennedy, attempted to portray the alternative defence policy it was offering as being more in agreement with American policy, thereby implying that its programme was more enlightened and that a Labour government would work effectively and in greater harmony with the New Frontier.

6. The General Election of 1964: Labour and 'Re-Negotiating' Nassau

... The Nassau agreement to buy Polaris know-how and Polaris missiles from the U.S.A. will add nothing to the deterrent strength of the Western Alliance.... We are not prepared any longer to waste the country's resources on endless duplication of strategic nuclear weapons. *We shall propose the re-negotiation of the Nassau agreement.* (Italics mine.) Our stress will be on the strengthening of our conventional regular forces so that we can contribute our share to NATO defence and also fulfil our peace-keeping commitments to the Commonwealth and the United Nations.

This passage of deceptive simplicity from the Labour party's election manifesto[2] sought to create the impression that a Labour government would give up Britain's nuclear weapons. Labour's critique of the 'independent deterrent', in recapitulation, was that it was neither independent because of its dependence on the United States, nor a deterrent because of its lack of credibility. Rather it was a pretence which encouraged the proliferation of nuclear weapons, gave no added influence to the country in world affairs, undermined the solidarity of the Western alliance, fostered unnecessary duplication in the West's nuclear armaments, constituted a costly waste in defence spending, and seriously weakened Britain's conventional forces and her contribution to NATO ground forces. The position of the Labour leadership since the cancellation of Blue Streak was that the effort to maintain the independent deterrent should be discontinued, not on the moral question important to the party's Left wing of whether Britain ought to possess nuclear weapons

---

[1] Kissinger, op. cit., p. 119.
[2] *Let's Go with Labour for the New Britain,* The Labour Party's Manifesto for the 1964 General Election (London, Transport House, 1964).

but on the practical ground that it was beyond the economic and technological capability of the nation. Consequently, after their obsolescence,
the V-bombers should not be replaced by a new delivery system, and in
this manner the independent deterrent would be tapered off. After the
Nassau Conference the debate between the two parties therefore focused
upon whether Britain should buy the Polaris missiles or 're-negotiate'
the Nassau Agreement.

What, in fact, was meant by 're-negotiating' the Nassau Agreement was
never clear in the period before the election because of the intentional
ambiguity of Labour's leaders. An essentially cautious and non-committal
man, Harold Wilson was elected leader of his party following the death of
Gaitskell in a three-cornered contest only six weeks after the Bahamas
meeting. In the past, as he attempted to straddle the two wings of the
Labour party, his views on defence had been equivocal. Having reached
the top of the slippery pole he set himself the task in his new position of
appearing to the British public and the American government as a
'responsible' statesman who supported the purposes of integrated defence
in NATO and the 'special relationship' with the United States—while
also imposing order and discipline within his own party in an area where
there had been much previous dissent and controversy. 'Re-negotiating'
the Polaris arrangement was not unwelcome in Washington where many
had come to regret the bargain struck at Nassau, especially as the negative
British attitude towards the MLF became clearer. To the Labour Left
it came to mean undoing a piece of Tory chicanery and throwing away
the devilish bomb; to the Labour Right it meant a step in constructive
alliance diplomacy. For the party's leadership the very nebulousness of
the term permitted it to retain maximum flexibility.

A careful examination of the statements of the Labour spokesmen
primarily responsible for giving voice to the party's views on defence
and foreign policy suggests that there was no common understanding or
agreement on giving up the option to buy Polaris missiles. On the contrary their somewhat conflicting statements were marked with implicit
reservations rather than a rash resolve to wind up the nuclear force
come what may. Patrick Gordon Walker, the shadow Foreign Secretary,
travelled the furthest down the path of de-nuclearization in an article
in which he wrote:

We do not, however, believe that Britain herself should seek to make *or possess*
(italics mine) nuclear weapons of her own. . . . The problem that faces us is
what we do when the V-bombers become obsolete. We think we should not
replace them with weapons bought from America.[1]

[1] 'The Labour Party's Defence and Foreign Policy', *Foreign Affairs*, Vol. XLII, No. 3,
April 1964, pp. 392–3.

Denis Healey, on the other hand, while saying that Polaris would not be acquired for a separate British nuclear force, indicated that they might be bought if there was an 'alliance requirement' for British Polaris submarines:

I cannot say whether or not we will cancel the Polaris submarine. What I will say is that we will certainly not continue the programme in its capacity as an independent British force and, secondly, if we decided that there was no alliance requirement for a British Polaris component we would not have the slightest difficulty in converting these submarines into hunter-killer submarines. . . .

We do not believe that it is a necessary or sensible use of our resources to spend more money on retaining an independent nuclear capacity. We have repeatedly said that we have no interest in the Polaris programme as a contribution to an independent British deterrent. Whether it is of any value as part of an alliance effort we cannot make up our minds until we negotiate the question with the United States.[1]

As a serious student of the issue, Healey personally believed that the Polaris programme would be continued under a Labour government. In the above statement during the debate on the last Defence White Paper before the election Healey did his best to keep open the line of retreat from a Labour commitment to give up the nuclear force.

Harold Wilson—whom *The Economist* saw as a 'deer among politicians who can put his verbal feet down without breaking twigs better than most of them'[2]—was extremely cagey in his statements on Labour's intentions. A government under his leadership would seek 'an anti-proliferation agreement limiting the ownership of nuclear weapons to the two major nuclear powers'. It would 're-negotiate the Nassau Agreement on the basis of our declared policy that our proper contribution to our Alliance, and that our most effective military strength in this country, is secured without the illusion which is created by nuclear missile-carrying submarines. . . . We would re-negotiate this Agreement to end the proposal to buy Polaris submarines from the United States.'[3]

What was the precise meaning of 're-negotiate', or, as Wilson sometimes preferred to say, 'de-negotiate'? It did not mean the simple cancellation of the Polaris sales arrangement, for Wilson repeatedly evaded questions designed to draw him out on whether he would 'cancel' it. Almost inherent in the phrase of 're-negotiating the Nassau Agreement' was the

[1] 690 H.C. Deb. col. 480–1 (26 February 1964). Healey's suggestion of cutting out the mid-section of the nuclear submarines that carry Polaris missiles and converting the hulls for use as hunter-killer submarines was an ingenious way to drop the plans for a Polaris submarine force without incurring cancellation costs or losing the shipyard workers' vote. See his letter to *The Economist*, 7 March 1964.

[2] 'The Polaris Option', 13 April 1963.

[3] 687 H.C. Deb. col. 443–4 (16 January 1964).

concept that Britain would give up its right to obtain Polaris missiles only in return for new rights. That is, a more mutually satisfactory nuclear arrangement within the alliance would be necessary as a *quid pro quo* for Britain to abandon the Polaris submarine nuclear force. Labour had its own proposals for a greater British participation in the formulation and implementation of American nuclear strategy. Presumably, without the acceptance of its proposals in a successful re-negotiation of Nassau, Britain would retain her right to purchase Polaris missiles. Labour's leaders were reluctant to define a course of action should they be unsuccessful in re-negotiating Nassau. Wilson himself was careful not to say flatly that he wanted Britain to get out of the nuclear business altogether. In retrospect one can see that the deliberate ambiguity and fuzzing in Labour's statements was designed to provide a base sufficiently broad to justify almost any action that might be taken by the party's leaders in the future. The statements were carefully worded to keep the options open on deciding what to do with the nuclear force after Labour came into office.

Yet the public and more than a few relatively sophisticated observers were under the impression throughout most of 1963–4 that Labour did indeed intend to give up the Polaris missile and make other far-reaching changes in defence policy. This can only be a tribute to the success of the smokescreen laid by Wilson and his colleagues. In a series of 'Election Papers' on the major issues before the electorate *The Times* said that defence policy constituted 'one of the deepest and most significant ideological differences between the parties of the right and left . . . [the differences] can be reduced in essence to that complicated interlocking pattern of ideas and emotions, fears and risks, that is often referred to with almost total incomprehension as the Bomb.' A Labour government, predicted *The Times*, 'would abandon plans to establish a fleet of missile carrying submarines and would therefore not maintain an independent nuclear striking force after the V-bomber force ceased to be effective.'[1] The existing nuclear arms, chiefly the V-bombers, would be assigned 'unequivocally' to NATO without reservations about their use in a nuclear role for national purposes and the Conservative government's plan to give the TSR-2 a nuclear capability would almost certainly be abandoned. Labour would seek greater influence on American strategic decision-making by integrating its existing nuclear weapons into the NATO alliance, and by shifting the balance of defence policy towards greater

[1] 'Paradox of Defence Policy', Election Paper No. 3, *The Times*, 13 April 1964. Interestingly, in a comparable series on 'Labour's Hidden Icebergs' in the *New Statesman* a contrary prediction was made, see Paul Johnson, 'Will Wilson Keep the Bomb?' *New Statesman*, 13 December 1963; see also Nora Beloff, 'Labour Unlikely to Scrap Bomb', *Observer*, 17 November 1963.

emphasis on increasing Britain's contribution to non-nuclear defences.[1]

What Labour really wanted, its defence spokesmen suggested, was an intimate participation in the evolution of the strategic thinking and contingency planning which would lie beneath an American decision to use its strategic nuclear force. 'We must try to reach a point', Gordon Walker said in the Commons, 'at which the President's decision—because those are the decisions that matter in the world—can only be made on the basis of an agreed, continuously worked out and elaborated nuclear strategy and doctrine.'[2] The assumption could be made that Labour would bargain away the right to purchase Polaris missiles and the future of the 'independent deterrent' in exchange for a far greater say in the formulation of American defence policy. This was most explicitly spelled out by the shadow Foreign Secretary in his article in *Foreign Affairs*:

We do not wish simply to cancel it [the Nassau Agreement]. We want to negotiate a far-reaching new arrangement with Washington. The opening of talks to this end would be one of the first acts of a Labour government.

We would want to have a real share with the United States in shaping nuclear policy and strategy and we accept, both as a fact and as something desirable, that the last decision must be in the hands of the President. But we want to participate fully, intimately and without limit in the formulation of the ideas, policy and strategy that together make up the doctrine upon which any particular decision of the President must depend. We would want to share in the decisions about the deployment and targeting of nuclear weapons and in future production plans. We would also seek to conclude agreements under which we could execute enough specialist work to benefit from the industrial fall-out that comes from production of nuclear weapons.

This would be to ask a lot from America. *But in exchange we would recognize and support the ultimate nuclear monopoly of the United States in the West.*[3] (Italics mine.)

Such a system of close consultations was also, as we have seen, Labour's preferred alternative to the multilateral force.

The general approach of the Labour party to defence and in particular the nuclear issue received widespread support in the press and in the intellectual community in the period after Nassau. Most of the responsible newspapers made a relatively serious effort to present to their readers the more significant questions at hand, perhaps feeling a greater necessity to do so because of the one-sided and unsatisfactory manner with which the Government was presenting its own case. More often than not they

[1] See Defence Correspondent, 'Guide to Labour Defence Policy: Abandoning of Polaris and Switch of TSR-2 Nuclear Role Seem Likely', *The Times*, 9 March 1964.

[2] 684 H.C. Deb. col. 496 (15 November 1963).

[3] Gordon Walker, op. cit., pp. 393–4.

criticized the nuclear pretensions of the Conservative government and sought to suggest ways in which Britain's nuclear dilemmas could be resolved. Though their support of Labour's defence proposals was often qualified, it is significant that in contrast to public opinion as registered in the polls the Government did not carry with it most of the press— including *The Times*, which often sustains the Government of the day.[1] In addition, the Liberal party proposed a defence policy quite similar to that of Labour, though more sophisticated.[2]

In the spring and summer of 1964 there was a subtle but very definite change in the thinking of Wilson, Healey, and some of their colleagues who were likely to hold office in a Labour government. This was a result of a hard re-examination of defence policy as the election drew nearer and as the prospects of achieving power appeared very good. The chief result of this educational process was the recognition that, after Labour examined the Ministry of Defence's data and secret files, the Polaris programme might well continue pretty much along its then current line and that relatively little would probably be done to expand the conventional capabilities of the military service.[3]

One question which up to then had not received serious study was— how does a country 'cease' to be a nuclear power? Labour's thinking had been heavily influenced by the belief that in ceasing to be a military nuclear power, and in giving a monopoly of nuclear weapons in the West to the United States, Britain would by her example help to stop proliferation. Upon further examination, however, the illusion was dispelled that a country could stop being a nuclear power at the stroke of a pen. On the contrary, to convince a sceptical world that Britain had unilaterally renounced her nuclear capability raised the same problems as multilateral nuclear disarmament.

As Leonard Beaton pointed out in a timely and influential pamphlet, a Labour government would have to destroy, along with the existing

[1] See especially, 'The Bomb', *Observer*, 17 November 1963; 'Britain's Bomb: Keep or Renounce?' *The Economist*, 15 February 1964; 'The Deterrent Issue', *Sunday Times*, 17 November 1963; 'Good Ally', *The Times*, 23 January 1963; Defence Correspondent, 'Britain Without Skybolt', *The Times*, 8 and 9 January 1963; Defence Correspondent, 'Realistic Tactics for Britain', *The Times*, 2 August 1963.

[2] See 'Defence in the 1960's' a detailed analysis drawn up in the format of a defence white paper, prepared by a group of Liberals interested in defence matters under the chairmanship of Jo Grimond. Published in *Current Topics*, Vol. II, No. 7, February 1963, Liberal Party Research and Information Department.

[3] The conclusion that there was a transition in Labour's thinking in 1964 is based upon my observations in London at the time and interviews with Labour ministers after the election.

nuclear stockpiles, all the production and research establishments which could be engaged in the nuclear weapons programme.[1] These he listed as:

1. the thermonuclear bomb stockpile (perhaps 300)
2. the atomic bomb stockpile (perhaps 1,200)
3. any stocks of plutonium or enriched uranium which may exist
4. the Capenhurst gaseous diffusion plant
5. the Calder Hall/Chapelcross plutonium reactors
6. nuclear reactors which are now used for power rather than plutonium production
7. the Windscale plutonium separation plants.

In addition, decisions would have to be made on all existing and planned delivery systems for British nuclear weapons:

1. Mark II Vulcan and Victor bombers with Blue Steel missiles
2. other V-bombers
3. Canberra bombers
4. Buccaneer bombers
5. Scimitar fighter-bombers
6. the Polaris submarine programme
7. the TSR-2 bomber programme
8. orders for Phantom fighter-bombers

Such a list would still exclude other possible delivery systems such as military and civil transport aircraft. To give convincing assurance to the world that Britain had 'ceased' to be a nuclear power, that it had not retained secret stocks of weapons or fissile materials, and that the accumulated knowledge of years of experience in such matters as bomb design and uranium separation methods was not again being put to use for military purposes required nothing less than a system of international inspection.

Another subject of re-examination was the exact substance of the greater sense of participation in the making of American strategic policy which Labour said it would accept in exchange for giving up Britain's nuclear role. Labour had said that it wanted to participate fully at earlier stages in the evolution of American policy, but given the nature of the policy process in Washington it was never made clear how this should be done. Would Britain have a seat on the National Security Council? Or a special adviser in the White House? Or uniformed officers in the Pentagon? Or witnesses before the Congressional committees? Would the Prime Minister have a veto or merely a right of consultation? The fact was that there were already in existence a number of arrangements designed to give Britain that sense of participation. These included: the Joint Strategic

[1] *Would Labour Give Up the Bomb?* published by the *Sunday Telegraph*, August 1964, pp. 12–14.

Planning System at the headquarters of the United States Strategic Air Command at Omaha, Nebraska, where British officers participated in targeting decisions; a large number of informal bilateral arrangements between various ministries of the two Governments; and an understanding whose origin could be traced back to the Quebec Agreement of 1943, that the two heads of state would consult each other, if possible, before firing a nuclear weapon. Britain still did not have a share in the Pentagon's weapons research and development decision-making process, or in the military planning of the staff of the Joint Chiefs. But to have such a role would have required an American willingness to make a fundamental reappraisal of its concepts of sovereignty during an era when history had made it the leader of a great alliance. The subsequent creation of the Nuclear Planning Group within NATO was a move in the direction Labour had earlier proposed.

Furthermore, there were several assumptions implicit in the declaratory Labour position which were of somewhat questionable validity. A defence policy that envisaged placing all the nuclear power of the Atlantic alliance in American hands should have as its natural corollary a foreign policy closely aligned with that of Washington, for it is difficult to see how military power could be integrated without a parallel co-ordination of foreign policy. The concentration of nuclear power in one country is likely to enhance that country's influence over its partners. Yet sentiment in the Labour party was running in favour of a more identifiably 'British' foreign policy, less dominated by the United States, which would give a Labour Britain a more 'constructive' role in world affairs. Another long-standing Labour assumption was that a British renunciation would contribute to halting the spread of nuclear weapons. But nuclear developments just across the English Channel made this assumption less likely. The leaders of the Labour party, who were very anxious to have a prominent role in the negotiations for a non-proliferation treaty, came to feel as they approached power that the British nuclear role did in some measure make it more certain that their voice would be heard. A unilateral cancellation of the Polaris Sales Agreement was not going to improve London's bargaining position on the MLF, or its influence on the outcome of a nuclear sharing settlement in Europe.

As a result of this fresh reappraisal of the value of the nuclear force made by the party's top echelon during the middle months of 1964, and also because public opinion polls continued to show that in terms of electoral strategy Labour was on the wrong side of the issue, an attempt was made to neutralize it. In the official three-week campaign period Wilson devoted only one speech to the 'independent deterrent', though he spoke more often of the Conservatives' neglect of the Royal Navy and of conventional forces. Tory speakers, and Sir Alec especially, often raised the issue in their speeches but Labour focused its attention on domestic affairs. Significantly, the Conservative manifesto started with defence policy while Labour left the subject to the last section of its manifesto. Labour's tactics were essentially defensive, in order to play down the issue, in contrast to the Conservatives' attempt to make it dominant.[1]

Thus Labour settled down to attacking the pretensions of grandeur which it found in the Government's nuclear policy rather than the substance of the policy itself. It no longer criticized the existence of the nuclear force, but the extravagant claims the Douglas-Home government made for it—such as the 'fiction' of an 'independent deterrent', or the claim that the possession of nuclear weapons was a pre-condition of any influence in the world. Labour insisted that the Conservatives' constant reiteration of the need for 'independence' was undermining the alliance and, through a suggestive process, promoting proliferation. It also charged Conservative governments since 1951 with a record of mismanagement of defence unequalled since the Crimean War. The very fact that there had been nine Ministers of Defence in thirteen years was depicted as evidence that the Tories had been playing politics with Britain's security. Incompetent administration had caused an appalling waste in defence programmes; the long list of cancelled projects testified to many errors of judgement and an unwillingness to deal firmly with special interests. In its 'New Britain' the Labour government would put defence on a sound basis and ensure the nation received value and security for its money.

The differences on defence between the two parties were therefore more apparent than real. There was a similarity of outlook on Britain's role in NATO and on the basic purposes and organization of the alliance. The electorate was not offered a choice on the indicative question of national service. On the nuclear issue the two parties were drawing together. Should they be successful at the polls, the Conservatives were likely to place less emphasis on the theoretical independence of the nuclear force and more on its contribution to the Western deterrent. Wilson just before the election refused to commit himself on what would happen if his attempt to 're-negotiate' Nassau failed and what he would do in this case with the Polaris submarines. But with its usual perception *The Economist* observed that:

In a very English way, without anybody saying anything, the argument about Britain's nuclear status looks as if it is being softly, fuzzily and rather satisfactor-

---

[1] See Butler and King, *The British General Election of 1964*, pp. 130–1; yet Lord Attlee in introducing Wilson on his final television appeal said of Prime Minister Douglas-Home, 'Well, if a man had any personality, he could put across British policy without a nuclear bomb in his hand.'

ily compromised. . . . If one goes under the surface of public remarks, it begins to look entirely possible that things are changing. . . . One's guess nowadays is that if the Labour party came to power next month it might well decide to go ahead and build Polaris submarines (if they could not be converted into hunter-killers) and then try to solve the problem by putting the submarines under some sort of joint allied command.[1]

A week before the election a *Times* leader, 'Not A Bomb Apart', predicted that the 're-negotiation' of the Nassau Agreement would probably amount to no more than the commitment of the Polaris submarines to an allied force as an alternative to the MLF.[2]

The great nuclear debate which had engaged Britain for almost a decade was slowly coming to an end. After years of shadow boxing around the issue, Labour did not care to admit that its Government might end up with a nuclear force, just as the Conservatives did not wish to acknowledge that the 'nuclear deterrent' might not be fully 'independent'. Yet there remained no great clash of principle on nuclear weapons between the parties and the ground was being set for an effective compromise on the question of the next generation of Britain's nuclear force.

It remains to be asked whether Labour while in opposition deliberately misled the American government as to its true intentions, for following the election and the decision to retain the Polaris sales arrangement there were responsible officials in Washington who thought they had been deceived. Certainly Wilson did make a determined effort to cultivate American support after his emergence as leader of the Labour party. A trip to Washington in April 1963, followed by another in March 1964, in which he attempted to give the image that he could work intimately with the American President, assisted him in making the transition in British eyes from politician to statesman.[3] Close rapport with the President was seen as an electoral asset in Britain. For Wilson it was also very important to dispel the neutralist image which he had acquired earlier when he had made more than his fair share of anti-American speeches.

In his Washington visits Wilson, and Gordon Walker in his own trip of February 1964, suggested that the defence policy of a Labour government would dovetail with what Washington wanted. They said that they did not think that the Conservative government was making the best use of its resources by spending them on the nuclear force, thereby

---

[1] 'Britain's Bomb', 12 September 1964.

[2] *The Times*, 7 October 1964; see also the article by Roy Jenkins, the future Minister of Aviation, in the *Daily Telegraph*, 25 September 1964.

[3] See Henry Brandon, 'Wilson Wooed and Won the Americans', *Sunday Times*, 7 April 1963.

making it impossible to bring the BAOR up to agreed NATO force levels. One of the first steps of a Labour government would be to recast Britain's defence programme so as to alter the nuclear/conventional balance by increasing the quantity and quality of conventional forces. If only by implication, there was to be a basic change in Britain's nuclear role. Admiration was expressed for the strategic analysis which underlay McNamara's concept of the centralized control of nuclear weapons within the alliance, and for the new analytical techniques which the Kennedy administration had brought to the Pentagon. It may well be that Labour went furthest in 're-negotiating' Nassau in what it said in Washington and wrote for American audiences.[1]

But if Washington was led to believe that Britain would give up the nuclear force completely, it was a victim of its own lack of sensitivity to the intricacies of domestic British politics. In this period, which coincides with the apogee of the MLF lobby, there was a certain tendency towards 'wish-fulfilment' thinking among those responsible for European affairs in the State Department.[2] Thus some Washington officials did believe that Britain was ready to move out of the nuclear field. Their understanding of the matter might have been more accurate had they paid greater attention to the nuances of the internal political debate in Britain, given harder analysis to how a nation 'ceases' to be a nuclear power, and examined in depth the incentives and motives behind the long history of the British nuclear force.

[1] See the account of Wilson's speech at the National Press Club, *The New York Times*, 2 April 1963. See also, Harold Wilson, 'Britain's Policy if Labour Wins', *Atlantic*, Vol. CCXII, No. 4, October 1963, pp. 61–5; Gordon Walker, op. cit., *passim*.

[2] The American press was also guilty of 'wish-fulfilment' and this may have added to the misreading by some Washington officials. Cyrus Sulzberger, for example, wrote: 'If Labor wins Britain's next election it plans to get this country out of the atomic military business. This doesn't just mean abandoning an independent deterrent. It means phasing out manufacture of all nuclear arms, tactical or strategic.' *The New York Times*, 25 March 1963.

PART FOUR

The Dénouement
1964–1970

10 | The Labour Government and the Nuclear Force

Governing is choosing. While in opposition an alternative government can develop policies toward issues without the restraints that accompany the responsibilities of those who hold power. Problems that seem relatively simple, solutions that appear reasonably attractive, take on new dimensions and complexities when one becomes responsible for them. Politicians discover that they have less room in which to turn around than they once had expected. The most immediate question facing the new Labour government in the defence-foreign affairs realm after it came into office in October 1964 was whether to join the proposed multilateral force. Some American officials had let it be known in no uncertain terms that they 'expected' the British commitment to the MLF within a matter of weeks, by December. This was the 'practical' issue on which the Wilson government was forced to make its first choice on Britain's nuclear role, for its response to the MLF proposal could not be separated from its attitude towards its own nuclear force. Implicit in Labour's counter-proposal to the MLF—the suggestion for an Atlantic Nuclear Force (ANF)—was the continuation of the British Polaris programme.

In this chapter we discuss first the ANF proposal and its fate. Then we evaluate, in a broader context, the explicit and implicit elements of the decision to continue the nuclear force, asking how it was politically master-minded. Third, we look at the construction of the Polaris force as an Anglo-American project, examining the decisions made by the Labour government concerning the size of the force and the possible acquisition of the Poseidon missile. Here we also discuss the cost, capabilities, and targeting plans of the Polaris submarines. The chapter closes by examining the Wilson government's attitude towards planning for the next generation of the British nuclear force and possible nuclear collaboration with France.

The reader will want to bear in mind, however, that nuclear questions were only one part of the broad scale reappraisal of Britain's defence policy undertaken during the stewardship of Minister of Defence Denis Healey. The dominating question of defence policy during Labour's years in power was how the nation's military capabilities could be brought into balance with its economic resources and foreign policy objectives. This was often posed in the form of what should be Britain's proper role East of Suez. It was to this—the Wilson government's initial inclination to emphasize Britain's traditional worldwide role and her potentialities for 'peacekeeping', followed by the reappraisal of the Far East role and the series of decisions to reduce the military presence there, and the consequent priority given to Britain's participation in European defence—that the attention of Westminster, Whitehall, and the interested public was turned.[1] Meanwhile, however, important decisions were taken in the nuclear weapons field and work went quietly ahead on the completion of the second generation of the nuclear force.

1. The Proposal for an Atlantic Nuclear Force

Labour entered office in the midst of an atmosphere of climax, if not of crisis, on the MLF. Seven years of discussion on nuclear sharing in NATO and two years of intense debate on the MLF were coming to a head because of the insistence of some State Department officials that a decision must be taken by December 1964, in order to have time to get the necessary legislation through the Bundestag before the German election campaign in 1965 could upset the entire applecart. With the MLF timetable requiring a quick decision, the new Labour ministers and their defence experts met at Chequers the weekend of 20–22 November to formulate their policy. Labour's objections to the MLF were discussed in the previous chapter. But the alternative suggested by Labour while it was still in opposition, the concept of greater allied participation in the decision-making on the strategy and organization of the American strategic nuclear force through a broad system of consultations, was not sufficiently concrete to be acceptable as a useful alternative to the MLF at this time.

The proposal for an Atlantic Nuclear Force which emerged out of the Chequers meeting, and which was presented by Prime Minister Wilson to President Johnson in Washington, had a dual purpose: first, to offer an alternative to the MLF which would be consistent with British political interests and financial resources; second, to provide a 'basket' into which to place the British nuclear force in such a manner that the Labour government could claim to have fulfilled its presumed election pledge of renouncing the 'independent deterrent'. The ANF, as outlined by Wilson in the Commons on 16 December, would have had the following components: the British V-bomber force (except for aircraft earmarked for possible deployment outside the NATO area); the British Polaris submarines; at least an equal number of United States Polaris submarines; any forces which France may decide to subscribe; and 'some kind of a

---

[1] The debate on the priorities of defence policy is examined in my article 'Britain's Defence Dilemmas', *The Atlantic Community Reappraised,* Proceedings of the Academy of Political Science, Vol. XXIX, No. 2, November 1968, pp. 64–79.

mixed-manned and jointly owned element in which the existing non-nuclear powers could take part'. The mixed-manned component would preferably consist of existing or planned land-based missiles and aircraft (such as the F-111 and TSR-2 fighter-bombers) rather than a new fleet of surface ships with Polaris missiles. A new strategic force of Polaris-equipped vessels (i.e., the MLF) was thought to be the 'least desirable way of applying the mixed-manned principle'.[1]

The British national element, the Polaris submarines and the V-bombers, would be committed to the force 'as long as the Alliance lasts'. The Atlantic Nuclear Force would be under a single authority in which all countries taking part would be entitled to be represented; this authority would be closely linked to NATO, but like the MLF would not be part of the cumbersome NATO machinery. The ANF went further than the MLF in confronting the difficult problems of control. The United States, Britain, and France, if she took part, would have a veto over the use of all elements in the force and over any changes which might at any time be proposed in the control system. In addition, 'any other country participating would also have a veto if it wanted, though collectively they could, if they so desired, exercise their veto as a single group'. The effect of this system of multiple vetoes was to give all the member countries a veto over the release of any of the nuclear weapons of the ANF. Wilson indicated that he was opposed to the concept of a 'European clause' and to any scheme by which the American veto on the use of strategic weapons could be withdrawn. In so doing, he implied agreement with the contention that a united Europe possessing nuclear arms not subject to an American veto would amount to proliferation. To ensure that the ANF could not be represented as fostering the dissemination of nuclear weapons, Wilson proposed that the basic charter contain clauses under which the nuclear countries undertake not to disseminate nuclear weapons and the non-nuclear countries undertake not to acquire them or to gain national control over nuclear weapons. In addition, there would be a specific prohibition against nuclear weapons passing into the control or owner-ship of any group of non-nuclear countries that might be formed.[2]

This complicated proposal was the product of a good deal of British pragmatism. By enlarging the MLF to the wider conception of the ANF, the Wilson government was attempting to form a package which would

---

[1] The British at first suggested the mixed manning of the underground control centres of some of the solid-fuel Minuteman ICBM missiles in the United States but this was rejected by Washington as unacceptable for security reasons.

[2] 704 H.C. Deb. col. 432–7 (16 December 1964). See also, 'Guide to Nuclear Force Proposals', *The Times*, 11 December 1964. *The Times* leader, the day following Prime Minister Wilson's presentation to the Commons of the ANF, depicted it as 'about as complicated as the Cyprus constitution or the Nigerian political party structure'.

solve its own nuclear dilemmas as well as those of the alliance. Britain would have a major role in the ANF (proportionally greater than it would have had in the MLF) through its large contribution of V-bombers, Polaris submarines, and possibly the TSR-2, but without the fresh, additional financial commitment which the MLF required. Having just squeezed through a run on sterling and a serious financial crisis shortly after coming into office, the Government was anxious to avoid the expense of new weapons. In this respect the ANF was extraordinarily similar to the 'Thorneycroft proposals' of the previous Government in that both were based upon the use of existing weapons systems. Originally Labour defence spokesmen had indicated they would accept a reduced Polaris surface vessel fleet of ten ships to constitute the mixed-manned element, instead of the twenty-five proposed by the MLF, but this idea was dropped after the Chequers meeting. The inclusion of a contingent of American Polaris submarines gave the ANF a broader base than the MLF in that this would serve to increase the co-ordination of targeting between the ANF and the United States nuclear forces, and would call for more consultation on nuclear strategy among the members of the force than previously had been the case in NATO.

The British made it clear, however, that their Polaris submarines would remain a nationally owned and manned contingent. The Prime Minister assured the Commons that 'there will not be any system of locks which interferes with our right of communication with a submarine or our right to withdraw the submarine.'[1] Mixed-manning of the British Polaris submarines was looked upon with strong distaste as were the even more unacceptable suggestions made in some quarters that electronic locks be put on the warheads, or that the Polaris submarines be sold to the ANF or MLF for the mixed-manned element.

Yet Wilson was able to present the ANF to Labour's Left wing as fulfilling the election pledge of re-negotiating the Nassau Agreement. The commitment of Britain's Polaris submarines to the ANF for the duration of the alliance was claimed to be the equivalent of the renunciation of the 'independent nuclear deterrent'.[2] The stated rationale for this questionable assumption was that Britain was foreclosing the option to act independently. Labour ministers said that the ANF represented a more definite commitment to NATO and to arms control than the policy of the previous Government. Yet in the Nassau Agreement the Conservative

[1] 704 H.C. Deb. col. 694 (17 December 1964).

[2] At the conclusion of his December meeting with President Johnson, Wilson told the press that the re-negotiation of the Nassau Agreement was under way. 'The disposal of Britain's nuclear deterrent', wrote *The Times*, 10 December 1964, 'an act of national abnegation surely unprecedented, appears to have begun.' See also Healey's statement, 704 H.C. Deb. col. 607–8 (17 December 1964).

government had assigned the Polaris force to NATO subject only to withdrawal when 'supreme national interests' were at stake. Labour's formula permitted withdrawal of the force in the event of the breakdown of the alliance. Though there might be a distinction, there was not much of a real difference between these two formulae, for the alliance would, in effect, be in a state of suspension if there was a crucial difference of opinion over a matter of supreme national interest.

Labour ministers did not put emphasis on the insoluble 'right of withdrawal', as the Macmillan-Home cabinets did, thus further fostering the impression that the status of the 'independent deterrent' was being altered.[1] But the hard fact remained that it would be impossible to stop a British government from retrieving its contribution to the ANF if it really wanted to as long as it was not mixed-manned. It could be reasoned that as long as the United States remained involved in Western Europe it was unlikely that the vital interests of the United States and the United Kingdom would diverge; should the American commitment to the alliance dissolve, NATO would erode to the point that Britain could justify with ease the withdrawal of its Polaris fleet. Meanwhile, Wilson could claim that the ANF was his plan to dispose of the British independent deterrent. It was true that in the absence of an agreement on the ANF, Britain would be left with the same nuclear force as before—but it would not be *his* fault if other countries refused to accept the Labour government's plan!

It is probable that an agreement on some type of an ANF/MLF arrangement could have been reached in December 1964, if Washington had insisted upon it. The British were caught between the possibility of a purely American-German accord on the MLF, or if this did not occur, the danger of a nuclear arrangement between a frustrated Germany and an ambitious France. Both were undesirable from London's point of view, since the former would weaken British influence in Washington and make Bonn its most intimate ally, while the latter was even more dangerous since it would increase Germany's nuclear knowledge, create the danger of an anti-Anglo-Saxon 'third force' in Europe, and be a cause of valid apprehension for the Soviet Union. Despite continuing differences of opinion between Britain, Germany, and the United States over the make-up of an integrated nuclear force, an agreement could well have been forged between these countries plus Italy and some of the smaller European nations in late 1964.

[1] Public acceptance that some change was under way and confusion about it was reflected in a Gallup poll in February 1965, four months after the election. To the question, 'Do you know whether we have an independent nuclear deterrent or not?' 41% replied they did not know, 30% thought Britain had a deterrent and 29% thought it did not. Data from British Institute of Public Opinion.

But the surprising result of the Wilson-Johnson meeting of 7–9 December 1964, was the cessation of the pressure for the MLF/ANF. Immersing himself deeply in the subject for the first time in preparation for the meeting with the new British prime minister, President Johnson took note of the lack of Congressional support for the MLF (whose charter would have to be ratified by the Congress), the grave misgivings within the administration and among the attentive public, the open hostility of the French, the division of opinion in Bonn, the lack of enthusiasm in a number of other European capitals, and the increasing opposition of the Soviet Union. With no strong European support for the plan and no requirements on the basis of national security for an early agreement, the President decided to delay so as to explore other alternatives which would be more satisfactory to both Germany and Britain, gain French approval, and command more support in general. The President ordered the executive branch through an NSC memorandum to cease pressing the MLF upon the allies and it was suggested to Wilson that he take the initiative in forging an agreement with the Germans. Thus the net effect of the initial presentation of the ANF proposal was to defuse the MLF controversy by making the situation much more flexible (wags said the ANF torpedoed the MLF, making the first case in history when a non-existent fleet sank another non-existent fleet) and to hand over to Wilson the responsibility for fashioning an Atlantic nuclear organization.

President Johnson, accepting the counsel of his White House advisers, had taken care not to repeat the Nassau experience of appearing to settle the problems of the Western alliance on an exclusively Anglo-American basis.[1] He placed great stress on not offending the French or the Germans by appearing to make an agreement with the British without German support and at least acquiescence from the French. Subsequently, the American notion emerged that a way must be found to give Germany a status of equality with Britain in nuclear matters. This was a strange idea for some Englishmen to accept. Quite apart from the United Kingdom's long historical involvement with nuclear energy, which had no counterpart in Germany, the defence roles of the two nations were basically asymmetrical. Germany had no extra-territorial responsibilities; Britain was still shouldering world-wide defence commitments at considerable expense. Talk of equality between the two countries was difficult to reconcile with some long-cherished assumptions about Britain's special place in the alliance.[2]

Wilson discovered during the course of 1965 that the ANF was not

---

[1] See the text of the joint communiqué, *U.S. Department of State Bulletin*, Vol. LI, No. 1331, 28 December 1964, pp. 902–4.

[2] See 'Equality Among Allies', *The Economist*, 12 December 1964.

attractive to Germany because it maintained the condition of nuclear inequality. The Germans were being asked to believe that they were attaining equality through their contribution to the mixed-manned force within the ANF and through their participation in the control system. But Britain and France were to have withdrawable national nuclear contingents which Germany would not have, thus retaining the original discrimination in nuclear arms. This role of relative minor importance for Germany was built into the politics of a potential nuclear arrangement. The ANF was designed to keep the door open for a France which was not likely to come in except on the basis of a retrievable contingent. But it was also constructed to provide room for a Germany which, because of the opposition of the Soviet Union and most Europeans, could not be permitted to have a withdrawable nuclear force. This dilemma was compounded by Wilson's decision to withhold part of the British strategic force for use outside Europe, and his guarded hints of a British nuclear role in Asia which would presumably be independent of the restraints of a multinational nuclear accord.

The ANF was also unattractive to many on the continent because of the Labour government's plan for a system of multiple vetoes, including Wilson's firm insistence upon an immutable American veto in perpetuity. As originally presented the ANF would have had so many safety catches that its credibility would be in serious question. But even if the number of vetoes could have been reduced through a system of weighted voting, France was likely to have opposed any new form which predicated a permanent American veto. Yet the Labour party would not have accepted any plan under which the American veto disappeared. Its continuing distrust of West Germany made it impossible for Wilson to suggest any formula which might eventually move the German finger closer to the trigger. Accordingly, the ANF proposal alienated many of the supporters of European unity and of an eventual European nuclear force because of its rejection of the option for a 'European clause' under which the American participation might some day be withdrawn following achievement of a higher level of political unity and military self-sufficiency among the Western European nations. With American pressure on the MLF removed and with a disinclination on the part of Washington officials to transfer their lobbying activities to support of the ANF, little headway was made when Wilson met Chancellor Erhard in March 1965. A hiatus ensued while awaiting the German elections of September during which opposition to the MLF/ANF increased in Bonn. The S.P.D. became concerned that the prospects for German reunification would be seriously compromised if Germany participated in a new nuclear force over strenuous Soviet objections; within the governing C.D.U. there was a growing reluctance to part company with France; and Franz Josef Strauss' C.S.U. opposed any agreement which barred a European nuclear force.

Meanwhile more optimistic prospects for a treaty halting the spread of nuclear weapons put the ANF proposal in a new light. Following the first Chinese atomic detonation in October 1964, a new sense of urgency pervaded arms control discussions. The Eighteen Nation Disarmament Conference in Geneva, which had been moribund for several years, came to life when the Soviet Union showed an unexpected interest in a treaty to prohibit the dissemination of nuclear weapons. Whatever be the Russian motives—it could be argued with some cogency that the Russians were interested in, among other things, blocking an MLF/ANF accord which would give the Germans some role in nuclear affairs—there was a marked eagerness in London to reach a non-proliferation agreement. Success in achieving arms control agreements had a peculiarly high dividend in British domestic politics. Ever since the 1959 proposal for a 'Non-Nuclear Club', the belief that a Labour government should play a leading role in pushing through a treaty to bar the spread of nuclear weapons had been gospel to the Labour party.

This attitude, combined with a sincere concern regarding the dangers of world-wide proliferation and a desire to forge a new accord with the Soviet Union which would help offset the eroding influence of Vietnam upon the East-West relationship, led the Labour government to put great emphasis on the importance of a non-proliferation treaty. Accordingly such an agreement was given priority over a new nuclear organization for the alliance. During the first half of 1965 the Soviet Union waged a diplomatic offensive against the MLF/ANF concepts by insisting that any arrangement which would give West Germany any knowledge, ownership, or voice in the control of nuclear weapons would destroy all hopes for a non-proliferation treaty. The fact that the proposed ANF charter, unlike the MLF, contained specific non-dissemination clauses appeared to be unnoticed in Moscow. Despite the State Department's claim that neither the MLF nor the ANF would increase the number of 'nuclear entities', the Soviets continued to view any 'hardware solution' as an obstacle to a treaty. The British were determined not to embark on any course of action which was not compatible with non-proliferation.

When Foreign Secretary Michael Stewart visited Washington in October 1965, he implied, to Secretary Rusk's dismay, that the Labour government would be willing to drop the ANF proposal if the Soviets would agree to a treaty.[1] And at Geneva the chief British negotiator, Lord Chalfont, who had played an important part in devising the ANF

[1] *The Times*, 12 October 1965; Henry Brandon, 'Shifts in Nuclear Aims', *Sunday Times*, 17 October 1965.

formula a year earlier at Chequers, took the view that retention of a European clause in the American draft treaty was undesirable. In effect what was happening was that in giving non-dissemination priority over the ANF, the British were aligning themselves with the then still minority view within the Washington establishment. The State Department continued to think it essential to weave Germany inextricably into the Western alliance through a multilateral nuclear arrangement, but a growing body of opinion including the Arms Control and Disarmament Agency and some Congressional critics such as Senator Frank Church argued that it was more important to achieve a non-proliferation treaty and to work towards a European political settlement by not insisting upon the retention of the European clause.[1]

So having somewhat unenthusiastically offered the ANF proposal to counter the MLF project, the Labour government a year later, more enthusiastically, withdrew it from serious consideration. The British never pressed the ANF hard upon their allies for they were never enamoured, as were the Americans, with a multilateral, hardware solution for the alliance's political problems. The diminution of nuclear anxieties in Germany (the Foreign Office had always insisted that the German interest in nuclear weapons and in 'equality' with Britain was less pronounced than Washington claimed), the withdrawal of pressure for the MLF, and the appearance of a non-proliferation treaty on the horizon, paved the way for a new approach to nuclear sharing. In retrospect the ANF, like the MLF, was a transitional concept, now carried away to some Valhalla of unused initials. The next proposal placed before the alliance, that of a special committee of defence ministers to provide for close consultations in nuclear strategic planning, was quite similar to what Labour defence spokesmen had been suggesting since their early opposition to the MLF. First as the 'McNamara Committee', and then transformed into the present Nuclear Planning Group of NATO, this consultative arrangement left the British nuclear force in the same unfettered position it was in under the previous Conservative government.

2. Deciding to Continue the British Nuclear Force

In section 6 of Chapter 9 we saw that as the leaders of the Labour party prepared during 1964 for a likely victory in the coming General Election they re-examined their declaratory defence policy with a view as to what

---

[1] See Lord Chalfont, 'The Politics of Disarmament', *Survival*, Vol. VIII, No. 2, November 1966, pp. 342–9; William C. Foster, 'New Directions in Arms Control and Disarmament', *Foreign Affairs*, Vol. XLIII, No. 4, July 1965, pp. 587–601; Senator Frank Church, 'U.S. Policy and the "New Europe"', *Foreign Affairs*, Vol. XLV, No. 1, October 1966, pp. 49–57.

they might find themselves doing upon achieving office. In this manner they came to realize, but not to acknowledge too openly, that a Labour government would probably continue the nuclear force. Certainly it would not be discarded before a general nuclear settlement was reached in Europe. Nor was it clear as to how Britain could 'cease' to be a nuclear power in a convincing manner, or what would be the benefits of such an action, even if feasible. Furthermore, the handful of politicians about to take on the responsibility for leading Britain in the international arena were not convinced that Britain's diplomatic influence would be increased if it were to jettison the most powerful military arms known to man, which also had come to be equated in the modern world with a high order of prestige and status.

Probably, then, Labour's decision to maintain the British nuclear force was implicitly taken before the election of October 1964. But in fact there never was a 'decision' in the sense of a one-time determination of a question. When the Labour ministers met at Chequers for their first major defence review there was no discussion of the merits or demerits of starting the process of de-nuclearizing Britain. Neither was there discussion of cancelling the agreement to purchase Polaris missiles from the United States. Nor was specific attention given to how the Nassau Agreement should be 're-negotiated'. Rather, attention was focused on the formation of the ANF plan to serve as a counter-proposal to the much disliked MLF. In retrospect, the ANF provided the smokescreen for Labour's nuclear reversal. When the smoke had cleared it was obvious that Britain was and would remain for at least some time a nuclear power. In retaining the arrangement to purchase the as yet undelivered Polaris missiles the decisive step had been taken—virtually without discussion.[1]

What were the reasons given by the Labour government for continuing the nuclear force? How was the Wilson cabinet's reversal of the Labour party's defence policy as understood by the mass of its supporters made palatable to them? What were some of the underlying motivations of Messrs. Wilson, Healey, and Gordon Walker which help to explain their actions? In what ways were the Whitehall perceptions of the role of the British nuclear force changed, and in what manner was the public attitude transformed after 1964? These are some of the questions to which we now turn.

Let us first look at some of the reasons explicitly given for maintaining the nuclear force. First, not long after taking hold of the reins of government it became known that Labour officials had discovered that work on the Polaris submarines had passed the 'point of no return'. The

[1] Interviews. See also Harold Wilson, *Labour Government 1964–70: A Personal Record* (London, Michael Joseph and Weidenfeld & Nicolson, 1971), pp. 40–2.

outgoing Conservative government was said to have sewn up the contracts for the manufacture of the submarines so tightly that the compensation costs in case of cancellation would have equalled the total planned costs of the vessels. Furthermore, three of the submarines were said to have reached a stage of construction which would make it impossible to convert them into nuclear hunter-killer type submarines except at heavy expense.[1] This was not a very convincing argument, for no British government is so hamstrung that its contracts could not be re-negotiated. But it did serve as a reminder to the labour unions that cancelling the submarines would reduce the work at the already impoverished shipyards and create further unemployment. Consequently, even communist-dominated unions did not want work on the submarines brought to a halt. The Government did, however, withdraw the order for a fifth Polaris submarine in February 1965, but this was mainly an economy measure.

A second reason was the sudden emergence of a possible mission for Polaris submarines in the Far East. This was part of a larger debate on Britain's proper role East of Suez, a role which was highly valued by the Wilson government in its early years. Suggestions were made that the Polaris submarines, when completed, should be deployed in the Indian Ocean area to provide a nuclear guarantee to India. Certainly by coincidence China's first nuclear explosion took place on the day the Labour party was elected to office. Although the Chinese breakthrough could have been foreseen, China's emergence as a nuclear power did not have its public impact in Britain until then. The threat to India incumbent in China's acquisition of nuclear weapons was thus a dramatic new factor which strengthened the Wilson government's hand in retaining the nuclear force. One must recall that the Labour party took unusual pride in the Attlee government's creation of an independent Indian state. The new Labour government could now tell the party's Left wing with considerable persuasion that divesting Britain of her nuclear force, just when India might need it to safeguard her security, made little sense. Prime Minister Shastri, of India, in London just prior to Wilson's trip to Washington in December 1964, was said to have discussed with him the question of nuclear guarantees in the Far East.

Two purposes could be assigned to the creation of a nuclear guarantee for India. The first was the containment of China through the deterrence of a massive Chinese conventional assault on India's northern border, or through the deterrence of a Chinese nuclear strike. Second, and quite separate, was the notion that the establishment of a nuclear guarantee for India would dissuade her from deciding to build her own nuclear weapons,

[1] *Financial Times*, 30 October 1964; *Sunday Times*, 29 November 1964.

thus inhibiting the spread of nuclear capabilities in Asia. The security of India and the prevention of proliferation were both purposes which could rally support among many of the very same people who in years past protested against British nuclear arms. Both aims were alluded to in the first Defence White Paper of the Labour government issued in February 1965. Under a section entitled 'The Threat', the risk of a major nuclear war arising out of a direct conflict between the Soviet Union and the West was said to be 'almost entirely excluded as a result of the present state of mutual deterrence'. Similarly, because of the high risk that any conflict in Europe would escalate, 'deliberate aggression, even on a limited scale, is unlikely in this theatre'. In the Far East, however:

The Chinese nuclear explosion casts a new shadow over the future making it more difficult to forecast the trend of political development in an area where we have Commonwealth and treaty responsibilities to assist our friends.

The Chinese explosion must remind us that the stability so far achieved in relations between Soviet and Western alliances might rapidly be jeopardised by the spread of nuclear weapons to countries which do not now possess them. . . . *Our nuclear policy must help to provide some reassurance to non-nuclear powers* (italics added).[1]

Although it was not specifically said that Britain was considering stationing a nuclear force in the Far East, this statement and Wilson's exclusion of part of the V-bomber force from the ANF for duty outside the NATO area were assumed to imply as much.[2]

The possible placement of the Polaris nuclear force in the Far East raised a number of salient questions. One could ask if the Polaris submarines could be a credible deterrent to a massive Chinese conventional invasion of India. Would a British government be likely to break the nuclear threshold which had existed since 1945 by making the first use of nuclear weapons, save in the event of a direct threat to its, or NATO's, territorial security? Even as a second-strike force the Polaris submarines might lack credibility in certain circumstances. If, for example, Peking announced following a Chinese nuclear strike on India that any retaliatory British nuclear attack on China would be met by a reprisal against, say, Japan or Australia, would Britain be willing to launch her Polaris missiles? Moreover, the eventual Chinese capacity to threaten Western Europe with intercontinental missiles placed further doubts on the credibility of a British deterrent.

The usefulness of nuclear guarantees for inhibiting nuclear proliferation was even more problematic. Nations are likely to make the decision to

[1] *Statement on the Defence Estimates: 1965*, Cmnd. 2592, p. 7.
[2] See, for example, 'Labour's Bomb and the White Man's Burden', *Observer*, 28 February 1965. British carrier forces in the Indian Ocean area have been known to be nuclear-equipped and V-bomber squadrons have been located for periods of time in Singapore.

acquire nuclear weapons for a number of reasons of which military security is only one. In the case of India considerations of prestige and avoidance of loss of status in Asia played a prominent part in the nuclear debate. A British nuclear guarantee would carry with it less credibility than an American or Soviet, or joint Superpower, guarantee and even that, were it possible, might not assuage the Indian need for prestige vis-à-vis her competitors for the leadership of Asia. In the 1960s the possibility of nuclear guarantees had less appeal to Indians than to the non-Indians who were concerned about nuclear spread in that part of the world. Senior Indian officials spoke with considerable scorn of uninvited proposals for guarantees which emanated, in particular, from London. It would also have to be recognized that the psychological effect of placing the British Polaris submarines in the Indian Ocean might be different from what one might expect. For some nations it might be provocative while for others it might appear as confirmation that Great Power status can indeed be equated with nuclear capability. In either case the British action could prove to be an incentive, rather than a discouragement, to nuclear spread.

The third justification for retaining the nuclear force, and one of greater pertinence, was that in the Polaris submarines Britain was obtaining a first class weapons system at an extraordinarily cheap price. This deflated for the coming decade at least the argument, which had been made for many years, that Britain could not afford to maintain a nuclear force. The 1966 White Paper revealed that the expected operating costs of the Polaris force would be under two per cent of the total defence budget.[1] The total expense of the four submarines including missiles, support installations, and training facilities was expected to come to £350 million, which was less than the £500 million spent on the V-bomber force and it was purchased at a time when electronics and aircraft were still relatively cheap. This low cost was explained by the fact that the British Polaris submarines, unlike the V-bombers, were heavily subsidized by the United States through its massive expenditure on the research and development of the Polaris missile system towards which Britain made a relatively insignificant contribution. For this very favourable arrangement the Labour government could thank Harold Macmillan. After looking at the Ministry of Defence's records Denis Healey was able to conclude that the Polaris submarines would be good value for the money and that his defence budget would have room for them. This enabled him to keep the submarines, as he probably had always hoped to do.

We now turn to the unstated, implicit motives for retaining the nuclear force. First, the Labour government recognized that the configuration

[1] *Statement on the Defence Estimates: 1966*, Part I, Cmnd. 2901, p. 9.

of the problem of nuclear spread had altered since the time in the 1950s when it could be argued that Britain by voluntarily renouncing her nuclear arms could strongly influence other countries to desist from acquiring them. At that time the more likely candidates for the nuclear club were thought to be European nations. Now with the emergence of China as a nuclear power and its consequent impact on India and Japan, and the construction of nuclear reactors in Israel with its effect on the Middle East, the dangers of nuclear proliferation were largely seen in a worldwide context. It was probably too late for Britain to arrest the acquisition of nuclear weapons by other countries simply by giving a moral lead in voluntarily renouncing her own. Thus in October 1966, Lord Chalfont, then Labour's Minister for Disarmament, in presenting British arms control policy at a United Nations meeting asked dubiously who would follow suit and how would it affect the policies and attitudes of other governments if Britain were to 'abandon its nuclear capability and throw all its nuclear weapons into the sea'.[1] The irony is that Lord Chalfont was using the same argument that previous Conservative governments had used in rejecting the Labour party's contention that maintenance of the 'independent deterrent' was serving to encourage proliferation.

The 'force de frappe' also stood as a reminder of Britain's reduced ability to set an example by renouncing her nuclear arms. Little support could be conjured in London for any act of self-abnegation which would leave France as the only European nuclear power. This was not because France was thought to present a security problem to Britain but because the Anglophobia of the Fifth Republic sharpened Anglo-French rivalry, rekindled the British national pride, and made the British more conscious of the necessity to husband their resources in order to strengthen their negotiating position on such matters as entrance into the Common Market and nuclear co-operation in Europe.

Second, therefore, the nuclear force was seen as an important bargaining asset and diplomatic instrument. It gave Britain a principal role—and veto—in the construction of nuclear sharing arrangements. Who could deny that without nuclear weapons of her own Britain would not have been as successful in staving off the MLF? The nuclear force would put Britain in a central position in the chartering of a European deterrent should this ever come about. Nuclear collaboration with France might serve as the ticket of admission into the E.E.C. Britain's nuclear status gave her a special position in negotiations on nuclear arms control and other disarmament matters. To give up the nuclear force unilaterally would be to obtain no new authority or bargaining power in the crisis management of international politics. There was no way to foretell in

[1] General Assembly, First Committee, U.N. Doc. A/C.1/PV 1432, p. 18, 26 October 1966.

what ways Britain's nuclear status might prove to be an invaluable bargaining instrument in the future.

The third and most important implicit reason for retaining the nuclear force was that the Labour ministers responsible for handling the nation's foreign relations acknowledged that it somehow intangibly enhanced Britain's influence. The fundamental aim of a British government is to find ways to have its voice heard. True, the linkage between arms and influence is open to question. But it would be even more difficult to prove that by scrapping her nuclear weapons Britain would be increasing her influence and prestige. Britain's status as a nuclear power strengthened her role in the shaping of Europe and the formulation of NATO strategy. At times Prime Minister Wilson spoke as if it also gave Britain a position of power and influence in the Far East.

Having criticized the Conservatives for keeping the nuclear force for reasons of prestige and influence, the Labour government was now doing likewise for many of the same reasons. Wilson could not have been unaware that public opinion following an initial period of confusion shortly after the election continued to support the nuclear force.[1] Once having achieved office, Labour was now adopting the policy of the centre. Modern British political parties, in order to retain power, must adopt the views and attitudes at the centre of the nation's political thought.

It would not be correct, however, to conclude that Labour simply continued the 'independent deterrent' policy of the past Conservative government. The Labour government claimed that the 'independent deterrent' did not exist and never had. Two months after the election Wilson announced in the Commons that it was a Conservative myth which he was now about to expose. The Polaris submarines would not be independent, he said, because in addition to relying upon the United States for certain components of the submarines, Britain would be dependent upon the supply of fissionable materials from America for its warheads for the Polaris missiles. Moreover, the British warheads would be untested in the atmosphere because of the Test Ban Agreement, so that the nuclear force would be dependent either upon tests carried out earlier by the United States or on untested warheads. The Polaris submarine force would therefore not constitute a reliable 'independent deterrent'.[2]

[1] In September 1965, in answer to the question: 'How important do you think it is for the Government to keep Britain strong in nuclear arms?' 28% answered 'very important', 32% 'important', 23% 'not important', 17% 'don't know'. Poll from the British Institute of Public Opinion.

[2] 704 H.C. Deb. col. 701-4 (17 December 1964); see also, 707 H.C. Deb. col. 1572-3 (4 March 1965). The United Kingdom received enriched uranium from the United States in

The Labour government spoke of the British nuclear force in a different
tone from that of the Macmillan and Douglas-Home governments, and
in a different style. There was less emphasis on national control and more
on alliance requirements. 'Independence' was understated rather than
overestimated. Wilson's task was to assuage the sentiments of the Left
wing of his party; Douglas-Home had fanned the chauvinistic flames of
the Right wing of the Tories. Labour ministers spoke of their intention
to 'internationalize', or at other times to 'collectivize', the nuclear force.
The 1966 Defence White Paper stated that it was the Government's
'aim to internationalize our nuclear strategic forces in order to discourage
further proliferation and to strengthen the alliance'.[1] Accordingly under its
proposal for an Atlantic Nuclear Force the United Kingdom had offered
'to internationalize the bulk of our nuclear strategic forces, including the
entire Polaris submarine fleet, by committing them *irrevocably to NATO
for the duration of the alliance*.'[2] (Italics mine.) In answer to a parliamentary question, Wilson said:

We intend to collectivise our nuclear position whether in the Atlantic, Pacific
or anywhere else. . . . We do not intend to preserve the myth of the independent
deterrent . . . it would be part of a collective security agreement with no pretence
at independent national status.[3]

Until the nuclear force could actually be merged into a collective arrangement, however, the main difference between the policies of the two governments was more verbal than substantive.

The decision to continue the nuclear force was carefully engineered
by Wilson so as not to cause a revolt within the Labour party's often
rebellious Left wing. The charge that the force was not an 'independent
deterrent', the subtle change in words and emphasis in describing it,
were designed as much for the ears of the Labour back bench as anybody's.
In addition, Wilson brought three prominent former unilateralists into
the cabinet, Frank Cousins, Anthony Greenwood, and Barbara Castle,
but without giving them portfolios related to defence. By bringing these
potential rebels into the cabinet he silenced his opposition, for there was
no man of sufficient stature remaining on the back benches to lead a revolt.
Political craftsman that he was, Wilson played upon the narrow five-vote

exchange for its plutonium, but its production of enriched uranium could be increased to a
sufficient output by reopening the Capenhurst plant. Wilson may therefore have been referring
to tritium, a radioactive material used in thermonuclear warheads, particularly in advanced
compact war-heads such as those used for Polaris missiles.

[1] *Statement on Defence Estimates: 1966*, Part I, Cmnd. 2901, p. 5.

[2] Ibid., Part II, p. 23.

[3] 729 H.C. Deb. col. 276–7 (24 May 1966).

majority of his first Government to keep the Left wing under discipline. Any serious dissension would have been suicidal. A former shadow Labour defence spokesman, Reginald Paget, plaintively informed his front bench in March 1965, that he was 'still waiting for some explanation of why the Labour party defence policy, which we worked out over a number of years together, has been abandoned, and the Conservative party adopted in its stead'.[1] But at the Blackpool Labour party conference, a year after the party had taken office, there was no criticism of the decision to continue the Polaris programme. Discontent was siphoned off on the Government's failure to dissociate itself from American policy on Vietnam, on uneasiness over the expense of the British military presence East of Suez, and by the Government's determination to cut military expenditures. Wilson's foreign and defence policy was essentially like Bevin's in its support of the United States and collective defence, and in its greater support from the opposition benches than from Labour's neutralist and pacifist members. It was made possible by Gaitskell's hard-won victory over the unilateralists in 1960–1.

The Conservative opposition also unwittingly came to the assistance of Wilson by helping him convince the Labour backbenchers that the nuclear force was being downgraded, if not discarded. Confused by Labour's use of the ANF proposal as a smokescreen, Douglas-Home, then still the Tory leader, indignantly accused the Prime Minister in December 1964, of abandoning the 'independent deterrent'.[2] This ensured for Wilson the support of the Labour Left and made the Tories look somewhat ridiculous for refusing to consider anything but totally unfettered independence. By the following February they were sardonically offering their congratulations to the Prime Minister for having adopted the Conservative defence policy.

After early 1965 the 'great debate' on the British nuclear deterrent came to a standstill as the issue faded away. There was no longer an important difference of views between the two parties. Moreover it was in the Wilson government's interest to keep the waters calm, since the whole subject was one of intense embarrassment within the party. After having gone on to build the Polaris fleet the Labour party did not even mention nuclear weapons in its manifesto before the General Election of 1970. Yet one should note that if Wilson had 're-negotiated Nassau' by cancelling the Polaris programme the Conservatives were prepared to start a massive campaign of protest. Similarly, for Wilson to have relinquished ultimate control or ownership of the nuclear force would have put strategic policy back into the centre of political debate. The Tories in opposition wanted to retain the British nuclear force badly

[1] 707 H.C. Deb. col. 1367 (3 March 1965).
[2] 704 H.C. Deb. col. 592–600 (17 December 1964).

enough not to chide Labour for having continued the past Conservative policies to the point of forcing Wilson to take more radical action. Nevertheless, it became generally accepted following the 1964 election that the pre-eminence given by Conservative governments to the 'independent deterrent' was no longer party policy. Thus the party's policy statement released after Edward Heath's accession to the Tory leadership placed far less emphasis on nuclear independence and more on the NATO alliance and Britain's role in a European partnership.[1] In conclusion, the Conservatives formerly possessed a nuclear force but claimed they had an 'independent deterrent'; the Labour government now charged that there was no 'independent deterrent' but begrudgingly admitted it owned a nuclear force.

3. Polaris, Poseidon, and the Dilemma of Anglo-French Collaboration

In late 1970 H.M.S. *Revenge*, the fourth and the last of the presently planned British Polaris submarines, joined the fleet. One source of irony and confusion in the nuclear age is that the time between the political decision on a weapons system and its actual production or delivery is so great that even if it has not become obsolete, the political context of the original decision may have been reversed. The decision to acquire Polaris was opposed by the Labour party which was pledged not to extend the life of the nuclear force beyond the V-bombers. Labour's leaders had suggested, following the Nassau conference, that once in power they would 're-negotiate' the agreement reached there. These were the same men who subsequently took ministerial responsibility for the remarkably rapid and successful completion of the Polaris submarine construction programme.

Shortly after the Nassau conference the Admiralty Board authorized the creation of a Polaris Executive Staff to take supervision for the entire Polaris project. This group was modelled somewhat along the lines of the Special Project Office of the U.S. Navy which developed the American Polaris submarines, although it did not have the same degree of autonomy within the Admiralty as did the American counterpart. Rear Admiral Mackenzie was appointed Chief Polaris Executive and headed a staff of close to 500, mostly located at Bath. Many of the modern management techniques developed for the U.S. Polaris programme were adopted,

---

[1] Conservative Party, 'Putting Britain Right Ahead', reprinted in the *Guardian*, 7 October 1965; see also, Critchley, 'Ending the Myth of Nuclear Independence', pp. 29–30.

thereby permitting stringent time and financial controls to be imposed upon the British project. The first British Polaris submarine, the H.M.S. *Resolution,* began operational patrol in June 1968, followed by the H.M.S. *Repulse* and the H.M.S. *Renown* in the next year.

The submarines themselves are of British manufacture, as are the nuclear warheads of the missiles. Under the terms of the Polaris Sales Agreement the British bought the Polaris missiles and their associated equipment. The United States specifically excluded from the agreement, however, transmission of information on the design of the Polaris missile system. The required technical data to cover installation, operation, and maintenance of the missiles was, of course, included. Also bought from American manufacturers were the launching system, components of the inertial navigation system, the fire control system, some of the communications equipment, and even the high stress steel for the submarine hulls.

The construction of the submarines was truly an Anglo-American enterprise. The test firing of the missiles was held off Cape Kennedy. Close working contacts were kept between the Polaris Executive Staff and the Special Projects Office. These will be maintained since the Polaris Sales Agreement does not end with the initial building of the ballistic missile submarines, but provides for the transfer of information on all future developments of the Polaris system, except those relating to penetration aids. Moreover, the Nassau Agreement provides that Polaris missiles be made available to Britain on a 'continuing basis'. It is not clear what would happen if the use of Polaris missiles was discontinued by the United States after all the American submarines were converted to Poseidon.

The size of the Polaris fleet in 1970 is the minimum necessary to assure that at least one submarine is at sea in an operational state at all times. Polaris submarines require one month's refit after each sixty day patrol and an extensive refitting at longer intervals. A majority of the time it should be possible to have two submarines at station. At moments of tension or developing crisis, when sufficient warning is available, it might be possible to have three Polaris submarines on patrol. Nevertheless, such a limited number raises doubts concerning the reliability of the Polaris fleet. What would happen should one be involved in an accident in peacetime or be detected by an enemy in war? Five submarines were planned by the previous Conservative government, but the Wilson government in its first months cancelled the fifth submarine in order to save money, particularly dollars which were a foreign exchange drain, and perhaps also to make amends to some in the Left wing of the party for not cancelling all of them. Although strong pressure did exist within the service for restoring the fifth submarine, a 'Future Fleet Working

Party' of the Royal Navy recommended in 1966 that higher priority be accorded to naval aircraft and other types of vessels for the more traditional fleet.

The Polaris flotilla was 'assigned' to the Supreme Allied Commander in Europe (SACEUR) by the Labour government, as ambiguously provided for in the Nassau Agreement, but the right of withdrawal is now undisputed. Targets have been allocated by the Joint Strategic Nuclear Targeting Committee which sits in Omaha, Nebraska, at the headquarters of the U.S.A.F. Strategic Air Command. In addition to this alliance plan there presumably exists a British targeting plan in the event of a conflict in which the United States does not take part.

Each submarine has sixteen A-3 Polaris missiles with a range of over 2,500 nautical miles. Each missile is fitted with a British multiple re-entry system. The number of warheads on each British Polaris A-3 missile has not been revealed, but if it is the same as its American counterpart, each missile has some combination of up to three separate warheads and decoys. Although the missiles have multiple re-entry vehicles (MRV) they are not independently targeted, and therefore are not the better known MIRVs. This means that each missile, even if it carries a cluster of warheads and decoys, can only hit the area of a single target, rather than a number of separate targets. The yield of the warheads has not been published but from the total payload carried by the missile it has been deduced that each warhead is in the neighbourhood of 200–300 kilotons.[1] If this is correct, then each Polaris submarine carries an explosive power roughly equal to all that released in the Second World War. One Polaris missile alone, bursting accurately on target, is capable of devastating a city the size of Moscow. The versatility of the Polaris submarines is evident where one considers that the A-3 missile is capable of hitting any spot on earth from some point at sea.

The most significant decision made by the Labour government concerning the nuclear force—apart from not cancelling the Polaris acquisition altogether—was the decision not to attempt to obtain Poseidon missiles from the United States. Because of concern about the ability of Polaris A-3 to penetrate Soviet Anti-Ballistic Missile (ABM) defences, the United States decided to place Poseidon C-3 missiles in 31 of its 41 missile submarines. This advanced delivery system carries multiple independently targeted re-entry vehicles (MIRVs), which send perhaps a dozen warheads plus decoys to quite separate targets. Accordingly ABM defences are put under far greater strain, since each offensive warhead can be spaced so that it must be intercepted by an individual defensive missile. Thus, a compara-

---

[1] Ian Smart, *Advanced Strategic Missiles: A Short Guide,* Adelphi Paper No. 63, London, Institute for Strategic Studies, December 1969, p. 23.

tively small number of MIRVs can attempt to exhaust, and therefore penetrate, a relatively heavy defensive system.

The Pentagon's decision raised the question of whether Britain should follow developments in American sea-launched ballistic missile technology, acquiring new systems, redesigning British warheads, and converting existing submarines or constructing new ones as required by the new missile systems. The British Polaris submarines could probably have been retrofitted for Poseidon, but only at very great expense. The availability of Poseidon was quite another problem. British officials took the position of assuming that Poseidon could be purchased from the United States under the terms of the Nassau Agreement as a natural follow through to Polaris. This assumption, however, was never tested at the official level in Washington. An American agreement to provide Poseidon may not have been as readily obtained as some people expected. Finally, the acquisition of Poseidon would probably only have made sense if it were used in order to launch MIRVs. Since warheads were not included in the Nassau Agreement, it might have been necessary to undertake a long and expensive research and development programme, culminating, if necessary, in underground tests.

These reasons undoubtedly influenced the decision not to ask for Poseidon. Another question which should have weighed heavily was whether Poseidon was then needed for the purpose of British strategic doctrine. The British nuclear force has a counter-city doctrine, that is, it is designed to deter by threatening the enemy's population and industrial centres. Therefore, unlike the United States, Britain does not attempt to maintain elements of a counter-force strategy whose aim is to restrict damage by knocking out the enemy's strategic forces.[1] As long as the Soviet Union did not have an effective ABM defence of all of its principal cities, Polaris A-3 missiles were likely to pose a credible threat. At the time there was no indication that the Soviet Union was further expanding its relatively limited and ineffective ballistic missile defences. Accordingly it could be reasonably maintained that for British purposes, unlike those of the United States, the necessity of Poseidon had not been proved. Moreover, it was possible to postpone a decision while waiting to see what the Soviet Union would be doing concerning ABM and also what the next American generation of strategic delivery system, after Poseidon, might be.

To what extent strategic considerations such as these influenced the Poseidon decision is not clear. In any case, it was decided at the political level that the expense of Poseidon was too great. Wilson was probably also influenced by the likelihood that some in the Labour party would have objected. A positive decision on Poseidon might have reopened the

[1] Within the NATO alliance targeting plans, the British force may have a counter-force role.

internecine Labour party debate on the entire question of Britain's possession of nuclear weapons.

The Labour government did proceed, however, with various measures
to improve the effectiveness of the Polaris A-3. After some deliberation,
research and development of the British MRV to replace the single warhead which had originally been planned was authorized. Steps were also
taken to harden the re-entry cone and to improve the ability of penetration
aids to confuse enemy defences.

The cost of the Polaris construction programme was remarkably
cheap, given the strategic and political value of the results. This was due,
of course, to the fact that the fundamental research and development was
earlier undertaken by the United States and because there was a high order
of co-operation between the two countries throughout the programme.
Although full cost accounting data has not been made available, the Under
Secretary for the Navy indicated in 1969 that the total cost of the programme was estimated to be £350 million. Since the cost of the four
submarines came to £156 million and the purchase of the Polaris missiles
is said to have been for £51·7 million, the remaining £142·3 million are
probably accounted for by the Polaris base at Faslane Bay, pay for personnel and training, and possibly also the nuclear warheads. The running
cost of the Polaris fleet is also remarkably low. According to the Defence
Estimates for 1970–1 it was £32 million out of a total of £2,280 million,
or less than 1·5 per cent of the defence budget.[1]

The Royal Navy officially took over responsibility for Britain's strategic
nuclear force from the R.A.F. in July 1969, after the third Polaris submarine
became operational. The previous year the once mighty and autonomous
Bomber Command came to an end as it was merged with Fighter Command into the new R.A.F. Strike Command. Although hardly noticed
at the time, this was an occasion which had great symbolic significance.
The doctrine of independent air power based on manned bombers which
had been formulated by Trenchard during World War I, the validity
of which was questioned in consequence of its results during the Second
World War, but which was given a new lease with the advent of the
atom bomb, had come to an end, at least in operational terms. This
doctrine had been a major component of British strategic thought for
almost half a century. The last Victor squadrons were disbanded in 1968
and the remaining Vulcans, only fifty in number, were given a tactical
role after the Navy acquired 'the deterrent'. Because of the cancellation
of the TSR-2 in 1965, the decision in 1968 not to purchase the F-111

---

[1] *Statement on the Defence Estimates: 1970*, Cmnd. 4290, p. 36. This makes the Polaris generation of the nuclear force far cheaper than the V-bombers, which cost 15–20% of the defence
budget.

from the United States, and the abandonment of plans for an Anglo-French variable geometry aircraft, Britain entered the 1970s with no plans for a long-range strategic nuclear aircraft in the future.

Although the Labour government saw through to completion the second generation of the nuclear force, what it failed to do was to engage in much planning for a successor to the Polaris submarines. There was a tendency to put off, or shy away from, considerations of what should come next. Britain's possession of nuclear weapons was hardly discussed in public and treated like an embarrassing or distasteful subject—as indeed it was to those who had been led to believe that the weapons would be given up and that responsibility for nuclear deterrence would be left to the United States. Little reference was made in Labour's Defence White Papers to the strategic and political significance of the nuclear force which was being successfully completed, in marked contrast to the often inflated statements of the previous Conservative years.

Nevertheless, the cabinet did decide in 1968 to continue research and development on nuclear weapons, particularly in warhead technology. The principal limitation imposed was to avoid the need for underground testing. Some ministers were in favour of reducing or even discontinuing the military research programme and of concentrating instead on civil nuclear research and development, in which Britain already had a flourishing industry. Counter-arguments evidently included considerations involving foreign policy. Primacy in military nuclear research in Western Europe, it was argued, should not be lost to the French. Secondly, a reduction of such research would undoubtedly lead to a diminution in the number and level of contacts on nuclear affairs with American officials. This was viewed as politically undesirable, since maintenance of the special relationships in nuclear matters depended in part on Britain's having something to offer to the United States, even if only a shared body of knowledge.

Intermittently consideration was given to the possibility of co-operation with France in some aspect of nuclear technology. This had been a perennial subject of speculation for over a decade, but it was given renewed attention by the Labour government after the departure of de Gaulle. In the following French electoral campaign Pompidou hinted that the future of common European defence lay in agreement between France and Britain; this was followed after the election by an indication of interest in Anglo-French nuclear collaboration on the part of Jacques Chaban Delmas, the new Prime Minister. The 'force de frappe' was known to be creating a heavy financial strain on the defence budget, as was the civilian nuclear power programme. The turbulent events of the spring of 1968 brought about an economic squeeze which forced a postponement of French nuclear testing and a slow down in the development of projected nuclear weapons. Plans for an ICBM were cancelled the following year. Moreover, the climate for nuclear co-operation was thought to be improving as the new French Chief of Staff, General Fourquet, dropped the *tous azimuts* strategy. According to this strategy of armed neutrality, French nuclear doctrine was to be so independent as to consider all foreign states as potential objects of nuclear retaliation.

Collaboration on so vital a matter as nuclear affairs, however, requires a measure of agreement on the political objectives of defence policy. Unofficial soundings across the English Channel in the following months and a visit of General Fourquet to London in November 1969 made it evident that the views of the two Governments were still far apart on the political premisses of collaboration. On the technological level there was much to recommend collaboration in that the two nuclear programmes were complementary to each other. Britain had considerably more knowledge of sophisticated warhead design and the production of miniaturized thermonuclear warheads. France, on the other hand, had a lead in the field of solid fuel missile propulsion. There could be technological benefits to both countries in collaboration; this is further discussed in the concluding chapter.

On the political level, on the other hand, there was no common agreement. The British position was that any arrangement for collaboration must be agreed upon within the alliance framework and have at least the tacit blessing of the United States. Nuclear targeting, for example, must be integrated with NATO's general targeting plans. This was not something which the Gaullist government in Paris could accept, since it conflicted with much of the political rationale and strategic theory of French policy. French representatives remained absent from the Nuclear Planning Group where NATO's nuclear strategy was discussed, and there was no indication of an early return of France to full participation in NATO.

The Labour government was, therefore, cautious and restrained in approaching the opportunity of nuclear collaboration with France. Wilson took the position that there was no connection, and should not be any, between nuclear co-operation with France and Britain's application for entry into the European Economic Community. There was a feeling that France had far more to gain from Britain in technological knowledge and assistance than did Britain from France. The results of joint procurement on aircraft and other projects had been mixed, and too often the source of misunderstandings. Whitehall officials were reluctant to take any steps which would upset their counterparts in Washington, or which would damage Britain's relations with the other countries of Western Europe. France was interested in collaboration in order to assist a national nuclear force which was seen as the symbol, perhaps the pride, of her independence. But Britain was not prepared to enter into anything outside the parameters of her relationship with the United States and her position within the Atlantic alliance.

Nevertheless, the Labour years were marked by a reorientation of Britain's defence policy towards Europe. It was no longer maintained that one thousand British soldiers East of Suez were as desirable as a thousand soldiers in Germany. The withdrawal from Asian and Middle East commitments permitted a concentration on Britain's participation in European defence. Minister of Defence Healey took the lead in attempting to establish a 'European defence identity' within NATO and in promoting an intra-European dialogue which would enable the European members of NATO to present a collective view to Washington. The motives for such initiatives could not, of course, be disengaged from the wider aim of political acceptability on the continent for a nation that was seeking entry into the European Economic Community. The 1969 White Paper candidly stated that the 'essential feature of our current defence policy is a readiness to recognise that political and economic realities reinforce the defence arguments for concentrating Britain's military role in Europe.'[1] The defence decisions of the previous three years, Healey told a press group in introducing the White Paper, 'set the seal on the transformation of Britain from a world power to a European power'. As the leading nuclear power after the two Superpowers it could be expected that Britain's knowledge and experience in nuclear matters would eventually make a still more important contribution to European defence. As Britain drew nearer to Europe in the late 1960s there was an assumption, if only implicit, that the nuclear force would one day become part of some form of a European nuclear arrangement.

A nuclear force, once possessed, is not easily shed. Contrary to the expectations of some, the Labour party once in office found compelling reasons for maintaining the British force. A multinational arrangement to 'envelop' the independent nuclear force was sought, but not found. The Wilson government scuttled the MLF with its own proposals for an Atlantic Nuclear Force but then was unable to have the ANF accepted by its allies. The Government, nevertheless, managed to create the impression that there had been a basic change of direction by asserting that the nuclear force was no longer 'independent', and by adroitly handling unilateralist sentiment. The second generation of the nuclear force was built, somewhat uncomfortably but expeditiously. The Wilson cabinet,

[1] *Statement on the Defence Estimates: 1969*, Cmnd. 3927 p. 1.

perhaps embarrassed, was cautious in making new commitments to more advanced weapons technology or to nuclear collaboration with France. Yet in failing to 're-negotiate' the Nassau Agreement and in continuing the construction of the Polaris flotilla, the Labour government assured that Britain would have an independent nuclear force for at least another decade—and probably longer.

PART FIVE
Conclusions

1. Conclusions: A Summary

Nuclear weapons are more than modern military arms; they become part of complex political and social phenomena. In the case of Britain, the creation and continuation of an independent nuclear force can best be understood in the context of a once Great Power in decline, attempting to adjust to reduced circumstances. At the time the nuclear force was originally developed, Britain's self-image was that of an imperial, self-sufficient Great Power with a major worldwide role. Although she did not possess the same economic and military resources as the two principal Superpowers, Britain was thought to be more than just a European power because of her global interests and responsibilities. Due to the weakness of the continental countries after the war, and also of Japan and China, Britain had no serious rival for third place among the nations of the world. The germinal decisions—to accept the Maud Committee's recommendation in 1941 that an atomic bomb project be commenced, the decision of 1947 to build a British atomic bomb independently—were taken by statesmen who retained this traditional conception of Britain's world role. Though she had become a junior partner of the United States during the course of the war, Britain thought of herself as a small Superpower rather than as a strong middle power.

This habit of mind continued roughly until Suez. By then the concept of the 'independent deterrent' had evolved and been accepted, and the V-bomber force was becoming operational. As recognition slowly grew that though Britain was a power with world interests she could no longer be a world power, the nation adjusted to the second rank of powers by reducing her military forces to a level it was thought could be afforded. Concurrently, the nuclear force took on new roles: in addition to its security function, the 'independent deterrent' became at once both a symbol of Britain's Great Power claim and a disguise for her diminished status. It was perceived as helping to maintain the nation's international influence while her power in relation to other states was decreasing.

This helps explain why considerations of prestige, pride, and status have been important in Britain's nuclear history. But it is an error to conclude, as many have, that the nuclear force has guaranteed security less than status. It is true that for many years the emphasis placed implicitly on the nuclear force as the protector of Britain's Great Power status increased almost symmetrically with the waning of the nation's power. It is also true that the prestige justifications given for the 'independent deterrent' grew as the difficulties of maintaining a credible second-strike nuclear deterrent mounted. But one of the salient characteristics of the nuclear age is that, more so than in the past, military power has been politicized and international politics have become militarized. To engage in debate, as has so often been done, on whether the British nuclear force has been maintained for reasons of status *or* security is sterile and fruitless. The answer is both and the 'mix' has varied at different times.

One of the primary motivations for the nuclear force was the desire to gain influence over American policy and strategy, and in recent years over the affairs of Europe. The reaction of Britain to the termination of the intimate wartime alliance, as signified by the dissolution of the combined boards and the passage of the McMahon Act, was to seek a new vehicle for making a bilateral political alliance necessary. The atomic energy programme was spurred to a considerable extent by the desire to use it as a means for restoring close relations with the United States. It is interesting to note that the British were not successful in reviving the former nuclear partnership with the United States until they achieved independently their first atomic detonation. Only after the Monte Bello tests in 1952 and the demonstration of a thermonuclear capability in 1957 were the doors of nuclear collaboration gradually re-opened with the 1954 and 1958 revisions to the American atomic energy legislation. This lesson has undoubtedly not remained unnoticed by the French and potential nuclear powers.

The advent of the missile age augmented the desire for wielding influence in Washington, for it was there more than ever that the decisions crucial to Britain's security would be taken. British nuclear weapons were neither the sole nor the primary source of British influence, but it was thought that the nuclear force provided a means for exerting influence in an operational manner on American strategic planning, or on the conduct of a crisis, which was not available to non-nuclear powers presumably lacking the necessary military and technological sophistication. Having been thus placed within the shadow of the overriding American power, the British Prime Minister would have special access to the ear of the President on a wide range of political matters, including the American response to a crisis in Europe, the conduct of a general war, and the negotiation of arms control and disarmament measures. An unstated but significant assumption of much British thinking was the superior wisdom of Britain's counsel and the restraint it exercised upon American impetuousness. The British method of achieving influence made an interesting contrast with that of the French. Paris was prone to demonstrate opposition through open disagreement, thereby often failing to alter American policy; London usually had greater success through intensive consultations and pragmatic accommodation.

Those who held power, whether politicians in office or civil servants, also viewed the nuclear force as an important bargaining asset and instrument of diplomacy. This was particularly true as the question of Britain's future European relationship came to the fore in the sixties, and as it became increasingly uncertain that the dispersion of nuclear capabilities could be arrested. After one cast away some of the more specious 'ticket at the top table' justifications for nuclear arms used by the Conservatives in the General Election of 1964, one was left with the undeniable fact that the existence of the nuclear force did ensure that greater regard was given to Britain's point of view on such issues as the MLF and the non-proliferation treaty. Moreover, the nuclear force would give Britain a decisive role in shaping a future European deterrent, an Anglo-French nuclear force, or any other European nuclear arrangement, and might also serve as the price of entry into the Common Market. The Wilson government was acutely aware of this: to cancel the Polaris submarine programme unilaterally, that is without a suitable *quid pro quo*, would not have improved Britain's bargaining power in the arena of international politics.

The primary strategic doctrine of the British nuclear force—the concept of the 'independent nuclear deterrent'—was formulated not before the bomb was developed, but after it entered the national arsenal. The fact that the nuclear capability preceded the military rationale as to how it might be used has led some commentators to conclude, mistakenly, that considerations of national security were unimportant in the development of the nuclear force. It is often asserted that nuclear weapons were developed without a strategy or a declared enemy in sight. A deeper examination reveals that the original stimulus had come from the threat of Nazi Germany and the chance that it was working on its own atomic bomb. The Maud Committee had felt that the atomic bomb might become the decisive factor in the war and its report enabled the United Kingdom to recognize and act upon the implications of uranium research before an equivalent action was taken by the American government.

The post-war decision to manufacture the bomb independently was made at a time when Britain stood vulnerable and alone. The British Isles, with their concentrated industrial centres and a population density more than twenty times that of the United States, made an ideal atomic target. The decision was made before the renewal of the American involvement in Europe through the Marshall Plan and NATO, and after the rupture of the special relationship following the abrupt halt of lend-lease and the cessation of atomic collaboration—the latter having caused particularly deep resentment among senior Whitehall officials. The possibility of a permanent return to isolationism, which was raised by the American behaviour of 1945 to 1947, could not be excluded and suggested that Britain could not rely safely upon the protection of the United States for her security. Within the British atomic energy programme, the manufacture of bombs had clear priority until after they became available in quantity to the R.A.F. The civil uses of atomic energy did not receive much attention until the mid-fifties. The vulnerability of the United States to nuclear devastation, which resulted from the development of intercontinental ballistic missiles by the Soviet Union, further supported the determination of British governments not to allow themselves to be totally dependent upon the American nuclear guarantee for the protection of vital British interests. Nuclear weapons did not grant complete security, but they were thought to give a greater measure of security than if they were not possessed.

The effectiveness and credibility of the nuclear force as a deterrent to the Soviet Union—the V-bombers were the only major strategic nuclear delivery system until the late 1960s—was always open to reasonable doubt. The doubts were augmented by a declaratory strategy of massive retaliation, which was often presented in stark and extreme language, and the support given to the early use of nuclear weapons in the context of alliance strategy. The dependence upon a counter-city strategy, which is probably an inherent characteristic of small independent nuclear forces, tended to discourage the theoretical refinement of nuclear doctrine by British Defence Ministers. The official estimates that a conflict would escalate rapidly to the nuclear level were not made because of ignorance, or undue regard for the delicate nature of the balance of deterrence. Rather, they were the only declaratory policy possible for a government that was unwilling to enlarge significantly its contribution to NATO conventional forces.

Still it cannot be judged that the nuclear force was at all times incredible. Credibility depends upon a host of variables: the identity of the enemy, his priority of values and decision-making process; his offensive power and its ability to penetrate defences; his defensive system and its effectiveness. It further depends upon whether the force is designed to commit an ally to one's defence through a 'catalytic' or 'trigger' function, or whether the force attempts to provide full deterrence on its own. Thus the credibility of the nuclear force depended upon *whom* was being deterred from doing *what* and under *which* circumstances. The threat of just one nuclear weapon reaching Moscow or Leningrad might be sufficient to deter the Soviet Union from undertaking a wide range of actions. If the destruction of one or two of its cities constituted for the Soviet Union a sufficient level of 'unacceptable damage' to deter it from launching an attack upon Britain, then it could be argued that the V-bombers and later the Polaris submarines provided an effective deterrent. Even if one granted that the British 'deterrent' was lacking in credibility against the Soviet Union—and many would not—because of the risk of Soviet retaliation, this did not reduce its value against a China or France or a non-nuclear country.

The nuclear force was therefore an insurance against the uncertainties of the future. It broadened the options available to Britain. Insurance was provided for a day when the United States, because of the then prevailing strategic context, might not be willing or able to deter an attack on Britain. And in an age of nationalism the 'independent British deterrent' became a symbol of military autonomy and national sovereignty.

Britain's nuclear force must also be viewed within its historical setting. The momentum of military and scientific impulses made the development of the force appear to Whitehall officials as a natural and inevitable historical evolution. It might have been a far more difficult and surprising decision not to acquire nuclear weapons than to develop them.

The Royal Air Force had a firmly espoused doctrine of strategic bombing long before the invention of the atomic bomb. Nuclear deterrence was seen by Bomber Command as a logical continuation of the belief in the efficacy of strategic bombardment which had inspired Lord Trenchard, and which had been used to justify the birth of the R.A.F. during the First World War as the first separate air force. Britain's experience in the bomber business, and her advanced and skilled aircraft industry, left few doubts as to the feasibility of maintaining a nuclear delivery capability. The complexities of vulnerability and the rising costs which were to accompany the coming technological revolution in aircraft, electronics, and missiles were not seen as presenting insurmountable obstacles. Thus, the V-bomber, like the Dreadnought of an earlier era, was seen as the 'dominant weapon', the possession of which made possible a reduction in manpower and in other types of military arms. In the twentieth century air power, coupled with nuclear weapons, was to replace the sea power of the nineteenth century as the prime agent for Britain's world role.

Similarly, it seemed natural that Britain should develop the most modern and effective military weapon possible because of her long tradition of leadership in science and technology. Britain had been a pioneer in both atomic energy and jet propulsion; the scientific and industrial capacity to continue existed. Already during the last two years of the Second World War, while Britain was participating in the Manhattan Project and after it appeared likely that an American atomic bomb would be created, much thought was being given to the United King-

WNP

dom's own post-war nuclear programme. A comprehensive atomic energy project, which was to include the production of fissile materials, was established shortly after the end of the war. The performance requirements for the R.A.F.'s first jet bomber, the Canberra, were issued as early as 1944. At the time that Britain went into the long-range missile field with Blue Streak, it was argued that this was necessary in order to keep up with a new branch of modern technology which would have important 'spill over' benefits with industrial application. In more recent years advocates of a British space programme, or of a British-made ballistic missile, have based their case in part on the undesirability of falling further behind in modern technology.

Thus, one can discern the impact of military and scientific pressures. Large weapons projects take on a momentum of their own. In the early stages there is the self-feeding drive of tasks begun; in later stages the psychological need of task completion. Forward steps are taken by small increments and it is difficult to refrain voluntarily from doing what appears technologically feasible. Once an 'independent deterrent' was thought to be within reach, the temptation to go after it was almost irresistible. This helps explain the R.A.F.'s determination to continue the nuclear force with Blue Streak, Skybolt, Blue Steel, and the TSR-2 after the quicksand of vulnerability became evident. A national nuclear weapons programme becomes a beehive of vested interests. The R.A.F. without the deterrent mission was seen as losing much of its *raison d'être*. One reason there was never much support in Whitehall for ceasing to be a nuclear power is that having made a large national investment in nuclear weapons it was easier to continue, sometimes by throwing good money after bad, than to reverse the train of events which had been set in motion.

A prime incentive for the nuclear force was the belief that nuclear weapons were 'cheaper', that they could provide more security for less money and manpower. To some extent this was a rationalization for the reduction in conventional military forces made necessary by the rise in the costs of maintaining and equipping forces at home and abroad. Britain turned to primary reliance on a declaratory strategy of nuclear deterrence following her inability to meet the rearmament goals originally set after the outbreak of the Korean war without a serious dislocation of the economy. The Global Strategy Paper of Churchill and Slessor, which predated and subsequently influenced the adoption of the Eisenhower 'New Look', was motivated by the desire to project nuclear deterrence as the way to reduce forces while remaining at least equally strong. The Macmillan government justified the termination of national service by the availability of the 'independent deterrent'. After the 1964 General Election the Labour government did not reverse the nuclear/conventional balance of British forces, as its earlier position might have led one to expect, in part because of the increased expenditures this would involve.

Defence policy in Britain for most of the time since the Second World War has been made through a Procrustean method. The critical question in determining the amount spent on defence has too often *not* been 'what military capabilities are necessary to implement our foreign policy?', but rather, 'what can we afford to spend on defence given the prevailing economic and domestic political conditions?' It has been generally assumed that, except for an extreme national emergency, the proportion of the GNP devoted to defence could not be significantly increased. A second assumption following the end of national service was that its reintroduction was politically unacceptable. The strategic consequence of these two assumptions, in a period of spiralling defence costs, was a greater dependence upon nuclear arms. In effect, security policy was forced into a nuclear straitjacket as the strategy was moulded to fit into acceptable defence budgets.[1]

Because of the multiple incentives and interests thus far discussed, the nuclear force became a major domestic political issue and was the subject of a 'Great Debate' over a number of years, both between the political parties and within the parties. Attention was drawn in the debate to: disparity between aspirations and capabilities of the force; distortion caused by the nuclear force in the composition of the military services; duplication of American nuclear armoury; difficulties in selecting and developing the right strategic weapons. These conditions were in a large measure created, and certainly seriously aggravated, by the limited economic resources available for supporting an 'independent deterrent'. In contrast to the United States, Britain could not afford a large research and development base, neither could she purchase all forms of defence. In particular, Britain was forced to choose a single major strategic delivery system rather than being able to have the luxury of several systems as in the United States or the Soviet Union. Consequently decisions on weapons systems, as well as their underlying strategic assumptions, often became involved in the domestic political debate.

One must ask what were the consequences for the nuclear force of having the nuclear debate couched in party terms, especially between 1960 and 1964 when Labour was in opposition to the Government's policy. On the whole it did not seem to bring much enlightenment to the complex issues and made for an unsatisfactory national debate. The role

[1] Defence budgets until the mid-sixties sought to conceal rather than to reveal the amounts spent on the strategic nuclear force. My rough estimate for total expenditures on the force between 1945 and 1970 is £3,200 million ($9 billion). This is based on the limited data available and on interviews, and includes nuclear facilities and warheads, bombers, missiles (Blue Steel and Polaris), and cancelled projects (Blue Streak, Skybolt, and TSR-2).

of the opposition is to embarrass the government, to create public disdain for its policies by identifying their weaknesses and failures, and to present an alternative programme. In response the government is forced to champion and to justify its policies, sometimes by saying things it knows to be somewhat unreasonable and would privately prefer not to articulate. In matters of war and peace, when foreign powers as well as domestic voters are listening, this can be dangerous. Yet some fatuous, though not inconsequential, statements on nuclear strategy were made in the heated atmosphere of the House of Commons or on election platforms. New weapons systems, such as Blue Streak and TSR-2, were prematurely enthroned in the Defence White Papers because of political considerations. And a lot of inflated claims were made in the months between the Nassau Conference and the 1964 General Election. All in all, the nuclear debate may have shed more confusion than light on Britain's own understanding of her nuclear role in the world.

Moreover, the politicization of the nuclear force produced unwanted side effects. It reduced the flexibility of the Government in making vital weapons decisions. Undoubtedly Blue Streak would have been cancelled earlier had not Duncan Sandys been induced to continue it longer than it should have been in the hope of being able to rebut the opposition's criticisms. The cancellation of Skybolt produced a domestic political crisis: it was absolutely essential for Macmillan to return from Nassau with a suitable replacement such as Polaris, for his position as leader of the Tories and perhaps even the continuation of the Conservatives in office was in serious jeopardy. At the time of both transitions, from Blue Streak to Skybolt and from Skybolt to Polaris, the Macmillan government's prestige and the credibility of its independent nuclear deterrent policy were at stake. The TSR-2 might have been cancelled earlier and with less cost if it had not acquired an added political significance after the end of Skybolt. Political considerations therefore heavily influenced the outcome of the weapons decisions. It is conceivable, though not certain, that the Conservative governments would have been less rigid in their determination to preserve the 'independent deterrent' had they not been welded into their policy by the heat of domestic politics, including the pressure of their own back benches.

The strong emphasis on independent nuclear deterrence which was written into the 1957 and 1958 Defence White Papers was not without significant domestic political undertones, for this strategy was considered necessary to justify the ending of national service, a measure which Macmillan considered essential after Suez for the recovery of electoral support before the next national election. Hardly noticed at the time was the fact that the Government's declaratory strategy had jumped several years ahead of its action capability, for the V-bomber force was not fully operational with thermonuclear bombs until as late as 1961. Moreover, the Conservative leaders knew well that the British public found assertions of military strength and Great Power status exhilarating. The public opinion polls consistently showed support for the continuation of the nuclear force. Thus defence policy was partially designed to please the home front and thereby meet the needs of the party.

This was equally true of the Labour party which backed the nuclear policy until 1960. Following the demise of Blue Streak it appeared to become politically profitable for Labour to espouse the position that Britain should no longer attempt to remain an independent nuclear power. This was a compromise designed to conciliate the deep split on unilateral disarmament which was tearing the party asunder. It sought to accommodate the pacifists by giving them part of what they wanted, not on the moral issue, but on the practical grounds that the inevitable trend of technology was placing the cost of advanced strategic delivery systems beyond Britain's means. Labour was thereupon in a good position to embarrass the Government when planned weapons systems were cancelled and to charge it with mismanagement of defence. But when Labour was returned to office, and was forced to acknowledge that the Polaris submarines could keep the nuclear force going inexpensively for more than a decade, it adopted the views at the large centre of the nation's political spectrum. Plans for the Polaris flotilla were retained, though there was less talk of its theoretical independence.

One characteristic of the nuclear age is the growing civilian influence in areas once regarded as primarily military. Because of the possible instantaneousness of annihilation, political leaders must be ready to make immediate life and death decisions. National security policy involves political choice as much as professional military expertise. Nuclear weapons have given a new importance to a nation's declaratory defence policy, as distinct from its military tactics. Not only is the decision to become a nuclear power primarily a political one; the elected leader is also forced to assume a greater role in the selection of weapons systems and the judgements on their use. In the process, nuclear arms become a political issue. Because security policy involves issues of the greatest national importance, it cannot somehow be above or apart from politics.

2. Conclusions: Four Paradoxes of Britain's Nuclear Experience

The British nuclear force has been as much a product of political, economic, military, scientific, and bureaucratic interests, pressures, and perspectives as it has been of strategic analysis and theoretical logic. This has resulted in a number of paradoxes, of which we now discuss four.

A. *Nuclear Proliferation.* Britain's position in relation to nuclear proliferation has had a unique significance: the United Kingdom was the first second-ranking nation in the post-war international system to acquire a nuclear capability. Britain was also the first country to have a serious domestic debate about giving up her nuclear weapons. The British were in many ways the first to recognize nationally the dangers inherent in the spread of nuclear capabilities. The 1959 proposal of the Labour party for a 'Non-Nuclear Club' had no parallel in the election platforms of the major political parties of the other nuclear powers. The first book-length study of nuclear dispersion came from London.[1] Yet, paradoxically, Britain probably did far more harm than good for the cause of non-proliferation.

By their rhetoric and by their actions, British statesmen encouraged the French to follow suit. British atomic developments and justifications for the strategic force were seized upon by those in France who argued for a French nuclear force. The British and French nuclear forces had an unsettling effect in Germany and on the rest of Europe—and perhaps much further, for nuclearism is a contagious disease. It is most improbable that we will be able to find a direct causal linkage between the 6th, 10th, and 20th nuclear powers, should they come, and Britain. But two conclusions are in retrospect now clear. First, the 'optimum' opportunity for limiting the nuclear club was probably between 1949 and 1952, before Britain had demonstrated her atomic capability and when only the United States and the Soviet Union were nuclear powers. In this respect it is interesting to ponder what would have happened if the United States and Britain had merged their respective nuclear programmes into a joint effort as was being discussed in the 1949 negotiations. Britain would not have become an atomic power in the sense of the national manufacture of nuclear weapons, but would have possessed its own stockpile of weapons under its autonomous custody. The precedent set for other nations would have been more ambiguous. Second, most of the political and strategic arguments given by British governments to justify the creation and continuation of the 'independent deterrent' could be applied with equal validity by many other countries to their own national interests. And often they were.

We will never know to what extent Britain started this type of a nuclear chain reaction. According to one interesting but unsubstantiated report, Russian officials indicated to Western diplomats that before 1960 one faction in the Soviet Union had sought to build up China as a second

[1] Beaton and Maddox, op. cit.

Communist nuclear power in order to offset the British nuclear capability in the West.[1] In addition to her direct impact on France, Britain consistently encouraged NATO to rely quite heavily on a nuclear strategy. This in turn increased the assumed desire of the non-nuclear members of the alliance to have a role in a European strategic nuclear defence system and thereby contributed to the years of controversy and debate over the MLF and ANF.

Understandable as was the creation of the nuclear force in the late 1940s and early 1950s, Britain may have made a profound mistake in not subjecting her nuclear course to intensive review from then on. There appears to have been a lack of analysis and perception within the highest levels of government in the mid-1950s of the consequences of Britain's actions in terms of their effect on proliferation. Yet it was in the mid-1950s that Britain by her example in voluntarily renouncing nuclear arms, possibly in return for an agreement that no other country would start making them, might have created an effective anti-proliferation strategy. (One exception was the quiet, unsuccessful 1954 intervention of Nigel Birch, then Parliamentary Secretary to Minister of Defence Macmillan. In a hitherto unknown confidential paper addressed to Macmillan and Foreign Secretary Selwyn Lloyd, he set forth arguments against the development of the British thermonuclear bomb on the grounds that it would complicate disarmament efforts and encourage proliferation.) Defence did not receive adequate intellectual attention, except from a handful of critical commentators who had little influence on policy, until the reaction set in to the 'Sandys' White Paper of 1957. It is significant that between 1950 and 1957 there were eight different Ministers of Defence. In the United States, also, there was little perception of Britain's key situation with respect to proliferation at the times that the atomic energy legislation was amended in 1954 and 1958 to permit the granting of substantial nuclear assistance to Britain.

By the time that the spread of nuclear weapons came to be recognized as a major world problem, in the late 1950s and early 1960s, it was too late. France had become a nuclear power and China was well on the way. The international context of proliferation had changed so that Britain could now do far less by her unilateral example to arrest it. Renunciation of atomic arms only made sense as part of a multinational arrangement. It was most improbable that Britain would leave France as the sole nuclear power in Europe. Thus, the British and French nuclear programmes over a period of a decade strongly interacted with each other: the British nuclear force, and the privileged nuclear relationship with the United States, were a thorn in the side of France which strongly stimulated the

[1] *The New York Times*, 21 May 1965.

French nuclear decision; subsequently no London government could opt out of the nuclear field, or even merge its force into a larger framework, unless Paris did likewise.

Moreover in the mid-1960s the danger of proliferation became world-wide because of the emergence of China as a nuclear power and the continuation of tensions in the Middle East, as well as the growing stocks of plutonium in nations that had civil nuclear reactors. It was all the more unlikely, therefore, that Britain would resign from the nuclear club just as the applicant list, consisting of other second level powers, appeared to be lengthening. One must wonder what lesson those potential nuclear nations drew from Britain's great nuclear debate and the Wilson government's retention of the nuclear force. Looking at the Labour party's deeds, rather than its rhetoric, they might have concluded that nuclear arms do have value after all.

B. *Independence* versus *Interdependence*. Upon his return to London Airport from the Nassau Conference Prime Minister Macmillan announced that the Nassau Agreement 'preserved both the concepts of independence and interdependence'.[1] The latent contradiction in this claim has stood as a persistent paradox throughout much of the history of the nuclear force. Britain accepted technological interdependence with the United States, yet sought to maintain political and strategic independence. In gradually allowing herself to become dependent upon the United States for strategic delivery systems, Britain placed herself in a dilemma. This was vividly illustrated at Nassau where Macmillan, in effect, found himself arguing that America had an obligation to provide Britain with a weapon which could put the United Kingdom in a position to involve the United States in a nuclear war against its will.

A second irony has followed from the first in the rhetoric of independence. Britain was a consistent proponent of NATO and the Atlantic alliance and gave its support to military integration, collective action, and the leadership of the United States within the alliance. But it also insisted on maintenance of its independence of action, on the undesirability of becoming wholly dependent for defence upon the United States, and on the necessity of retaining her own nuclear arms. The difficulties in reconciling loyalty to the alliance and to her principal ally with the aspirations for independence at times weakened and confused British defence policy.

Accordingly London never used the nuclear force in order to create or manipulate an 'independent' foreign policy. The contrast of Britain's Atlantic orthodoxy with French attitudes is evident. De Gaulle continu-

[1] *Keesings Contemporary Archives*, 5–12 January 1963, p. 19175.

ously used the 'force de frappe' as a political symbol of France's independence from the integrationist aspects of the Atlantic alliance. No
doubt this policy was given added credibility by the technological independence of the French nuclear force. An important lesson of the British
experience in the nuclear era is that nations which become dependent on
another state's strategic technology do lose some of their perceived political
independence.

The tenacious clinging to independence none the less accurately reflected
the post-war British attitude towards the United States, which in truth has
been bitter-sweet. On the one hand, the Anglo-American alliance was the
centrepiece of British foreign policy. On the other, the British people,
having been independent for over nine hundred years, did not wish to see
themselves as servants or satellites, even of their best ally. The diminution
of the United Kingdom's position in the world produced a sense of frustra-
tion in British society—as was evident after Suez. In the same manner the
relationship of dependency led to a feeling of resentment—as following
the Skybolt cancellation. In common, Suez and Skybolt fostered mistrust
of the United States and were followed by renewed demands for nuclear
independence. As far back as the period of collaboration in the Manhattan
Project Whitehall officials were acutely sensitive to the desirability of
retaining Britain's freedom of action in nuclear matters.

The disparate claims for both interdependence and independence
resulted in illogicalities when applied to the operational requirements of
the nuclear force and to its strategic doctrine. Although the targeting
plans of Bomber Command were integrated with those of SAC, the
V-bombers remained under British national control and were said to be
always capable of independent action. Yet in their deterrent role the
V-bombers were dependent upon the American early warning system,
and in later years they had to rely substantially upon intelligence gathered
by American reconnaissance satellites on Soviet anti-aircraft dispositions
in order to hope to get through Russian air defences. The Polaris submarines presumably also use data from American space satellites. In its
strategic doctrine the nuclear force was said to constitute an 'independent
deterrent', while almost simultaneously it was described as a 'contribution
to the Western deterrent'. The latter phrase was a euphemism designed
in part to cover the fact that the nuclear force was not likely to be used
except in conjunction with the American strategic force. Much of the
confusion surrounding the Nassau Agreement resulted from the unsuccessful attempts to reconcile interdependence with independence in the Polaris
generation of the British nuclear force through the Agreement's multilateral and multinational clauses. Today, the Polaris flotilla is 'assigned'
to NATO but the right of unilateral withdrawal is fully accepted.

The quest for the maintenance of an 'independent deterrent' resulted, ironically, in a deepening technological dependency upon the United States. The V-bombers were wholly British manufactured, but each of the major strategic delivery systems planned to follow the bombers was dependent upon American technology. Blue Streak benefited considerably from information received from American companies on rocket engines and the small gyroscopes used for guidance. Skybolt would have attached an American missile to a British aircraft. With Polaris reliance upon the United States has almost become complete. As mentioned earlier, in addition to the Polaris missiles themselves, the launching system, components of the inertial navigation system, the fire control system, some of the communications equipment, and even the high stress steel for the submarine hulls have been purchased from American manufacturers. Thus Britain in the 1960s tied herself to the American order of priorities in research, development, and production, and became dependent upon American satellite intelligence and radio communications systems. In so doing she has undoubtedly lost a measure of her strategic independence.

C. *Alliance Relationships*. Britain's role as a nuclear power, and the existence of the nuclear partnership with the United States, may have been injurious to her long-term interests to the extent that it encouraged Britain to feel that she could avoid Europe. Self-identity as the second nuclear power in the West, and a self-image of continuing worldwide responsibilities, encouraged Britain to refuse to join the Schuman Plan in 1950, to refrain from supporting the abortive European Defence Community in 1954, to hold back from the European Economic Community in its early and formative years, and to reject beforehand the possibility of eventually permitting an MLF/ANF scheme to transform itself into a European nuclear force.

The special relationship with the United States induced Britain to look first to America rather than to Europe. For two decades under Labour and Conservative governments the Anglo-American alliance was the sheet anchor of British foreign policy. Britain aimed to be America's chief lieutenant in NATO and she had far closer ties with Washington than with any European country. Of course the origins of this unique alliance were to be found deep in the roots of history, tradition, shared interests, and common values. The strategic nuclear relationship was only one aspect of the broadly conceived 'special relationship', but it was a most visible and tangible symbol for the outside world. The preferential treatment given to the United Kingdom in the exchange of atomic information and materials, the assistance with strategic delivery systems, the co-ordination of Bomber Command and the Strategic Air Command outside the central framework of NATO, were all integral parts of the cement of the 'special relationship'.

This discouraged the growth of co-operation with Europe. Even before the limited return to nuclear collaboration with the United States in 1954, Whitehall officials were reluctant to enter into an atomic arrangement with France because of the negative impact it would have in Washington; negotiations initiated in 1955 by the Commissariat à l'Énergie Atomique for British help in the construction of a gaseous diffusion plant in France were reportedly given up for a similar reason. American assistance with Blue Streak made the development of missile co-operation with Europe more difficult, and the granting of Skybolt and Polaris seemed to make it less necessary. In his meetings with de Gaulle at Chateau des Champs and Rambouillet in 1962 Macmillan appeared more interested in maintaining the special relationship with the United States than in entering into a new defence and nuclear partnership with France, even if it were in time to become the basis of a European defence scheme. And at Nassau the British clearly demonstrated that they preferred the 'Atlantic' concept to its 'European' rival.

In consequence British foreign policy developed a schizophrenic quality. This was especially true after 1960, the year in which the first tentative steps were being taken towards entry into the Common Market while at the same time Britain, in replacing Blue Streak with Skybolt, accepted dependence upon the United States for her primary nuclear delivery system. Britain looked to Europe for her future *economic* partners—and simultaneously looked to the United States for her future *strategic* partner. These two major strands of foreign policy, if pursued, were likely to conflict: the Nassau Conference, not surprisingly, was seen suspiciously by many Europeans as another Anglo-Saxon cabal in which Britain renewed the lease on her American relationship while the Common Market question was still unsettled. Thus the transatlantic strategic connection tended to cut across, and thereby render more difficult, the growth of economic and military co-operation with Europe.

Moreover the nuclear ties with the United States undoubtedly were a source of resentment in continental Europe. Especially before France became a military nuclear power, Britain's claim of nuclear independence separated her qualitatively and therefore psychologically from Europe. The 1957 Defence White Paper, for example, was not well received on the continent where the end of conscription and the increased reliance on nuclear deterrence were viewed as a weakening of Britain's commitment to collective defence. De Gaulle's bid for a three-power directorate within the alliance upon his return to power was based upon the fact that France was about to break the Anglo-Saxon monopoly on atomic weapons in the West, and his view that the political direction of the alliance should be exercised by three and no longer by two.

Having said this, it is pertinent and necessary to note further that over much of the period since 1940 nuclear affairs have been a souring element in the Anglo-American relationship. The tangled record of negotiations on nuclear matters between the two countries confirms the perceptive observation of two decades ago that 'even if we take Anglo-American friendship for granted, effective collaboration is something which has to be achieved.'[1] One needs only to recall the series of misunderstandings before the Quebec Agreement of 1943, the rupture symbolized by the McMahon Act of 1946, the unsuccessful negotiations of 1949 to renew collaboration, the Skybolt cancellation, and the controversy over the MLF, to be reminded of the irritants in the partnership.

The Anglo-American relationship has been more important to Britain than to the United States since the Second World War and for this reason, primarily, it is the British who usually undertook the burden of keeping it 'special'. The annals are filled with records of the frequent visits of British Prime Ministers and cabinet officials to Washington, sometimes to the embarrassment of American officials anxious not to affront their other allies by appearing to give the United Kingdom too much deference. One must conclude that on the whole the British were successful in their exploitation of the bilateral relationship: the Quebec Agreement, the 1954 and 1958 revisions in the American atomic energy legislation, the offer of Polaris missiles at Nassau, the sinking of the MLF—these were all British successes in altering prior American policy. In each case, one might note, the Prime Minister went to see the President and persuaded him to reverse or ignore the policy positions of some of his advisers.

Yet the British probably tended to overestimate their over-all influence on American policy. Because of the disparities in power and global responsibility, the 'special relationship' as viewed from Washington often looked less important than it appeared in London. Conversely, the United States overestimated the extent of Britain's pliability. Washington officials ruefully discovered that they had only a limited capacity to influence the nuclear affairs of the United Kingdom despite its condition of semi-dependency upon the United States. Thus Britain never subscribed to the strategy of 'flexible response' and the arguments for the strengthening of conventional forces in Europe, nor would it support the raising of the nuclear threshold in NATO strategy. Similarly, while becoming

[1] William T. R. Fox and Annette B. Fox, *Britain and America in the Era of Total Diplomacy*, Memorandum No. 1 (Princeton, Center of International Studies, Princeton University, 1952), p. 1.

dependent upon the United States for Polaris missiles, Britain rejected strong American pressures for a Polaris-type solution to the alliance's presumed nuclear sharing problem. Despite all the intimate transatlantic contacts, Washington often remained amazingly insensitive to the nuances of the nuclear element in British politics, as the Skybolt cancellation illustrated well.

D. *The 'Frontier' of Science and Technology*. Britain became the victim of her own past success in science and technology. Because she had always occupied a position of leadership in advanced science and technology, Britain after the Second World War tried to keep pace with the United States and the Soviet Union by attempting to remain on the 'frontier' of defence technology. Thus Britain entered the ballistic missile field in its early stages when many of the technical and financial factors were unknown or underrated. The failure of Blue Streak—the nation's first and only strategic ballistic missile—was thought to indicate, however, more than failure in a single weapon project. The cancellation of Blue Streak was widely interpreted as meaning that long-range missile technology was beyond the nation's economic means. In consequence, Britain became dependent upon the United States and subsequently, in the 1960s, had no significant missile programme of her own. France, in contrast, by entering the missile field later and learning from the mistakes and dead-ends of others was able to avoid many of the pitfalls. By the late 1960s France had a relatively successful missile programme and a healthier, more self-reliant aerospace technology than the United Kingdom.

The British experience offers some interesting observations concerning the interaction of innovations in technology with nuclear strategy. In the first post-war years it was not generally foreseen that the cost of maintaining an adequate and credible means of delivery would be in time far greater than the cost of manufacturing atomic bombs. Following the development of missiles, however, it came to be recognized that maintaining a credible nuclear force was more complex and expensive than had earlier been envisaged. Nuclear weapons now needed to be delivered by ballistic missiles or by 'stand-off' bombs such as Blue Steel. Long-range bombers in order to be able to get through enemy ground-to-air missile defence needed a low-level strike capability. Polaris submarines may need MIRVs in order to penetrate Soviet ABM defences. The added technical requirements for maintaining an invulnerable deterrent created a sharp rise in the cost factor. To give some examples from the British experience: the cost of one V-bomber in 1961 was eight times that of a strategic bomber of 1946 vintage; the TSR-2 would have cost twenty times more to develop and ten times more to produce than the Canberra which it was to replace;

the necessity of 'hardening' Blue Streak by placing the missile underground more than doubled its expected costs. At the time the V-bombers were being developed it was not foreseen that they would be required to move from their bases within a four-minute alert. Similarly, when Blue Streak was initially on the drawing boards as a fixed site above ground missile the later evident high accuracy of Soviet missiles was not expected. A nation in deciding as a matter of policy to maintain an 'independent deterrent' commits itself to competing with its potential opponent's rate of technological innovatioh, and this is unpredictable.

In the first post-war decade Britain entered into technological competition with the other two nuclear powers without having either their resources or a clear understanding that this was more difficult than merely joining the nuclear club. There were only two 'supertechnical' powers in the world and the United Kingdom never succeeded in joining their ranks. In theory it is dangerous in an age of rapid technological progress to place all one's security expectations on one weapon, but Britain did not have the economic resources to develop and produce simultaneously several different advanced strategic delivery systems. Instead, it had to choose the most promising prospect and hope for the best. The choice had to be made earlier than a comparable choice in the United States because Britain had less money to spend for research and development of alternative systems. Britain had to choose between a land-based missile *or* a supersonic bomber *or* a missile firing submarine; it could not develop a Minuteman, a Skybolt, and a Polaris all at once. As Minister of Defence Duncan Sandys explained to the Commons: 'We cannot put our money on all the horses, like the Americans can, and we therefore have to back our fancy.'[1]

In the process, a number of unfortunate weapons decisions were made. The method by which the principal strategic systems were selected is justifiably open to criticism. All too often parochial service interests, the needs of industry, and short-term political considerations took precedent over long-range cost-effectiveness calculations and analysis. The erratic pattern of weapons acquisition can be seen in the major upheavals in procurement policy that took place between 1957 and 1968. In 1957 great emphasis was placed on nuclear-tipped missiles (Blue Streak) and the long-range bomber (Avro 730) was cancelled; in 1959 the manned bomber was reinstated (TSR-2); in 1960 Blue Streak was abandoned as the principal delivery system of the nuclear force to be replaced by Skybolt, appended to the existing V-bombers; in 1962 after considerable sums of money had been spent on refitting the V-bombers for Skybolt the missile was cancelled and the Polaris system was purchased; in 1965 the TSR-2 was cancelled to be replaced by the American F-111 fighter-

[1] 600 H.C. Deb. col. 1139 (25 February 1959).

bomber; in 1965 also, the indigenous P-1154 vertical take-off and landing fighter was cancelled and in 1967 plans for an Anglo-French variable geometry aircraft were abandoned. Finally, with the retrenchment from the Far East and under severe economic pressures, the Labour government cancelled the F-111 in early 1968. The costs of the cancelled projects in money and in technological effort was very high indeed.

In retrospect the single most critical weapons decision error may have been the failure to opt for a British nuclear ballistic missile submarine in the late 1950s, by which time there was little remaining doubt about the feasibility of such a system. This would have permitted Blue Streak to have been cancelled earlier, Blue Steel would have been dropped, the order for the Mark II V-bombers cancelled and a highly effective British-made missile could have been developed in their place. Moreover, the road to the Nassau Conference through the Skybolt cancellation would have been avoided and the MLF episode, so disruptive to the alliance, might not have occurred. In addition, the Labour party would not have been given the suitable opportunity to come out in opposition to the continuation of the nuclear force. But, for reasons earlier given, neither the Royal Navy nor the R.A.F. wanted the Government to opt for Polaris and a seaborne system was rejected in favour of air force plans for the nuclear force.

A serious distortion in British thinking on the nation's ability to develop strategic missile systems resulted from the unhappy experience with Blue Streak. The missile was cancelled because of the sharp rise in its costs, which in turn was the result of the increase in its vulnerability due to Soviet missile progress and the consequent new requirements for assuring its invulnerability. The Conservative government, as part of the Sandys 'New Look' of 1957, had placed great importance on Blue Streak as the core of the 'independent deterrent'. Its cancellation in April 1960 had a great impact. The conclusion was widely drawn that Britain could not afford to develop her own strategic delivery systems. Indeed, many thought that Britain's experience with Blue Streak indicated that in the age of missiles no middle power would be able to create and maintain an 'independent deterrent' of its own. This partially explained the willingness to become dependent upon the United States.

In hindsight it is now clear that Britain's travails were caused principally by proceeding on an advanced missile in a parallel time frame with the United States, rather than being able to learn from the trials and errors of her more affluent ally. At the time the liquid fuel Blue Streak was started solid fuels were on the horizon, but there was still some uncertainty whether solid fuels would prove sufficiently stable for use in long-range missiles. For political and defence policy reasons Britain felt impelled to proceed with the liquid fuel missile before the answer on solid fuels was available. Moreover,

Britain, because she was vulnerable earlier than the United States to Soviet missiles, was compelled to undertake pioneering research in underground 'hardening' and plans for Blue Streak were expensively revised to have it placed in a silo. The poor cost history of Blue Streak, however bad, was probably no worse than its American equivalent, the Atlas.

At the time Britain was the only European nation to attempt to develop ballistic missiles. France waited, though not primarily for reasons of scientific prescience. France was thus able to benefit from some of the knowledge that had been accumulated by other nations about guidance systems, missile fuels, et cetera. In addition, by watching for which paths to avoid, based on the experience of other countries, France inherited good guidelines with which to make its selection of delivery systems. By 1970 France was nearing completion of a land-based solid fuel IRBM and had built a missile-firing nuclear submarine although it was not yet in operational condition. Britain had no serious strategic missile programme of her own—but her technical capability for such could not be doubted, given the political will.

Through her bilateral arrangements with the United States, Britain has purchased a strategic weapons system which will enable her to remain a nuclear power at least through the 1970s. These weapons cost far less than they would have if developed independently. For this reason, and because technological co-operation within the alliance may be desirable in principle, the arrangement may well be justified. But it should be recognized that it has also produced a psychology of dependence upon the United States. After producing the first generation of the nuclear force, the V-bombers, Britain never succeeded in building a second generation of its own; Britain has never developed a major strategic missile independently. The embarrassed position of Macmillan following the Skybolt cancellation illustrates that there is a price to pay for this lack of self-sufficiency. Of the five nuclear powers to date, Britain is the only one without a strategic missile production programme.

France has had a more consistent policy. Whatever may have been the arguments against her decision to become an independent nuclear power, once that policy was set she proceeded to develop strategic delivery systems essentially on her own, though alone not always by choice. The necessity to work out technology unaided has given France a capability and independence she might not otherwise have possessed. At one time it was assumed by the British that France would run into the same difficulties that earlier beset them.[1] But time has proved this assump-

---

[1] George Brown: 'All the facts of life from which we have been unable to escape will apply to them', 684 H.C. Deb. col. 190 (13 November 1963); see also Strachey, *On the Prevention of War*, p. 129.

tion to be wrong. Whereas the industrial base necessary to support missile technology has gradually narrowed in Britain, France has developed a growing self-sufficiency. According to present plans, France is likely to spend more than four times as much as Britain on her military nuclear programme between 1970 and 1975. This is of significance in an age in which national security is closely linked to technological prowess.

3. Polaris: Present Status, Future Obsolescence

Let us now turn to the present status of the nuclear force and its prospects for the future. Britain entered the 1970s having just completed a strategic nuclear force of four Polaris submarines. The normal life span of the submarines themselves, not including missiles or the ability of the warheads to penetrate enemy defence, is approximately twenty years, which gives them until at least the late 1980s. In addition, the British military nuclear capability includes the Canberra bombers, the Buccaneer bombers, the ageing Vulcan bombers, the F-4 Phantom fighter-bombers and two planned aircraft, the Jaguar Anglo-French strike/trainer and the MRCA, multi-role combat aircraft, being constructed by a consortium of nations. Each of these aircraft has a tactical nuclear capability, but they are not part of the strategic force.

The Polaris flotilla consists of four submarines each of which has sixteen A-3 missiles with a range of over 2,500 nautical miles. The missiles are tipped with multiple re-entry vehicles (MRVs), of British design, which are not independently targeted. Because of the refitting required after each sixty day patrol, and the more extensive overhaul after longer intervals, it is only possible to assure having one submarine on operational patrol at all times, although most of the time there should be two. The nuclear force is 'assigned' to NATO, as agreed at Nassau, with the right of withdrawal when 'supreme national interests' are at stake. Target plans have been made in co-ordination with the alliance through the Joint Strategic Planning System at Omaha, Nebraska, but Britain is assumed also to have a targeting plan of its own.

Submarines are particularly suitable for Britain as the principal weapon system for the nuclear force in the 1970s. In moving the force out to sea they draw counter-force fire away from the densely populated British Isles. Land-based missiles such as Minuteman are far less attractive for a nation of limited territory and high industrial concentrations. Moreover, Britain has excellent ready access to the high seas and has well protected anchorage areas, such as Faslane Bay in the Clyde, where the Polaris base is located.

X<small>NP</small>

One of the great attractions of the Polaris submarines is that they are a second-strike weapon. For some time they are likely to remain invulnerable, so that their assured ability to retaliate in a general war situation increases the credibility of the deterrent. Even if in comparison with America's forty-one ballistic missile submarines the British force appears to be 'mini', its destructive power is considerable and should not be underrated. A single submarine should be able to destroy a dozen Soviet cities. Because they are able to travel in a concealed manner all over the world's seas with relatively little chance of detection, Polaris submarines provide great accessibility to potential enemy targets. Indeed in theory there is no spot on the globe immune from a Polaris A-3 missile. For the present, Polaris submarines constitute a desirable nuclear force of unquestioned deterrent value; it is of the future that there is some doubt.

The obsolescence of the Polaris submarines will depend upon the deployment of ABM defences and progress in anti-submarine warfare (ASW). A great deal of money and effort has been put in recent years into research in ASW techniques and undoubtedly considerable advances have been made. But thus far, at least, the ability to detect long-range nuclear powered submarines remains extremely limited. Although an occasional submarine may be located, it is no easy task to locate quickly and correctly identify at moments of crisis a number of submarines armed with sea-launched ballistic missiles, particularly if they have taken evasive action, such as placing themselves under the Polar ice caps. Most experts who have looked at the task of tracking and detection in the deep seas believe that, given the magnitude of the problem, advances in ASW will not make Polaris submarines vulnerable for quite some time.

The potential challenge posed by ABM is far more serious. The presently limited Soviet ABM deployment of uncertain quality, in combination with air defence, is unlikely to be very effective against the British Polaris submarines. But a moderate or 'thick' Soviet ABM would pose real penetration difficulties, and this could be achieved by the middle-to-late 1970s. This would be especially true if Britain does not acquire a MIRV capability and more sophisticated penetration aids. In such circumstances a growing Soviet defensive capability would present obstacles earlier and far greater to Britain—and, incidentally, to France also—than to American offensive forces.

One must be careful, however, not to downgrade the European nuclear forces too quickly. No doubt it is true that the new strategic systems, ABM and MIRV in particular, serve as a stark reminder of the technological dominance of the Superpowers. It raises them still more firmly to a category of their own among the nuclear powers. Contrary to the assumptions of some analysts, however, it does not necessarily follow that ABM and

MIRV will make smaller nuclear forces obsolete. As we have seen earlier, the British nuclear force has a counter-city doctrine and does not attempt damage limitation by neutralizing the opponent's offensive forces. Neither does it need to reach all the adversary's population centres, or even any one particular city, in order to inflict 'unacceptable damage'. The threat to do marginal damage to the Soviet Union, to destroy one or two medium-sized cities, may well be sufficient for the required level of deterrence. Moreover, the ability to threaten a nation not possessing ballistic missile defences, China to take an obvious example, would not be diminished.

Much of our analysis thus far depends on the outcome of the strategic arms limitation talks (SALT) between the United States and the Soviet Union, which have yet to reach an agreement as of this writing. An agreement on a low level of ABM, or on banning ABM altogether, would enhance the credibility of Britain's nuclear force and lengthen the utility of its present generation. An outcome which led to a comprehensive ABM deployment in the Soviet Union would undermine its credibility. It is very unlikely that the Polaris submarines in their present number and capability would be able to swamp Soviet missile defences. Still, the threat of the British nuclear force's ability to get through missile defences, even if only partially, will remain a factor to reckon with for some time. Britain during the 1970s is likely to continue to rank third in the world in ability to penetrate sophisticated missile defences with nuclear war-heads.

4. Prospects for the Future

Planning should now be underway for the strategic environment likely to exist in the 1980s. Because of the long lead time necessary, strategic delivery systems now take an average of six years for research and development. This means that Britain should be prepared to make some important decisions around 1974 if she is to be assured a relatively viable nuclear force in the following decade. If the Soviet Union proceeds to expand and upgrade its ABM defences, then the late 1970s could already present penetration difficulties for the Polaris submarines.

Whitehall planners and Westminster politicians, in reaching their decisions, will have to grapple with some fundamental questions. Does Britain wish to remain dependent upon the United States for its strategic delivery systems? If not, should Britain seek self-sufficiency by embarking on a strategic missile programme of its own? Or should Britain attempt to develop a collaborative arrangement with another nation, or group of nations, for the joint development and production of nuclear weapons?

Should Britain seek a collaborative arrangement with France? With other European nations? Would the United States agree to continue some sort of special nuclear relationship with the United Kingdom if this is Britain's choice? Assuming that Britain enters the E.E.C., should the primary consideration in deciding on the future of the nuclear force be her attempt to become a good 'European'? Should, therefore, London take the initiative in proposing a European nuclear force or at a more modest level, Anglo-French nuclear collaboration following admission into the European Community? Would London be willing to incure the displeasure of Washington, if this seems necessary, in order to forge nuclear links on the continent? What importance should be attached to the Chinese nuclear force, the first threat ever posed to Britain from outside Europe? Finally, what type of deterrence should Britain, or Europe-cum-Britain, seek to achieve in the coming strategic environment with its possible emphasis on defence as well as offence? Such questions are not open to simple answers!

Three sets of considerations will have to be taken into account as the alternatives are weighed and preferences are ordered. The first of these will involve a range of factors which form the international political context of British policy. Central here is the question of Britain's future in Europe. If the negotiations on entry into the Common Market are successful, and Britain is brought into the E.E.C., the European element of British policy will undoubtedly be strengthened. It is difficult to conceive of a real *entente nucléaire* between Paris and London while Britain continues to remain outside the Common Market. Once in the E.E.C., however, Britain would be likely to want to use her knowledge and experience in nuclear matters, and her position of comparative strength in defence technology, to help shape the future course of the continent.[1]

Equally important is the steadfastness of the American commitment to the security of Western Europe. One of the incentives in the decision to create an independent nuclear force in 1946–7, as we have seen, was the concern that existed before the inception of NATO and the Marshall Plan that the United States would return to isolationism. The early postwar atomic programme was a form of insurance against this possibility. In the 1970s the concern will again surface, though in a different form, and it will be heightened if there is a major withdrawal of American troops from West Germany and a more general reduction in American

[1] The potentialities and limitations of Britain's future role in Europe, with particular reference to strategy and technology, as well as the alternatives to Europe, are further discussed in the author's *Britain and European Security: Issues and Choices for the 1970s*, in Volume II, 'Arms Control and European Security in the 1970s', Report prepared for the U.S. Arms Control and Disarmament Agency by the Institute of War and Peace Studies, Columbia University.

interest in Europe. The ingredients for a reduced American military involvement in Western Europe undoubtedly exist in the social and economic difficulties of American society, which make for a preoccupation with domestic problems, and in the widespread view that the prosperous European NATO countries are not carrying a fair share of the burden of their own defence. A sense of disengagement also stems from the retrenchment of responsibilities resulting from the traumatic American experience in Vietnam. A perception in Western Europe of a diminution in the American commitment to its security is likely to spur initiatives not for augmenting conventional forces but, because of the lowering of the nuclear threshold, for greater dependence upon Europe's own nuclear deterrence capabilities.

Finally, the international political context of British policy will be affected by the developing nature of East-West relations. An expectation of continuing détente and gradual reconciliation in Europe, through an expansion of economic, technological, and political contacts and perhaps a European Security Conference, will somewhat lessen the resolve of political leaders to maintain past levels of defence spending. On the other hand, a concern for the future of relations with the U.S.S.R. because of a stagnant Soviet economy, persistent social and political repression in Eastern Europe and Russia, a continuing increase in strategic nuclear forces and expenditures on global military capabilities, Russian risk taking in the Middle East and elsewhere, coupled with worry about the conservative and unimaginative nature of the Soviet leadership, will lead to a somewhat different appraisal of what is required. Bridging these contrasting, though not necessarily mutually exclusive, expectations will be the worry that the United States and the Soviet Union will increasingly give priority to their dealings with one another, and that with the emergence of a Superpower 'condominium' the interests of America's European allies may suffer.[1]

This brings us to the second set of considerations which will inform British policy: ones relating to the strategic environment. The character and potential long-term impact of SALT, as of this writing, is not yet clear. But as viewed from Europe the simple fact that the SALT dialogue now is well under way places the central strategic balance, around which the structure of international relations in most of the industrialized world is built, in a somewhat new perspective. A rough parity in the strategic nuclear capabilities of the Superpowers now exists and will probably be codified through SALT. As the perception of this parity sinks into the

[1] For a more extensive discussion of the evolution of East-West relations, see the author's 'Reconciliation in Europe: A Western Approach to the European Security Conference', *Interplay*, Vol. 3, No. 10, July 1970, pp. 16–20.

consciousness of the European public, the credibility of the American security guarantee to Europe, especially that part of it dependent on the first use of strategic nuclear weapons, may become even further open to question.

One must also ask what would be the consequences if both the United States and the Soviet Union move on to a higher technological plateau with the deployment of ABM and MIRV. Such a step would reduce the effectiveness of the British nuclear force, in terms of its ability to penetrate enemy defences. But as we have seen earlier, it would not necessarily be a fatal blow to its deterrence function since barring an extremely 'thick' Soviet ABM deployment it will still be credible for some counter-city purposes. Accordingly it is wrong to conclude, as some commentators have done, that ballistic missile defences will be the death blow to the European nuclear forces. Nevertheless, their credibility will have been somewhat reduced and the new strategic environment would create added technological and financial requirements for their next generation.

The impact of ballistic missile defences upon the viability of the American security guarantee to Europe is difficult to gauge because it is so much a matter of perceptions. Two competing speculations are possible. On the one hand, the Safeguard deployment could be perceived as increasing the credibility of the guarantee in that the retaliatory force might be insured against destruction, and an eventual area defence of the population would strengthen American resolution in times of crisis. Alternatively, however, the United States could be seen as withdrawing into a 'fortress America' mentality, and losing interest in her allies after having developed the protective cover of ABM. A third 'scenario' may well come closer to what might occur: the United States continues with its ABM programme in fits and starts, but sufficient doubt persists concerning its effectiveness that on balance there is little impact upon perceptions of the reliability of the American guarantee.

Soviet and American deployment of ABM and MIRV could also introduce a new element of European inferiority into the strategic environment. It is most unlikely that the West European states would respond by building an ABM system for their own defence, even if American assistance were to be made available. A European ABM would be for the purpose of defending its population since there will be few 'hard' targets, such as European land-based nuclear retaliatory forces. But the task of constructing an effective system of area defence would probably present insurmountable difficulties. The close geographical proximity of Western Europe to the Soviet Union necessitates an extremely rapid and technically efficient ABM system, but even if it were feasible to create it at great costs, the Soviet Union could respond by threatening 'unacceptable damage' with alternate forms of offensive forces, such as manned bombers and cruise missiles. The cost of a European ABM system would be much greater than the expense which the Soviet Union would incur by improving its offensive capabilities sufficiently to neutralize it. Moreover, the political as well as the command and control problems of organizing a European ABM would be formidable. Such a system would almost certainly require nuclear warheads and, because of the close proximity to Soviet nuclear forces, a decision to use ABMs would have to be made within seconds of the launching of an attack.

Thus a deployment of ABM and MIRV by the Superpowers, particularly if it were on a large scale, could leave Western Europe with a sense of nuclear nakedness. The Soviet Union with its IRBMs, medium-range strategic bombers, tactical nuclear weapons, and ICBMs that can be retargeted for a shorter range, maintains a massive capability against Western Europe. This may increase the fear that Western Europe will be held as a 'hostage' by the Soviet Union against American actions and policies around the world. One need only recall the concern about possible Soviet pressure on Berlin at the time of the Cuban missile crisis in 1962. In addition, with both Superpowers partially secure behind their missile defences but in all likelihood still vulnerable to each other, there may develop a concern that the Superpowers will adopt strategies of 'controlled' nuclear warfare with the European continent as the potential battlefield.

In such circumstances Britain would have an interest in retaining the means to break up such rules of engagement. The Superpowers may have a common interest in declaring their own territories off limits, and because Western Europe remains so closely linked to the United States it could well become the prize to be fought over. This would not be out of maliciousness but for want of a better nuclear strategy on the part of the two musclebound giants. But there is no reason why Britain should not then retain the capacity to threaten to spread a European nuclear war to the homelands of the Superpowers. This would be a credible threat since if carried out under the circumstances of the country already being devastated, Britain would have little left to lose. Such a role for the British nuclear force in an ABM strategic environment would be a variant of the classic function of threatening to 'trigger' the awesome American nuclear forces. The independent nuclear capability would help Britain to avoid becoming a 'hostage' to the Soviet Union and give her leaders greater flexibility in an era of ever greater Superpower nuclear dominance.

The third set of considerations which will influence policy on the continuation of the nuclear force involves the future of the Anglo-American special relationship in nuclear affairs. British policy-makers will want to try to ascertain to the best extent possible whether they can expect to receive from the United States another generation of strategic systems, after Polaris submarines, or if they can plan on assistance in warhead design, for example on MIRVs. This will not be an easy task, for this study illustrates the extent to which such decisions, ever since the Quebec Agreement of 1943, have been as much the result of timing, politics and personality as orderly and rational decision-making. Nevertheless, London will want intermittently to test the climate in Washington, since changing perceptions of American-European problems and of arms control may alter policies in the United States.

It will be very important that the British also give hard thought to whether and how they wish to continue the special nuclear relationship. It should be recognized that along with its very considerable technological benefits in the past have come some not insubstantial political costs. The French have always viewed the bilateral nuclear ties with suspicion. Some French leaders have tended to see this nuclear relationship as the acid test of Britain's political loyalties. Thus in the past de Gaulle's failure in his 1958 bid for equal treatment through a three power directorate, and Britain's choice at Nassau of the United States as her future nuclear partner, undoubtedly contributed to keeping the United Kingdom barred from the Common Market. If Britain is to be fully accepted by the continental countries as a European state, she may have to strengthen her European identity by a corresponding loosening of her close ties across the Atlantic.

Considerations of expense cannot help but be a weighty factor in Whitehall's deliberations since the development of strategic delivery systems takes an enormous bite out of any nation's defence budget. A second Nassau Agreement, one which gave Britain a successor to Polaris, could save a tremendous financial expenditure. It need not if it simply leads to the availability of a better system at a high cost. But in either case it would also continue and deepen the condition of dependency upon the United States in the maintenance of the nuclear force. This has both technological and political disadvantages. Britain would fall that much further behind in having a strategic weapons industry of her own. And, unless there was an adjustment in American nuclear sharing policy, roadblocks would be maintained on nuclear co-operation with France.

At the end of 1974 the U.S.-U.K. nuclear exchange agreement signed after the 1958 amendments were adopted will become subject to termination. The clauses dealing with exchange of information on nuclear weapons will continue automatically for another five years unless denounced by December 1973. The provisions for exchange of weapons-grade fissile materials will terminate unless extended. It should not be assumed that these accords will be automatically renewed in routine manner, although this could occur as it has already once. There exists a school of argument in the United States which for a number of reasons opposes the favourable discriminatory treatment given to Britain. The privileged access given to London is seen as harmful to America's relations with France. The extension of the nuclear accords is viewed as affirming the importance of nuclear weapons in the eyes of non-nuclear nations and therefore also harmful to the cause of non-proliferation. Finally, the continuation of the special nuclear relationship is seen as psychologically deflecting Britain from her true European destiny.[1] If such arguments gain influence, then Washington will want to consider the U.S.–U.K. nuclear accords in the context of its entire European policy and the defence arrangements of the Atlantic alliance as a whole.

With these three sets of considerations in mind—the international political context of British policy, the coming strategic environment, and the Anglo-American special nuclear relationship—we can now examine more specifically the options open to Britain for the medium-range future of the nuclear force. It is likely that Britain's choices on strategic weapons systems will involve fundamental decisions about her future alliance relationships. In the past Britain has attempted simultaneously to remain an independent nuclear power, to maintain a special relationship with the United States, and to become a 'European power'. It is not certain that she will be able to continue indefinitely this difficult balancing act. Britain's nuclear decisions will be influenced by the broadest political considerations regarding the choice of her future political, economic, and military partners, and their choice of her. But in a more specific sense the critical questions will be: what degree of nuclear self-sufficiency, especially in strategic delivery systems, does Britain wish to possess? If Britain is to have nuclear partners, who will they be and under what circumstances?

In answering these questions there are six major alternative policies which Britain can follow.

1. To dispose of first things first, Britain could unilaterally give up the nuclear force. This could be done in one of several ways. A simple decision could be made not to replace the Polaris submarines when they wear

---

[1] See the admonitions of George Ball on the 'disadvantages' of the special relationship, and his plea that in the future, following on the 1958 Amendments, Skybolt, and Nassau, the U.S. not make a 'fourth mistake', op. cit., pp. 98–100.

out in the 1980s. If this was seen as taking too long in coming, the missile systems could be taken out of the boats at any time and the submarines converted to an attack role. Another possibility would be to sell the Polaris flotilla to the U.S. Navy.

None of these possibilities is likely to occur. For the reasons discussed extensively in this study and briefly summarized earlier in the conclusions, there is only a remote chance that Britain will unilaterally cease to be a nuclear power in the next decade or two. After a ten year national debate on Britain's independent possession of nuclear weapons we can see in retrospect that the watershed was reached with the Labour government's quiet decision in 1964–5 not to 're-negotiate' Nassau by cancelling the agreement with the United States for the purchase of Polaris missiles. Whatever may have been the merits in the past of the arguments for phasing out the military nuclear business—and they were considerable—Britain will not, through an act of self-abnegation, now leave France as the sole nuclear power in Europe.

As to non-proliferation, the once widespread belief that Britain, by voluntarily renouncing her nuclear arms, could strongly influence other countries to desist from acquiring them, has lost much of its validity. Today the N.P.T. is the heart of the anti-proliferation strategy; the countries to be influenced are less those of Western Europe than of Asia and the Middle East, and these states, being primarily concerned with regional security and prestige, are not going to be much influenced by exemplary action on the part of Britain. Nor is it clear how a nation can convince the world that it has 'ceased' to be a military nuclear power, even if it wishes to, except through a system of comprehensive international inspection of plants, stockpiles, military facilities, underground caverns, and so on.

Finally, it is quite possible that Britain's nuclear capability will play some role, perhaps a major one, in the evolution of her future relationships in Europe and the future organization of Western defence. Neither Westminster politicians nor Whitehall planners are likely to forget that in their nuclear force they possess an important asset in future international bargaining. Unless there is a surprising transformation in the present international system, it is unlikely that Britain will on her own give up nuclear weapons over roughly the next twenty years. Beyond that, prediction is hardly ever wise.

2. A second option would be to pursue a policy of deliberate technological independence—a policy not to be derided since it is the chosen course of all the other nuclear powers. France's example is being watched with great interest and some envy—'French missiles will carry the tricolour, Britain's the stars and stripes'. Although the French may not achieve

their ambitious goals and their timetable may incur considerable slippage, present plans call for an independently constructed *force de dissuasion* equipped with thirty-six Mirage IV bombers, eighteen land-based IRBMs located on the Plateau d'Albion, and five missile-firing nuclear submarines. Britain has not been developing long-range missiles since the cancellation of Blue Streak in 1960. Since then Britain has fallen considerably behind in the technology of strategic missilery. A persuasive case can therefore be made for a new British missile programme on the basis of technological advancement and on the need for staying in advanced research and development. This could be underpinned by arguments based on national security and perhaps, indirectly, even national pride.

A policy favouring self-reliance in the future would, however, have to be made in the context of a more varied range of choices. One possibility would be to develop MIRVs for the existing Polaris fleet. This was once seriously considered by the U.S. Navy for its own Polaris submarines. A British MIRV on Polaris would probably carry fewer and smaller warheads than those developed for Poseidon, but improvements in accuracy might well compensate for this. Though Polaris tipped with MIRV is a technologically feasible option it might require altering the present fire control and computer systems as well as a nuclear warhead testing programme. Thus there would be quite some expense in addition to the cost of developing the British MIRV itself. The requirement for MIRV is, of course, dependent upon the deployment of at least a moderate ABM area defence by the Soviet Union. If this does not occur then, as we have discussed earlier, the present Polaris generation with its counter-city doctrine will retain its viability for as far ahead as we can presently foresee. In such circumstances the Polaris force could simply be continued in its present form with whatever further improvements can be achieved in penetration aids.

Another possibility, a new British developed strategic missile, would probably only make sense if it were sea-launched. A mobile land-based missile, an IRBM moved by road or rail around the Scottish Highlands, for example, is conceivable. But in all likelihood it would be politically unacceptable since it would make the British Isles a lightening rod susceptible to a Soviet counter-force threat. Moreover, as far as we can look ahead in strategic technology, sea-based deterrent forces appear to have a considerable edge over land-based ones in retaining their invulnerability. If it were decided as a matter of national policy to develop a long-range missile it might therefore be quite similar to the American Poseidon. The past experience of close co-operation with the United States on Polaris would be of invaluable assistance. Although Britain was not given the Polaris design plans themselves, she did learn a great deal through the construction programme, and of course is now acquiring experience in running missile-firing submarines. A British-made missile similar to Poseidon would be very expensive and technologically consuming, but it need not be beyond the nation's capabilities.

Still another available choice should not be totally overlooked. There has been a tendency in recent years to write off manned long-range aircraft as incongruous with the advanced missile era. But estimates of the value of such deep penetration aircraft might again rise if the Soviet Union deploys a comprehensive anti-ballistic missile system. In such circumstances manned bombers might be used to fly under Soviet ABM screens. It is likely that a Soviet response to American MIRVs which involved going all out for missile defences would curtail the amount of money and effort expendable for air defence against large numbers of low-intrusion and fast-strike aircraft. If so, Britain might consider taking advantage of the high technology plateau of the Superpowers by basing her deterrent on a simpler and yet reasonably effective weapon. With the demise of the TSR-2 and the curtailment of the V-bombers, the R.A.F. has no deep-strike aircraft and none is currently planned. A new bomber might be well suited to Britain's industrial capacity and past strategic doctrine, and should therefore at least be seriously considered.

3. A third alternative would be to seek to renew the present dependency upon the United States. This might be the least expensive policy but it could incur not inconsequential political costs. Continuing dependence cannot in the long run but have a restrictive influence upon British foreign policy. And it is hardly compatible with the political and economic arguments for pursuing a greater role in Europe. The first thing that would need to be done would be to ascertain the conditions under which the special nuclear relationship might be extended; as we have seen this might not be so readily accomplished.

Assuming that this course were followed—and in many ways it is the most 'natural' given past history—what weapons might Britain want to receive? Poseidon in combination with the American MIRV would be an obvious choice. Poseidon would perhaps only make sense if fitted with MIRVs since otherwise it would not be used at its full potential. On the other hand, the American MIRV alone might be adapted for use on the British Polaris.

Another possibility would be the construction of some additional submarines containing American Polaris missiles. This would increase the credibility of the nuclear force as a deterrent since it would be easier to inflict 'unacceptable damage'. Even two more submarines would make a substantial difference, since it would double the number of submarines that can be guaranteed at sea at all times.

In this regard what the United States does with its ten Polaris submarines that are not being retrofitted with the Poseidon system is a matter of some importance to Britain. Obviously Britain could benefit from being sold a few of them. A related question is what happens to the support and maintenance operations which are carried out in the United States for all Polaris missiles, including Britain's. If the American Polaris missiles are scrapped, then Britain will have to take over the Polaris support maintenance at great expense because the facilities would have to be continued for so small a number of missiles. Obtaining a new strategic system might then, on balance, be more desirable.

Attention should therefore be turned to the next generation of sea-based deterrence, a completely new and advanced submarine which is now in the stage of developmental studies in the United States. This is still known by its acronym, ULMS, standing for Underwater Long Range Missile System. The ULMS submarine would be larger and quieter than existing submarines and would be capable of attaining greater depths. Its new MIRVed missile would have a range of over 5,000 miles and approximately twenty missiles would be carried in each submarine. Due to the increased range of the missile, the undersea area in which ULMS could hide would be greatly expanded, perhaps by a factor of ten compared to Poseidon. This new system has yet to be approved for production, but given that the sea increasingly appears as the best environment for a retaliatory strategic force, its future looks promising. ULMS would be very expensive, with up to 25 billion dollars as a possible total cost for the programme. Britain's interest would clearly be dependent upon the terms she could receive. Moreover, the ULMS submarine could hardly be ready before 1980, which could present a problem for Britain if the penetration capability of the Polaris A-3 is threatened before then.

4. A fourth option would be nuclear collaboration with France. This will undoubtedly be a matter of great interest to both Governments in the coming years, and the subject of much analysis and speculation. An *entente nucléaire* between Britain and France does have an inherent logic since many of the interests of the only two nuclear powers of Europe do coincide. For both countries the almost inevitable reduction of American forces in Europe and the continuing strategic dialogue between the Superpowers will require a re-evaluation of the role of European nuclear forces in the defence of Western Europe. And both countries also will be faced with the task of maintaining credible nuclear forces within an increasingly technologically advanced strategic environment.

An analysis of the possibilities for Anglo-French nuclear collaboration must be separated into two parts. One is the potential for an exchange of knowledge of nuclear weapons, including that about their production, and the transfer of existing nuclear materials and technology. The other is the possibility of co-operation on the operational use of nuclear weapons, that is, their targeting and deployment. The latter is particularly important since it is affected by concepts of national sovereignty and should be consistent with alliance relationships. Although technological needs may present the original basis for collaboration, it is the political requirements of policy which in the final analysis, as we shall see, are paramount.

If one looks at the technology of the British and French strategic nuclear programmes, one finds that they are remarkably complementary and therefore suitable for a series of exchanges. Britain is far ahead in the design of warheads, having exploded her first thermonuclear device over a decade before France and having also acquired much design information from the United States. France, for her part, needs assistance in warhead miniaturization and is greatly interested in the British experience with MRV warheads. The sophistication of warheads is, of course, the crucial factor in the ability to penetrate anti-ballistic missile defences. With regard to missile propulsion the situation is reversed. France is ahead in the production of solid fuel ballistic missiles, having designed them for the 18 IRBM Silos in Haute-Provence and for installation in her missile-launching submarines. Because of the expected availability of Skybolt and Polaris, Britain has had no strategic missile programme of her own since 1960. As to guidance technology, comparative strength is difficult to judge. Although Britain has acquired a great deal of knowledge through the Polaris programme, France has done more independent work in some areas of guidance.

Since existing strengths and weaknesses are roughly complementary, the technical basis for an agreement on collaboration undoubtedly does exist. The benefits of a straight technological exchange would not, however, be equally distributed. At the present juncture in their nuclear programmes, France would gain the most. This is because the two national nuclear programmes are at very different stages. Whereas Britain has very recently completed the Polaris flotilla and has no other strategic systems planned, all the French missile-launching submarines will not be operational before the mid-1970s and the first land-based IRBMs have yet to enter into service. An early agreement on technological assistance could save considerable money and time for France even in developing her present generation of systems. For Britain it is too late, and in any case the assistance came from the United States. This is part of the explanation for the French interest in collaboration in recent years and the relative British lack of enthusiasm.

Joint development of a post-Polaris system would be quite another matter and is likely to be attractive to both countries. In the construction of the third generation nuclear force (the first for both was bombers) it might be possible to bring together British warhead knowledge with French missile propulsion experience. Such a combination would permit a substantial saving of expenditures for what is likely to be a very costly strategic system since it may have to be designed to be capable of penetrating missile defences. Anglo-French nuclear collaboration on the next generation of both their nuclear forces might encompass joint research and development, common testing, and the co-operative production of the system, or some variation of these. Collaboration might also be broadened to include work on nuclear hunter-killer submarines, the production of enriched nuclear fuel and weapons-grade nuclear materials, and the manufacture of tactical nuclear weapons.

The political understanding necessary for Anglo-French collaboration may be more difficult to achieve than the technological basis. Nuclear weapons not being like consumer products, the manufacturer will produce only if he retains some influence over how his product is to be employed. Thus collaboration would entail agreement on nuclear targeting and force deployments as well as some common understanding concerning political aims.

In the mid-1970s Britain and France will have missile-firing submarine forces which are remarkably symmetrical. They will have four and five boats respectively, carrying in each case sixteen missiles per boat. An Anglo-French force of nine submarines could assure a minimum of four on patrol at any time, and more often than not five. Since this would provide a greater threat to the Soviet Union than either force separately, it would enhance the credibility of the deterrence capability of either nation.

Such an Anglo-French force could be constituted by the co-ordination of targeting plans, patrol missions, some joint communications and intelligence, and possibly co-operation in maintenance facilities. Command and control arrangements would remain national, however, as would the ownership of the boats. Each national contingent would be left able to recapture total freedom of action whenever vital interests were at stake. The decision to fire would thus be solely a national one—as indeed it must be so long as nations are not prepared to give up a vital element of their sovereignty—control over their military forces.

There are major political inhibitions in such an arrangement, and the first is created by the special nuclear relationship with the United States. The 1958 agreement on nuclear exchange forbids either country to transfer knowledge and secret information obtained from the other to a third party. Although Britain has without doubt originated a good deal of valuable data through her own research, it would be almost impossible to disentangle fully such indigenous information from that obtained from the United States. Nevertheless, some British-produced data could certainly be isolated and passed on to France without American permission. Doubts arise as to whether this would be a wise thing to do if it irritated the U.S. government and especially the Congress. With so much of Britain's nuclear programme linked to that of her ally, and the full range of future options dependent upon a continuation of these close ties, there would seem to be a high value placed upon maintaining the spirit as well as the legal terms of the Agreement. Whitehall officials have long been sensitive to this and, unless there is a major re-orientation of defence policy, they are unlikely to propose an accord with France which could upset the Joint Committee on Atomic Energy of the U.S. Congress.

The divergent views on the Atlantic alliance currently held by France on the one hand, and by Britain and the United States on the other, create a still more formidable political inhibition. Britain in recent years has been of the view that nuclear policy should be discussed in the Nuclear Planning Group of NATO and that European nuclear forces should be targeted in co-ordination with those of the United States. Accordingly, an Anglo-French force should fall within the alliance framework. This has been contrary to the French view which sees NATO as too much under American influence and which therefore seems to equate the co-ordination of forces within NATO with loss of national autonomy.

An Anglo-French force *outside* NATO would, however, have grave disadvantages. The United States would not support it and consequently the restrictive provisions of the Anglo-American exchange agreement would come into play. Such a nuclear contingent outside NATO would also not be acceptable to the West Germans since it would not be committed to their defence and might thus stir a wave of interest in national atomic weapons. Moreover, it would be of concern to the other NATO members as a step away from the common defence of Western Europe and might thus induce the unravelling of the alliance. Outside NATO, and without the support of the United States, an Anglo-French force would have reduced credibility and would sharply open to question the continuation of the American security guarantee to Western Europe.

For these reasons the present political obstacles to Anglo-French nuclear collaboration seem formidable. So long as France insists on unblemished nuclear independence an arrangement satisfactory to the two countries as well as to the Federal Republic and the United States seems unlikely.

Still, the trend is not unfavourable towards an eventual accord. In recent years, France has dropped the *tous azimuts* strategy of armed neutrality and her nuclear doctrine has moved closer to that of the alliance. With the death of de Gaulle and the passage of time, France's role in the world will be reassessed and some of the more Gaullist conceptions of the alliance are likely to be modified.

The French strategic nuclear programme has fallen considerably behind in recent years, in large measure because of the enormous expense involved. The land-based IRBMs have been reduced in number, and the missile-firing nuclear submarines are running three years behind the original schedule. French administrators and scientists, looking at the technology ahead, especially the need for improved penetration capabilities in case of further Soviet ABM deployment, have for some time been interested in nuclear collaboration. Britain for her part has gradually become more European. Prime Minister Heath and some other influential Conservatives have for a number of years expressed an interest in Anglo-French nuclear collaboration. Various pressures are coalescing towards a greater European role within NATO and a reduction in the American military predominance. This might eventually create the conditions for a wider European effort in nuclear deterrence.

5. A fifth option for Britain, one that has been frequently mentioned in the context of Britain's entry into Europe, would be participation in a European nuclear deterrent. The military and political requirements of a valid European deterrent, one which by definition would be capable of balancing the Soviet Union and which would no longer necessitate reliance upon the American nuclear umbrella, are worth briefly examining. They suggest that the chances of a credible European deterrent emerging in the next decade or two are slim indeed.

Such a European force would have to assure the thirteen European members of NATO, perhaps less if the 'flanks' were excluded, protection against a superpower nuclear threat. Coverage of the seven countries of the Western European Union alone would include a population of 250 million and an area of 544,000 square miles. The contribution of the British and French nuclear forces as presently existing or planned would be a start, but only that. To bring a European nuclear deterrent anywhere near up to the superpower scale might necessitate a strategic force of something like 30 nuclear submarines with Poseidon missiles carrying MIRVs. Once totally dependent upon itself, Europe might feel the need to insure against the obsolescence of any one particular strategic system and produce a mix of sea and mobile land-based strategic forces. In order to have a damage-limiting capability, a European force would need counter-force strategic weapons, with all the added guidance and penetration requirements that this entails. In addition, separate satellite and other intelligence systems would have to be created. Finally, a wide spectrum of tactical nuclear weapons and conventional forces would be necessary to deal with piecemeal threats and limited war situations in order to make possible a graduated response to a less than all out attack. The cost of such a varied deterrence capability would send European defence budgets skyrocketing and would involve a very great expenditure of scientific and technological resources.

Still more daunting, however, would be the political requisites for a viable European nuclear deterrent. The command and control arrangements for such a force would require a central political authority capable of deciding on the use of the force on behalf of Europe. No nation in the present European system will be prepared to place its survival in the hands of another political entity since the use of the deterrent could invite the destruction of its homeland. The necessary psychological cohesion, political unity, and institutional loyalty are lacking. Only a President of Europe with individual authority in a nuclear crisis could endow a European deterrent with full credibility, yet this is clearly not possible in the foreseeable future. A European nuclear deterrent must probably await the formation of a Federal Europe.

6. We are thus brought to the sixth and final option, an Atlantic solution through a major restructuring of NATO. This would involve a European pillar within the alliance entrusted with greater responsibilities for Europe's defence. This might parallel the progress in the widening and deepening of the European Economic Community. Co-operation within Europe across the spectrum of defence activities—conventional and nuclear—would be increased and the American military role and psychological dominance correspondingly reduced.

In so far as nuclear weapons are concerned, the British and French strategic forces might become subject to the advisory guidelines of a European Nuclear Committee (E.N.C.). This would permit the formulation of a European perspective on planning for contingencies, nuclear strategy, and political guidelines on the use of nuclear weapons. A unified European view might thereby be presented to the United States. Such consultations might also include discussions about the next generation of the European nuclear forces. Command and control decisions would still remain in the hands of the respective national authorities although nuclear planning, both targeting and strategy, would be co-ordinated with the United States.

The E.N.C. would give the non-nuclear countries a sense of participation and responsibility. This would be particularly significant for the Federal Republic of Germany, as the only major West European power without an independent nuclear capability. A change of French policy would be necessary, but, as seen earlier, this is far from inconceivable with the passage of time, especially if such an intra-European grouping succeeds in shedding the psychological weight of the American yoke. In time, if the notion that the British and French forces were truly 'Europe's force' took hold, the non-nuclear countries might contribute to their maintenance either through joint production of delivery systems or through common financing. This arrangement would not involve a breach of the Non-Proliferation Treaty since it would not include a transfer of nuclear weapons or their control to non-nuclear powers. The proposed E.N.C. is, of course, only one possible means of enhancing the European element within the alliance and of giving the European nations larger participation in their nuclear defence.

A great deal would depend upon the attitude of the United States. The conditions and priorities of the 1970s and 1980s will differ from the previous decade when the United States discouraged European nuclear forces, especially France's and the German potential for one, and attached great weight to centralized command and control. In the past it was argued in Washington that de Gaulle's co-operation could not be 'bought'; nor should he be 'rewarded' for his attacks on NATO and the dollar. Perhaps that was right for the times, but France, we hope, will now gradually be returning to the alliance system. If Paris agrees to joint targeting, the 'force de frappe' should no longer be seen as a challenge to American policy.

Similarly, past concern over non-proliferation no longer seems relevant in the same manner. France is a nuclear power; her example has not encouraged Germany to emulate her; and the real dangers of the spread of nuclear weapons are now outside Europe. The N.P.T., the SALT dialogue between the Superpowers, the progress towards European economic integration, the opening of new contacts between Western and Eastern Europe, and the forthcoming reduction in the American military presence in Western Europe are all creating new circumstances. Consideration should be given to a more constructive U.S. policy of aiding the European nuclear forces so as to integrate them into a polity of Western deterrence. This might, in the long run, be the best way for the United States to retain its influence in the affairs of Europe.

Accordingly, the United States might do well to look benevolently upon Anglo-French nuclear co-operation provided that the *entente nucléaire* existed *within* the framework of the Atlantic alliance, possibly as the pedestal of a strengthened European pillar. Such a policy could be given substance by releasing Britain from some of the restraints of the Anglo-American nuclear agreement so as to permit her to exchange knowledge and materials with France. The ten American Polaris submarines not to be converted for Poseidon missiles might be sold to the European Nuclear Committee, with the understanding that they would be operated by Britain and France on behalf of Europe. Still another type of aid would be a direct offer to Britain and France of technological help in the maintenance of their nuclear forces and in the construction of the next generation.

In return for such a change of policy, the United States could reasonably expect that all European nuclear forces be put at the service of the alliance. French forces would thus have to be jointly targeted with those of the United States and Britain and there would have to be a closer understanding on strategic doctrine than exists at present. This should not be an insurmountable obstacle, since the differences which existed in the Gaullist era were often rooted more in political symbolism and strategic 'theology' than in fundamentally divergent national interests. Two additional criteria, somewhat antithetical, would have to be satisfied. West Germany as a key participant in the E.N.C. would have to give its full support and should not feel unreasonably discriminated against. At the same time, the Soviet Union would have to be persuaded that such an arrangement would not provide Bonn with control over nuclear weapons and, more generally, that there is no valid reason why it should aggravate East-West relations in Europe.[1]

Britain in the years ahead should seek to maintain its close involvement with the United States while developing a trusting relationship with France. In practical terms this would mean Anglo-French-American collaboration in nuclear policy. Whether this could best be brought about by an *entente nucléaire* which was 'blessed' by Washington, or by direct American assistance to London and Paris separately is difficult to assess at this stage. The goal should be a European nuclear role within the Atlantic alliance which fortifies the European pillar, and which serves as a step towards greater European political integration without damaging the partnership with the United States.

The future of the nuclear force now awaits political decisions. Unlike much of the past, however, it is the politics of today which will determine the strategy and the technology of tomorrow. Whichever of the above alternatives, or combination thereof, may ultimately be chosen, it is certain that Britain's nuclear innocence has been lost beyond recall. With a quarter of a century's experience behind her, Britain will retain her nuclear force in some form. If the force is not absorbed into a multinational arrangement, Britain will remain an important nuclear power in an international system of possibly many nuclear powers. To give up the nuclear force unilaterally would be unnecessarily to foreclose options in a highly unpredictable world.

[1] The above is contained in a proposal on future U.S. policy in the author's 'Nuclear Diplomacy: Britain, France, and America', *Foreign Affairs*, Vol. XLIX, No. 2, January 1971.

Tables

TABLE 1

*Great Britain: Military Defence Expenditures as a Proportion of Gross
National Product and Central Government Expenditures*

Calendar year	Gross National Product	Central Government expenditures on current account		Defence expenditures as a proportion of:	
		Total[a]	Military defence[b]	GNP	total current expenditures
		(millions of pounds sterling)		(per cent)	
1947	11,021	3,154	930	8·4	29·5
1948	11,070	3,291	740	6·7	22·5
1949	11,784	3,495	770	6·5	22·0
1950	12,466	3,539	827	6·6	23·4
1951	13,731	3,951	1,102	8·0	27·9
1952	14,817	4,519	1,465	9·9	32·4
1953	15,952	4,707	1,548	9·7	32·9
1954	16,921	4,834	1,543	9·1	31·9
1955	19,277	4,962	1,490	7·7	30·0
1956	20,892	5,261	1,570	7·5	29·8
1957	22,092	5,484	1,543	7·0	28·1
1958	23,063	5,816	1,488	6·5	25·6
1959	24,253	6,159	1,534	6·3	24·9
1960	25,721	6,611	1,598	6·2	24·2
1961	27,468	7,146	1,700	6·2	23·8
1962	28,852	7,581	1,819	6·3	24·0
1963	30,637	8,059	1,871	6·1	23·2
1964	33,268	8,475	1,963	5·9	23·2
1965	35,765	9,273	2,085	5·8	22·5
1966	38,047	10,038	2,174	5·7	21·7
1967	40,026	11,319	2,363	5·9	20·9
1968	42,873	12,438	2,391	5·6	19·2
1969	45,625	12,966	2,280	5·0	17·6
1970	50,429	14,246	2,420	4·8	17·0

[a] Current expenditures on goods and services; subsidies; current grants for social security benefits, education, etc.; debt service; current grants to local authorities; current grants to overseas countries and international organizations.

[b] Current expenditures on goods and services; current grants to personal sector; current grants abroad.

Source: Great Britain, Central Statistical Office, *National Income and Expenditure* (London, H.M.S.O., various years).

TABLE 2

British Defence Expenditures, 1946/47–1969/70

Year ending 31 March	Expenditures, in millions of pounds sterling					Allocation by department, in per cent			
	Total	Army	Navy	Air	Other[a]	Army	Navy	Air	Other[a]
1946/47	1,653·4	717·0	266·9	255·5	414·0	43·4	16·1	15·5	25·0
1947/48	853·9	383·6	194·3	181·9	94·1	44·9	22·8	21·3	11·0
1948/49	753·2	346·7	162·7	186·9	56·9	46·0	21·6	24·8	7·6
1949/50	740·7	291·8	186·8	201·6	60·5	39·4	25·2	27·2	8·2
1950/51	777·4	309·0	190·0	225·1	53·3	39·7	24·4	29·0	6·9
1951/52	1,110·2	422·3	271·3	322·3	94·3	38·0	24·5	29·0	8·5
1952/53	1,403·7	525·0	333·4	421·3	124·0	37·4	23·8	30·0	8·8
1953/54	1,364·5	487·8	324·1	416·4	136·2	35·7	23·8	30·5	10·0
1954/55	1,435·9	477·0	345·8	463·6	149·5	33·2	24·1	32·3	10·4
1955/56	1,404·9	462·9	337·7	431·1	173·2	33·0	24·0	30·7	12·3
1956/57	1,525·1	498·9	342·6	471·5	212·1	32·7	22·5	30·9	13·9
1957/58	1,429·7	387·9	353·0	474·0	214·8	27·1	24·7	33·2	15·0
1958/59	1,467·7	433·0	373·7	465·7	195·3	29·5	25·5	31·7	13·3
1959/60	1,475·7	428·2	364·6	485·1	197·8	29·0	24·7	32·9	13·4
1960/61	1,595·8	482·8	389·2	532·0	191·8	30·3	24·4	33·3	12·0
1961/62	1,688·7	508·4	413·8	547·3	219·2	30·1	24·5	32·4	13·0
1962/63	1,766·6	528·5	438·1	569·7	230·3	29·9	24·8	32·3	13·0
1963/64	1,791·7	489·0	433·6	499·2	369·9	27·3	24·2	27·9	20·6
1964/65	1,909·0	506·6	473·9	491·8	436·7	26·5	24·8	25·8	22·9
1965/66	2,055·9	553·7	512·0	533·0	457·2	26·9	24·9	25·9	22·2
1966/67	2,114·9	573·3	586·4	514·1	441·1	27·1	27·7	24·3	20·9
1967/68	2,254·4	620·3	648·0	536·4	449·7	27·5	28·7	23·8	20·0
1968/69	2,232·0	591·4	674·7	562·3	403·6	26·5	30·2	25·2	18·1
1969/70	2,204·5	600·5	638·7	559·4	405·9	27·2	29·0	25·4	18·4

[a] Comprises central defence expenditures; the expenditures for defence items of the Ministry of Aviation, the Ministry of Technology, and the Atomic Energy Authority; and the expenditures for defence items of the Ministry of Public Building and Works, which prior to 1963/64 were allocated among the three services.

Source: Great Britain, Central Statistical Office, *Annual Abstract of Statistics* (London, H.M.S.O., various years).

Appendix

A. *The Quebec Agreement*

ARTICLES OF AGREEMENT governing collaboration between the authorities of the U.S.A. and the U.K. in the matter of Tube Alloys.

Whereas it is vital to our common safety in the present War to bring the Tube Alloys project to fruition at the earliest moment; and whereas this may be more speedily achieved if all available British and American brains and resources are pooled; and whereas owing to war conditions it would be an improvident use of war resources to duplicate plants on a large scale on both sides of the Atlantic and therefore a far greater expense has fallen upon the United States;

It is agreed between us

First, that we will never use this agency against each other.

Secondly, that we will not use it against third parties without each other's consent.

Thirdly, that we will not either of us communicate any information about Tube Alloys to third parties except by mutual consent.

Fourthly, that in view of the heavy burden of production falling upon the United States as the result of a wise division of war effort, the British Government recognize that any post-war advantages of an industrial or commercial character shall be dealt with as between the United States and Great Britain on terms to be specified by the President of the United States to the Prime Minister of Great Britain. The Prime Minister expressly disclaims any interest in these industrial and commercial aspects beyond what may be considered by the President of the United States to be fair and just and in harmony with the economic welfare of the world.

And Fifthly, that the following arrangements shall be made to ensure full and effective collaboration between the two countries in bringing the project to fruition:

(a) There shall be set up in Washington a Combined Policy Committee composed of:

The Secretary of War	(United States)
Dr. Vannevar Bush	(United States)
Dr. James L. Conant	(United States)
Field-Marshal Sir John Dill, G.C.B., C.M.G., D.S.O.	(United Kingdom)
Colonel the Right Hon. J. J. Llewellin C.B.E., M.C., M.P.	(United Kingdom)
The Honourable C. D. Howe	(Canada)

The functions of this Committee, subject to the control of the respective Governments, will be:

    (1) To agree from time to time upon the programme of work to be carried out in the two countries.

(2) To keep all sections of the project under constant review.

(3) To allocate materials apparatus and plant, in limited supply, in accordance with the requirements of the programme agreed by the Committee.

(4) To settle any questions which may arise on the interpretation or application of this Agreement.

(b) There shall be complete interchange of information and ideas on all sections of the project between members of the Policy Committee and their immediate technical advisers.

(c) In the field of scientific research and development there shall be full and effective interchange of information and ideas between those in the two countries engaged in the same sections of the field.

(d) In the field of design, construction and operation of large-scale plants, interchange of information and ideas shall be regulated by such *ad hoc* arrangements as may, in each section of the field, appear to be necessary or desirable if the project is to be brought to fruition at the earliest moment. Such *ad hoc* arrangements shall be subject to the approval of the Policy Committee.

Approved

19 August 1943

Franklin D. Roosevelt

Winston Churchill

B. *The Nassau Agreement*

Statement on Nuclear Defense Systems—21 December 1962

(1) The President and the Prime Minister reviewed the development program for the Skybolt missile. The President explained that it was no longer expected that this very complex weapons system would be completed within the cost estimate or the time scale which were projected when the program was begun.

(2) The President informed the Prime Minister that for this reason and because of the availability to the United States of alternative weapons systems, he had decided to cancel plans for the production of Skybolt for use by the United States. Nevertheless, recognizing the importance of the Skybolt program for the United Kingdom, and recalling that the purpose of the offer of Skybolt to the United Kingdom in 1960 had been to assist in improving and extending the effective life of the British V-bombers, the President expressed his readiness to continue the development of the missile as a joint enterprise between the United States and the United Kingdom, with each country bearing equal shares of the future cost of completing development, after which the United Kingdom would be able to place a production order to meet its requirements.

(3) While recognizing the value of this offer, the Prime Minister decided, after full consideration, not to avail himself of it because of doubts that had been expressed about the prospects of success for this weapons system and because of uncertainty regarding date of completion and final cost of the program.

(4) As a possible alternative the President suggested that the Royal Air Force might use the Hound Dog missile. The Prime Minister responded that in the light of the technical difficulties he was unable to accept this suggestion.

(5) The Prime Minister then turned to the possibility of provision of the Polaris missile to the United Kingdom by the United States. After careful review, the President and the Prime Minister agreed that a decision on Polaris must be considered in the widest context both of the future defense of the Atlantic Alliance and of the safety of the whole Free World. They reached the conclusion that this issue created an opportunity for the development of new and closer arrangements for the organization and control of strategic Western defense and that such arrangements in turn could make a major contribution to political cohesion among the nations of the Alliance.

(6) The Prime Minister suggested and the President agreed, that for the immediate future a start could be made by subscribing to NATO some part of the forces already in existence. This could include allocations from United States Strategic Forces, from United Kingdom Bomber Command, and from tactical nuclear forces now held in Europe. Such forces would be assigned as part of a NATO nuclear force and targeted in accordance with NATO plans.

(7) Returning to Polaris the President and the Prime Minister agreed that the purpose of their two governments with respect to the provision of the Polaris missile must be the development of a multilateral NATO nuclear force in the closest consultation with other NATO allies. They will use their best endeavours to this end.

(8) Accordingly, the President and the Prime Minister agreed that the U.S. will make available on a continuing basis Polaris missiles (less warheads) for British submarines. The U.S. will also study the feasibility of making available certain support facilities for such submarines. The U.K. Government will construct the submarines in which these weapons will be placed and they will also provide the nuclear warheads for the Polaris missiles. British forces developed under this plan will be assigned and targeted in the same way as the forces described in paragraph 6.

These forces, and at least equal U.S. forces, would be made available for inclusion in a NATO multilateral nuclear force. The Prime Minister made it clear that except where Her Majesty's Government may decide that supreme national interests are at stake, these British forces will be used for the purposes of international defense of the Western Alliance in all circumstances.

(9) The President and the Prime Minister are convinced that this new plan will strengthen the nuclear defense of the Western Alliance. In strategic terms this defense is indivisible, and it is their conviction that in all ordinary circumstances of crisis or danger, it is this very unity which is the best protection of the West.

(10) The President and the Prime Minister agreed that in addition to having a nuclear shield it is important to have a non-nuclear sword. For this purpose they agreed on the importance of increasing the effectiveness of their conventional forces on a worldwide basis.

Bibliography

PUBLIC DOCUMENTS

1. *Great Britain. Command Papers*

Cmd. 6743. *Statement Relating to Defence: 1946.*
Cmd. 7042. *Statement Relating to Defence: 1947.*
Cmd. 7327. *Statement Relating to Defence: 1948.*
Cmd. 7849. *Mutual Defence Assistance Agreement Between the United Kingdom and the United States.*
Cmd. 7895. *Statement on Defence: 1950.*
Cmd. 8162. *Air Estimates for 1951–52.*
Cmd. 8768. *Statement on Defence: 1953.*
Cmd. 8986. *The Future Organization of the United Kingdom Atomic Energy Project.*
Cmd. 9075. *Statement on Defence: 1954.*
Cmd. 9076. *Air Estimates for 1954–55.*
Cmd. 9388. *The Supply of Military Aircraft.*
Cmd. 9389. *A Programme of Nuclear Power: 1955.*
Cmd. 9391. *Statement on Defence: 1955.*
Cmd. 9555. *Agreement for Co-operation Regarding Atomic Information for Mutual Defence Purposes.*
Cmd. 9560. *Agreement for Co-operation on the Peaceful Uses of Atomic Energy.*
Cmd. 9691. *Statement on Defence: 1956.*
Cmnd. 124. *Defence: Outline of Future Policy: 1957.*
Cmnd. 363. *Report on Defence: Britain's Contribution to Peace and Security: 1958.*
Cmnd. 476. *Central Organization for Defence: 1958.*
Cmnd. 537. *Agreement for Co-operation on the Uses of Atomic Energy for Mutual Defence Purposes.*
Cmnd. 859. *Amendment to Agreement between the Government of the United Kingdom of Great Britain and Northern Ireland and the Government of the United States of America for Co-operation on the Uses of Atomic Energy for Mutual Defence Purposes of July 3, 1958.*
Cmnd. 952. *Report on Defence: 1960.*
Cmnd. 1288. *Report on Defence: 1961.*
Cmnd. 1639. *Statement on Defence, 1962: The Next Five Years.*
Cmnd. 1936. *Statement on Defence: 1963.*
Cmnd. 1995. *Polaris Sales Agreement.*
Cmnd. 2097. *Central Organization for Defence: 1963.*
Cmnd. 2270. *Statement on Defence: 1964.*
Cmnd. 2592. *Statement on the Defence Estimates: 1965.*
Cmnd. 2853. *Report of the Committee of Inquiry into Aircraft Industry.*
Cmnd. 2901. *Statement on Defence Estimates: 1966.* Part I. *The Defence Review.*
Cmnd. 2902. *Statement on Defence Estimates: 1966.* Part II. *Defence Estimates: 1966–67.*
Cmnd. 3203. *Statement on the Defence Estimates: 1967.*
Cmnd. 3357. *Supplementary Statement on Defence Policy: 1967.*

Cmnd. 3438. *Fuel Policy.*
Cmnd. 3540. *Statement on the Defence Estimates: 1968.*
Cmnd. 3701. *Supplementary Statement on Defence Policy: 1968.*
Cmnd. 3927. *Statement on the Defence Estimates: 1969.*
Cmnd. 4290. *Statement on the Defence Estimates: 1970.*

2. *Other Government Publications*

France. *Journal Officiel,* Assemblée Nationale, 25 October 1960.
Great Britain. British Information Services, New York. *Anglo-American Co-operation,* 1958.
Great Britain. British Information Services. *Nuclear Energy in Great Britain,* 1962.
Great Britain. Ministry of Supply and Central Office of Information. *Britain's Atomic Factories: The Story of Atomic Energy Production in Britain,* K.E.B. Jay (ed.), London, H.M.S.O., 1954.
Great Britain. Ministry of Supply and Central Office of Information. *Harwell: the British Atomic Energy Research Establishment, 1946–1951,* London, H.M.S.O., 1952.
Great Britain. *Parliamentary Debates* (5th series). (Commons), Vol. CDXIII-DCCCIV (1945–70).
Great Britain. *Parliamentary Debates* (5th series). (Lords), Vol. CXXXVII-CCCXI (1945–70).
Great Britain. Office of the Minister of Science. *Report of the Committee on the Management and Control of Research and Development,* London, H.M.S.O., 1961.
Great Britain. Treasury. *Statements Relating to the Atomic Bomb,* London, H.M.S.O., 1945.
U.S. Atomic Energy Commission. *In the Matter of J. Robert Oppenheimer,* Washington, GPO, 1954.
U.S. Congress, Joint Committee on Atomic Energy. *Hearings to Amend the Atomic Energy Act of 1946,* 83rd Cong., 2nd Sess.
U.S. Congress, Joint Committee on Atomic Energy. *Senate Report, 1954,* 85th Cong., 2nd Sess.
U.S. Congress. *Public Law 703,* 83rd Cong., 2nd Sess.
U.S. Department of State, 'Declaration of Common Purpose'. *Department of State Bulletin,* Vol. XXXVII, 11 November 1957.
U.S. Department of State. 'Exchange of Notes Concerning an Agreement for the Supply of Intermediate Range Missiles to the United Kingdom', *Department of State Bulletin,* Vol. XXXVIII, 17 March 1958.
U.S. Department of State. *Foreign Relations of the United States: The Conferences at Malta and Yalta, 1945,* Washington, GPO, 1955.
U.S. Department of State. 'Joint Communiqué and Attached Statement on Nuclear Defense Systems', *Department of State Bulletin,* Vol. XLVIII, No. 1229, 14 January 1963.
U.S. House of Representatives, Committee on Armed Services. *Hearings on Military Posture,* 88th Cong., 1st Sess., Washington, GPO, 1963.

U.S. Senate, Committee on Foreign Relations. *Hearings on the Nomination of Christian A. Herter to be Secretary of State,* 86th Cong., 1st Sess.
U.S. Senate. *Congressional Record.* 81st Cong., 2nd Sess., Vol. XCVI, Part 7, 10 July 1950, 9762–3.

BOOKS

ACHESON, DEAN, *Present at the Creation,* New York, W. W. Norton & Co., Inc., 1969.
ADAMS, SHERMAN, *Firsthand Report: The Story of the Eisenhower Administration,* New York, Harper & Brothers, 1961.
ALLEN, HARRY CRANBROOK, *The Anglo-American Predicament,* London, Macmillan, Ltd., 1960.
—, *Great Britain and the United States: A History of Anglo-American Relations,* London, Odhams Press, 1955.
AMRINE, MICHAEL, *The Great Decision: The Secret History of the Atomic Bomb,* New York, G. P. Putnam's Sons, 1959.
ARON, RAYMOND, *The Great Debate: Theories of Nuclear Strategy,* New York, Doubleday & Co., Inc., 1965.
ATTLEE, CLEMENT R., *As It Happened,* London, Heinemann, Ltd., 1954.
—, *Purpose and Policy,* London, Hutchinson & Co., n.d.
Atomic Challenge—A Symposium consisting of BBC talks by: Prof. J. D. Cockcroft, Prof. M. L. Oliphant, Sir George Thomson, Group Capt. G. L. Cheshire, Prof. P. M. S. Blackett, Sir Henry Dale, Bertrand Russell, The Rt. Hon. Sir John Anderson, *et al.,* London, Winchester Publications, Ltd., n.d.
BADER, WILLIAM B., *The United States and the Spread of Nuclear Weapons,* New York, Pegasus, 1968.
BAGEHOT, WALTER, *The English Constitution* (introduction by R. H. S. Crossman), London, Fontana Books, 1963.
BALL, GEORGE W., *The Discipline of Power,* Boston, Atlantic-Little, Brown & Co., 1968.
BATCHELDER, ROBERT C., *The Irreversible Decision, 1939–1950,* Boston, Houghton Mifflin Co., 1962.
BAXTER, III, JAMES PHINNEY, *Scientists Against Time,* Boston, Little, Brown & Co., 1946.
BEATON, LEONARD, *Must the Bomb Spread?* London, Penguin Books, 1966.
BEATON, LEONARD, AND MADDOX, JOHN, *The Spread of Nuclear Weapons,* London, Chatto & Windus Ltd., 1962.
BEER, SAMUEL H., *British Politics in the Collectivist Age,* New York, Alfred A. Knopf, 1965.
BELL, CORAL, *The Debatable Alliance: An Essay in Anglo-American Relations,* London, Oxford University Press, 1964.
BELOFF, MAX, *New Dimensions in Foreign Policy,* London, George Allen & Unwin, Ltd., 1961.
BELOFF, NORA, *The General Says No: Britain's Exclusion from Europe,* London, Pengiun Books, 1963.

BERTIN, LEONARD, *Atom Harvest: A British View of Atomic Energy*, London, Secker & Warburg, Ltd., 1955.

BIRKENHEAD, EARL OF, *The Prof in Two Worlds*, London, Collins, Sons & Co., Ltd., 1961.

BLACKETT, PATRICK M.S., *Atomic Weapons and East-West Relations*, Cambridge, Cambridge University Press, 1956.

—, *Fear, War and the Bomb: Military and Political Consequences of Atomic Energy*, New York, McGraw-Hill Book Company, 1949.

—, *Studies of War: Nuclear and Conventional*, New York, Hill & Wang, 1962.

BOWIE, ROBERT R., *Shaping the Future: Foreign Policy in an Age of Transition*, New York, Columbia University Press, 1964.

BOYD, FRANCIS, *British Politics in Transition 1945–63*, New York, Frederick A. Praeger, 1964.

BOYLE, ANDREW, *Trenchard*, London, Collins, 1962.

BRAND, CARL, *The British Labor Party: A Short History*, Stanford, Stanford University Press, 1964.

BROWN, NEVILLE, *Nuclear War: The Impending Strategic Deadlock*, London, Frederick A. Praeger, 1964.

BRYANT, ARTHUR, *Triumph in the West: A History of the War Years Based on the Diaries of Field-Marshal Lord Alanbrooke, Chief of the Imperial General Staff*, London, Collins, 1959.

BUCHAN, ALASTAIR, *NATO in the 1960's* (revised ed.), New York, Frederick A. Praeger, 1963.

BUCHAN, ALASTAIR (ed.), *A World of Nuclear Powers?* Englewood Cliffs, New Jersey, Prentice-Hall, Inc., 1966.

BUCHAN, ALASTAIR, AND WINDSOR, PHILIP, *Arms and Stability in Europe: A British-French-German Enquiry*, London, Chatto & Windus, 1963.

BULL, HEDLEY, *The Control of the Arms Race* (2nd ed.), New York, Frederick A. Praeger, 1962.

BURN, DUNCAN, *The Political Economy of Nuclear Energy*, London, The Institute of Economic Affairs, 1967.

BUSH, VANNEVAR, *Modern Arms and Free Men*, New York, Simon & Schuster, 1949.

—, *Pieces of the Action*, New York, William Morrow & Co., 1970.

BUTLER, DAVID E., *The British General Election of 1951*, London, Macmillan, Ltd., 1952.

—, *The British General Election of 1955*, London, Macmillan, Ltd., 1955.

BUTLER, DAVID E., AND KING, ANTHONY, *The British General Election of 1964*, London, Macmillan, Ltd., 1965.

—, *The British General Election of 1966*, London, Macmillan, Ltd., 1966.

BUTLER, DAVID E., AND ROSE, RICHARD, *The British General Election of 1959*, London, Macmillan, Ltd., 1960.

BYRNES, JAMES F., *All in One Lifetime*, New York, Harper & Brothers, 1958.

—, *Speaking Frankly*, New York, Harper & Brothers, 1947.

CAMPS, MIRIAM, *European Unification in the Sixties: from the Veto to the Crisis*, New York, McGraw-Hill Book Company, 1966.

CHURCHILL, WINSTON S., *The Second World War*, Vol. I, *The Gathering Storm*, London, Cassell & Co. Ltd., 1948.

CHURCHILL, WINSTON S., *The Second World War*, Vol. III, *The Grand Alliance*, London, Cassell, 1950.

—, *The Second World War*, Vol. IV, *The Hinge of Fate*, London, Cassell, 1951.

—, *The Second World War*, Vol. VI, *Triumph and Tragedy*, London, Cassell, 1954.

CLARK, RONALD W., *The Birth of the Bomb*, New York, Horizon Press, 1961.

—, *Tizard*, Cambridge, M.I.T. Press, 1965.

CLEVELAND, HAROLD VAN B., *The Atlantic Idea and its European Rivals*, New York, McGraw-Hill Book Company, 1966.

COLLIER, BASIL, *The Defence of the United Kingdom*, History of the Second World War: United Kingdom Military Series, London, H.M.S.O., 1957.

COMPTON, ARTHUR HOLLY, *Atomic Quest: A Personal Narrative*, New York, Oxford University Press, 1956.

CONANT, JAMES B., *Anglo-American Relations in the Atomic Age*, London, Oxford University Press, 1952.

—, *My Several Lives*, New York, Harper & Row, 1970.

COOTE, COLIN, AND BATCHELOR, DENZIL (eds.), *Churchill's Maxims and Reflections*, London, Eyre & Spottiswoode, Ltd., 1947.

DALTON, HUGH, *High Tide and After: Memoirs, 1945–1960*, London, Frederick Muller Ltd., 1962.

DEAN, GORDON, *Report on the Atom* (2nd ed.), New York, Alfred A. Knopf, 1957.

DE KADT, EMANUEL J., *British Defence Policy and Nuclear War*, London, Frank Cass & Co., 1964.

DICKIE, JOHN, *The Uncommon Commoner: A Study of Sir Alec Douglas-Home*, London, Pall Mall Press, 1964.

DIVINE, DAVID, *The Blunted Sword*, London, Hutchinson, 1964.

—, *The Broken Wing: A Study in the British Exercise of Air Power*, London, Hutchinson, 1966.

DONOVAN, ROBERT J., *Eisenhower: The Inside Story*, New York, Harper & Brothers, 1956.

DRIVER, CHRISTOPHER, *The Disarmers: A Study in Protest*, London, Hodder & Stoughton, Ltd., 1964.

EDEN, ANTHONY, *Full Circle: The Memoirs of Anthony Eden*, London, Cassell, 1960.

—, *The Reckoning: The Memoirs of Anthony Eden*, London, Cassell, 1965.

EHRMAN, JOHN, *Grand Strategy*, Vol. VI, *United Kingdom History of the Second World War*, London, H.M.S.O., 1956.

EISENHOWER, DWIGHT D., *Mandate for Change, 1953–1956*, New York, Doubleday & Co., 1963.

—, *Waging Peace, 1956–1961*, New York, Doubleday & Co., 1965.

ENTHOVEN, ALAIN C., AND SMITH, K. WAYNE, *How much is Enough? Shaping the Defense Program, 1961–1969*, New York, Harper & Row, 1971.

EPSTEIN, LEON D., *Britain—Uneasy Ally*, Chicago, University of Chicago Press, 1954.

—, *British Politics in the Suez Crisis*, Urbana, University of Illinois Press, 1964.

FEDDEN, SIR ROY, *Britain's Air Survival*, London, Cassell, 1957.

FEIS, HERBERT. *Between War and Peace, The Potsdam Conference*, Princeton, Princeton University Press, 1960.

—, *Japan Subdued: The Atom Bomb and the End of the War in the Pacific*, Princeton, Princeton University Press, 1961.

FINER, SAMUEL E., *Anonymous Empire: A Study of the Lobby in Great Britain,* London, Pall Mall Press, 1958.

FINER, S. E., BERRINGTON, H. B., AND BARTHOLOMEW, D. J., *Backbench Opinion in the House of Commons, 1955–59,* London, Pergamon Press, 1961.

FITZSIMMONS, MATTHEW A., *The Foreign Policy of the British Labour Government, 1945–51,* South Bend, Notre Dame University Press, 1953.

FLETCHER, RAYMOND, *£60 a Second on Defence,* London, MacGibbon & Kee, Ltd., 1963.

FOX, WILLIAM T. R., AND FOX, ANNETTE B., *NATO and the Range of American Choice,* New York, Columbia University Press, 1967.

FURNISS, JR., EDGAR S., *De Gaulle and the French Army: A Crisis in Military-Civil Relations,* New York, The Twentieth Century Fund, 1964.

GARDNER, RICHARD N., *Sterling-Dollar Diplomacy,* Oxford, Clarendon Press, 1956.

GELBER, LIONEL M., *The Rise of Anglo-American Friendship,* London, Oxford University Press, 1938.

GILPIN, ROBERT, *France in the Age of the Scientific State,* Princeton, Princeton University Press, 1968.

GOLDSCHMIDT, BERTRAND, *l'Aventure atomique,* Paris, Fayard, 1962.

—, *Les Rivalités atomiques,* Paris, Fayard, 1967.

GOUDSMIT, SAMUEL A., *Alsos,* New York, Henry Schuman, Inc., 1947.

GOWING, MARGARET, *Britain and Atomic Energy 1939–1945,* London, Macmillan, Ltd., 1964.

GREEN, HAROLD P., AND ROSENTHAL, ALAN, *Government of the Atom: The Integration of Powers,* New York, Atherton Press, 1966.

GRETTON, VICE ADMIRAL SIR PETER, *Maritime Strategy,* London, Cassell, 1965.

GRIMOND, JO, *The Liberal Challenge,* London, Hollis & Carter, 1963.

GROUEFF, STEPHANE, *Manhattan Project: The Untold Story of the Making of the Bomb,* Boston, Little, Brown & Co., 1967.

GROVES, LESLIE R., *Now It Can Be Told: The Story of the Manhattan Project,* New York, Harper & Brothers, 1962.

HALPERIN, MORTON H., *China and the Bomb,* New York, Frederick A. Praeger, 1965.

HANCOCK, W. K., and GOWING, MARGARET, *British War Economy,* London, H.M.S.O., 1949.

HARROD, ROY F., *The Prof: A Personal Memoir of Lord Cherwell,* London, Macmillan, Ltd., 1959.

HARTLEY, ANTHONY, *A State of England,* London, Hutchinson, 1963.

HEWLETT, RICHARD G., and ANDERSON, JR., OSCAR E., *A History of the United States Atomic Energy Commission,* Vol. I, *The New World 1939–1946,* University Park, Pennsylvania State University Press, 1962; HEWLETT AND DUNCAN, FRANCIS, Vol. II, *Atomic Shield, 1947–1952,* 1969.

HIGHAM, ROBIN, *The Military Intellectuals in Britain: 1918–1939,* New Brunswick, Rutgers University Press, 1966.

HSIEH, ALICE LANGSLEY, *Communist China's Strategy in the Nuclear Age,* Englewood Cliffs, New Jersey, Prentice-Hall, Inc., 1962.

HUNTINGTON, SAMUEL P., *The Common Defense,* New York, Columbia University Press, 1961.

IRVING, DAVID, *The German Atomic Bomb: The History of Nuclear Research in Nazi Germany,* New York, Simon & Schuster, 1967.

ISMAY, LORD, *The Memoirs of General the Lord Ismay*, London, Heinemann, 1960.

Jane's All the World's Aircraft, 1960–61, London, S. Low, Marston & Co., 1961.

JAY, K. E. B., *Atomic Energy Research at Harwell*, New York, Philosophical Library, 1955.

JUNGK, ROBERT, *Brighter than a Thousand Suns: The Moral and Political History of the Atomic Scientists*, London, Victor Gollancz, 1959.

KAUFMANN, WILLIAM W., *The McNamara Strategy*, New York, Harper & Row, 1964.

KING-HALL, STEPHEN, *Defence in the Nuclear Age*, London, Victor Gollancz, 1958.

—, *Power Politics in the Nuclear Age*, London, Victor Gollancz, 1962.

KINGSTON-MCCLOUGHRY, AIR VICE-MARSHAL E. J., *Defence: Policy and Strategy*, London, Stevens & Sons, Ltd., 1960.

—, *Global Strategy*, New York, Frederick A. Praeger, 1957.

KISSINGER, HENRY A., *Nuclear Weapons and Foreign Policy*, New York, Harper & Brothers, 1957.

—, *The Troubled Partnership*, New York, McGraw-Hill Book Company, 1965.

KLEIMAN, ROBERT, *Atlantic Crisis: American Diplomacy Confronts a Resurgent Europe*, New York, W. W. Norton & Co., 1964.

KOHL, WILFRID L., *French Nuclear Diplomacy*, Princeton, Princeton University Press (forthcoming).

KRAMISH, ARNOLD, *Atomic Energy in the Soviet Union*, Stanford, Stanford University Press, 1959.

—, *The Peaceful Atom in Foreign Policy*, New York, Harper & Row, 1963.

LAPP, RALPH E., *The New Force*, New York, Harper & Brothers, 1953.

LAYTON, CHRISTOPHER, *European Advanced Technology: A Programme for Integration*, London, George Allen & Unwin, 1969.

LEAHY, WILLIAM D., *I Was There*, New York, Whittlesey House, 1950.

LIDDELL HART, BASIL HENRY, *Defence of the West*, London, Cassell, 1950.

—, *Deterrent or Defence*, London, Stevens, 1960.

LILIENTHAL, DAVID E., *Change, Hope and the Bomb*, Princeton, Princeton University Press, 1963.

—, *The Journals of David E. Lilienthal*, Vol. II, *The Atomic Energy Years, 1945–1950*, New York, Harper & Row, 1964.

LORT PHILLIPS, COLONEL PATRICK, *Towards Sanity*, Carmarthen, Radical Publications, 1960.

MACMILLAN, HAROLD, *Riding the Storm, 1956–1959*, London, Macmillan, Ltd., 1971.

—, *Tides of Fortune, 1945–1955*, London, Macmillan, Ltd., 1969.

MANDER, JOHN, *Great Britain or Little England?* London, Penguin Books, 1963.

MARTIN, CHARLES NOEL, *The Atom: Friend or Foe?*, London, George G. Harrap & Co., 1962.

MARTIN, LAURENCE W., *The Sea in Modern Strategy*, New York, Frederick A. Praeger, 1967.

MAYHEW, CHRISTOPHER, *Britain's Role Tomorrow*, London, Hutchinson, 1967.

MCKENZIE, ROBERT T., *British Political Parties: The Distribution of Power Within the Conservative and Labour Parties* (2nd revised ed.), London, Mercury Books, 1963.

MCLIN, JON B., *Canada's Changing Defense Policy, 1957–1963*, Baltimore, The Johns Hopkins Press, 1967.

MCNEILL, WILLIAM H., *America, Britain, and Russia: Their Co-operation and Conflict, 1941–1946*, London, Oxford University Press, 1953.

MELVILLE, SIR HARRY, *The Department of Scientific and Industrial Research*, London, George Allen & Unwin, 1962.

MENDL, WOLF, *Deterrence and Persuasion: French Nuclear Armament in the Context of National Policy, 1945–1969*, London, Faber and Faber, Ltd., 1970.

MILLIS, WALTER (ed.), *Forrestal Diaries*, New York, Viking Press, 1951.

MONTGOMERY OF ALAMEIN, FIELD-MARSHAL THE VISCOUNT, *The Memoirs of Field-Marshal the Viscount Montgomery of Alamein*, London, Collins, 1958.

MORRISON, HERBERT (LORD OF LAMBETH), *Government and Parliament: A Survey from the Inside*, London, Oxford University Press, 1954.

—, *Herbert Morrison: An Autobiography*, London, Odhams Press, 1960.

MULLEY, FREDERICK W., *The Politics of Western Defence*, London, Thames & Hudson, Ltd., 1962.

MURRAY, THOMAS E., *Nuclear Policy for War and Peace*, Cleveland, World Publishing Company, 1960.

NEUSTADT, RICHARD E., *Alliance Politics*, New York, Columbia University Press, 1970.

NEWHOUSE, JOHN, *De Gaulle and the Anglo-Saxons*, New York, The Viking Press, 1970.

NICHOLAS, HERBERT G., *Britain and the U.S.A.*, Baltimore, The Johns Hopkins Press, 1963.

—, *The British General Election of 1950*, London, Macmillan, Ltd., 1951.

NICOLSON, HAROLD, *Public Faces*, London, Constable & Co. Ltd., 1932.

NIEBURG, HAROLD L., *Nuclear Secrecy and Foreign Policy*, Washington D.C., Public Affairs Press, 1964.

NOEL-BAKER, PHILIP, *The Arms Race: A Programme for World Disarmament*. London, Stevens & Sons, Ltd., 1958.

NORTHEDGE, F. S., *British Foreign Policy: The Process of Readjustment 1945–61*. New York, Frederick A. Praeger, 1962.

OSGOOD, ROBERT E., *NATO: The Entangling Alliance*, Chicago, University of Chicago Press, 1962.

PAWLE, GERALD, *The War and Colonel Warden*, London, George G. Harrap & Co., Ltd., 1963.

PAYNE, GEORGE LOUIS, *Britain's Scientific and Technological Manpower*, Stanford, Stanford University Press, 1960.

POSTAN, M. M., *British War Production: History of the Second World War*, London, H.M.S.O., 1952.

POSTAN, M. M., HAY, D., AND SCOTT, J. D., *Design and Development of Weapons: History of Second World War*, London, H.M.S.O., 1964.

RASMUSSEN, JORGEN SCOTT, *The Liberal Party: A Study of Retrenchment and Revival*, London, Constable, 1965.

ROBERTS, HENRY L., AND WILSON, PAUL A., *Britain and the United States: Problems in Cooperation*, New York, Harper & Brothers, 1953.

ROSECRANCE, RICHARD N., *Defense of the Realm: British Strategy in the Nuclear Epoch*, New York, Columbia University Press, 1968.

ROSECRANCE, RICHARD N., *The Dispersion of Nuclear Weapons*, New York, Columbia University Press, 1964.

RUSSELL, BERTRAND, *Common Sense and Nuclear War,* London, George Allen & Unwin, 1959.

—, *Has Man a Future?* London, George Allen & Unwin, 1961.

—, *Unarmed Victory*, London, Penguin Books, 1963.

RUSSETT, BRUCE H., *Community and Contention: Britain and America in the Twentieth Century*, Cambridge, Mass., M.I.T. Press, 1963.

SAMPSON, ANTHONY, *Macmillan: A Study in Ambiguity,* London, Allen Lane The Penguin Press, 1967.

SAUNDBY, AIR MARSHAL SIR ROBERT, *Air Bombardment*, New York, Harper & Brothers, 1961.

SCHEINMAN, LAWRENCE, *Atomic Energy Policy in France under the Fourth Republic*, Princeton, Princeton University Press, 1965.

SCHILLING, WARNER R., HAMMOND, PAUL Y., AND SNYDER, GLENN H., *Strategy, Politics and Defense Budgets*, New York, Columbia University Press, 1962.

SCHLESINGER, JR., ARTHUR M., *A Thousand Days: John F. Kennedy in the White House*, Boston, Houghton Mifflin Co., 1965.

SCOTT, J. D., *Vickers: A History*, London, Weidenfeld & Nicolson, Ltd., 1962.

SELZNIK, PHILIP, *Leadership in Administration*, Evanston, Row, Peterson & Co., 1957.

SHERWOOD, ROBERT E., *Roosevelt and Hopkins*, New York, Harper & Brothers, 1948.

SHINWELL, EMANUEL, *Conflict Without Malice*, London, Odhams Press, 1955.

—, *The Labour Story*, London, MacDonald & Co., 1963.

SLESSOR, SIR JOHN, *Strategy for the West*, London, Cassell, 1954.

—, *The Central Blue: Recollections and Reflections,* London, Cassell, 1956.

—, *The Great Deterrent*, London, Cassell, 1959.

—, *What Price Coexistence?: A Policy for the Western Alliance*, London, Cassell, 1962.

SMITH, DUDLEY, *Harold Wilson: A Critical Biography*, London, Robert Hale Ltd., 1964.

SNOW, C. P., *Science and Government*, London, Oxford University Press, 1960.

SNYDER, WILLIAM P., *The Politics of British Defense Policy, 1945–1962*, Columbus, Ohio State University Press, 1964.

SORENSEN, THEODORE C., *Kennedy*, New York, Harper & Row, 1965.

STANLEY, TIMOTHY W., *NATO in Transition,* New York, Frederick A. Praeger, 1965.

STRACHEY, JOHN, *On the Prevention of War*, London, Macmillan, Ltd., 1962.

—, *The End of Empire*, London, Victor Gollancz, 1959.

STRAUSS, LEWIS, *Men and Decisions,* Garden City, New York, Doubleday & Co., 1962.

TEDDER, MARSHAL OF THE ROYAL AIR FORCE THE LORD, *Air Power in War*, London, Hodder & Stoughton, 1947.

TEMPLEWOOD, VISCOUNT, *Empire of the Air: The Advent of the Air Age, 1922–29*, London, Collins, 1957.

TRUMAN, HARRY S., *Memoirs:* Vol. I, *Year of Decisions*; Vol. II, *Years of Trial and Hope*, New York, Doubleday & Co., 1955.

VANDENBERG, JR., ARTHUR H. (ed.), *The Private Papers of Senator Vandenberg*, Boston, Houghton Mifflin Co., 1952.

VERRIER, ANTHONY, *An Army for the Sixties: A Study in National Policy, Contract and Obligation*, London, Secker & Warburg, Ltd., 1966.

WALTZ, KENNETH N., *Foreign Policy and Democratic Politics: The American and British Experience*, Boston, Little, Brown and Co., 1967.

WEBSTER, SIR CHARLES, AND FRANKLAND, NOBLE, *The Strategic Air Offensive Against Germany, 1939–1945*, Vol. I-IV, History of the Second World War; United Kingdom Military Series, London, H.M.S.O., 1961.

WHEELER-BENNETT, JOHN W., *John Anderson: Viscount Waverly*, London, Macmillan, Ltd., 1962.

WILLIAMS, FRANCIS, *A Prime Minister Remembers*, London, Heinemann, 1961.

WILSON, HAROLD, *Purpose in Politics: Selected Speeches*, London, Weidenfeld & Nicolson, 1964.

—, *Labour Government 1964–70: A Personal Record,* Michael Joseph and Weidenfeld & Nicolson, 1971.

WILSON, H. H., and GLICKMAN, HARVEY, *The Problem of Internal Security in Great Britain, 1949–1953*, New York, Doubleday & Co., 1954.

WOODHOUSE, C. M., *British Foreign Policy Since the Second World War,* London, Hutchinson, 1961.

WORCESTER, RICHARD, *Roots of British Air Policy*, London, Hodder & Stoughton, 1966.

WRIGHT, SIR MICHAEL, *Disarm and Verify*, London, Chatto & Windus, 1964.

YOUNG, WAYLAND, *Strategy for Survival*, London, Penguin Books, 1959.

YOUNGER, KENNETH, *Changing Perspectives in British Foreign Policy*, Chatham House Essays, No. 7, London, Oxford University Press, 1964.

ZUCKERMAN, SIR SOLLY, *Scientists and War: The Impact of Science on Military and Civil Affairs*, London, Hamish Hamilton, 1966.

ARTICLES AND PERIODICALS

ANATOLYEV, G., 'Britain and European Security', *International Affairs* (Moscow), No. 2, February 1966, 42–5.

BARCLAY, C. N., 'Atomic Warfare', *Brassey's Annual*, London, William Clowes & Sons, 1952.

BEATON, LEONARD, 'Facts about Skybolt', *New Scientist*, No. 275, 22 February 1962, 430–1.

—, 'Labour's Defence Policy: Learning to Love the Bomb', *The Statist*, Vol. CLXXXVII, No. 4530, 8–9.

—, 'Men and/or Missiles', *Crossbow*, Summer 1958.

BROWN, NEVILLE, 'Britain's Strategic Weapons: 1. Manned Bombers', *The World Today*, Vol. XX, July 1964, 293–8.

—, 'Britain's Strategic Weapons: 2. The Polaris A-3', *The World Today*, Vol. XX, August 1964, 358–64.

—, 'British Arms and the Switch Towards Europe', *International Affairs*, Vol. XLIII, No. 3, July 1967, 468–82.

BRUNDRETT, SIR FREDERICK, 'Rockets, Satellites and Military Thinking', *Journal of the Royal United Service Institution,* Vol. CV, August 1960, 332–43.

BUCHAN, ALASTAIR, 'Britain and the Bomb', *Reporter*, Vol. XX, 19 March 1959, 23–5.

• —, 'Britain and the Nuclear Deterrent', *Political Quarterly*, Vol. XXXI, No. 1, January–March 1960, 36–45.

—, 'Britain Debates the "Balance of Terror"', *Reporter*, Vol. XVIII, 3 April 1958, 8–11.

• —, 'Defence on the New Frontier', *Political Quarterly*, Vol. XXXIII, No. 2, April–June 1962.

—, 'Europe and the Atlantic Alliance: Two Strategies or One?' *Journal of Common Market Studies*, Vol. I, No. 3, Spring 1963, 224–55.

• —, 'Nassau Reconsidered', *New Republic*, 2 March 1963.

• —, 'Partners and Allies', *Foreign Affairs*, Vol. XLI, No. 4, July 1963.

—, 'Research and Opinion', *Brassey's Annual*, London, 1964.

—, 'Should NATO Become a Nuclear Power?' *Reporter*, Vol. XXII, 14 April 1960, 21–3.

• —, 'The Changed Setting of the Atlantic Debate', *Foreign Affairs*, Vol. XLIII, No. 4, July 1965, 574–86.

• —, 'The Choice for British Defence Policy', *International Journal*, Vol. XVIII, No. 3, Summer 1963, 281–90.

—, 'The Odds Against Gaitskell', *Reporter*, Vol. XXIII, 22 December 1960, 30–3.

—, 'Their Bomb and Ours: Some Concluding Remarks on the Nuclear Paradox', *Encounter*, Vol. XII, No. 1, January 1959, 11–18.

—, 'Wanted: A European Deterrent', *Reporter*, Vol. XXI, 15 October 1959, 28–30.

BULL, HEDLEY, 'The Many Sides of British Unilateralism', *Reporter*, 16 March 1961, 35–7.

BUSH, VANNEVAR, 'Churchill and the Scientists', *Atlantic Monthly*, Vol. CCXV, No. 3, March 1965, 94–100.

BUZZARD, REAR ADMIRAL SIR ANTHONY W., 'Massive Retaliation and Graduated Deterrence', *World Politics*, Vol. VIII, January 1956, 228–37.

—, 'The H Bomb: Massive Retaliation or Graduated Deterrence?' *International Affairs*, Vol. XXXII, No. 2, April 1956, 148–58.

CALDER, RITCHIE, 'The Non-Nuclear Club', *Bulletin of Atomic Scientists*, Vol. XVI, April 1960, 123–6.

CHALFONT, LORD (Alun Gwynne-Jones), 'The Next Ten Years: A Review of British Defence Policy', *Hawk*, December 1962, 24–32.

—, 'The Politics of Disarmament', *Survival*, Vol. VIII, No. 2, November 1966, 342–9.

CHURCH, FRANK C., 'U.S. Policy and the "New Europe"', *Foreign Affairs*, Vol. XLV, No. 1, October 1966, 49–57.

COCKBURN, R., 'Science and War', *Journal of the Royal United Service Institution*, Vol. CI, No. 601, February 1956.

COCKCROFT, SIR JOHN, Review of Margaret Gowing's, *Britain and Atomic Energy, 1939–1945*, in *Disarmament and Arms Control*, Vol. III, Spring 1965, 87–91.

COWLEY, SIR JOHN, 'Future Trends in Warfare', *Journal of the Royal United Service Institution*, Vol. LV, No. 617, 1960, 4–16.

CRITCHLEY, JULIAN, 'Ending the Myth of Nuclear Independence', *Crossbow*, Vol. VIII, No. 31, April–June 1965, 29–30.

• CROSSMAN, RICHARD H. S., 'The Nuclear Obsession', *Encounter*, July 1958, Vol. XI, No. 1, 3–10.

• DAWSON, RAYMOND, AND ROSECRANCE, RICHARD, 'Theory and Reality in the Anglo-American Alliance', *World Politics*, Vol. XIX, No. 1, October 1966, 21–51.

DAY, A. C. L., 'The Economics of Defence', *Political Quarterly*, Vol. XXXI, No. 1, January–March 1960, 57–65.

DE SOUTTER, D. M., 'The Royal Air Force in Time of Growth and Change', *Brassey's Annual*, London, 1957.

' DE WEERD, HARVEY A., 'Britain's Changing Military Policy', *Foreign Affairs*, Vol. XXXIV, No. 1, October 1955.

• DULLES, JOHN FOSTER, 'Challenge and Response in United States Foreign Policy', *Foreign Affairs*, Vol. XXXVI, No. 1, October 1957, 25–43.

—, 'The Evolution of Foreign Policy', *Department of State Bulletin*, Vol. XXX, No. 761, 25 January 1954.

EDMONDS, MARTIN, 'International Collaboration in Weapons Procurement: The Implications of the Anglo-French Case', *International Affairs*, Vol. XLIII, No. 2, April 1967, 252–64.

EPSTEIN, LEON D., 'Britain and the H-Bomb, 1955–1958', *The Review of Politics*, Vol. XXI, August 1959, 511–29.

—, 'Cohesion of British Parliamentary Parties', *American Political Science Review*, Vol. L, June 1956, 360–77.

—, 'Who Makes Party Policy: British Labor, 1960–61', *Midwest Journal of Political Science*, Vol. VI, No. 2, May 1962, 165–82.

'Eyewitness', *Brassey's Annual*, London, 1947.

EYRAUD, MICHAEL, 'La Controverse nucléaire au sein de l'alliance atlantique', *Strategie*, No. 1, Été 1964.

FALLS, CYRIL, 'The Minister and the Soldier', *Illustrated London News*, 21 November 1959.

FIELD, THOMAS F., 'Britain's Deterrent and the Decision to Abandon the Blue Streak Missile', *Fifteen Nations*, February–March 1962, 27–31.

FONTAINE, ANDRÉ, 'What is French Policy?' *Foreign Affairs*, Vol. XLV, No. 1, October 1966.

FOSTER, WILLIAM C. 'New Directions in Arms Control and Disarmament', *Foreign Affairs*, Vol. XLIII, No. 4, July 1965, 587–601.

FOXLEY-NORRIS, WING COMMANDER C. N., 'The Role of the Bomber', *Brassey's Annual*, London, 1954.

• FRANKLAND, NOBLE, 'Britain's Changing Strategic Position', *International Affairs*, Vol. XXXIII, No. 4, October 1957, 416–26.

GAITSKELL, HUGH, *et al.*, 'Prospects of Mankind', *The Listener*, Vol. CXIV, 6 October 1960, 543–8.

GIBBS, NORMAN H., 'Blue Streak . . . End or Beginning?' *Air Force*, June 1960, 51–6.

—, 'Britain's Defense Budget', *Air Force*, June 1956.

—, 'Britain's Defense Dilemma', *Air Force*, July 1959, 85–8.

—, 'Britain's New Defense Policy', *Air Force*, June 1957.

GIBBS, NORMAN H., 'British Labour Party's Defense Program—New or Old?' *Air Force/Space Digest*, June 1965.

—, 'The Way Ahead for the Western World's Deterrent', *Fifteen Nations*, No. 15, October–November 1960.

GOLDBERG, ALFRED, 'The Atomic Origins of the British Nuclear Deterrent', *International Affairs*, Vol. XL, No. 2, July 1964, 409–29.

—, 'The Military Origins of the British Nuclear Deterrent', *International Affairs*, Vol. XL, No. 4, October 1964, 600–18.

GOOLD-ADAMS, RICHARD, 'Conventional Forces and British Defence Policy', *Political Quarterly*, Vol. XXXI, No. 1, January–March 1960, 26–35.

—, 'Those Against the H-Bomb', *Brassey's Annual*, London, 1958, 90–7.

GORDON WALKER, PATRICK C. 'The Labour Party's Defense and Foreign Policy', *Foreign Affairs*, Vol. XLII, No. 3, April 1964, 391–8.

GOTT, RICHARD, 'The Evolution of the Independent British Deterrent', *International Affairs*, Vol. XXXIX, No. 2, April 1963, 238–52.

GROOM, A. J. R., 'U.S.–Allied Relations and the Atomic Bomb in the Second World War', *World Politics*, Vol. XV, No. 1, October 1962, 123–37.

HARTLEY, ANTHONY, 'The British Bomb', *Survival*, Vol. VI, No. 4, July–August 1964, 170–81.

HARVEY, IAN, 'The Services from Parliament', *Brassey's Annual*, London, 1955.

HEALEY, DENIS, 'Britain and NATO' in *NATO and American Security*, Klaus Knorr (ed.), Princeton, Princeton University Press, 1959, 209–35.

—, 'Interdependence', *Political Quarterly*, Vol. XXXI, No. 1, January–March 1960, 46–56.

—, 'The Sputnik and Western Defence', *International Affairs*, Vol. XXXIV, No. 2, April 1958, 145–56.

HILSMAN, ROGER, 'NATO: The Developing Strategic Context', in *NATO and American Security*, Klaus Knorr (ed.), Princeton, Princeton University Press, 1959.

HINDELL, KEITH, AND WILLIAMS, PHILIP, 'Scarborough and Blackpool', *Political Quarterly*, Vol. XXXIII, No. 3, July–September 1962, 306–20.

HINTON, SIR CHRISTOPHER, 'British Developments in Atomic Energy', *Nucleonics*, Vol. XII, January 1954, 6–8.

—, 'The Chairman's Inauguration of the Conference', *Journal of the British Nuclear Energy Conference*, Vol. I, No. 1, January 1956.

HOWARD, MICHAEL, 'Air Power and Limited War', *Encounter*, April 1962; reprinted in *Survival*, Vol. IV, No. 3, May–June 1962, 132–6.

—, 'Britain's Defenses: Commitments and Capabilities', *Foreign Affairs*, Vol. XXXIX, October 1960, 81–91.

—, 'Central Defence Organization in Great Britain, 1959', *Political Quarterly*, Vol. XXXI, No. 1, January–March 1960.

—, 'Organisation for Defence in the United Kingdom and the United States, 1954–1958', *Brassey's Annual*, London, 1959.

—, 'Strategy in the Nuclear Age', *Journal of the Royal United Service Institution*, Vol. CII, November 1957, 473–82.

HUGHES-HALLETT, VICE ADMIRAL J., 'Thoughts on the New British Defence Policy', *Brassey's Annual*, London, 1957.

JUST, WARD S., 'The Scrapping of Skybolt', *Reporter*, Vol. XXXVIII, 11 April 1963, 19–21.

KERSHAW, ANTHONY, 'The Services from Parliament', *Brassey's Annual*, London, 1962.

MADDOX, JOHN, 'The Problems of Continuous Innovation', *Survival*, Vol. IV, No. 3, May–June 1962, 102–5.

MARQUAND, DAVID, 'England's Labor Party and Its Discontents', *Commentary*, Vol. XXX, December 1960, 489–96.

· MARTIN, LAURENCE W., 'The Market for Strategic Ideas in Britain: The "Sandys Era"', *American Political Science Review*, Vol. LVI, No. 1, 1962, 23–41.

MEGRET, MAURICE, 'L'Angleterre et le "Deterrent National"', *Revue de Défense Nationale*, Mars 1961, 423–36.

MENDL, WOLF, 'The Background of French Nuclear Policy', *International Affairs*, Vol. XLI, No. 1, January 1965, 22–36.

' MIDDLETON, DREW, 'The Deeper Meaning of British Neutralism', *The New York Times Magazine*, 11 December 1960.

MONTGOMERY OF ALAMEIN, FIELD-MARSHAL THE VISCOUNT, 'A Look Through A Window at World War III', *Journal of the Royal United Service Institution*, Vol. XCIX, No. 596, November 1954, 507–23.

MOUNTBATTEN OF BURMA, ADMIRAL OF THE FLEET THE EARL, 'Britain's Armed Forces', *NATO Letter*, Vol. XIII, No. 5, May 1965, 23–5.

MURPHY, CHARLES J. V., 'A New Strategy for NATO', *Fortune*, Vol. XLVII, January 1953, 80–5.

—, 'A Strategy for the Pacific', *Fortune*, January 1966; reprinted in *Survival*, Vol. VIII, No. 3, March 1966, 85–91.

✗NEUSTADT, RICHARD E., 'Memorandum on the British Labour Party and the MLF', *New York Review of Books*, Vol. XI, No. 10, 5 December 1968, 37–46, or the *New Left Review*, September–October 1968, 11–21.

'Nuclear Weapons and the West', a symposium, *International Affairs* (Moscow), No. IX, September 1964, 53–66.

OGORKIEWICZ, R. M., 'Failings of the Weapon Development System', *Brassey's Annual*, London, 1963, 85–91.

OWEN, SIR LEONARD, 'Nuclear Engineering in the United Kingdom—The First Ten Years', *Journal of the British Nuclear Energy Society*, Vol. II, No. 1, January 1963, 23ff.

PIERRE, ANDREW J., 'Britain's Defense Dilemmas' in *The Atlantic Community Reappraised*, Proceedings of the Academy of Political Science, Vol. XXIX, No. 2, November 1968.

—, 'Nuclear Diplomacy: Britain, France, and America', *Foreign Affairs*, Vol. XLIX, No. 2, January 1971, 283–301.

—, 'Reconciliation in Europe: A Western Approach to the European Security Conference', *Interplay*, Vol. 3, No. 10, July 1970, 16–20.

SCHILLING, WARNER R., 'The H Bomb Decision: How to Decide Without Actually Choosing', *Political Science Quarterly*, Vol. LXXVI, March 1961, 24–46.

SIMPSON, JOHN, 'Lessons of the British Polaris Project: An Organizational History', *Journal of the Royal United Service Institution*, March 1969, 46–50.

SLESSOR, SIR JOHN, 'A New Decade for Defence', *The Listener*, Vol. LXIII, No. 1610, 199–201.

SLESSOR, SIR JOHN, 'Air Power and the Future of War', *Journal of the Royal United Service Institution*, Vol. XCIX, No. 595, August 1954, 343–58.

—, 'British Defense Policy', *Foreign Affairs*, Vol. XXXV, No. 4, July 1957, 551–63.

—, 'The Place of the Bomber in British Policy', *International Affairs*, Vol. XXIX, July 1953, 302–8.

—, 'The Revolution in Strategy', *The Listener*, Vol. LI, No. 1302, 243, and No. 1303, 283–5.

—, 'Trenchard and the Birth of the Royal Air Force', *Journal of the Royal United Service Institution*, Vol. CVII, No. 627, August 1962, 216–19.

SNOW, C. P., Editorial in *Discovery*, New Series, Vol. II, No. 18, September 1939, 443–4.

SPEIER, HANS, 'Soviet Atomic Blackmail and the North Atlantic Alliance', *World Politics*, Vol. IX, April 1957, 307–28.

SPROUT, HAROLD AND MARGARET, 'Retreat from World Power: Processes and Consequences of Readjustment', *World Politics*, Vol. XV, No. 4, July 1963, 655–88.

STRACHEY, JOHN, 'Is Our Deterrent Vulnerable?—A Discussion of Western Defence in the 1960s', *International Affairs*, Vol. XXVI, No. 1, January 1961, 1–8.

—, 'Nuclear Chess', *Encounter*, Vol. XI, No. 2, August 1958, 3–6.

TAYLOR, JOHN R., 'The RAF—Today and Tomorrow', *Air Power*, Vol. V, July 1958, 283–91.

THOMSON, SIR GEORGE, 'Britain's Drive for Atomic Power', *Foreign Affairs*, Vol. XXXV, No. 1, October 1956, 95–104.

THORNEYCROFT, PETER, 'Labour Policy Will Destroy Our Only Effective Defense', *NATO's Fifteen Nations*, August–September 1964, 27–9.

THURSFELD, H. G., 'The Lessons of War', *Brassey's Annual*, London, 1946.

'U.S. Bases in Britain' (notes of the month), *The World Today*, Vol. XVI, No. 8, August 1960, 319–25.

VERRIER, ANTHONY, 'British Defense Policy Under Labor', *Foreign Affairs*, Vol. XLII, No. 2, January 1964, 282–92.

—, 'Defence and Politics after Nassau', *Political Quarterly*, Vol. XXXIV, No. 3, July–September 1963, 269–78.

WADE, O. L., 'The Services in 1952–1953', *Brassey's Annual*, London, 1953.

WARNER, GEOFFREY, 'The Nassau Agreement and NATO', *The World Today*, Vol. XIX, February 1963, 61–9.

'Week of Cuba', *Encounter*, Vol. XX, No. 1, January 1963, 84–95.

WHITESTONE, COMMANDER N. E., 'Progress with Polaris', *Brassey's Annual*, London, 1966, 129–34.

WILLIAMSON, G. W., 'Aircraft Development', *Brassey's Annual*, London, 1952.

WILSON, HAROLD, 'Britain's Policy if Labour Wins,' *Atlantic*, Vol. CCXII, No. 4, October 1963, 61–5.

WILSON, MAJOR-GENERAL B. T., 'The Modern Relationship of Statesmen and Military Leaders', *Brassey's Annual*, London, 1958.

YOOL, AIR VICE-MARSHAL W. M., 'Changing Patterns of the Royal Air Force', *Brassey's Annual*, London, 1953, 327–33.

—, 'Royal Air Force Problems', *Brassey's Annual*, London, 1955.

YOOL, AIR VICE-MARSHAL W. M., 'The Evolution of Strategic Bombing', *Brassey's Annual*, London, 1957.

—, 'The Royal Air Force Today', *Brassey's Annual*, London, 1954.

—, 'The Task of the Royal Air Force', *Brassey's Annual*, London, 1952.

YOUNGER, KENNETH, 'Public Opinion and British Foreign Policy', *International Affairs*, Vol. XL, January 1964, 22–33.

ZUCKERMAN, SIR SOLLY, 'Judgement and Control in Modern Warfare', *Foreign Affairs*, Vol. XL, No. 2, January 1962, 196–212.

—, 'Science and the Services', *Brassey's Annual*, London, 1961, 36-40.

REPORTS AND PAMPHLETS

BEATON, LEONARD, *The Western Alliance and the McNamara Doctrine*. Adelphi Papers No. 11, London, Institute for Strategic Studies, August 1964.

—, *Would Labour Give Up the Bomb?*, Sunday Telegraph pamphlet, August 1964.

Bow Group, Conservative Party, *A Smaller Stage: Britain's Place in the World*, London, Bow Group, 1965.

—, *Stability & Survival: A Bow Group Discussion about Defence Policy*, London, Bow Group, 1961.

BRODIE, BERNARD, *The American Scientific Strategists*, RAND Memorandum P-2979, Santa Monica, The RAND Corporation, October 1964.

BROWN, NEVILLE, *Britain and World Security*, London, Fabian Society Research Series No. 258, December 1966.

—, *Britain in NATO*, London, Fabian Society Tract No. 357, November 1964.

—, *British Arms and Strategy 1970–80*, London, Royal United Service Institution, May 1969.

BUCHAN, ALASTAIR, *The Multilateral Force: An Historical Perspective*, Adelphi Papers No. 13, London, Institute for Strategic Studies, October 1964.

BULL, HEDLEY, *Strategy and the Atlantic Alliance: A Critique of United States Doctrine*, Policy Memorandum No. 29, Princeton, Center of International Studies, Princeton University, September 1964.

COCKCROFT, SIR JOHN, 'Nuclear Power in the United Kingdom', in *Atoms for Power*, papers of the Twelfth American Assembly, Columbia University, 17–20 October 1957.

Conservative Party, *Sixty-Ninth Annual Report of the National Union of Conservative and Unionist Associations*, London, 1948.

—, *The Deterrent*, 1962.

The Control of Western Strategy. Adelphi Papers No. 3, London, The Institute for Strategic Studies, April 1963.

DE WEERD, HARVEY A., *Britain and the Alliance*, RAND Memorandum P-2779, Santa Monica, The RAND Corporation, August 1963.

—, *Britain's Defense New Look Five Years Later*, RAND Memorandum P-2562, March 1962.

—, *British Defense Policy: An American View*, RAND Memorandum P-2390, 3 August 1961.

—, *British Defense Policy and NATO*, RAND Memorandum P-2814, October 1963.

—, *The Labour Party and Unilateralism*, RAND Memorandum RM 2914–PR, 1962.

FOX, WILLIAM T. R., AND FOX, ANNETTE BAKER, *Britain and America in the Era of Total Diplomacy*, Memorandum No. 1, Center of International Studies, Princeton University, 1952.

GOLDSTEIN, WALTER, *The Dilemma of British Defense: The Imbalance Between Commitments and Resources*, Mershon National Security Program, Pamphlet No. 3, Ohio State University Press, April 1966.

GOOLD-ADAMS, RICHARD (rapporteur), *The British Army in the Nuclear Age*, Report of Army League Study Group, 1959.

HARLOW, C. J. E., *The European Armaments Base: A Survey: Part Two, National Procurement Policies*, No. 2 of *Defence, Technology and the Western Alliance*, London, Institute for Strategic Studies, 1967.

HEALEY, DENIS, *A Labour Britain and the World*, Fabian Society Tract 352, January 1964.

—, *The Race Against the H Bomb*, London, Fabian Society Tract 322, March 1960.

LABOUR PARTY, *Report of the Fifty-Fourth Annual Conference of the Labour Party*, London, Transport House, 1955.

—, *Report of the Fifty-Sixth Annual Conference of the Labour Party*, London, Transport House, 1957.

—, *Report of the Fifty-Ninth Annual Conference of the Labour Party*, London, Transport House, 1960.

—, *Report of the Sixtieth Annual Conference of the Labour Party*, London, Transport House, 1961.

—, *Disarmament and Nuclear War: The Next Step*, Declaration by the Labour Party and the Trades Union Congress, London, Transport House, 24 June 1959.

—, *Let's Go with Labour for the New Britain*, The Labour Party's Manifesto for the 1964 General Election, London, Transport House, 1964.

—, *Policy for Peace*, London, Transport House, 1961.

—, *The Great Defence Scandal*, London, Transport House, 1960.

LIBERAL PARTY, Research and Information Department, 'Defence in the 1960s', *Current Topics*, Vol. II, No. 7, February 1963.

—, 'Defence—The Liberal Answer', 1964.

LIBERAL PARTY, *Liberal Assembly Resolution*, adopted at Southport, 1957. The Liberal Party Organization, London.

—, *Liberal Assembly Resolution*, adopted at Torquay, 1958. The Liberal Party Organization, London.

—, *Liberal Assembly Resolution*, adopted at Eastbourne, 1960. The Liberal Party Organization, London.

—, *Liberal Assembly Resolution*, adopted at Edinburgh, 1961. The Liberal Party Organization, London.

—, *Liberal Assembly Resolution*, adopted at Llandudno, 1962. The Liberal Party Organization, London.

—, *Liberal Assembly Resolution*, adopted at Brighton, 1963. The Liberal Party Organization, London.

—, *Liberal Assembly Resolution*, adopted at London, 1964. The Liberal Party Organization, London.

MARTIN, L. W., *Ballistic Missile Defence and the Alliance*, Paris, The Atlantic Institute, May 1969.

MARTIN, L. W., *British Defence Policy: The Long Recessional,* Adelphi Papers No. 61, London, Institute for Strategic Studies, November 1969.

The Nuclear Deterrent in the Context of Anglo-American Relations, Report of a Conference held under the auspices of the Ditchley Foundation, 27–30 September 1963.

OSGOOD, ROBERT E., *The Case for the MLF,* Washington, Washington Center for Foreign Policy Research, 1964.

PIERRE, ANDREW J., *Britain and European Security: Issues and Choices for the 1970s,* Vol. II, 'Arms Control and European Security in the 1970s', Report prepared for the U.S. Arms Control and Disarmament Agency by the Institute of War and Peace Studies, Columbia University, 1970.

RAISON, TIMOTHY, *The Missile Years,* Conservative Party Centre pamphlet No. 203, June 1959.

ROTHSTEIN, ROBERT L., *On Nuclear Proliferation,* Occasional Paper, School of International Affairs, Columbia University, 1966.

ROYAL INSTITUTE OF INTERNATIONAL AFFAIRS, *Atomic Energy: Its International Implications,* A Discussion by a Chatham House Study Group, London, Broadwater Press, 1948.

—, *British Security,* A Report by a Chatham House Study Group, London, Oxford University Press, 1946.

—, *Defence in the Cold War,* Report by a Chatham House Study Group under Chairmanship of Major General Sir Ian Jacob, London, 1950.

—, *On Limiting Atomic War,* Report of a Study Group, London, November 1956.

SMART, IAN, *Advanced Strategic Missiles: A Short Guide,* Adelphi Paper No. 63, London, Institute for Strategic Studies, December 1969.

SMYTH, HENRY DE WOLF, *Atomic Energy for Military Purposes: The Official Report on the Development of the Atomic Bomb under the Auspices of the United States Government, 1940–1945* (released 1945, reprinted by Princeton University Press, 1948).

SOCIETY OF BRITISH AEROSPACE COMPANIES, *Keep Britain Flying: The Case for Britain's Aerospace Industry,* London, 1965.

STRACHEY, JOHN, *Scrap All the H Bombs,* London, Transport House, 1958.

—, *The Pursuit of Peace,* London, Fabian Tract No. 329, December 1960.

WILLIAMS, GEOFFREY, GREGORY, FRANK, AND SIMPSON, JOHN, *Crisis in Procurement: A Case Study of the TSR-2,* London, Royal United Service Institution, 1969.

WOLFE, THOMAS W., *Soviet Commentary on the French 'Force de Frappe',* RM-4359-I.S.A., Santa Monica, RAND Corporation, January 1965.

YOUNG, ELIZABETH. *Nations and Nuclear Weapons,* London, The Fabian Society Tract No. 347, July 1963.

YOUNG, WAYLAND, *Bombs and Votes,* London, Fabian Society Tract No. 354, May 1964.

YOUNGER, KENNETH, *Britain's Role in a Changing World,* London, Fabian Society Tract No. 327, 1960.

Index